EASTERN ORTHODOX THEOLOGY

Eastern Orthodox Theology

A Contemporary Reader

SECOND EDITION

Edited by
Daniel B. Clendenin

PATERNOSTER PRESS

Baker Academic

A Division of Baker Book House Co
Grand Rapids, Michigan 49516

© 1995, 2003 by Daniel B. Clendenin

Published by Baker Academic
a division of Baker Book House Company
P.O. Box 6287
Grand Rapids, Michigan 49516-6287
www.bakeracademic.com
and
Paternoster Press
an imprint of Authentic Media
P.O. Box 300, Carlisle, Cumbria CA3 0QS, UK
www.paternoster-publishing.com

Second printing, August 2004

Printed in the United States of America

Library of Congress Cataloging-in-Publication Data
Eastern Orthodox Theology : a contemporary reader / [edited by] Daniel B. Clendenin—
   2nd ed.
      p.   cm.
   Includes bibliographical references and index.
   ISBN 0-8010-2651-2 (pbk.)
   1. Orthodox Eastern Church—Doctrines. I. Clendenin, Daniel B.
BX320.3.E27 2003
230′. 19—dc21   2003052313

British Library Cataloguing in Publication Data
A catalogue record for this book is available from the British Library.
UK ISBN 1-84227-234-9

Contents

Preface to the Second Edition

One of the best ways to get to know a viewpoint is to allow its advocates to speak for themselves. This anthology does just that; it introduces Eastern Orthodox Christianity with selections from its leading voices on the most important aspects of its tradition. I also have added my own voice to this reader in the companion volume *Eastern Orthodox Christianity: A Western Perspective*. As with the present volume, I have also edited this book by adding an epilogue that explores Orthodoxy's dialogue with Protestantism in general and evangelicalism in particular.

In this revised edition, I have included all of the readings of the original edition, and then two more. These new readings address one of the more interesting and important aspects of Christian ecumenism of the past two decades, the growing interface between the evangelical and Orthodox traditions.

I would like to thank Cam Anderson, national director for the Graduate and Faculty Ministry of InterVarsity, for his encouragement to take time out from my campus ministry responsibilities at Stanford University in order to undertake these revisions. Brian Bolger at Baker Academic prodded me along the way with encouragement and sound advice.

Preface to the First Edition

The great Orthodox liturgical scholar Alexander Schmemann once observed that despite some interaction between Eastern Orthodox and Western Christians, the Orthodox heritage had never really been "integrated" into the consciousness of Westerners, many if not most of whom still view Orthodoxy as "marginal, exotic, [and] oriental." Similarly, in the preface to his book *Journeys to Orthodoxy*, which is a series of autobiographical accounts by converts to Orthodoxy, Thomas Doulis notes that even today Orthodox Christianity remains "the great unknown among American religious denominations."

This collection of readings is intended to rectify, at least in some small way, this unfortunate state of affairs, and to introduce Western believers, both Catholic and Protestant, to the rich tradition of Eastern Orthodox Christianity. Specifically, the readings have been selected to introduce some of the distinctive themes and most important modern theologians of Orthodoxy.

This volume has been designed as a companion to my exposition of Orthodoxy, *Eastern Orthodox Christianity* (Grand Rapids: Baker, 1994). In that volume I offer an apologia for the study of Orthodoxy, present a brief history of Eastern Christianity, and then focus on four major theological themes—apophaticism, icons, Scripture and tradition, and theosis. A final chapter offers a Protestant evaluation of Orthodox theology.

But can the Orthodox tradition be learned from a book? The story is told of a Protestant believer who asked an Orthodox priest to explain his theological beliefs. The priest responded that it would be better to ask "not what we believe, but how we worship." Above all things Orthodoxy is a liturgical tradition which takes quite literally the maxim, usually attributed to Pope Celestine I (422–32), *"Lex orandi est lex credendi et agendi"* ("the rule of prayer is the rule of belief and action"). While Westerners tend to learn their theology from books in the library, Orthodoxy specializes in learning theology from the liturgy and worship in the sanctuary. Of course, as the selections of this anthology show, Orthodoxy enjoys an extraordinarily rich intellectual legacy (just as Western Christians are not bereft of rich liturgies), one that extends as far back as the great champion of trinitarian orthodoxy, Athanasius, and continues unabated today. Still, readers of the following essays must not mistake scholarly analyses of Orthodoxy for the liturgical experience of worship that is so characteristic of its heritage.

Numerous people offered their help and advice in the production of this volume. I would especially like to thank John Breck and Paul Meyendorff of St. Vladimir's Orthodox Theological Seminary, James Stamoolis of Wheaton College, Bradley Nassif of the Society for the Study of Eastern Orthodoxy and Evangelicalism, librarian Keith Wells of Trinity Evangelical Divinity School, and editors Jim Weaver and Ray Wiersma of Baker Book House.

Part 1
Theology as Worship:
Liturgy and Sacraments

The Earthly Heaven

Timothy (Kallistos) Ware

Timothy Ware (b. 1934) graduated from Magdalen College, Oxford, where he studied classics, philosophy, and theology. After joining the Orthodox church in 1958, he was ordained a priest in 1966, taking monastic vows at the Monastery of Saint John the Theologian on Patmos and receiving the new name of Kallistos. In 1982 he was consecrated as titular bishop of Diokleia and appointed assistant bishop in the Orthodox Archdiocese of Thyateira and Great Britain. Since 1966 he has been Spalding Lecturer in Eastern Orthodox Studies at Oxford University, where in 1970 he became a fellow at Pembroke College. Since 1973 he has been a member of the Anglican-Orthodox Joint Doctrinal Commission. In addition to his many works, Ware is one of the three translators of the new five-volume English edition of the Philokalia *(1979–), an extremely significant collection of mystical Orthodox texts dating from the fourth to the fifteenth century. First published in 1963, his work* The Orthodox Church, *from which the following selection is taken, has been frequently reprinted, most recently in 1993. It has become a classic introduction to the history, faith, and worship of Orthodox Christianity.*

"The Earthly Heaven" is the first of two chapters in which Ware considers Orthodox worship and sacraments. Citing a famous passage from the twelfth-century Russian Primary Chronicle (the earliest text of Russian history) about the conversion of the Slavic people to Orthodoxy rather than to Islam or Catholicism, Ware demonstrates how beauty and liturgical worship are of central importance to all of Orthodox life and thought. The text is particularly instructive about the Orthodox conception of the relationship of theological doctrine to worship.

From Timothy Ware, *The Orthodox Church* (Baltimore: Penguin, 1963), 269–80. Copyright © 1963 by Penguin Books Ltd. Reproduced by permission of Penguin Books Ltd.

Doctrine and Worship

There is a story in the *Russian Primary Chronicle* of how Vladimir, prince
of Kiev, while still a pagan, desired to know which was the true religion,
and therefore sent his followers to visit the various countries of the world
in turn. They went first to the Muslim Bulgars of the Volga, but observing
that the Bulgars when they prayed gazed around them like men possessed,
the Russians continued on their way dissatisfied. "There is no joy among
them," they reported to Vladimir, "but mournfulness and a great smell;
and there is nothing good about their system." Traveling next to Germany
and Rome, they found the worship more satisfactory, but complained that
here too it was without beauty. Finally they journeyed to Constantinople,
and here at last, as they attended the divine liturgy in the great Church of
the Holy Wisdom, they discovered what they desired. "We knew not
whether we were in heaven or on earth, for surely there is no such splendor
or beauty anywhere upon earth. We cannot describe it to you; only this we
know, that God dwells there among humans, and that their service surpasses the worship of all other places. For we cannot forget that beauty."

In this story can be seen several features characteristic of Orthodox
Christianity. There is first the emphasis upon divine beauty: "we cannot
forget that beauty." It has seemed to many that the peculiar gift of Orthodox peoples—and especially of Byzantium and Russia—is this power of
perceiving the beauty of the spiritual world, and expressing that celestial
beauty in their worship.

In the second place it is characteristic that the Russians should have
said, "We knew not whether we were in heaven or on earth." Worship, for
the Orthodox church, is nothing else than "heaven on earth." The holy
liturgy is something that embraces two worlds at once, for both in heaven
and on earth the liturgy is one and the same—one altar, one sacrifice, one
presence. In every place of worship, however humble its outward appearance, as the faithful gather to perform the Eucharist, they are taken up into
the "heavenly places"; in every place of worship when the holy sacrifice is
offered, not merely the local congregation is present, but the church universal—the saints, the angels, the Mother of God, and Christ himself.
"Now the celestial powers are present with us, and worship invisibly"[1]—
"This we know, that God dwells there among humans."

Orthodox, inspired by this vision of "heaven on earth," have striven to
make their worship in outward splendor and beauty an icon of the great
liturgy in heaven. In the year 612, on the staff of the Church of the Holy
Wisdom, there were 80 priests, 150 deacons, 40 deaconesses, 70 sub-

---

1. These words are sung at the great entrance [an offertory procession in which the
bread and wine are brought to the altar] in the Liturgy of the Presanctified.

deacons, 160 readers, 25 cantors, and 100 doorkeepers; this gives some faint idea of the magnificence of the service which Vladimir's envoys attended. But many who have experienced Orthodox worship in very different outward surroundings have felt, no less than those Russians from Kiev, a sense of God's presence among humans. Turn, for example, from the *Russian Primary Chronicle* to a letter written by an Englishwoman in 1935:

> This morning was so queer. A very grimy and sordid Presbyterian mission hall in a mews over a garage, where the Russians are allowed once a fortnight to have the Liturgy. A very stage property iconostasis and a few modern icons. A dirty floor to kneel on and a form along the wall. . . . And in this two superb old priests and a deacon, clouds of incense and, at the Anaphora [offering of the eucharistic elements], an overwhelming supernatural impression.[2]

There is yet a third characteristic of Orthodoxy which the story of Vladimir's envoys illustrates. When they wanted to discover the true faith, the Russians did not ask about moral rules or demand a reasoned statement of doctrine, but watched the different nations at prayer. The Orthodox approach to religion is fundamentally a liturgical approach, which understands doctrine in the context of divine worship. It is no coincidence that the word *Orthodoxy* should signify alike right belief and right worship, for the two things are inseparable. It has been truly said of the Byzantines, "Dogma with them is not only an intellectual system apprehended by the clergy and expounded to the laity, but a field of vision wherein all things on earth are seen in their relation to things in heaven, first and foremost through liturgical celebration."[3] In the words of George Florovsky: "Christianity is a liturgical religion. The Church is first of all a worshipping community. Worship comes first, doctrine and discipline second."[4] Those who wish to know about Orthodoxy should not so much read books as follow the example of Vladimir's retinue and attend the liturgy. As Christ said to Andrew, "Come and see" (John 1:39).

Because they approach religion in this liturgical way, Orthodox often attribute to minute points of ritual an importance which astonishes Western Christians. But once we have understood the central place of worship in the life of Orthodoxy, an incident such as the schism of the Old Believers will no longer appear entirely unintelligible; if worship is the faith in action, then liturgical changes cannot be lightly regarded. It is typical that

---

2. *The Letters of Evelyn Underhill*, ed. Charles Williams (London, 1943), 248.

3. George Every, *The Byzantine Patriarchate* (London, 1947), ix.

4. George Florovsky, "The Elements of Liturgy in the Orthodox Catholic Church," *One Church* 13.1–2 (1959): 24.

a Russian writer of the fifteenth century, when attacking the Council of Florence, should find fault with the Latins, not for any errors in doctrine, but for their behavior in worship:

> What have you seen of worth among the Latins? They do not even know how to venerate the church of God. They raise their voices as the fools, and their singing is a discordant wail. They have no idea of beauty and reverence in worship, for they strike trombones, blow horns, use organs, wave their hands, trample with their feet, and do many other irreverent and disorderly things which bring joy to the devil.[5]

Orthodoxy sees humanity above all else as liturgical creatures who are most truly themselves when they glorify God, and who find their perfection and self-fulfilment in worship. Into the holy liturgy which expresses their faith, the Orthodox peoples have poured their whole religious experience. It is the liturgy which has inspired their best poetry, art, and music. Among Orthodox, the liturgy has never become the preserve of the learned and the clergy, as it tended to be in the medieval West, but it has remained *popular*—the common possession of the whole Christian people:

> The normal Orthodox lay worshipper, through familiarity from earliest childhood, is entirely at home in church, thoroughly conversant with the audible parts of the Holy Liturgy, and takes part with unconscious and unstudied ease in the action of the rite, to an extent only shared in by the hyper-devout and ecclesiastically minded in the West.[6]

In the dark days of their history—under the Mongols, the Turks, or the Communists—it is to the holy liturgy that the Orthodox peoples have always turned for inspiration and new hope; nor have they turned in vain.

The Outward Setting: Priest and People

The basic pattern of services is the same in the Orthodox as in the Roman Catholic Church: there is, first, the *holy liturgy* (the Eucharist or mass); secondly, the *divine office* (i.e., the two chief offices of matins and vespers, together with the six "lesser hours" of nocturn, prime, terce, sext, none, and compline);[7] and thirdly, the *occasional offices*—that is, services intended

5. Quoted in Nicolas Zernov, *Moscow, the Third Rome* (London, 1937), 37. I cite this passage simply as an example of the liturgical approach of Orthodoxy, without necessarily endorsing the strictures on Western worship which it contains!

6. Austin Oakley, *The Orthodox Liturgy* (London, 1958), 12.

7. In the Roman rite nocturn is a part of matins, but in the Byzantine rite nocturn is a separate service. Byzantine matins is equivalent to matins and lauds in the Roman rite.

for special occasions, such as baptism, marriage, monastic profession, royal coronation, consecration of a church, burial of the dead. In addition to these, the Orthodox church makes use of a great variety of lesser blessings.

While in many Anglican and almost all Roman Catholic parish churches, the Eucharist is celebrated daily, in the Orthodox church today a daily liturgy is not usual except in cathedrals and large monasteries; in a normal parish church it is celebrated only on Sundays and feasts. But in contemporary Russia, where places of worship are few and many Christians are obliged to work on Sundays, a daily liturgy has become the practice in many town parishes.

The divine office is recited daily in monasteries, large and small, and in some cathedrals, as well as in a number of town parishes in Russia. But in an ordinary Orthodox parish church it is sung only on weekends and at feasts. Greek churches hold vespers on Saturday night, and matins on Sunday morning before the liturgy; in Russian parishes matins is usually "anticipated" and sung immediately after vespers on Saturday night, so that vespers and matins, followed by prime, together constitute what is termed the vigil service or the all-night vigil. Thus while Western Christians, if they worship in the evening, tend to do so on Sundays, Orthodox Christians worship on the evening of Saturdays.

In its services the Orthodox church uses the language of the people: Arabic in Antioch, Finnish in Helsinki, Japanese in Tokyo, English (when required) in London or New York. One of the first tasks of Orthodox missionaries—from Cyril and Methodius in the ninth century, to Innocent Veniaminov and Nicolas Kasatkin in the nineteenth—has always been to translate the service books into native tongues. In practice, however, there are partial exceptions to this general principle of using the vernacular: the Greek-speaking churches employ, not modern Greek, but the Greek of New Testament and Byzantine times, while the Russian church still uses the ninth-century translations in Church Slavonic. Yet in both cases the difference between the liturgical language and the contemporary vernacular is not so great as to make the service unintelligible to the congregation. In 1906 many Russian bishops in fact recommended that Church Slavonic be replaced more or less generally by modern Russian, but the Bolshevik Revolution occurred before this scheme could be carried into effect.

In the Orthodox church today, as in the early church, all services are sung or chanted. There is no Orthodox equivalent to the Roman low mass or to the Anglican "said celebration." At every liturgy, as at every matins and vespers, incense is used and the service is sung, even though there may be no choir or congregation, but the priest and a single reader alone. In their church music the Greek-speaking Orthodox continue to use the ancient Byzantine plainchant, with its eight tones. This plainchant the Byzantine missionaries took with them into the Slavonic lands, but over the centuries it has become extensively modified, and the various Slavonic churches have each developed their own style and tradition of ecclesiastical music. Of these traditions the Russian is the best known and the most immediately attractive to Western ears; many consider Russian church music the finest in all Christendom, and alike in the Soviet Union and in the emigration there are justly celebrated Russian choirs. Until very recent times all singing in Orthodox churches was usually done by the choir; today a small but increasing number of parishes in Greece, Russia, Romania, and the diaspora are beginning to revive congregational singing—if not throughout the service, then at any rate at special moments such as the creed and the Lord's Prayer.

In the Orthodox church today, as in the early church, singing is unaccompanied and instrumental music is not found, except among certain Orthodox in America—particularly the Greeks—who are now showing a penchant for the organ or the harmonium. Most Orthodox do not use hand or sanctuary bells inside the church; but they have outside belfries, and take great delight in ringing the bells not only before but at various moments during the service itself. Russian bell-ringing used to be particularly famous. "Nothing," wrote Paul of Aleppo during his visit to Moscow in 1655, "nothing affected me so much as the united clang of all the bells on the eves of Sundays and great festivals, and at midnight before the festivals. The earth shook with their vibrations, and like thunder the drone of their voices went up to the skies. . . . They rang the brazen bells after their custom. May God not be startled at the noisy pleasantness of their sounds!"[8]

An Orthodox church is usually more or less square in plan, with a wide central space covered by a dome. (In Russia the church dome has assumed that striking onion shape which forms so characteristic a feature of every Russian landscape.) The elongated naves and chancels, common in cathedrals and larger parish churches of the Gothic style, are not found in Eastern church architecture. There are as a rule no chairs or pews in the central part of the church, although there might be benches or stalls along the walls. An Orthodox normally stands during church services (non-Orthodox visitors are often astonished to see old women remaining on their feet for several hours without apparent signs of fatigue); but there are moments when the congregation can sit or kneel. Canon 20 of the first ecumenical council forbids all kneeling on Sundays or on any of the fifty days between Easter and Pentecost; but today this rule is unfortunately not always strictly observed.

8. Paul of Aleppo, *The Travels of Macarius*, ed. Laura Ridding (London, 1936), 27, 6.

It is a remarkable thing how great a difference the presence or absence of pews can make to the whole spirit of Christian worship. There is in Orthodox worship a flexibility, an unselfconscious informality, not found among Western congregations, at any rate north of the Alps. Western worshipers, ranged in their neat rows, all in their proper places, cannot move about during the service without causing a disturbance. A Western congregation is generally expected to arrive at the beginning and to stay to the end. But in Orthodox worship people can come and go far more freely, and nobody is greatly surprised if they move about during the service. The same informality and freedom also characterize the behavior of the clergy. Ceremonial movements are not so minutely prescribed as in the West; priestly gestures are less stylized and more natural. This informality, while it can lead at times to irreverence, is in the end a precious quality which Orthodox would be most sorry to lose. They are at home in their church—not troops on a parade ground, but children in their Father's house. Orthodox worship is often termed "otherworldly," but could more truly be described as "homely"; it is a *family* affair. Yet behind this homeliness and informality there lies a deep sense of mystery.

In every Orthodox church the sanctuary is divided from the rest of the interior by the *iconostasis*, a solid screen, usually of wood, covered with panel icons. In early days the chancel was separated merely by a low screen three or four feet high. Sometimes this screen was surmounted by an open series of columns supporting a horizontal beam or architrave; a screen of this kind can still be seen at Saint Mark's in Venice. Only in comparatively recent times—in many places not until the fifteenth or sixteenth century—was the space between these columns filled up, and the iconostasis given its present solid form. Many Orthodox liturgists today would be glad to follow Father John of Kronstadt's example, and revert to a more open type of iconostasis; in a few places this has actually been done.

The iconostasis is pierced by three doors. The large door in the center—the holy or royal door—when opened affords a view through to the altar. This door is closed by double gates, behind which hangs a curtain. Outside service time, except during Easter week, the gates are kept closed and the curtain drawn. During services the gates are sometimes open, sometimes closed; occasionally when the gates are closed the curtain is drawn as well. Many Greek parishes, however, no longer close the gates or draw the curtain at any point in the liturgy; in a number of churches the gates have been removed altogether, while other churches have followed a course which is liturgically far more correct—keeping the gates, but removing the curtain. Of the two other doors, that on the left leads into the chapel of the *prothesis* or preparation (here the sacred vessels are kept, and here the priest prepares the bread and the wine at the beginning of the liturgy); that on the right leads into the *diakonikon* (now generally used as a vestry, but originally the place where the sacred books, particularly the Book of the Gospels, were kept together with the relics). Laypeople are not allowed to go behind the iconostasis, except for a special reason such as serving at the liturgy. The altar in an Ortho-dox church—the holy table or throne, as it is called—stands free of the east wall, in the center of the sanctuary; behind the altar and against the wall is set the bishop's throne.

Orthodox churches are full of icons—on the screen, on the walls, in special shrines, or on a kind of desk where they can be venerated by the faithful. When Orthodox people enter a church, their first action will be to buy a candle, go up to an icon, cross themselves, kiss the icon, and light the candle in front of it. "They be great offerers of candles," commented the English merchant Richard Chancellor, visiting Russia in the reign of Elizabeth I. In the decoration of the church, the various iconographical scenes and figures are not arranged fortuitously, but according to a definite theological scheme, so that the whole edifice forms one great icon or image of the kingdom of God. In Orthodox religious art, as in the religious art of the medieval West, there is an elaborate system of symbols involving every part of the church building and its decoration. Icons, frescoes, and mosaics are not mere ornaments designed to make the church look nice, but have a theological and liturgical function to fulfil.

The icons which fill the church serve as a point of meeting between heaven and earth. As each local congregation prays Sunday after Sunday, surrounded by the figures of Christ, the angels, and the saints, these visible images remind the faithful unceasingly of the invisible presence of the whole company of heaven at the liturgy. The faithful can feel that the walls of the church open out upon eternity, and they are helped to realize that their lit-urgy on earth is one and the same with the great liturgy of heaven. The mul-titudinous icons express visibly the sense of heaven on earth.

The worship of the Orthodox church is communal and popular. Any non-Orthodox who attends Orthodox services with some frequency will quickly realize how closely the whole worshiping community, priest and people alike, are bound together into one; among other things, the absence of pews helps to create a sense of unity. Although most Orthodox congregations do not join in the singing, it should not therefore be imag-ined that they are taking no real part in the service; nor does the iconosta-sis—even in its present solid form—make the people feel cut off from the priest in the sanctuary. Indeed, many of the ceremonies take place in front of the screen and thus in full view of the congregation.

Orthodox laity do not use the phrase "to hear mass," for in the Ortho-dox church the mass has never become something done by the clergy for the laity, but is something which clergy and laity perform together. In the medieval West, where the Eucharist was performed in a learned language not understood by the people, men came to church to adore the host at the elevation, but otherwise treated the mass mainly as a convenient occasion for saying their private prayers.[9] In the Orthodox church, where the liturgy has never ceased to be a common action performed by priest and people together, the congregation do not come to church to say their private prayers, but to pray the public prayers of the liturgy and to take part in the action of the rite itself. Orthodoxy has never undergone that separation between liturgy and personal devotion from which the medieval and postmedieval West has suffered so much.

Certainly the Orthodox church, as well as the West, stands in need of a liturgical movement; indeed, some such movement has already begun in a small way in several parts of the Orthodox world (revival of congregational singing; the gates of the holy door left open in the liturgy; a more open form of iconostasis, and so on). Yet in Orthodoxy the scope of this liturgical movement will be far more restricted, since the changes required are very much less drastic. That sense of corporate worship which it is the primary aim of liturgical reform in the West to restore has never ceased to be a living reality in the Orthodox church.

There is in most Orthodox worship an unhurried and timeless quality, an effect produced in part by the constant repetition of litanies. Either in a longer or a shorter form, a litany recurs several times in every service of the Byzantine rite. In these litanies, the deacon (if there is no deacon, the priest) calls the people to pray for the various needs of the church and the world, and to each petition the choir or the people reply, "Lord, have mercy"— *Kyrie eleison* in Greek, *Gospodi pomilui* in Russian—probably the first words in an Orthodox service which the visitor grasps. (In some litanies the response is changed to "Grant this, O Lord.") The congregation associate themselves with the different intercessions by making the sign of the cross and bowing. In general the sign of the cross is employed far more frequently by Orthodox than by Western worshipers, and there is a far greater freedom about the times when it is used. Different worshipers cross themselves at different moments, each as he or she wishes, although there are of course occasions in the service when almost all sign themselves at the same time.

We have described Orthodox worship as timeless and unhurried. Most Western people have the idea that Byzantine services, even if not literally timeless, are at any rate of an extreme and intolerable length. Certainly Orthodox functions tend to be more prolonged than their Western counterparts, but we must not exaggerate. It is perfectly possible to celebrate the Byzantine liturgy, and to preach a short sermon, in an hour and a

9. All this, of course, is now being changed in the West by the liturgical movement.

quarter; in fact, in 1943 the patriarch of Constantinople laid down that in parishes under his jurisdiction the Sunday liturgy should not last over an hour and a half. Russians on the whole take longer than Greeks in their services, but in a normal Russian parish of the emigration, the vigil service on Saturday nights lasts no more than two hours, and often less. Monastic offices of course are more extended, and on Mount Athos at great festivals the service sometimes goes on for twelve or even fifteen hours without a break, but this is altogether exceptional.

Non-Orthodox may take heart from the fact that Orthodox are often as alarmed as they by the length of services. "And now we are entered on our travail and anguish," writes Paul of Aleppo in his diary as he enters Russia. "For all their churches are empty of seats. There is not one, even for the bishop; you see the people all through the service standing like rocks, motionless or incessantly bending with their devotions. God help us for the length of their prayers and chants and masses, for we suffered great pain, so that our very souls were tortured with fatigue and anguish." And in the middle of Holy Week he exclaims: "God grant us His special aid to get through the whole of this present week! As for the Muscovites, their feet must surely be of iron."[10]

10. Paul of Aleppo, *Travels of Macarius*, ed. Ridding, 14, 46.

Concerning the Sacraments

John Karmiris

Born in 1904, John Karmiris graduated from the University of Athens, where he studied theology and Greek literature. He later studied theology at the Universities of Bonn and Berlin. He received his Ph.D. in theology from the University of Athens, where after 1937 he served as professor of theology. Although considered a bit scholastic by some Orthodox thinkers, the following piece gives a succinct overview of the Orthodox position on the sacraments. With his heavy reliance upon patristic notation, Karmiris's piece also typifies standard Orthodox theological method.

That justifying and sanctifying divine grace which abides in the church is administered by the church to the people by means of the holy mysteries, which are divinely instituted ceremonies that deliver, by visible means, mysteriously transmitted invisible grace. Thus it is that the sacraments, when they are worthily received, become instruments, means of transmission, of divine grace. They are "efficacious instruments of grace for those who participate in them,"[1] enabling faithful participants to become communicants in the redemptive work of the Savior; they are not fine means

From John Karmiris, *A Synopsis of the Dogmatic Theology of the Orthodox Catholic Church*, trans. George Dimopoulos (Scranton, Pa.: Christian Orthodox Edition, 1973), 100–112.

1. Dositheus, *Confession*, 15, quoted in John Karmiris, *The Dogmatical and Symbolical Texts of the Orthodox Catholic Church*, 2 vols. (Athens, 1951, 1953), 2:758.

of the commandments of God. Through the action of the sacraments, the salvific power of God completes in us the process of sanctification. This is accomplished in all who are truly faithful by the grace and power of the Holy Spirit. It is for this reason that the sacraments occupy such a prominent position in the Orthodox conscience. Indeed, "the whole meaning of the church is realized in the sacraments, the church being, at the same time, the fullness of the body of Christ and members in particular."[2]

The sacraments are seven in number, and include baptism, chrismation, Holy Eucharist, repentance, ordination, marriage, and holy unction. Three of them (baptism, chrismation, and ordination) are nonrepeatable; the remaining four (Holy Eucharist, repentance, marriage, and holy unction) may be repeated;[3] that is to say, they may be administered more than once to the same person. Each sacrament transmits its own particular grace. Baptism and chrismation transmit justifying and regenerating grace; repentance and unction transmit grace which is for the healing of soul and body; ordination and marriage enable us to perform certain specific functions; and the Holy Eucharist feeds and satisfies us spiritually.

The completeness, the wholeness, of the sacraments is contingent upon their divine order and institution by the Lord, who is the invisible celebrant and our "initiator." It is contingent also upon the canonical position of the officiating clergy and upon the effect, both *ex opere operato* and *ex opere operantis*. In no way is the efficacy of the sacrament contingent upon the faith or moral qualifications of either celebrant or recipient,[4] yet every magical and mechanical action is excluded in the perfor-

---

2. Nicholas Cabasilas *Interpretation of the Divine Liturgy* 37–38, in *Patrologia Graeca* (PG), ed. J. P. Migne, 162 vols. (Paris, 1857–66), 150.452–53. The church understands the sacraments, not as symbols, but as the very heart of the members of the body, as the root of the branches (to use the Lord's picture of the vine and branches). The objection to the word *symbol* is based on the fact that the sacraments transmit, not a picture or abstract representation, but the reality of their subject. (E.g., in the Eucharist, we actually have communion with the body and blood of Christ.) Through these means, the faithful actually participate in the life of Christ, who is the actual head of the body, and their dependence upon him is not symbolic, but very real.

3. It is to be noted that the "ineffaceable character" (*character indelibilis*) of certain sacraments, as held by the Latins, has not found acceptance in the Orthodox church. (See K. Dyobouniotes, *The Sacraments of the Eastern Orthodox Church* [Athens, 1913], 24–30.) However, the ancient Eastern fathers do teach an "indissoluble seal, the eternal seal of the Holy Spirit." (See Cyril of Jerusalem *Procatechesis* 16.17 [PG 33.365]; and Basil the Great *On Holy Baptism* 13.5 [PG 31.433].)

4. "He, though the priests be exceedingly vile, works all things that are his, and will send the Holy Spirit. For neither does the pure [priest] draw down the Holy Spirit by his own purity, but it is grace that worketh all. . . . For the things which are placed in the hands of the priest it is with God alone to give; and however far human wisdom may reach, it will

mance of the sacrament. We see then, first of all, that the priest, as performer of the sacrament, is simply the instrument of the invisible and actual celebrant, the Lord himself. (Hence it is that, in the Holy Eucharist, the priest prays that God will "make this bread the precious body of thy Christ," only because "Thou art the Offerer and the Offered, the Acceptor and the Distributed."[5]) Secondly, the accomplishment of the sacrament is not dependent upon the people; they need only prepare themselves in order that the sacrament might be personally efficacious to them, according to the words of the Scripture: "For he that eateth and drinketh unworthily, eateth and drinketh damnation to himself" (1 Cor. 11:29). Thus the sacraments are effectively accomplished independently of the faith of those accepting them. Furthermore, the Orthodox Catholic Church believes that divine grace is not dispensed outside of the true church, and thus the church does not recognize in their fullness sacramental acts which are performed outside of her, except in extraordinary circumstances (and then by "economy" [a special exemption from the norm] and condescension she recognizes the sacraments of those heterodox who come to her).[6]

The Orthodox church accepts the above-mentioned seven sacraments, which were known from antiquity in the Orthodox East. They were always believed in, as testified by liturgical practice. The teaching concerning them, however, was not written down, as it was considered to be secret.[7] Neither did any cause impel the church to officially define the number of sacraments as being seven, inasmuch as no one ever happened to express any doubt concerning this. We have, however, sufficient witness from the ancient Orthodox fathers, and even from the heretical Nestorians and Monophysites, who separated themselves from the body of the ancient catholic church, yet continued to adhere to her teaching concerning the seven sacraments. Such was the common state of affairs in the East and West alike. Hence, during the schism no doubt was raised concerning the number of the sacraments, no attempt being made by either East or West to increase or reduce their number.[8]

---

appear inferior to that grace. . . . Neither angel nor archangel can do anything with regard to what is given from God. But the Father, the Son, and the Holy Ghost dispenseth all, while the priest lends his tongue and affords his hands" (Chrysostom *Homilies on John* 84.4 [PG 59.472]; see also Gregory of Nazianzus *Orationes* 40.26 ["On Holy Baptism," PG 36.396]; Jeremiah II, *Answer I to the Lutherans*, in Karmiris, *Dogmatical and Symbolical Texts*, 1:391ff.).

5. Liturgy of Chrysostom, in Karmiris, *Dogmatical and Symbolical Texts*, 1:255–60.

6. See John Karmiris, *How Heterodox Who Come to Orthodoxy Should Be Accepted* (Athens, 1954).

7. Karmiris, *Dogmatical and Symbolical Texts*, 1:41–42.

8. John Karmiris, *Orthodoxy and Protestantism* (Athens, 1937), 148ff.

Baptism

By means of holy baptism, the "bath of regeneration" and renewing of the Holy Spirit, believers shed the sinful garments of the old man and are clothed in Christ, entering through him, as through a door, into the church, the kingdom of grace. We are thus regenerated, renewed, and re-created, our nature being made over into the divine image, so that we become members of the mystical body of Christ, children of God by grace, and partakers of the divine nature through participation in the Holy Spirit. According to Chrysostom, "It is through baptism that we received remission of sins, sanctification, communion of the Spirit, adoption, and life eternal."[9] And according to Basil the Great, baptism is "the ransoming of captives, the forgiving of their debts, the regeneration of the soul, the bright garment, the unassailable seal, chariot to heaven, the cause of the kingdom, the gift of adoption."[10]

Indeed, through this sacrament those who believe are cleansed of original sin and all actual sins (if they be adults). All of these sins are totally uprooted and obliterated, together with their guilt and their due punishment, the very body of sin (excepting only concupiscence) being reconciled to God, justified, made worthy by grace of the divine adoption. Those baptized thus become citizens and members incorporate in the body of the church, in the mystical body of Christ, which is actually formed through baptism. We would emphasize again that it is through baptism that we receive explicit, complete, and utter remission of original sin, which is by this means uprooted, obliterated, together with any actual sins which the individual may have committed. Baptism brings about also the ontological destruction of the very body of sin, the source of death, since it was by sin that death passed to all (Rom. 5:12). According to the patriarch Dositheus, "There is no sin which cannot be absolved by baptism. The inclination to sin remains, but that is irrelevant. . . . All those sins committed prior to baptism, or during baptism, disappear, are counted as not existing, as though they had never been committed."[11] Consequently, baptism "frees us from all spot (of sin), and thus we become the holy temple of God and partakers of his divine nature through our participation in his Holy Spirit."[12]

In order for the sacrament of baptism to be considered valid, it is necessary that the person being baptized be immersed and raised up three times in water which has been sanctified. "In regard to canonical baptism

9. Chrysostom *Homilies on Acts* 14.3 (PG 60.285).
10. Basil the Great *On Holy Baptism* 13.5 (PG 31.433).
11. Dositheus, *Confession*, 16, in Karmiris, *Dogmatical and Symbolical Texts*, 2:760.
12. Cyril of Alexandria *On Luke* 22 (PG 72.904).

(and not the baptism of necessity, performed in a bed or similar special circumstance), the bishop or priest proclaims that 'the servant of God (name) is baptized in the Name of the Father, and of the Son, and of the Holy Spirit.'"[13] Only the baptism of necessity (emergency) can be performed by a deacon or a baptized layperson, whether man or woman. Baptism is a sacrament which, dogmatically, cannot be repeated because, just as in the natural life a person is born but one time, so also in the spiritual life a man can be reborn one time only: "So, then, as our Lord died once and for all, we also must be baptized once and for all."[14] For this reason we have suggested in another work[15] that heterodox converts to Orthodoxy should be rebaptized as rarely as possible, since by confessional zeal without knowledge it is easy to fall into the heresy of the Anabaptists, who deny the Christian dogma "I confess one baptism."[16]

Chrismation

Through chrismation baptized individuals receive the gifts of the Holy Spirit, together with a power which enables them to develop their new spiritual state, which they entered at baptism. For "with the visible chrism the body is anointed, and the soul is sanctified by the Holy and life-giving Spirit." Chrismation "is the Holy Spirit . . . Christ's gift of the Holy Spirit, the actualization of his divine presence."[17] Thus, while baptism grants us a new, or spiritual, nature in Christ, chrism further expands it, shaping the newly baptized into the form, the mold, of Christ. For this reason, in actual practice chrism is connected with baptism, and is granted to the Orthodox believer "immediately upon his arising from the waters of baptism."[18] It is exactly for this reason that baptism together with chrismation is granted to those "of tender years," that is, to children. With holy chrism prepared from sweet-smelling spices the bishop or priest anoints in the form of a

13. This canonical formula of baptism was known by the ancient church, as witness the councils and the Fathers, from among whom it is sufficient to refer to Basil, who says: "In three immersions, then, and with three invocations, the great mystery of baptism is performed, to the end that the type of death may be fully figured, and that by the tradition of the divine knowledge the baptized may have their souls enlightened" (On the Holy Spirit 15.35 [PG 32.129]).

14. Chrysostom Homilies on Hebrews 9.3 (PG 63.79); John of Damascus Exposition of the Orthodox Faith 11.9 (PG 64.117–1120).

15. Karmiris, Heterodox Who Come to Orthodoxy, 30.

16. Karmiris, Dogmatical and Symbolical Texts, 1:134.

17. Cyril of Jerusalem Lectures 3.3 (PG 33.1029).

18. Cyril of Jerusalem Lectures 3.1 (PG 33.1089). See also Canon 48 of Laodicea (Karmiris, Dogmatical and Symbolical Texts, 1:215): "The newly baptized should be anointed with the heavenly chrismation, in order to become partakers of Christ's kingdom."

cross various parts of the body of the newly baptized, and says, "The seal of the gift of the Holy Spirit, Amen." Chrismation, once canonically performed, cannot ever be repeated. The anointing of people who come to Orthodoxy out of the various heretical confessions is not a repetition of the sacrament of chrismation. It is granting the sacrament, for the first and only time, to one who in his heresy was deprived of a valid priesthood and valid chrism. Hence, in the ancient church "people who came out of any heresy were 'chrismated,' for they did not already possess the holy chrismation."[19]

Holy Eucharist

In the Holy Eucharist the faithful truly participate in the real body and blood of Christ. They are mystically united with and incorporated into him, becoming, according to the historically well-known descriptions of Ignatius of Antioch, "one body, one blood, Christ-bearers and temple-bearers." According to Cyril of Jerusalem, "by partaking of the body and blood of Christ, thou mayest be made of the same body and of the same blood with him. For thus we come to bear Christ in us, because his body and blood are distributed through our members; thus it is that, according to the blessed Peter, we become partakers of the divine nature."[20] The flesh of the Lord, received by the believers, through hypostatic union animates and deifies those who partake; without losing its own natural properties, it transmits to them and transplants into them the divine life. This union of Christ with his faithful results in the remission of the sins of the latter. This remission of sins results in immortality and eternal life, in accordance with the meaning of this prayer from the Liturgy of the Presanctified Gifts: "That partaking with a pure conscience, with faces unashamed, with hearts illumined, of these divine, consecrated gifts, and being quickened through them, we may be united unto thy Christ himself, our true God . . . [and] become the temple of thine all-holy and adorable Spirit, redeemed from every wile of the devil wrought by deed or word or thought, and obtain the good things promised unto us."[21]

According to the divine Liturgy of Chrysostom, the faithful communicate in the Holy Eucharist of the body and blood of Christ "for the purification of the soul, for the remission of sins, for the fellowship of the Holy Spirit, for the fulfilment of the kingdom of heaven (an inheritance)."[22] In the first place, the soul of the participant is purified and sanctified, spiritually nourished and mystically rendered incorruptible. Secondly, the communicant

19. Didymus of Alexandria On the Holy Trinity 2.15 (PG 39.720).
20. Cyril of Jerusalem Lectures 22.3 (PG 33).
21. J. Coar, Euchologion (Prayer Book): Sive Rituale Graecorum (Venice, 1730), 167.
22. Karmiris, Dogmatical and Symbolical Texts, 1:260, 261, 263.

receives the seed of incorruption, resurrection, immortality, and eternal life; taking in "the very body and blood of Christ,"[23] the participants progress further into sanctification as members of Christ's mystical body (the church), being linked with him and with each other through the Holy Communion through which they receive the divine life and deification.[24] According to Maximus the Confessor, Christ "transmits to us a divine life, making himself eatable. . . . The quality of this life is truly divine, for all who partake are deified."[25] According to John of Damascus, "men become partakers of and communicants in the divine nature; as many, that is, as receive the holy body of Christ, and drink his blood."[26] In the Holy Eucharist men are united with and incorporated into the God-man, receiving that divine quality necessary for their deification.[27]

The Orthodox Catholic Church accepts the real presence of Christ in the Holy Eucharist: the elements of bread and wine are changed into Christ's very body and blood[28] in such a way that he is hypostatically and essentially present in the sacrament. Here the Orthodox church clings tenaciously to the old tradition formulated by the seventh ecumenical council: "Neither the Lord nor his apostles anywhere stated that the bloodless sacrifice offered by the priest is an icon or picture . . . after consecration the very body and blood of Christ are truly present."[29] John of Damascus writes:

> The bread itself and the wine are changed into God's body and blood. But if you inquire as to how this takes place, it is enough for you to know that it is effected by the Holy Spirit . . . the manner of the change can in no way be researched. But one can put it well thus, that just as in nature bread, by eating, and wine and water, by drinking, are changed into the body and blood of the eater and drinker, yet not becoming a different body from the former one; so the bread of the table, and also the wine and water, are super-

23. Cyril of Jerusalem *Lectures* 22 (PG 33).

24. Chrysostom *Homilies on Corinthians* 24 (PG 61.200): "For as the bread consisting of many grains is made one so that the grains nowhere appear—they exist indeed, but because of their conjunction their difference is not seen; so are we conjoined both with each other and with Christ: there not being one body for thee, and another for thy neighbor to be nourished by, but the very same for all. . . . For we all partake of the one bread" (1 Cor. 10:17).

25. Maximus the Confessor *Hermeneia to Prayer* (PG 90.877).

26. John of Damascus *On the Divine Images* 3.26 (PG 94.1348).

27. Gregory of Nyssa *Catechism* 37 (PG 45.93–97).

28. Chrysostom *Homily on the Betrayal of Judas* 16 (PG 49.380).

29. *Acta Conciliorum*, ed. Jean Hardouin, 12 vols. (Paris, 1714–15), 4.309, 372. See also Theodore of Mopsuestia *On Matthew* 26:26—"He did not say, 'This is the symbol of my body and blood'; but 'this is my body, and this is my blood,' teaching us not to see the nature of the object, for, in becoming Eucharist, the objects are changed into the body and blood of Christ" (PG 66.713).

naturally changed by the invocation and presence of the Holy Spirit into the body and blood of Christ, and are not two, but one and the same. . . . Participation is spoken of, for through it we partake of the divinity of Jesus. Communion, too, is spoken of, and it is an actual communion, because through it we have communion with Christ and share in his flesh and divinity; yea, we have communion and are united with one another through it. For since we partake of the one bread, we all become one body of Christ and one blood, and members one of another, being of one body with Christ.[30]

Moreover, the Orthodox church accepts the permanent presence of the whole Lord in every part of the elements, and in every place in which the Eucharist is offered.

This sacrament is performed by a bishop or a presbyter using leavened (never unleavened) bread and wine, the latter being mixed with water. The change takes place, not by the means of repeating the Savior's words of institution, but through the direct invocation of the Holy Spirit: "Send down thy Holy Spirit upon us and upon these gifts here presented, and make this bread the precious body of thy Christ, and that which is in this cup the precious blood of thy Christ, changing them by thy Holy Spirit."[31]

The importance of this sacrament for our salvation is so great as to make it equally important with the sacrament of baptism. For this reason the Orthodox people, clergy and laity alike, all receive the Holy Communion in both species, following the required preparation. The communion in both species is based on Matthew 26:26–27, and even infants, according to John 6:53–54, participate immediately following their baptism, which practice (infant baptism) is based upon John 3:5.[32] It should be evident from all of the above that the Holy Eucharist is not a mere sacrament, but a sacrifice as well. It is a bloodless, conciliatory offering to God "in all and for all."[33] It is "for the whole world, for the holy, catholic, and

---

30. John of Damascus *Exposition of the Orthodox Faith* 4.13 (*PG* 94.1141ff.). It is obvious that, in the Orthodox teaching concerning this change, there is not room for the Latin theory of transubstantiation. That term has found acceptance by a few Byzantine theologians, who use it, however, only to convey the correct, patristic teaching. See John Karmiris, *External Influences upon the Confessions of the Seventeenth Century* (Athens, 1948), 56–61. "The Latin scholastic theory of transubstantiation neither became, nor can possibly become, acceptable to Orthodox theology and to the Orthodox church" (p. 126). Therefore, the opposing accusations of Wilhelm Niesel are inaccurate.

31. Liturgy of Chrysostom, in Karmiris, *Dogmatical and Symbolical Texts,* 1:260–61. Recent Orthodox theologians correctly unite both the words of institution and the epiclesis, so that they form one unique and indivisible whole.

32. See John Karmiris, *The Confession of Metrophanes Kritopoulos (with Replies to Godon) and His Dogmatic Teaching* (Athens, 1948), 77.

33. Liturgy of Chrysostom, in Karmiris, *Dogmatical and Symbolical Texts,* 1:260.

apostolic church"[34]—for all Orthodox Christians, those who are alive and those who sleep in hope of the resurrection to eternal life. The sacrifice will not be completed until the final judgment.[35] Naturally, it is understood that, in all of these things, nothing is added to the sacrifice of the cross, the saving fruit of which is communicated to participants in the Eucharist. Neither is repeated the Redeemer's death on the cross. His presence in the Eucharist is a mystical one, as "the Offerer and the Offered, the Acceptor and the Distributed,"[36] as sacrifice and victim, delivering to those who partake of the Holy Eucharist the saving fruits of his sacrifice on the cross.

Repentance

Through our repentance God forgives the sins we have committed after baptism, provided we have frankly repented of them, and have confessed them before the bishop or priest. Thus penance, the sacrament of repentance, is characterized as a second baptism. According to Athanasius, "sufficient repentance will absolve every sin."[37] God himself remits the sin, the officiating clergyman merely proclaiming the absolution. In any event, "we must confess our sins to those unto whom, in the providence of the mystery of God, confession was entrusted."[38] The forgiveness of sin procured through sincere and heartfelt repentance is complete and perfect, needing no additional fulfilment. The penalties imposed upon people who have confessed are a sort of spiritual medicine to ensure the beginning of moral recovery and healing, the uprooting of passion, the therapeutic, pedagogical, and corrective means of betterment, reinforcing repentant sinners in virtue, and making of them examples for others. These penalties then are totally without any conciliatory or satisfactory character. Totally contrary is the Latin teaching of penalties and punishments, external and temporal remission, the treasury of merits, the superabounding grace of our Lord's passion, the works of supererogation performed by the saints, and purgatorial fire, all of which the Orthodox church most strenuously rejects. Inasmuch as remission is granted on the basis of sincere repentance and confession, as we have seen, the imposed penalties are obviously neither essential nor supplementary to the sacrament. Their character is simply that of therapeutic medicine administered in proportion to the

34. Ibid., 262. The Orthodox liturgy in many places mentions the Holy Eucharist as a sacrifice, the sacrifice of the altar; see, e.g., pp. 247, 251, 254, 255, 258, 259, 260, 261, 262.

35. Confession of Peter Mogila, in Karmiris, *Dogmatical and Symbolical Texts*, 2:639; Liturgy of Chrysostom, in Karmiris, *Dogmatical and Symbolical Texts*, 1:261.

36. Liturgy of Chrysostom, in Karmiris, *Dogmatical and Symbolical Texts*, 1:255, 264.

37. Athanasius the Great *On Matthew* (PG 27.1388).

38. Basil the Great *Regulae brevius tractatae* 288 (PG 31.1284).

type of illness. It is not administered uniformly to all penitents, but at the discretion of the confessor. Thus the improvised teachings of the Latins can find no place in the Orthodox dogmatic system.

Ordination to the Priesthood

Through the sacrament of holy orders, or priesthood, by the laying on of hands by the bishop and the invocation of the Holy Spirit, the ministers of the church are specially consecrated. The ordination of three degrees of church hierarchy (bishop, presbyter, and dean) is abundantly witnessed to by the New Testament as well as by the sacred tradition. All three orders of the clergy continue canonically and uninterruptedly in the Orthodox church, the hierarchy of which traces its beginnings back through an unbroken succession to the apostles themselves. The sacrament of ordination possesses, in the Orthodox church, a great importance, and no one who is not in possession of the apostolic succession has any right to perform any sort of priestly or pastoral function.[39]

For this reason the Orthodox church did not originally recognize the validity of any sacrament performed outside of herself, nor did she recognize the ordinations of heterodox clergy. Nevertheless, through the means of "economy" she can recognize the ordination of a priest who comes to her from a heterodox church, as long as this church is in possession of apostolic succession, holds generally to the Orthodox view of the church (ecclesiology), and recognizes ordination to the priesthood as a sacrament, endeavoring to perform it canonically. Moreover, ordination to the priesthood is one of those sacraments that must never be repeated. No Orthodox priest who defects to a heterodox communion and later after sincere repentance returns may ever be reordained. Neither can an Orthodox priest who was canonically defrocked and subsequently restored be ordained a second time.[40]

Marriage

In the sacrament of marriage the free union between a man and woman is sanctified by the granting of divine grace so that the relationship might attain to its purpose. Indispensable to the performance of this sacrament

39. The Orthodox delegation to the Second Assembly of the World Council of Churches (Evanston, Ill.; 1954) maintained this position: "Only through Apostolic Succession is the mystery of Pentecost continued in the Church. The episcopal succession from the Apostles constitutes the historical reality of the Church, the organization of the Church, and one of the presuppositions for unity with her, over the centuries: the unity of the episcopacy, the unity of the faith" (*Ecclesia* 31 [1954]: 366).

40. Apostolic Canon 68, and also Council of Carthage 48 (57), in Karmiris, *Dogmatic and Symbolical Texts*, 1:210, 217.

are: (1) the free and willing consent of those who come to be married, both of whom should be Orthodox Christians; and (2) the blessing of the bishop or presbyter for the transmission of divine grace. Marriage is indissoluble, and divorce can be granted only on the grounds of fornication or the death of one of the marriage parties, as well as for some secondary reasons which were added later in the history of the church. After a marriage has been dissolved, the church, by economy, can permit a second or third marriage, but never a fourth. Marriage between blood relatives and between in-laws is forbidden. Mixed marriage between Orthodox and heterodox is tolerated on the condition that the marriage is solemnized in an Orthodox temple, and all children resulting from the marriage are baptized and raised Orthodox.

Holy Unction

By means of the sacrament of holy unction we invoke divine grace for the healing of our bodily and spiritual infirmities. This sacrament is performed by seven priests, who anoint various parts of the body with specially sanctified oil. It is usually administered to those who are ill (seriously or not) for the healing of their physical sickness, and also for the remission of sins, especially those that may have some connection with the present illness. In the Orthodox church, holy unction may be administered to any baptized person—young or adult, sick or healthy—and it can be repeated in cases of need. This is in contradistinction to the Roman Catholic sacrament, which since Peter Lombard and in opposition to James 5:14 is called extreme unction. The Orthodox church does not have a special unction for cases of utter crisis. We do not wait until the very end before calling a priest; rather, we hope for the recovery of the afflicted one. We pray that God would use this sacrament as the means of healing for the sick person. Thus unction is not limited to once per lifetime; it should be used as medicine—whenever there is need.[41]

41. Metrophanes Kritopoulos, *Confession*, in Karmiris, *Dogmatical and Symbolical Texts*, 2:544–55.

3

The Meaning and Content of the Icon

Leonid Ouspensky

The importance of icons in the Orthodox tradition might be symbolized by an experience recounted by Harvard theologian Harvey Cox. A Russian intellectual once asked his priest why there was not more doctrinal teaching in Orthodoxy to supplement its rich liturgical tradition. The priest responded by saying, "Icons teach us all we need to know." Far from serving merely as church art, icons are indispensable to the Orthodox understanding of Christian identity. Each year on the first Sunday of Lent a special Orthodox service commemorates the triumph of the veneration of icons over the iconoclasts in the year 843. Among other things, during this service anathemas are pronounced on all who would reject the decision of the seventh ecumenical council (Nicea, 787) that upheld the use of icons.

Leonid Ouspensky, who lived in Paris until his death in 1987, was one of the greatest iconographers and iconologists of his time. The following selection is a chapter of his two-volume classic text Theology of the Icon, a comprehensive tome which examines the history and theology of the icon from the catacomb art of the early church to the modern world.

From Leonid Ouspensky, *Theology of the Icon*, trans. Anthony Gythiel and Elizabeth Meyendorff, 2 vols. (Crestwood, N.Y.: St. Vladimir's Seminary Press, 1992), 1:151–94. Reprinted by permission.

A Key to Understanding the Icon:
The Kontakion of the Triumph of Orthodoxy

One of the best sources for discovering the meaning and the content of the icon is the teaching the church formulated in answering iconoclasm. In addition, the dogmatic foundation of the veneration of icons and the meaning and content of the liturgical image are particularly revealed by the liturgy of two feast days: the Feast of the Holy Face and the Feast of the Triumph of Orthodoxy, the latter being the feast of the victory of the icon and of the ultimate triumph of the dogma of the divine incarnation.

The basis for our study will be the kontakion (a short hymn honoring a saint) of the Triumph of Orthodoxy, which is a true verbal icon of the feast. This text, which is of an extraordinary richness and depth, expresses all of the church's teaching about images. It is believed that the text dates to no earlier than the tenth century, but it is possible that it is contemporary with the canon of the feast. If this is the case, it dates to the ninth century, that is, to the very moment of the Triumph of Orthodoxy. The canon was, in fact, written by Theophanes the Marked, a confessor of Orthodoxy during the second iconoclastic period. Theophanes eventually became metropolitan of Nicea and died circa 847. This canon is therefore written by a man who personally participated in the struggle to preserve the icon. It represents the totality of the church's experience, a concrete and real experience of divine revelation, an experience defended with blood.

Celebrating the triumph of the icon, the kontakion of the Triumph of Orthodoxy expresses in a concise, exact form, in a few sentences, the entire economy of salvation, and thereby the teaching on the image and its content.

> No one could describe the Word of the Father;
> But when he took flesh from you, O Theotokos (God-bearer),
> He consented to be described,
> And restored the fallen image to its former state by uniting it to
>   divine beauty.
> We confess and proclaim our salvation in word and images.

The first part of the kontakion tells of the abasement of the Second Person of the Holy Trinity, and thus of the christological basis of the icon. The words which follow reveal the meaning of the incarnation, the accomplishment of the divine plan for humans and consequently for the universe. It can be said that these phrases illustrate the patristic formula "God became man so that man might become God." The end of the kontakion expresses the human answer to God: confession of the saving truth of the incarnation, acceptance of the divine economy, and participation in the work of God and, therefore, achievement of salvation: "We confess and proclaim our salvation in word and images."

"No one could describe the Word of the Father; But when he took flesh from you, O Theotokos...."

The first part of the kontakion ("No one could describe the Word of the Father; But when he took flesh from you, O Theotokos . . .") can be summarized in the following way: The Second Person of the Holy Trinity becomes human and yet remains what he is, that is, fully God, possessing the fullness of divine nature, hence uncircumscribable in his divinity, for "no one could describe the Word of the Father." God assumes the human nature which he created; he borrows the human nature in its totality from the Mother of God; and without changing his divinity, without confusing it with humanity, he becomes God and man at the same time. "The Word became flesh so that the flesh could become word," according to Mark the Ascetic.[1] This is the humiliation, the *kenosis* of God; he who is absolutely inaccessible to humans, who is indescribable and unrepresentable, becomes describable and representable by assuming human flesh.

The icon of Jesus Christ, the God-man, is an expression of the dogma of Chalcedon in image; indeed, it represents the person of the Son of God who became man, who by his divine nature is consubstantial with the Father and by his human nature is consubstantial with us, "similar to us in everything except sin," in the expression of Chalcedon. During his life on earth, Christ reunited in himself the image of God and the image of the servant about whom Paul speaks (Phil. 2:6–7). The men who surrounded Christ saw him only as a man, albeit often as a prophet. For the unbelievers, his divinity is hidden by his form of a servant. For them, the Savior of the world is only a historical figure, the man Jesus. Even his most beloved disciples saw Christ only once in his glorified, deified humanity, and not in the form of a servant; this was before the passion, at the moment of his transfiguration on Mount Tabor. But the church has "eyes to see" just as it has "ears to hear." This is why it hears the Word of God in the Gospel, which is written in human words. Similarly, it always considers Christ through the eyes of an unshakable faith in his divinity. This is why the church depicts him in icons not as an ordinary man, but as the God-man in his glory, even at the moment of his supreme humiliation. Unshakable faith in Christ's divinity is precisely the reason why, in its icons, the Orthodox church never represents him simply as a man who suffers physically, as is the case in Western religious art.

The image of the God-man was precisely what the iconoclasts could not understand. They asked how the two natures of Christ could be represented. But the Orthodox did not even think of representing either the

---

1. Mark the Ascetic, "Epistle to the Monk Nicholas," in the Russian *Philokalia*, 5 vols. (1876–90), 1:420.

divine nature or the human nature of Christ. They represented his person, the person of the God-man who unites in himself the two natures without confusion or division.

It is characteristic that the kontakion of the Triumph of Orthodoxy is addressed not to one of the persons of the Holy Trinity, but to the Mother of God. This shows the unity in the church's teaching about Christ and the Mother of God. The incarnation of the Second Person of the Trinity is the fundamental dogma of Christianity, but the confession of this dogma is possible only by confessing the Virgin Mary to be the true Mother of God. Indeed, if the negation of the human image of God logically leads to the negation of the very meaning of our salvation, it is also true, on the other hand, that the existence and the veneration of the icon of Christ imply the importance of the Mother of God, whose consent, "Let it be to me according to thy word" (Luke 1:38), was the indispensable condition for the incarnation, and who alone permitted God to become visible and therefore representable. According to the Fathers, the representation of the God-man is based precisely on the representable humanity of his mother. "Since Christ was born of the indescribable Father," explains Theodore the Studite,

> he cannot have an image. Indeed, what image could correspond to the divinity whose representation is absolutely forbidden by Holy Scripture? But from the moment Christ is born of a describable mother, he naturally has an image which corresponds to that of his mother. If he could not be represented by art, this would mean that he was not born of a representable mother, but that he was born only of the Father, and that he was not incarnate. But this contradicts the whole divine economy of our salvation.[2]

This possibility of representing the God-man in the flesh which he borrowed from his mother is contrasted by the seventh ecumenical council with the absolute impossibility of representing God the Father. The fathers of the council repeat the authoritative argument of Pope Gregory II, contained in his letter to Emperor Leo III the Isaurian: "Why do we neither describe nor represent the Father of the Lord Jesus Christ? Because we do not know what he is. . . . And if we had seen and known him as we have seen and known his Son, we would have tried to describe him and to represent him in art."[3]

The reasoning of this council, as well as the words of Theodore the Studite, touches upon a subject that is very relevant and of great dogmatic

2. Theodore the Studite *Antirrheticus* 1.2, in *Patrologia Graeca* (PG), ed. J. P. Migne, 162 vols. (Paris, 1857–66), 99.417C.

3. In *Sacrorum Conciliorum Nova et Amplissima Collectio*, ed. G. D. Mansi, 31 vols. (Florence, 1759–98), 12.963E.

importance, namely, that there should be no image of God the Father, for he is not incarnate and is consequently invisible and nonrepresentable. The council thus emphasizes the difference between the representability of the Son, because he is incarnate, and the absolute impossibility of representing the Father. We have every right to conclude from this that, from the doctrinal point of view, the council confirms the impossibility of representing God the Father. Obviously, anything can be represented, since the human imagination has no limit. But the fact is that some things are not representable. Many things concerning God are not only not representable in image and not describable by words, but are even positively inconceivable to humans. It is precisely because of this inconceivable, unknowable character of God the Father that the council proclaims the impossibility of making his image. We have only one way of knowing the Holy Trinity. We know the Father by the Son ("He who sees me sees him who sent me," we read in John 12:45, and "He who has seen me has seen the Father," in John 14:9) and the Son by the Holy Spirit ("No one can say 'Jesus is Lord' except by the Holy Spirit," 1 Cor. 12:3). Consequently, we represent only what has been revealed to us: the incarnate person of the Son of God, Jesus Christ. The Holy Spirit is represented as it manifested itself: in the shape of a dove at the baptism of Christ, in the form of tongues of fire at Pentecost, and so on.

"...And restored the fallen image to its former state by uniting it to divine beauty...."

While the beginning of the kontakion of the Triumph of Orthodoxy speaks of the divine incarnation as the basis for the icon, the second part expresses the meaning of the incarnation and thus the meaning and contents of the New Testament image: "And restored the fallen image to its former state by uniting it to divine beauty." These words signify that the Son of God, in his incarnation, re-creates and renews in humans the divine image soiled by the fall of Adam.[4] Christ, the new Adam, the firstfruits of the new creation, of the celestial man, leads us to the goal for which the original Adam was created. To attain this goal, it was necessary to return to the beginning, to Adam's point of departure. In the Bible we read: "God said, Let us make man in our image, after our likeness" (Gen. 1:26). Therefore, according to the plan of the Holy Trinity, not only must man be the image of his Creator, but he must also be a like image and resemble God. But the descriptions in Genesis of the accomplished creative act no longer mention the likeness: "So God created man, he made

---

4. On this subject see, for example, Athanasius the Great *Oratio de incarnatione Verbi* (PG 25.120CD).

him in the image of God"—κατ᾽ εἰκόνα θεοῦ (Gen. 1:27; 5:1).[5] One could say that the text insists on the word *image* by repeating it from Genesis 1:26; the absence of the word *likeness* could not be more evident.[6]

The meaning of the biblical account of the plan of the Holy Spirit to create man "in the image and likeness" of God and the account of the creation "in the image" is understood by the Fathers in the sense that man, created in the image of God, is consequently called to realize his likeness to God. To be in the image of God is to have the possibility of acquiring the divine likeness. In other words, this likeness to God is assigned to man as a dynamic task to accomplish.

By baptism, grace restores the image of God to man; as for the divine likeness, grace outlines it later, with the efforts of man to acquire the virtues of which love is the highest, the supreme trait of the likeness to God.

> Just as painters clearly establish the resemblance of the portrait to the model by first tracing the outline in one color, then filling it in little by little with different colors . . . so also at baptism, the grace of God begins to remake the image to what it was when man came into existence. Then, when we begin to strive with all our will power towards the beauty of the likeness . . . divine grace makes virtue flourish upon virtue, elevating the beauty of the soul from glory to glory, bestowing upon it the mark of likeness.[7]

Man is a microcosm, a little world. He is the center of created life; and therefore, being in the image of God, he is the means by which God acts in creation. It is precisely in this divine image that the cosmic meaning of man is revealed, according to the commentary of Gregory of Nyssa. Creation participates in spiritual life through man. Placed by God at the head of all visible creatures, man must realize in himself the union and harmony of everything and unite all the universe to God, in order to make of it a homogeneous organism where God can be all in all—for the final goal of creation is its transfiguration.

But man did not accomplish his calling. He turned away from God; his will power weakened, and the inertia in his nature prevailed over his impetus toward God. This led to the disintegration of man, the microcosm, which consequently led to a cosmic disintegration, a catastrophe in all creation. The whole visible world fell into disorder, strife, suffering, death, and corruption. This world ceased faithfully to reflect divine beauty, because the divine image, man, inscribed at the center of the uni-

---

5. The references are to the Septuagint.

6. On this topic see Vladimir Lossky, "Image and Likeness," chap. 6 in *The Mystical Theology of the Eastern Church* (Crestwood, N.Y.: St. Vladimir's Seminary Press, 1976), 114ff.

7. Diadochus of Photiki *Oeuvres spirituelles* 89 (Paris, 1955), 149.

verse, was obscured. This was the exact opposite of man's vocation. God's plan, however, did not change. Because man by himself was incapable of reestablishing his nature in its primitive purity, the task which fallen man could no longer fulfil was accomplished by the new Adam, Christ. Simeon the New Theologian says on this subject:

> Man, such as God had created him, ceased to exist in the world; it was no longer possible for anyone to be like Adam was before his fall. But it was indispensable that such a man exist. God, therefore, wishing there to be a man such as he had created with Adam, sent his only Son to earth, who, having come, became incarnate, assuming perfect humanity in order to be a perfect God and a perfect man, and in order that the divinity could have a man worthy of him. This is the man. There has never been and never will be one like him. But why was Christ like this? To keep the law and the commandments of God, and to fight and conquer the devil.[8]

To save man from the ascendancy of original sin, it was therefore necessary to have a man such as God had created in the beginning, that is, a sinless man, because sin is an external thing superimposed on human nature. It is a contrivance of the created will, according to Gregory of Nyssa, a voluntary denial by creation of the fullness of life.

The incarnation of the Son of God is not only the re-creation of man in his primitive purity. It is also the realization of that which the first Adam did not know how to achieve. In the words of the fathers of the seventh ecumenical council: "God re-created man in immortality, thus bestowing upon him a gift which could no longer be taken away from him. This re-creation was more godlike and better than the first creation; it is an eternal gift."[9] This gift of immortality entails the possibility of attaining beauty and divine glory—"by uniting it [the fallen image] to divine beauty," says the kontakion. By assuming human nature, Christ impregnated it with grace, making it participate in divine life, and cleared the way to the kingdom of God for man, the way of deification and transfiguration. The divine image was reinstated in man in the perfect life of Christ. He destroyed the power of original sin by his freely accepted passion and led man to realize the task for which he was created: to achieve divine likeness. In Christ, this likeness is realized to a total, perfect degree by the deification of human nature. Indeed, the deification represents a perfect harmony, a complete union of humanity and divinity, of human will and divine will.

---

8. Homily attributed to Simeon the New Theologian, "First Oration," in *Homilies*, 3d Russian ed. (Moscow, 1892), 23.

9. Fifth session, in *Collectio*, ed. Mansi, 13.216A.

The divine likeness, therefore, is possible only for a renewed man in whom the image of God is purified and restored. This possibility is realized in certain properties of human nature and particularly in its freedom. The attainment of divine likeness is not possible without freedom, because it is realized in a living contact between God and man. Man consciously and freely enters into the plan of the Holy Trinity and creates in himself the likeness to God to the extent of his possibilities and with the help of the Holy Spirit. Thus the Slavonic word *prepodobnyi*, which literally means "very similar," is applied to the monastic type of holiness.[10] The rebirth of man consists in changing the present humiliated state of his nature, making it participate in the divine life, because, according to the classical phrase of Gregory of Nazianzus, who echoes Basil the Great, "Man is a creature, but he is commanded to become God." Henceforth, by following Christ, by integrating himself to Christ's body, man can reestablish in himself the divine likeness and make it shine forth in the universe. In the words of Paul, "We all, with unveiled face, beholding the glory of the Lord, are being changed into his likeness from one degree of glory to another" (2 Cor. 3:18). When we attain this goal, we participate in divine life and transform our very nature. We become the children of God, temples of the Holy Spirit (1 Cor. 6:19). By increasing the gifts of grace, we surpass ourselves and elevate ourselves higher than Adam was before his fall, for not only do we return to man's primitive purity, but we are deified, transfigured, "united to divine beauty"; we become gods by grace.

This ascension of man reverses the process of the fall and begins to deliver the universe from disorder and corruption, since the deification attained by the saint constitutes the beginning of the cosmic transfiguration to come.

The image of God is ineffaceable in man. Baptism only reestablishes and purifies it. The likeness to God, however, can increase or decrease. Being free, man can assert himself in God or against God. He can, if he wants, become a child of perdition. Then the image of God grows obscure in him, and in his nature he can achieve an abject dissimilarity, a caricature of God.

---

10. This word, created at the time of Cyril and Methodius to translate the Greek word ὅσιος, indicates the attainment of divine likeness by man. A corresponding expression does not exist in other languages. The opposite term ("dissimilar"), however, can be traced to a very distant epoch. Plato uses this term in a philosophical sense (ἐκπεσεῖν εἰς τὸν τῆς ἀνομοιότητος πόντον) in his *Politics* to express the "noncorrespondence" of the world to its Idea. Athanasius the Great already uses it in a Christian sense: "He who created the world, seeing it succumb to the storm and in danger of being swallowed up in the place of dissimilitude, seized the helm of the soul and came to its aid by correcting all of its transgressions." Augustine in his *Confessions* says, *"et inveni me longe esse a Te in regione dissimilitudinis"* (in *Patrologia Latina*, ed. J. P. Migne, 221 vols. [Paris, 1844–64], 32.742)—"and I found that I was far distant from you, in a region of total unlikeness," trans. Rex Warner (New York, 1983), 149.

The future transfiguration of the entire human nature, including that of the body, is prefigured for us in the transfiguration of the Lord on Mount Tabor: "He was transfigured before them, and his face shone like the sun, and his garments became white as light" (Matt. 17:2; cf. Mark 9:2–8; Luke 9:28–36). The Lord no longer appeared to his disciples in his "form of a servant," but as God. The whole body of Christ was transfigured, becoming, so to speak, the luminous clothing of his divinity. In his transfiguration "on Mount Tabor, not only divinity appeared to men, but humanity also appeared in divine glory."[11] The fathers of the seventh ecumenical council explain: "With regard to the nature of the transfiguration, it took place not in such a way that the Word left the human image, but rather in the illumination of this human image by his glory."[12] In the words of Gregory Palamas: "Thus Christ assumes nothing foreign, nor does he take on a new state, but he simply reveals to his disciples what he is."[13]

The transfiguration is a manifestation, perceptible by the whole human being, of the divine glory of the Second Person of the Holy Trinity, who, in his incarnation, is inseparable from his divine nature, which is common to both the Father and the Holy Spirit. United hypostatically, the two natures of Christ remain distinct one from the other ("without mixture or confusion," according to the formulation of Chalcedon), but the divine energies penetrate the humanity of Christ and make his human nature become resplendent by transfiguring it in a flash of uncreated light. This is "the kingdom of God [which] has come with power" (Mark 9:1).

According to the Fathers, Christ showed to his disciples the deified state to which all are called. Just as the body of our Lord was glorified and transfigured, becoming resplendent with divine glory and infinite light, so also the bodies of the saints are glorified and become luminous, being transfigured by the force of divine grace. Seraphim of Sarov not only explained, but directly and visibly revealed this likeness between man and God by transfiguring himself before the eyes of his disciple Nicholas Motovilov.[14] Another saint, Simeon the New Theologian, describes his own experience of this divine illumination in the following way: "The man whose soul is all on fire also transmits the glory attained internally to his body, just as a fire transfers its heat to iron."[15]

11. Metropolitan Philaret, "Homily 12," in *Complete Works* (in Russian) (Moscow, 1873), 99.

12. Sixth session, in *Collectio*, ed. Mansi, 12.321CD.

13. Gregory Palamas *Hagioriticus tomus* (PG 150.1232C).

14. I. Gorainoff, *Sérafin de Sarov* (Bellefontaine, 1973), 208–14.

15. Simeon the New Theologian *Catechesis* 83, in *Traités théologiques et éthiques*, ed. J. Darrouzès (Paris, 1967), 2:128–29.

Just as iron when it is united with fire becomes hot and yet remains iron, though it is purified, so also human nature when it comes into contact with grace remains what it is, remains whole. Nothing is lost. On the contrary, human nature is purified just as iron is purified when in contact with fire. Grace penetrates human nature, is united with it, and from this point on one begins to live the life of the world to come. This is why we can say that a saint is more fully human than the sinner is. Saints are free from sin, which is essentially foreign to human nature; they realize the primordial meaning of their existence; with their lives they participate in constructing and put on the incorruptible beauty of the kingdom of God. For this reason beauty, as it is understood by the Orthodox church, is not the characteristic beauty of a creature. It is a part of the life to come, when God will be all in all. "The Lord reigns; he is clothed with majesty" (Ps. 93:1), we hear in the prokeimenon (short anthem before Scripture reading) at vespers on Saturday evening. This is an image of the eternal life to come. Pseudo–Dionysius the Areopagite calls God beauty because, on the one hand, God bestows on all creatures a unique beauty, and, on the other hand, he adorns them with another beauty, with the true divine beauty. Every creature is, so to speak, marked with a seal of its Creator. But this seal is not yet the divine likeness, but only the beauty characteristic of the creature.[16] This beauty can be a path or a means of bringing us closer to God. Indeed, according to Paul, "ever since the creation of the world, his invisible nature, namely, his eternal power and deity, has been clearly perceived in the things that have been made" (Rom. 1:20). For the church, however, the value and the beauty of the visible world lie not in the temporary splendor of its present state, but in its potential transfiguration, realized by humans. In other words, true beauty is the radiance of the Holy Spirit, the holiness of and participation in the life of the world to come.

Thus the second part of the kontakion leads us to the patristic understanding of the icon and allows us to grasp the profound meaning of Canon 82 of the Quinisext Council (692): "We represent on icons the *holy flesh* of the Lord."[17] The fathers of the seventh ecumenical council explain this in the following words:

> Although the catholic church represents Christ in his human form (μορφή) through painting, it does not separate his flesh from the divinity which is joined to it. . . . When we make the icon of the Lord, we confess his deified flesh, and we recognize in the icon nothing except an image representing a resemblance to the prototype. It is for this reason that it receives its name; it participates only in this, and is therefore venerable and holy.[18]

16. Pseudo–Dionysius the Areopagite *De divinis nominibus* 4 (PG 3.701C).
17. *Epistolae* 2 (PG 98.157BD).
18. Sixth session, in *Collectio*, ed. Mansi, 13.344.

Theodore the Studite explains even more clearly: "The representation of Christ," he says, "is not in the likeness of a corruptible man, which is disapproved of by the apostles, but as he himself had said earlier, it is in the likeness of the incorruptible man, but incorruptible precisely because he is not simply a man, but God who became man."[19] These words of Theodore explaining the contents of the icon, and the words of the fathers of the seventh ecumenical council, reflect the christological teaching of Gregory of Nazianzus: "Let us not be deprived of our integral salvation by attributing only bones, veins, and the human exterior to the Savior. Let us keep man in his entirety and add the divinity."[20]

By comparing these texts, we see that the task of the New Testament image, as the Fathers understood it, consists precisely in portraying as faithfully and completely as possible the truth of the divine incarnation, insofar as this can be done by art. The image of the man Jesus is the image of God; this is why the fathers of the seventh ecumenical council, having his icon in mind, say: "In the same Christ, we contemplate both the inexpressible and the represented."[21]

As we can see, therefore, the icon is an image not only of a living but also of a deified prototype. It does not represent the corruptible flesh destined for decomposition, but transfigured flesh illuminated by grace, the flesh of the world to come (see 1 Cor. 15:35–46). It portrays the divine beauty and glory in material ways which are visible to physical eyes. The icon is venerable and holy precisely because it portrays this deified state of its prototype and bears his name. This is why grace, characteristic of the prototype, is present in the icon. In other words, the grace of the Holy Spirit sustains the holiness both of the represented person and of his icon, and this grace brings about the relationship between the faithful and the saint through the intermediary of the icon of the saint. The icon participates in the holiness of its prototype and, through the icon, we in turn participate in this holiness in our prayers.

The fathers of the seventh ecumenical council distinguished carefully between an icon and a portrait. The latter represents an ordinary human being, the former a man united to God. The icon is distinguishable from the portrait by its very content. This content calls for specific forms of expression which are characteristic of the icon alone, and which distinguish it from all other images. The icon indicates holiness in such a way that it need not be inferred by our thought but is visible to our physical eyes. As the image of the sanctification of man, the icon represents the reality which was revealed in the transfiguration on Mount Tabor, to the

19. Theodore the Studite *Adversus iconomachos* 7.1 (PG 99.488).
20. Gregory of Nazianzus *Ad Cledonium contra Apollinarium epistola* 1 (PG 37.184AB).
21. Sixth session, in *Collectio*, ed. Mansi, 13.244B.

extent that the disciples were able to understand it. This is why the liturgical texts, particularly for the Feast of the Holy Face (August 16), set up
a parallel between the content of the icon and the transfiguration:

> Falling to the ground on the holy mountain, the greatest of the apostles
> prostrated themselves upon seeing the Lord reveal the dawn of divine
> brightness, and now we prostrate ourselves before the Holy Face, which
> shines forth brighter than the sun. . . . Having illuminated the human im-
> age which had grown dark, O Creator, thou didst reveal it on Mount Tabor
> to Peter and to the Sons of Thunder; and now bless and sanctify us, O Lord
> who lovest mankind, by the brightness of thy most pure image.[22]

This parallel, which can also be illustrated by other texts, is certainly not
the fruit of simple poetic imagination, but is, rather, an indication of the
spiritual content of the icon. The icon of the Lord shows us that which was
revealed to the apostles on Mount Tabor. We contemplate not only the face
of Jesus Christ, but also his glory, the light of divine truth made visible to
our eyes by the symbolic language of the icon, "the accomplishment made
clear to everyone by paintings," as was stated at the Quinisext Council.

"...We confess and proclaim our salvation in word and images."

This spiritual reality of the icon assumes all its practical teaching value
in the last phrase of the kontakion of the Triumph of Orthodoxy: "We
confess and proclaim our salvation in word and images." Thus the kontakion ends with our answer to God, with the acceptance and confession
of the divine economy of salvation.

It is easy to understand how to confess salvation in words. The confession in image (or by deed) can be understood as the accomplishment of
the commandments of Christ. But there is something more here. We find
the clearest explanation of these words in the Synodicon of the Triumph
of Orthodoxy. This Synodicon contains a series of anathemas against the
heretical iconoclasts and a series of proclamations of eternal remembrance
of the confessors of Orthodoxy.[23] The third paragraph proclaims eternal
remembrance of "those who believe and who substantiate their words with

---

22. Second and third stichera, tone 4.
23. The oldest text of this Synodicon to have come down to us is a copy made in the
sixteenth century of an eleventh-century text. This text, called the Madrid text, was published by T. Ouspensky in 1891 in Russian (*Otcherki vizantiiskoi obrazovannosti* 89). The
seven paragraphs of this text summarize the entire dogmatic teaching on the icon, concluding with a proclamation of eternal remembrance of those of the Orthodox faith. In
counterpoint, five other paragraphs note the confessional errors of and anathematize those
who distort true doctrine. In the Russian church during the seventeenth century, this Synodicon was modified to such a degree that its entire dogmatic content about the icon

writings and *their deeds with representations*, for the propagation and affirmation of the truth by word and images." "Representations" implies that
there are deeds which should be represented. But the act of creating
images is also a "deed." This word takes on a double meaning: internal and
external deeds. In other words, it denotes the living experience of the
church, the experience which is expressed in words or in images by those
who have attained holiness. On the one hand, we can reestablish in and
through the grace of the Holy Spirit our likeness to God. We can transform ourselves by an internal effort (the spiritual *praxis*) and make of ourselves living icons of Christ. This is what the Fathers call "an active life,"
an internal deed. On the other hand, we can also, for the good of others,
translate our inner sanctification into images, either visible or verbal: "We
proclaim our salvation in words and images," says the kontakion. We can
therefore also create an external icon, making use of matter which surrounds us and which has been sanctified by the coming of God on earth.
Certainly, we can express the inner spiritual state by words alone, but such
a state is made apparent, visibly confirmed, *shown* by representation. Word
and image point to one another.

Relating everything we have said about the content of the icon to a text
in the first epistle of Paul to the Corinthians will help us to understand the
significance of the icon, for this text and the icon express the same teaching and the same experience. "How are the dead raised?" asks Paul. And
he answers, "You foolish man! What you sow does not come to life unless
it dies. And what you sow is not the body which is to be" (1 Cor. 15:35–
37). He compares our mortal body to the grain thrown to the ground. In
the course of this present life, the grain must germinate, that is, it must to
some extent enter the life to come. Similarly, we must enter the life of the
age to come in order to open ourselves to that form which it will please
God to give us in the general resurrection. "What is sown is perishable,
what is raised is imperishable. It is sown in dishonor, it is raised in glory. It
is sown in weakness, it is raised in power. It is sown a perishable body, it is
raised a spiritual body" (1 Cor. 15:42–44). Christ, the new Adam, renewed
and re-created our human nature in immortality.

> The first man Adam became a living being; the last Adam became a life-
> giving spirit. But it is not the spiritual which is first but the physical, and
> then the spiritual. The first man was from the earth, a man of dust; the sec-
> ond man is from heaven. As was the man of dust, so are those who are of

disappeared and its meaning was completely changed. The expression of Orthodox teaching was replaced by a series of general statements, for example, a statement of support for
the seventh ecumenical council. This text contains only one passage on the icon. This passage, which closely resembles a paraphrase of one of the canons of the Council of Trent
(1563), is of little interest since it is limited to a rejection of the accusation of idolatry.

the dust; and as is the man of heaven, so are those who are of heaven. Just as we have borne the image of the man of dust, we shall also bear the image of the man of heaven. I tell you this, brethren: flesh and blood cannot inherit the kingdom of God, nor does the perishable inherit the imperishable. [1 Cor. 15:45–50]

And a little further on, the apostle says, "For this perishable nature must put on the imperishable, and this mortal nature must put on immortality" (1 Cor. 15:53).

The light of the transfiguration on Mount Tabor is already the glory of the world to come. For the power which resurrects the saints after their death is the Holy Spirit. And, in fact, during their terrestrial life he vivifies not only their souls but also their bodies. This is why we say that the icon transmits not the everyday, banal face of man, but his glorious and eternal face. For the very meaning of the icon is precisely to depict the heirs of incorruptibility, the heirs of the kingdom of God, of which they are the firstfruits from the time of their life here on earth. The icon is the image of one in whom the grace which consumes passions and which sanctifies everything is truly present. This is why the flesh is represented completely differently from ordinary corruptible flesh. Absolutely devoid of all emotional explanation, the icon is a peaceful transmission of a certain spiritual reality. If grace enlightens the entire person, so that the entire spiritual and physical being is filled by prayer and exists in the divine light, the icon visibly captures an individual who has become a living icon, a true likeness of God. *The icon does not represent the divinity. Rather, it indicates the human's participation in the divine life.*[24]

There is, therefore, an organic link between the veneration of saints and that of the icons. This is why in a theology that has removed the veneration of saints (Protestantism), the sacred image no longer exists. Where the concept of holiness differs from that of Orthodoxy, the image moves away from tradition.

24. One sometimes hears non-Orthodox, and occasionally even certain Orthodox, say that if the Christian art of the West, that of the Roman church, leans towards Nestorianism, the Orthodox icon has nuances of Monophysitism. What we have already said about the content of the icon permits us to see the absurdity of this statement. Though one can say that Western art is really Nestorian because it represents only the human aspect of the sacred, that is, the terrestrial reality alone, the Orthodox icon has nothing to do with Monophysitism because it represents neither the divinity nor man absorbed by it. Rather, it represents man in the fullness of his terrestrial nature, purified from sin and united with the divine life. To accuse Orthodox art of Monophysitism is to completely misunderstand its content. For the very same reasons, one could accuse the Holy Scripture or the Orthodox liturgy of Monophysitism, because like the icon they express a double reality: that of the creature and that of divine grace.

The Content of the Icon

Historical Reality

Our analysis of the kontakion of the Triumph of Orthodoxy gives us a clearer understanding of the double realism of the New Testament sacred image. Just like the God-man, Jesus Christ, "in whom dwells all the fullness of the Godhead bodily" (Col. 2:9), so also the church, the body of Christ, is both a divine and human system. It unites two realities in itself: the historical, earthly reality and the grace of the Holy Spirit, the reality of the world and that of God. The purpose of sacred art is precisely to bear witness visibly to these two realities. It is realistic in these two senses, and thus the icon is distinguishable from all other things, just as the Holy Scripture is distinguishable from all other literary works.

The church piously preserves historical reality in the representation of Christ, the saints, and the events of the Bible. Only a surrender to the most concrete history can, by the grace of the Holy Spirit, turn an icon into a possible encounter with the person represented. "It is appropriate," Patriarch Tarasius wrote to the emperor and the empress, "to accept the precious icons of Jesus Christ, since he became the perfect man, provided such icons are painted with historic exactness, in conformity with the Gospel story."[25] The characteristic traits of the saints will therefore be carefully preserved; only such fidelity to the historical truth allows the iconography of the saints to be so stable. Actually, it is a matter not only of transmitting an image consecrated by tradition, but above all of preserving a direct and living link with the person whom the icon represents. This is why it is essential that an image reproduce, to the greatest degree possible, the traits of the person. Obviously, this is not always possible. Like the biographies of the saints, the physical traits of the saints are often more or less forgotten, and it is difficult to reconstruct them. The likeness therefore risks being imperfect. The unskillfulness of the painter can also lessen the likeness. However, it can never disappear completely. An irreducible minimum always remains which provides a link with the prototype of the icon. As Theodore the Studite writes, "Even if we grant that the image does not have the same form as the prototype because of insufficient artistic skill, still our argument would not be invalid. For veneration is given to the image not insofar as it falls short of similarity, but insofar as it resembles its prototype."[26] In other words, what is essential in this case is not what an icon lacks in resemblance to its prototype, but what it has in common with it. The iconographer may limit himself to a few characteristic traits. In the

25. In *Collectio,* ed. Mansi, 13.404D.
26. Theodore the Studite *Antirrheticus* 3.5 (PG 99.421; *On the Holy Icons,* trans. Catharine P. Roth [Crestwood, N.Y.: St. Vladimir's Seminary Press, 1981], 104).

majority of cases, however, the faithfulness to the original is such that a devout Orthodox can easily recognize the icons of their most revered saints, not to mention those of Christ and the Virgin. And even if some saint is unknown to them, they can always say to which order of sainthood the saint belongs, that is, martyr, bishop, monk, or whatever.

The Orthodox church has never accepted the painting of icons according to the imagination of the artist or from a living model, which would signify a conscious and total break from the prototype. The name which the icon bears would then no longer correspond to the person represented, and this would be a flagrant lie which the church could not tolerate. (This general rule has frequently been broken or abused in the past few centuries.) In order to avoid falsehood and a break between the image and its prototype, iconographers use old icons and manuals as models. The ancient iconographers knew the faces of the saints as well as they knew those of their close relatives. They painted them either from memory or by using a sketch or a portrait. Indeed, once a person had acquired a reputation for holiness, an image was made of him to distribute among the faithful immediately after his death, and thus before his official canonization and the discovery of his relics.[27] In this way all kinds of accounts, and particularly sketches and the evidence of contemporaries, were preserved on icons.[28]

Depiction of Holiness and Divine Grace

However, the historical reality alone, even when it is very precise, does not constitute an icon. Since the person depicted is a bearer of divine grace, the icon must portray his holiness to us. Otherwise, the icon would have no meaning. If, in representing the human aspect of the incarnate God, the icon portrayed only the historical reality, as does, for

27. N. P. Kondakov notes a characteristic case of the use of the portrait as a documentary basis for the icon. In 1558, when the relics of Nicetas, archbishop of Novgorod, were discovered intact, a posthumous portrait of the saint was made and sent to the ecclesiastical authorities with the following letter: "By the grace of the saint, lord, we have sent you on paper an image of St. Nicetas, bishop . . . ; following this model, lord, order that an icon of the saint be made." This was followed by details describing the outward appearance of Nicetas, his vestments, and so forth, to complete the portrait drawn on paper (*The Russian Icon* [in Russian], vol. 3, Part One, 18–19).

28. When the living tradition began to disappear, or more exactly, when people began to deviate from it, toward the end of the sixteenth century, the documentation which the iconographers used was systematized. It was then that manuals appeared with what are called *podlinniki*, with and without illustrations. These establish the standard iconography of the saints and the feast days and indicate the principal colors. When they are not illustrated, they contain brief descriptions which characterize the saints and also mention the colors. As documentation, these *podlinniki* are indispensable to iconographers. But in no way can one attribute to them the same significance as that of iconographic canons or the holy tradition, as certain Western authors do.

example, a photograph, the church would see Christ with the eyes of the nonbelieving crowd that surrounded him. But according to the commentary of Simeon the New Theologian, the words of Christ, "he who has seen me has seen the Father" (John 14:9), were addressed only to those who, while looking at Jesus the man, simultaneously contemplated his divinity:

> Indeed, if we were to conceive this vision as it relates to the body, then those who crucified him and spat upon him would also have seen the Father; thus, there would be no difference or preference between believers and unbelievers, since all have equally reached, and, evidently, will reach the desired beatitude.[29]

Vladimir Lossky expresses a similar thought:

> The "historical Christ," "Jesus of Nazareth," as He appears to the eyes of alien witnesses; this image of Christ, external to the Church, is always surpassed in the fullness of the revelation given to the true witnesses, to the sons of the Church, enlightened by the Holy Spirit. The cult of the humanity of Christ is foreign to Eastern tradition; or, rather, this deified humanity always assumes for the Orthodox Christian that same glorious form under which it appeared to the disciples on Mount Tabor: the humanity of the Son, manifesting forth that deity which is common to the Father and the Spirit.[30]

The precise difference between the contemplation of the church and secular vision is that in the visible the church contemplates the invisible, and in the temporal the eternal, which is revealed to us in worship. Like worship itself, the icon is a revelation of eternity in time. This is why in sacred art the naturalistic portrait of a person can be only a historical document; in no way can it reflect the liturgical image, the icon.

We have said that the icon expresses the spiritual experience of holiness, and there we also see the same authenticity as in the transmittal of the historical reality; we "are surrounded by so great a cloud of witnesses," in the words of Paul (Heb. 12:1), witnesses who communicate this experience of sanctification to us. Simeon comments, "One should call their testimony a narration of things seen, while the term *concept* (νόημα) is to be applied to an idea born in the mind."[31] Indeed, only a living, personal experience can bring forth the words, forms, colors, or lines which truly correspond to what they express. Simeon continues:

29. Simeon the New Theologian, in *Traités*, ed. Darrouzès, 2:86–87.
30. Lossky, *Mystical Theology*, 243.
31. Simeon the New Theologian, in *Traités*, ed. Darrouzès, 2:94–95.

Anyone who wants to tell something about, say, a house, a town, or a place
. . . , even a play . . . , must have seen and learned its content thoroughly; only
then can he speak with plausibility. For, if he has not seen it beforehand, what
could he say of his own devising? . . . Thus, if no one can speak of or give a
description of visible, earthly things without having seen them with his own
eyes, how then would anyone have the power to speak . . . about God, things
divine, and even the saints and servants of God, and about the vision of God
which appears ineffably in them? It is the latter which produces in their heart
an ineffable strength. Human words do not allow us to say more about it, unless one is illuminated first by the light of knowledge.[32]

The transfiguration of Christ occurred before only three witnesses, the
three apostles capable of receiving this revelation; and even they saw this
dawn of divine light only to the extent that they were able (that is, to the
extent of their inner participation in this revelation). We can draw an
analogy from the lives of the saints. When Seraphim of Sarov was transfigured before Motovilov, to whom he wished to show the aim of Christian life,
he explained to Motovilov that he was able to see this transfiguration only
because he participated in it himself to a certain extent. He would not have
been able to see the light of grace if he himself had not been enlightened. The
essentiality of personal enlightenment also explains why tradition asserts that
the evangelist Luke painted the icons of the Virgin after Pentecost. Without
this "light of knowledge," about which Simeon the New Theologian speaks,
without a direct participation in the sanctification and concrete evidence, no
science, no technical perfection, no talent can be of much help. Until the
Holy Spirit descended upon them, the apostles themselves (who, however,
had constantly seen Christ and believed in him) had no direct experience of
sanctification by the Holy Spirit, and consequently they were not able to
express it in word or image. This is why neither Holy Scripture nor a holy
image could appear before Pentecost. In the creation of an icon, nothing can
replace the personal, concrete experience of grace. Without such personal
experience, one can paint icons only by transmitting the experience of those
who had it. This is why the church, through the voice of its councils and its
hierarchs, ordains that icons be painted as they were formerly painted by the
holy iconographers. "To represent with colors which conform to tradition,"
says Simeon of Thessalonica, "is true painting; it is analogous to a faithful
copy of the Scriptures; and divine grace rests upon it, since what is represented is holy."[33] It is necessary to "represent with colors which conform to
tradition," because through tradition we participate in the experience of the
holy iconographers, in the living experience of the church.

32. Ibid., 96–99.
33. Simeon of Thessalonica *Dialogus contra haereses* 13 (*PG* 155.113D).

These words, like those of the seventh ecumenical council, emphasize the participation of the image in the holiness and glory of its prototype. The grace of God rests on the image, says John of Damascus, because "the saints were filled with the Holy Spirit during their lives. Even after their death the grace of the Holy Spirit lives on inexhaustibly in their souls, in their bodies which are in their tombs, in their writings, and in their holy images, not because of their nature, but as a result of grace and divine action."[34] The grace of the Holy Spirit lives in the image, which "sanctifies the eyes of the faithful," according to the Synodicon of the Triumph of Orthodoxy (paragraph 4), and which heals both spiritual and corporal illnesses: "We venerate thy most pure image, by which thou hast saved us from the servitude of the enemy," we sing at matins on the Feast of the Holy Face; "by representation, thou healest our illnesses."[35]

The means used by the icon to convey spiritual quality corresponds perfectly to the state which is to be communicated, and which has been described in words by the holy ascetic fathers. It is obvious that grace cannot be expressed by any human means. In real life, if we happen to meet a saint, we do not actually see his holiness. "The world does not see the saints, just as a blind man does not see light."[36] Consequently, we cannot represent this holiness, which we do not see; it cannot be portrayed by word, by image, or by any human means. In the icon, however, it can be portrayed with the help of forms, colors, and symbolical lines, by an artistic language established by the church and characterized by strict historical realism. This is why an icon is more than an image representing a certain religious subject. Such subjects can be represented in different ways. But the specific character of an icon consists more particularly in the *how* of the representation, that is, in the means by which the sanctified state of the represented person is portrayed.

According to the liturgy for the Feast of the Holy Face, we prostrate ourselves before the icon of the Savior, whose face "shines more brightly than the sun"; we ask to be "enlightened" by the image of Christ (see the stichera for August 16). We must remember that scriptural or liturgical comparisons with the perceptible world that are intended to teach us about the spiritual realm are only images and not adequate descriptions. And thus, speaking of the Evangelists' account of the transfiguration of Christ, John of Damascus justifies the inevitably insufficient comparison between divine grace and the light of the sun, emphasizing that it is impossible to represent the uncreated

---

34. John of Damascus *De imaginibus* 1.19 (PG 94[1].1249CD).

35. Feast of the Holy Face (August 16), magnification and ode 7 of the canon.

36. Metropolitan Philaret, "Sermon 57: For the Annunciation," in *Sermons* (in Russian) (Moscow, 1874), vol. 3.

by means of the created.[37] In other words, the material light of the sun can be only an *image* of the divine, uncreated light, and nothing more.

On the other hand, the icon must correspond to sacred texts which are absolutely explicit, that is, texts which are not a matter of poetic imagery or of an allegory, but of translating concrete reality. But how is spiritual illumination, a light "which shines brighter than the sun," surpassing, therefore, all the means of representation, to be depicted in the icon? By colors? But they are not sufficient to portray the natural light of the sun. How then could they represent the light which surpasses that of the sun?

In the writings of the Fathers, as well as in the lives of the saints, we often find evidence of a certain light which made the faces of the saints shine internally at the moment of their supreme glorification, just as the face of Moses glowed when he descended from the mountain, so much so that he had to cover it because the people could not stand the glare (Exod. 34:30; 2 Cor. 3:7–8). The icon conveys this phenomenon of light by a halo, which is a precise sign, in an image, of a well-defined event in the spiritual world. The light which shines from the glorified faces of the saints and which surrounds their heads, as well as the upper part of their bodies, naturally has a spherical shape. As Motovilov says, when speaking of the transfiguration of Seraphim: "Imagine, in the very center of the sun, in the most brilliant burst of its rays, the face of the man who speaks to you."[38] Since it is obviously impossible to represent this light as such, the only way to convey it in painting is to depict a disk, like a pattern, so to speak, of this luminous sphere. It is not a matter of placing a crown above the head of the saint, as is sometimes done in Western images, where this crown somehow remains external; rather, it is a matter of portraying the radiance of the face. The halo is not an allegory, but the symbolical expression of an authentic and concrete reality. It is an indispensable part of the icon— indispensable yet insufficient. Indeed, it expresses other things besides Christian holiness. The pagans also frequently represented their gods with halos, as well as their emperors, undoubtedly to emphasize the divine nature of the latter.[39] It is not, therefore, the halo alone which distin-

---

37. John of Damascus *Homilia in transfiguratione* (PG 94[3].545–46); see also Basil Krivochéine, "L'Enseignement ascétique et théologique de saint Grégoire Palamas," *Seminarium Kondakovianum* 8 (Prague, 1936): 135.

38. Quoted in Gorainoff, *Sérafin*, 209.

39. We cannot say what this light symbolizes for the pagans. On the one hand, the church recognizes a partial revelation outside of itself, and one may then conclude that the mystery of uncreated light could have been revealed to the pagans to a certain extent. In any case, they knew that divinity was connected with light. On the other hand, the writings of the Fathers reveal to us that the phenomenon of light can have a demonic origin as well, because the devil himself sometimes takes on the features of an angel of light.

guishes an icon from other images. The halo is only an iconographic device, an outward expression of holiness, a witness of the light.[40] For even if the halo should be effaced and no longer be visible, an icon still remains an icon, and is clearly distinguishable from all other images. By its forms and by all its colors, it shows us, in a symbolical manner of course, the inner state of the man whose face "shines brighter than the sun." This state of inner perfection is so inexpressible that the Fathers and ascetic writers characterize it only as an absolute silence. The effect of this illumination on human nature and particularly on the body can, however, be described to a certain extent and indirectly represented. Simeon the New Theologian used the image of fire united with iron. Other ascetics left us more concrete descriptions:

> When prayer is sanctified by divine grace, . . . the entire soul is drawn towards God by an unknowable force, which pulls the body with it. . . . In the man born to the new life, it is not only the soul, nor the heart alone, but also the flesh which is filled with spiritual consolation and bliss, with the joy of the living God.[41]

And:

> Incessant prayer and the teaching of the divine Scripture open the spiritual eyes of the heart which see the King of powers, and there is great joy, and the desire of God burns strongly in the soul; then the flesh is also carried away by the effect of the Spirit and the whole man becomes spiritual.[42]

In other words, when the usual state of dissipation, the thoughts and sensations of the fallen nature, are replaced in man by silent prayer, and man is illuminated by the grace of the Holy Spirit, the entire human being flows like molten lava in a single burst toward God. The entire human nature is spiritually exalted; and then, according to Pseudo–Dionysius the Areopagite, "the disorderly is set in order, the formless takes on form, and the man is radiant with a life full of light."[43] Thus "the peace of God, which passes all understanding" (Phil. 4:7) lives in man, this peace which characterizes the presence of the Lord himself. "In the time of Moses and Elias," says Macarius of Egypt,

---

40. What is in view here is something completely different from the square halo which can be seen on certain images. Formerly, this was a way to indicate that the person was painted when still alive.

41. Bishop Ignatius Brianchaninov, *Ascetic Essay*, vol. 1 (in Russian).

42. "A Most Useful Account of Abba Philemon," in the Russian *Philokalia*, 3:397.

43. Pseudo–Dionysius the Areopagite, *Ecclesiastical Hierarchy*, trans. Thomas L. Campbell (Lanham, Md.: University Press of America, 1983), 32.

when God appeared to them, a multitude of trumpets and powers preceded him and served the majesty of the Lord; but the coming of the Lord himself was different, manifested by peace, silence, and calm. For it is said: "And after the earthquake a fire, but the LORD was not in the fire; and after the fire a still small voice" (1 Kings 19:12). This shows that the presence of the Lord is made manifest by peace and harmony.[44]

While remaining a creature, man becomes God according to grace. The body of man, as well as his soul, participates in the divine life. This participation does not change him physically: "What we see does not change," says Gregory of Nyssa. "An old man does not become an adolescent, wrinkles do not disappear. What is renewed is the inner being, soiled by sin and grown old in bad habits. This being returns to its childlike innocence."[45] In other words, the body retains its structure, its biological properties, and the characteristic traits of the outward human appearance. Nothing is lost. Rather, everything is changed, and the body, entirely united with grace, is illuminated by its union with God. "The Holy Spirit, uniting with the intellect," says Anthony the Great,

> teaches it to keep the entire body, from head to toe, in order—the eyes, so that they can see purely, the ears so that they can hear in peace. . . , the tongue, so that it can speak only good, the hands, so that they are put into movement only to be lifted in prayer or to perform works of charity . . . , the stomach, so that it may keep eating and drinking within appropriate limits . . . , the feet, so that they may walk aright in the will of God. . . . Thus, the entire body becomes accustomed to goodness and is transformed by submitting itself to the power of the Holy Spirit, so that it finishes by participating to a certain extent in the characteristics of the spiritual body that it will receive at the resurrection of the just.[46]

The patristic passages just quoted are like so many verbal icons, even to the details which the teaching of Anthony makes us understand. This is why such passages are of utmost importance to our subject. The effect of the divine grace on the human body, and in particular on the senses, as described in words by Anthony, is shown to us in the icon. The analogy between the verbal description and the image is so obvious that it leads us to a very clear conclusion: There is an ontological unity between the ascetic experience of Orthodoxy and the Orthodox icon. Precisely this experience and its outcome are described and conveyed by the Orthodox

44. Macarius of Egypt, in the Russian *Philokalia*, 1:192.
45. Quoted in George Florovsky, *The Fathers of the Fourth and Fifth Centuries* (in Russian) (Westmead, 1972), 171.
46. Anthony the Great, in the Russian *Philokalia*, 1:21.

ascetics who are shown to us in the icons. With the help of colors, forms, and lines, with the help of symbolical realism, an artistic language unique in its genre, the spiritual world of the man who has become a temple of God is revealed to us. The order and inner peace to which the holy fathers testify are conveyed in the icon by outward peace and harmony. The entire body of the saint, in every detail, even the hair and the wrinkles, even the garments and all that surrounds him, is unified and restored to a supreme harmony. This harmony in the icon is a visible expression of (1) victory over the inner division and chaos in man, and (2), as we shall see, victory by man over the division and chaos in humanity and in the world.

The unusual details of appearance which we see in the icon—in particular in the sense organs (the eyes without brilliance, the ears which are sometimes strangely shaped)—are represented in a nonnaturalistic manner, not because the iconographer is unable to do otherwise, but because their natural state is not what he wants to represent. The icon's role is not to bring us closer to what we see in nature, but to show us a body which perceives what usually escapes human perception, that is, the spiritual world. The questions which Seraphim of Sarov insistently asked as he was transfigured before Motovilov illustrate this well: "What do you see?" "What do you feel?" For the light which Motovilov saw, the scent which he smelled, the heat which he felt, were not of the physical order. At that moment his senses were perceiving the effect that grace had on the physical world which surrounded him. The icon's nonnaturalistic manner of representing the organs of sense conveys the deafness, the absence of reaction to the business of the world, the detachment from all excitement, and the impassiveness that characterize those who have reached holiness. And, conversely, it conveys their acceptance of the spiritual world. The Orthodox icon expresses in an image the theme of a hymn for Holy Saturday: "Let all mortal flesh keep silent ... pondering nothing earthly-minded." Everything here is subordinate to the general harmony which expresses peace, order, and inner harmony. For there is no disorder in the kingdom of the Holy Spirit. God is "the God of peace and order," Simeon the New Theologian says.[47]

The Meaning and Purpose of the Icon

We have seen that the icon shows the saint's glorified state, his transfigured, eternal face. But the icon is made for us; given everything that has been said, it should be clear that in its coded language the icon speaks to us in the same way that the patristic passages that were quoted are con-

---

47. Catechetical instruction attributed to Simeon the New Theologian (in Russian), *Prayer* 15 (Moscow, 1892): 143.

cerned with the ascetic practices not only of the monks, but of all believers; for the acquisition of grace is a task assigned to all members of the
church. As a manifestation of the ascetic experience of Orthodoxy, the
icon has a crucial educational function, and therein lies the essential goal
of sacred art. Its constructive role lies not only in the teaching of the truths
of the Christian life, but in the education of the whole person.

The content of the icon forms a true spiritual guide for the Christian
life and, in particular, for prayer. Prayer is a conversation with God; this is
why it requires the absence of passions, deafness to and the nonacceptance
of external, worldly excitement. "And thus, brothers," Gregory of Nazianzus says,

> let us not perform what is holy in an impure manner, what is sublime in a
> lowly fashion, what is worthy of honor in a disgraceful way, and, in short,
> what is holy in a terrestrial manner. . . . With us all things are somehow
> holy: activity, movement, desire, speaking, as well as our manner of walking
> and our garments, even our gestures, because reason (λόγος) extends to
> everything and guides man according to God; this is how our celebration is
> spiritual and solemn.[48]

This is precisely what is shown by the icon. A reasonable guide for our
senses is indispensable, for through them evil enters the human soul: "The
purity of man's heart is disturbed by the disordered movement of images
which enter and leave by the senses of sight, hearing, touch, taste, and
smell, as well as the spoken word," says Anthony the Great.[49] This is why
the Fathers speak of the five senses as the doors of the soul: "Close all the
doors of your soul, that is, your senses," Abba Isaiah says, "and guard them
carefully, so that your soul does not accidentally go wandering through
them, or so that neither the cares nor the words of the world drown out
the soul." Praying before an icon or simply looking at it, we are constantly
reminded of what Abba Isaiah says: "He who believes that his body will be
resurrected on the judgment day must keep it without sin and free from all
stain and vice."[50] We must see to it that, in our prayer at least, we close
the doors of our soul and strive to teach our body (as the saint in the icon
taught his body) to keep itself aright in and by the grace of the Holy Spirit,
so that our eyes may "see with purity," "our ears may hear in peace," and
our "heart does not nurture evil thoughts." In other words, through the
image the church endeavors to help us redeem our nature, which has been
tainted by sin.

48. Gregory of Nazianzus Orationes 11 (PG 35.840A).
49. Anthony the Great, in the Russian Philokalia, 1:122.
50. Abba Isaiah, Homily 15, in the Russian Philokalia, 1:33.

In describing the Orthodox ascetic experience of prayer the Fathers use the image of "the narrow gate . . . that leads to life" (Matt. 7:14). It is as if one were standing at the beginning of a road which, instead of leading to a particular place, opens up into infinite fullness. A door that opens into the divine life is opened for the Christian. This is how Macarius, like many other ascetic authors, speaks of spiritual progress: "Doors are opened . . . and man enters the interior of many abodes; and as he enters, still other doors are opened before him, and he is enriched; and to the degree that he is enriched, new marvels are shown to him."[51] Once embarked on the path to which the narrow gate leads, the Christian sees endless possibilities and perspectives opening before him; and his path, far from becoming narrow, becomes wider. But in the beginning it is but a simple point in our hearts at which our whole perspective must be reversed. This is the authentic and literal meaning of the Greek word μετάνοια, which means "change of mind."

Thus the icon is both a means to holiness and a path to follow. It is itself a prayer. Visibly and directly it reveals to us the freedom from passion about which the Fathers speak. It teaches us "to fast with our eyes," in the words of Dorotheus.[52] And indeed, it is impossible "to fast with our eyes" before just any image, be it abstract, or even an ordinary painting. Only the icon can portray what it means "to fast with our eyes" and what this allows us to attain.

Thus the aim of the icon is not to provoke or glorify in us a natural human feeling. It is not emotive, not sentimental. Its intention is to attune us to the transfiguration of all our feelings, our intelligence, and all the other aspects of our nature. It does so by stripping them of all exaltation which could be harmful or unhealthy. Like the deification which it conveys, the icon suppresses nothing that is human: neither the psychological element nor a person's various characteristics in the world. Thus the icon does not fail to indicate the occupation which the saint was able to turn into a spiritual activity, whether an ecclesiastic occupation such as that of a bishop or a monk, or a worldly occupation, such as that of a prince, a soldier, or a physician. As in the Gospel, every aspect of the saint's life—thought, learning, and human feelings—is represented in its contact with the divine world; this contact purifies everything and consumes that which cannot be purified. Every manifestation of human nature, each phenomenon of life, is illumined, becomes clear, acquires its true meaning and place.

Just as we represent the God-man as being similar to us in all things *except sin*, so do we represent the saint as a person freed from sin. According to Maximus the Confessor, "Our flesh, like the flesh of Christ, is also freed from the corruption of sin. For just as Christ was without sin through

51. Macarius of Egypt, in the Russian *Philokalia*, 1:230.
52. Dorotheus, *Teachings and Messages Useful to the Soul* (in Russian), 7th ed. (Optina Pustyn, 1895), 186.

his flesh and his soul as a man, so can we who believe in him, and who have put on Christ through the Spirit, be in him without sin through our will."[53] The icon shows us precisely the body of a holy person "in the mold of his glorious body" (Phil. 3:21), a body which is freed from the corruption of sin, and which "in a certain manner partakes of the properties of the spiritual body it will receive at the resurrection of the just."

Orthodox sacred art is a visible expression of the dogma of the transfiguration. The transfiguration of man is understood and transmitted here as a well-defined, objective reality in full accordance with Orthodox teaching. What is shown to us is not an individual interpretation or an abstract or more or less deteriorated understanding, but a truth taught by the church.

The colors of the icon convey the color of the human body, but not the natural flesh tints, which simply do not correspond to the meaning of the Orthodox icon. For much more is involved than depicting the physical beauty of the human body. The beauty in the icon is spiritual purity, inner beauty; in the words of Peter, "let it be the hidden person of the heart, with the imperishable jewel of a gentle and quiet spirit, which in God's sight is very precious" (1 Peter 3:4). It is the beauty of the communion of the terrestrial with the celestial. It is this beauty-holiness, this divine likeness attained by man, that the icon portrays. In its own language, the icon conveys the work of grace which, according to Gregory Palamas, "paints in us, so to speak, on what is the image of God that which is in the divine likeness, in such a way that . . . we are transformed into his likeness."[54] The justification and the value of the icon do not, therefore, lie in its beauty as an object, but in that which it represents—an image of beauty in the divine likeness.

It is understandable that the light of the icon which enlightens us is not the natural brightness of faces depicted by color, but rather the divine grace which purifies man, the light of purified and sinless flesh. This light of the sanctified flesh must not be understood only as a spiritual phenomenon, nor as a uniquely physical phenomenon, but as the two together, a revelation of the spiritual flesh to come.[55]

53. Maximus the Confessor, *Active and Contemplative Chapters* 67, in the Russian *Philokalia*, 3:263.

54. Gregory Palamas, "To the Nun Xenia, on the Virtues and the Passions," in the Russian *Philokalia*, 5:300–301.

55. This perspective helps explain why the problem of representing the human body never arose in Orthodoxy as in Roman Catholicism after the decision of the Council of Trent (25th session): "The Holy Council wishes that all impurity be avoided, that images not be given provocative charms." The "impurity" that had to be avoided was the human body. Accordingly, the first thing that the Roman ecclesiastical authorities did was to prohibit the representation of the naked body in religious art. A real purge against nudity began. By order of Pope Paul IV, the figures of Michelangelo's *Last Judgment* were covered. Pope Clement VIII, renouncing half measures, decided to have the whole fresco obliterated,

The clothing, while keeping its distinctiveness and covering the body in a perfectly logical fashion, is represented in such a way so as not to conceal the glorified state of the saint. It emphasizes the work of man and becomes in some way the image of his vestment of glory, of his robe of incorruptibility. The ascetic experience, or rather its result, also finds here its outward expression in the severity of the often geometrical forms, in the lighting, and in the lines of the folds. They cease to be disordered. They change their appearance and acquire a rhythm and an order which is subordinate to the general harmony of the image. In effect, the sanctification of the human body is communicated to its clothing. We know that touching the clothing of Christ, of the Virgin, the apostles, and the saints brought healing to the faithful. One need only recall the Gospel story of the hemorrhaging woman or the healings that took place through the clothing of Paul (Acts 19:12).

The inner order of the man represented in the icon is naturally reflected in his posture and in his movements. The saints do not gesticulate. They are in prayer before the face of God, and each of their movements and the very posture of their bodies take on a hieratic, sacramental aspect. Usually, they are fully turned towards the spectator, or at least partially turned. This trait has characterized Christian art from its origins in the catacombs. The saint is present before us and not somewhere in space. Addressing our prayer to him, we must see him face to face. This is without a doubt the reason why the saints are almost never represented in profile, except in very rare cases when they are turned toward the center in complicated works. A profile does not allow direct contact; it is, as it were, the beginning of absence. This is why only persons who have not yet attained holiness are represented in profile, such as the wise men and the shepherds in the icon of the nativity.

It is the nature of holiness to sanctify that which surrounds it. It is in man and through man that the participation of all creatures in the divine eternal life is actualized and made manifest. Just as creation fell with the fall of man, so is it saved by the deification of man, for "it was not for its own purposes that creation had frustration imposed upon it, but for the purposes of him who imposed it, with the intention that the whole creation itself might be freed from its slavery to corruption and brought into the same glorious freedom as the children of God" (Rom. 8:20–21).

---

and was stopped only by the entreaties of the Academy of Saint Luke. Charles Borromeo, who firmly believed in the decisions of the Council of Trent, had the nude obliterated whenever he found it. Paintings and statues which did not seem modest enough were destroyed (see Emile Mâle, *L'Art religieux après le Concile de Trente* [Paris, 1932], 2). Painters themselves burned their own works. The very character of sacred art in the Orthodox church prevented such a situation there.

We have a sign which marks the beginning of the restoration of unity in the entire fallen creation. This is the sojourn of Christ in the desert: "He was with the wild beasts, and the angels served him" (Mark 1:13). The heavenly and earthly creatures destined to become the new creation in the God-man Jesus Christ are assembled around him. The thought of the unification of the entire universe in peace clearly informs all Orthodox iconography.[56] This union of all creatures, beginning with the angels down to the inferior creatures, is the renewed universe to come; in the icon, it is contrasted to the general discord, to the prince of this world. Peace and harmony restored, the church embracing the entire world—this is the central idea of Orthodox sacred art, which dominates architecture as well as painting.[57] This is why, in the icon, we find that everything which surrounds a saint changes its mien. The world that surrounds man—the bearer and announcer of the divine revelation—here becomes transformed and renewed, an image of the world to come. Everything loses its usual disorderly aspect, everything becomes a harmonious structure: the landscape, the animals, architecture. Everything that surrounds the saint bows with him to a rhythmic order. Everything reflects the divine presence and is drawn—and also draws us—towards God. The representations of the earth, the world of vegetation, and the animal world in the icon are not intended to bring us close to what we always see around us—a fallen world in its corruptible state—but to show that this world participates in the deification of man. The effect of holiness on the entire created world, especially on the wild animals, is often seen in the saints' lives.[58] Epiphanius, a disciple and biographer of Sergius of Radonezh, comments on the attitude of wild beasts toward the saint: "Let no one be astonished, for you know that when God dwells in a man and when the Holy Spirit rests in him, everything submits to him as to Adam before his fall, when Adam lived alone in the desert." The life of Isaac the Syrian states that the animals who came to him smelled in him the odor which Adam exhaled before his fall. Similarly, because of the effects of saints' holiness animals represented in an icon have an unusual appearance. While preserving the characteristic traits of their species, they lose their usual appearance. This would seem to be odd or awkward if we did not understand the profound language of the iconographers, who allude here to the mystery of paradise, which is, at the moment, inaccessible to us.

As for architecture in the icon, while subordinate to the general harmony, it plays a particular role. Like the landscape, it identifies the place

56. This thought is most particularly emphasized in certain icons which reveal the cosmic meaning of creation—for example, "Let everything that breathes praise the Lord," or "All creation rejoices in you."

57. Eugene Trubetskoy, *The Meaning of Life* (in Russian) (Berlin, 1922), 71–72.

58. For example, Isaac the Syrian, Mary of Egypt, Sergius of Radonezh, Seraphim of Sarov, and Paul of Obnorsk.

where the event takes place: a church, a house, a town. But the building (just like the cave of the nativity or that of the resurrection) never encloses the scene. It acts only as a background, so that the event does not occur *in* the building, but *in front of* it. This is because the very meaning of the events that the icons represent is not limited to their historical place, just as they surpass the moment in time when they occurred. It is only since the beginning of the seventeenth century that Russian iconographers, under the influence of Western art, have begun representing scenes which take place within a building.

Although the general meaning and composition of the icon link the architecture and the human figures represented, there is a great difference. The representation of the human body, although not naturalistic, is with very rare exceptions completely logical: Everything is in its place. The same is true of clothing: The way in which garments are treated, in which the folds fall, is quite logical. But the architecture, both in its forms and in its details, frequently defies all human logic. Though real architectural forms are the starting point, proportion is absolutely neglected; the doors and windows are not in their proper place and, besides, are completely useless because of their dimensions. Contemporary opinion sees a blind attachment of the iconographers to Byzantine and ancient forms which have become incomprehensible. But the true meaning of this phenomenon is that the action represented in the icon transcends the rationalistic logic and the laws of earthly life. Architecture, be it ancient, Byzantine, or Russian, is the element which best permits the icon to portray this. It is arranged with a certain pictorial "foolishness for the sake of Christ," which is in complete contradiction to "the spirit of gravity." Such architectural fantasy systematically frustrates reason, puts it back in its place, and emphasizes the metalogical character of faith.[59]

The strange and unusual character of the icon is similar to that of the gospel. For the gospel is a true challenge to every order, to all the wisdom of the world. "I will destroy the wisdom of the wise, and the cleverness of the clever I will thwart," says the Lord by the mouth of Isaiah, whom Paul quotes (1 Cor. 1:19). The gospel calls us to life in Christ; the icon represents this life. This is why it sometimes uses irregular and shocking forms, just as holiness sometimes tolerates extreme forms which seem like madness in the eyes of the world, such as the holiness of those who are fools in Christ. "They say that I am mad," said one of them, "but

59. The alogical character of architecture continued until the period of decadence (end of the sixteenth and beginning of the seventeenth centuries), when the understanding of iconographic language was gradually lost. From that time on, architecture became logical and proportioned. What is amazing is that today one finds truly fantastic masses of architectural forms.

without madness one does not enter into the kingdom of God. . . . To live according to the gospel one must be mad. As long as men are reasonable and of sober mind, the kingdom of God will not come to earth."[60] Madness for the sake of Christ and the sometimes provocative forms of icons express the same evangelical reality. Such an evangelical perspective inverts that of the world. The universe shown to us by the icon is ruled not by rational categories or by human standards, but by divine grace. Hence the hieratic nature of the icon, its simplicity and majesty, its quietness; hence also the rhythm of its lines and the joy of its colors. It reflects the ascetic effort and the joy of victory. It is sorrow transformed into the joy of the living God. It is the new order in the new creation.

The world which we see here no longer reflects daily banality. The divine light penetrates everything, and this is why the persons and the objects are not illuminated from one side or another by a source of light; they do not project shadows, because there are no shadows in the kingdom of God, where everything bathes in light. In the technical language of iconographers, "light" is the background of the icon.

In this study we have tried to show that, just as the symbolism of the first centuries of Christianity was a language common to the entire church, so also the icon is a language common to the entire church because it expresses the common Orthodox teaching, the common Orthodox ascetic experience, and the common Orthodox liturgy. The sacred image has always expressed the revelation of the church, bearing it in a visible form to the faithful, placing it before their eyes as an answer to their questions, as a teaching and a guide, as a task to accomplish, as a prefiguration and the firstfruits of the kingdom of God.

Divine revelation and its acceptance by man are the same action in two ways, so to speak. Apocalypse and gnosis, the path of revelation and that of knowledge, correspond to each other. God descends and reveals himself to man; man responds to God by lifting himself, by harmonizing his life with the attained revelation. In the image he receives the revelation, and by the image he responds to this revelation to the degree that he participates in it. In other words, the icon is a visible testimony to the descent of God to man as well as to the impetus of man toward God. If the word and the song of the church sanctify our soul by means of hearing, the image sanctifies by means of sight, which is, according to the Fathers, the most important of the senses. "The eye is the lamp of the body. So, if your eye is sound, your whole body will be full of light" (Matt. 6:22).

60. Archimandrite Spiridon, *Mes Missions en Sibérie* (Paris: Editions du Cerf, 1950), 39–40.

By word and by image, the liturgy sanctifies our senses. Being an expression of the image and likeness of God restored in man, the icon is a dynamic and constructive element of worship.[61] This is why the church, by the decision of the seventh ecumenical council, orders that icons be placed "on the same level as the images of the life-giving cross, in all of the churches of God, on vases and sacred vestments, on the walls, on wooden boards, in homes and in the streets." In the icon, the church recognizes one of the means which can and must allow us to realize our calling, that is, to attain the likeness of our divine prototype, to accomplish in our life that which was revealed and transmitted to us by the God-man. The saints are very few in number, but holiness is a task assigned to all, and icons are placed everywhere to serve as examples of holiness, as a revelation of the holiness of the world to come, a plan and a project of the cosmic transfiguration. Furthermore, since the grace attained by the saints during their lives continues to dwell in their images,[62] these images are placed everywhere for the sanctification of the world by the grace which belongs to them. Icons are like the markers on our path to the new creation, so that, according to Paul, in contemplating "the glory of the Lord, [we] are being changed into his likeness" (2 Cor. 3:18).

Men who have known sanctification by experience have created images which correspond to it and which truly constitute a "revelation and demonstration of that which is hidden," in the words of John of Damascus, just as the tabernacle revealed what had been shown to Moses on the mountain. These images not only reveal a transfigured universe to man, but also allow him to participate in it. It can be said that the icon is painted according to nature, but with the help of symbols, because the nature which it represents is not directly representable, namely, the world which will be fully revealed only at the second coming of the Lord.

---

61. It is far from being merely conservative and having a passive function only, as certain outside observers think.
62. John of Damascus De imaginibus 1.19 (PG 94[1].1249CD).

4

The Virgin and the Saints in Orthodoxy

Sergius Bulgakov

Sergius Bulgakov (1871–1944) was the son of an Orthodox priest. One year before his seminary graduation (1888), however, he lost his childhood faith and became an ardent Marxist and atheist. In 1894 he graduated from the Law School of Moscow State University. At the age of thirty he returned to his Orthodox faith and in 1918 was ordained as a priest, an experience he once described as "like going through fire, scorching, cleansing, and regenerating." Because of the Soviet Revolution in 1917, Bulgakov was forced to minister in faraway Simferopol in the Crimea. In 1923 he was exiled from Russia, never to return. After two years in Prague, he settled in Paris, where he helped fellow Russian émigrés to found the Saint Sergius Orthodox Theological Institute. Bulgakov served there as professor of theology and dean until his death in 1944.

The Orthodox Church, from which the following selection is taken, was designed to introduce Westerners to Orthodoxy, and became the most famous of Bulgakov's many writings. First published in Russian, and then in English in 1935, the book has become a classic. In his treatment of the veneration of Mary and the saints, Bulgakov distinguishes Orthodoxy from both Protestantism and Catholicism, and addresses the charges that such liturgical practices amount to nothing more than crass superstition or pagan syncretism which weakens the unique mediatorial role of Christ. In addition, he touches upon the doctrines of relics and angels.

From Sergius Bulgakov, *The Orthodox Church* (Crestwood, N.Y.: St. Vladimir's Seminary Press, 1988), 116–28. Reprinted by permission.

The Veneration of Mary

The Orthodox church venerates the Virgin Mary as "more honorable than the cherubim and beyond compare more glorious than the seraphim," as superior to all created beings. The church sees in her the Mother of God, who, without being a substitute for the one Mediator, intercedes before her Son for all humanity. We ceaselessly pray to her to intercede for us. Love and veneration of the Virgin is the soul of Orthodox piety, its heart, that which warms and animates its entire body. A faith in Christ which does not include his virgin birth and the veneration of his mother is another faith, another Christianity from that of the Orthodox church. Protestantism is this other sort of Christianity, with its strange and deeply rooted lack of feeling for the Mother of God, a condition which dates from the Reformation. In this lack of veneration for the Virgin, Protestantism differs in almost equal measure from both Orthodoxy and Catholicism. Hence even the Protestant comprehension of the incarnation loses some of its fullness and power.

The perfect union of divine and human in Christ is directly connected with the sanctification and the glorification of human nature, and thus, above all, with the Mother of God. Without this concept the incarnation becomes only something external, kenotic, a voluntary self-humiliation by the assumption of human nature as the price necessary to purchase the justification of humanity before God. Here the incarnation is only a means of redemption, which has become a bitter necessity because of sin—and hence the Virgin Mary is only an instrument for the incarnation, inevitable, but still something external, an instrument which is laid aside and forgotten when the need has passed. This failure to be mindful of the Virgin Mary is often found in Protestantism in such extreme beliefs as that the Virgin might have had other children by Joseph, or even in a denial of the virgin birth itself. The Orthodox church never separates mother and Son, she who was incarnated by him who was incarnate. In adoring the humanity of Christ, we venerate his mother, from whom he received that humanity and who, in her person, represents the whole of humanity. Through the grace of God, in her all the sanctity accessible to humanity after the fall is attained. The church of the Old Testament had for its purpose the elevation, the conservation, and the preparation of a holy humanity worthy to receive the Holy Spirit, that is, worthy of the annunciation. That holy humanity was attained in the person of the Virgin. Hence Mary is not merely the instrument, but the direct positive condition of the incarnation, its human aspect. Christ could not have been incarnate by some mechanical process that violated human nature. It was necessary for that nature itself to say for itself by the mouth of the most pure human being: "Behold the handmaid of the Lord; be it unto me according to thy word" (Luke 1:38). At that moment the Holy Spirit descended upon her; the annunciation was the Pentecost of the Virgin, and the Spirit completely sanctified and abode with her.

The Orthodox church does not accept the Catholic dogma of 1854—the dogma of the immaculate conception of the Virgin, in the sense that she was exempt at birth from original sin. This would separate her from the human race, and she would then have been unable to transmit to her Son humanity.[1] But Orthodoxy does not admit in the all-pure Virgin any individual sin, for that would be unworthy of the dignity of the Mother of God. The connection between the Virgin and her Son does not cease with his birth. It continues in the same degree that the divine and human are inseparably united in Christ. During the earthly ministry of our Lord, the Virgin, infinitely humble, remains in the background. She leaves it only to take her place near the cross of Golgotha with him; she shares his passion. She is also the first to participate in his resurrection. The Virgin Mary is the center, invisible but real, of the apostolic church; it is in her that the secret of primitive Christianity is hidden, as well as that of the Evangel of the Spirit, written by John, whom Christ, as he hung upon the cross, gave her for a son. The church believes that, dying a natural death, she was not subject to corruption, but, raised up by her Son, she lives in her glorified body at the right hand of Christ in the heavens. In her is realized the idea of Divine Wisdom in the creation of the world, and Divine Wisdom in the created world. It is in her that Divine Wisdom is justified, and thus the veneration of the Virgin blends with that of the Holy Wisdom. In the Virgin there are united Holy Wisdom and the Wisdom of the created world, the Holy Spirit and the human hypostasis. Her body is completely spiritual and transfigured. She is the justification, the end, and the meaning of creation. She is, in this sense, the glory of the world. In her, God is already all in all.

Living in heaven in a state of glory the Virgin remains the mother of the human race for which she prays and intercedes. This is why the church addresses to her its supplications, invoking her aid. She covers the world with her veil, praying, weeping for the sins of the world; at the last judgment she will intercede before her Son and ask pardon from him. She sanctifies the whole natural world; in her and by her the world attains transfiguration. In a word, the veneration of the Virgin marks with its imprint all Christian anthropology and cosmology and all the life of prayer and piety.

Prayers addressed to the Virgin occupy a large place in the Orthodox service. Besides the feasts and the days specially consecrated to her, every office contains innumerable prayers addressed to her, and her name is con-

1. On the Orthodox cult of the Virgin, see Sergius Bulgakov, *The Unburned Bush* (in Russian) (Paris, 1927).

stantly spoken in the temple together with the name of our Lord Jesus Christ. Her icons are found before us on the iconostasis and in different places in the church and in the houses of the faithful. There exist numerous types of these icons, the originals of which are considered miraculous. This warmth natural to the cult of the Virgin comes from her humanity and her feminine nature. I sometimes think that the coldness of atmosphere of some Protestant churches results from the absence of just this warmth. In her and by her the feminine receives, in connection with the Holy Spirit, a place in piety. The deep veneration of the Virgin in Orthodoxy sometimes shocks outside observers because it seems analogous with paganism. Such critics discover the prototype of the Virgin in Isis and other female divinities. But even if it were admitted that paganism had a certain obscure prescience, the difference between these goddesses and the Virgin, who is a glorified creature, completely deified, is too evident to warrant any comparison. It must be remarked that the nuances which characterize the cult of the Virgin in the West (the chivalric cult of the Madonna, of the *belle dame*) are entirely unknown to the sober spirit of Orthodoxy, which rejects the least hint of eroticism.

The Cult of the Saints

The cult of the saints occupies a considerable place in Orthodox piety. The saints are our intercessors and our protectors in the heavens and, in consequence, living and active members of the church militant. Their blessed presence in the church manifests itself in their pictures and their relics. They surround us with a cloud of prayer, a cloud of the glory of God. This cloud of witnesses does not separate us from Christ, but brings us nearer, unites us to him. The saints are not mediators between God and humans—this would set aside the unique Mediator, which is Christ—but they are our friends, who pray with us and aid us in our Christian ministry and in our communion with Christ. Sometimes veneration of saints is seen as approaching the pagan cult of heroes or demigods, even to be equivalent to pagan polytheism. The parallel is not at all as far-fetched as it seems, however. Paganism, with all its superstitions and delusions, could have contained important premonitions, "foreshadowings," which for divine reasons remained unknown to the Old Testament church. This may be the case of the veneration of demigods, who were truly gods by grace, and who were known to the pagan world but unknown to Old Testament Judaism. It would have been a temptation beyond its strength for Judaism to diverge toward polytheism from the strict monotheism in which the chosen people were nurtured. Only after the coming of Christ could the unbridgeable chasm, as well as the closeness, between Christ and "those who belong to Jesus Christ" (Gal. 5:24) become clear. The dogmatic basis for the veneration of saints lies precisely in this link. The church is the body of Christ, and those who are saved in the church receive the power and the life of Christ; they are deified. They become gods by virtue of grace; they become christs in Jesus Christ.

Although our lot will be decided finally at the last judgment of Christ, already at the so-called preliminary judgment, which takes place after death for each person, the designation for glory and a crown of holiness becomes clear. It glows on the brow of a godly person even in his lifetime, for the judgment is only an open confirmation of his real state. Life eternal in God begins here, in the flux of time; but on departure from this life it becomes the defining principle of existence.

Orthodoxy does not believe that the glorification of the saints is founded on the special merits of the saints before God—merits supererogatory or necessary—a recompense which they have received, and which they can in turn use for the benefit of those who have not sufficient merit. That proud conception would truly put the saints in the rank of demigods. The saints are those who by their active faith and love have become like God, and show forth the image of God in its power, those who have obtained for themselves abundant grace. In this purification of the heart by a heroic effort of mind and body lies the road to salvation for everyone in whom Christ abides: "It is no longer I who live, but Christ who lives in me" (Gal. 2:20). In the words of the Lord: "If a man loves me, he will keep my word, and my Father will love him, and we will come to him and make our home with him" (John 14:23). On this road to salvation there are quantitative distinctions between persons which become qualitative and decisive for one's eternal fate. Beyond this threshold our salvation is accomplished as a decisive self-determination, and then begins the growth in grace, corresponding for each of us to our personal image and the type of our spiritual personality. Sanctity has as many forms as there are human individualities. The sublime work of holiness always has an individual and creative character. The church knows divers degrees of sanctity or spiritual aspects of salvation: prophets, apostles, martyrs, doctors, venerable monks, soldiers, and kings. And certainly this list is not complete; each epoch (ours among them) reveals new aspects of holiness in addition to those already existing. Besides, not all the saints are known to the world; there are those whom our Lord permits to remain unknown to us. There is a Feast of All Saints where all the saints together are commemorated, both those who are glorified and those who are not.

Saints can help us, not by force of their deserts but by force of the spiritual freedom in love that they have acquired through their spiritual efforts. This freedom gives them the power to represent us before God in prayer, and also in effective love for human beings. God accords to the saints, as to the angels, the power to accomplish his will by active though invisible aid accorded to humans. They are the church invisible which lives with the same life as the church visible. They are the hands of God by which God performs his works. This is why it is given to the saints to do deeds of love even after their death, not as works necessary to their salvation—for their salvation is already attained—but to aid their brothers in the way of salvation.

The extent of the power of the saints' effective participation corresponds to the extent of their spirit and to the magnitude of their efforts, "for star differs from star in glory" (1 Cor. 15:41). While there are degrees in sanctity, the members of the human race, being subject to original sin, cannot have levels of distinction comparable to the great and saving power of Christ's redemptive sacrifice. Even the pure Virgin bears witness to "God my Savior" (Luke 1:47). But our incomparability in this respect certainly does not remove distinctions in the forms of acquiring natural human gifts which are granted (ability for learning, for art, for practical skills, etc.); this is all the more true of spiritual life. Spiritual effort is a creative endeavor to acquire the Holy Spirit. It is achieved by becoming free from sin, which is granted to us by mastering a redemptive sacrifice. If we were passively indifferent to this effort, the division into sheep and goats at the day of judgment would not take place. Judgment presupposes distinctions in the achievement of sanctity.

The existence of the saints in the church is not only possible, but necessary for us. Each soul must have its own direct contact with Christ, its own conversation with him, its own life in the Savior. And in this there cannot be any mediator, just as there is none in our participation in the Eucharist: each person receives the body and blood of the Lord and is mystically joined with him. But the soul which clings individually to Christ should not be isolated. The sons of men, who belong to the same human race, cannot and should not be shut up in isolation. And thus it is that before the Christ who taught us to say "Our Father" we find ourselves together, with all our brothers, either those who are here with us on earth or those who are already with the saints. This is "the communion of saints." We are conscious, at one time, both of the immediate nearness and dearness of Christ and of the presence of our Lord and Judge. It is naturally necessary to hide ourselves in awe before the Judge of all, and here we take refuge beneath the protection of the Virgin and the saints. For they belong to our race and kind. With them we may speak in our language of human frailty, and thus, in mutual comprehension, stand shoulder to shoulder with them before the terrible judgment seat of God.

Of course, in our prayers addressed to the saints a certain interior spiritual perspective must be observed. The saints should not veil from us the grandeur of Christ; and our life in Christ, and through him in the Holy Trinity, should not be diminished. The conscience of the church shows us the right degree to maintain. But it cannot be denied that in practice superstition and the lack of religious teaching can bring us near to polytheism and near a syncretism where pagan vestiges tranquilly exist side by side with Christianity. But this is not due to the cult of the saints in itself. Those who reject this cult suffer great spiritual loss; while remaining near to Christ, they lose their true relation to him. They are destined to remain spiritually without a family, without race, without home, without fathers and brothers in Christ. They traverse the way of salvation all alone, each one for himself without looking for examples and without knowing communion with others. Certainly all this is not accomplished without a vigorous logic, and the authority and example of the saints of the church are replaced by the teaching of the doctors (for example, the apostles). But from these latter only teaching is received; it is impossible to pray with them or to them.

How does the church learn the mystery of the judgment of God about the saints? In other words, how is the glorification of the saints attained? In general, the answer to this question is as follows: this glorification becomes self-evident to the church. Special signs, different in each case, miracles, the incorruptibility of relics and, above all, evident spiritual aid testify to the saints. By an official act of canonization the church authorities testify to facts already evident to the ecumenical conscience of the church, and make legal the veneration of a given saint. As a matter of fact, this glorification (local or general) always precedes the juridical canonization which confirms it. In Orthodoxy, the act of canonization does not call for so meticulous a procedure as in Catholicism. Canonization is effected by an act of ecclesiastical authority—ecumenical or local. The source of sanctity is never exhausted in the church, which has known saints in all times of its existence. And doubtless the future will manifest new aspects of sanctity, each conformable to the life of its epoch.

One consequence of the cult of the saints is the veneration of their relics. Sometimes even bodily incorruption is revered as a sign of sanctity. Incorruption, however, is by no means a general rule, nor is it essential for canonization. The relics of the saints, when they are preserved, are very specially venerated. To indicate a particular instance, portions of relics are placed in the antimension, the silken napkin on which the liturgy is celebrated. This is in remembrance of the primitive church, where the liturgy was celebrated on the tombs of the martyrs. From the dogmatic point of view, the veneration of relics (as well as that of the icons of saints) is founded on faith in a special connection between the spirit of the saint and his human remains, a connection which death does not destroy. In the case of the saints the power of death is limited; their souls do not altogether leave their bodies, but remain present in spirit and in grace in their relics, even in the smallest portion. The relics are bodies already glorified in earnest of the general resurrection, although still awaiting that event. They have the same nature as that of the body of Christ in the tomb, which, although it was dead, deserted by the soul, and awaiting resurrection, still was not altogether abandoned by his divine spirit.

Each day of the ecclesiastical year is consecrated to the memory of a saint or saints. The lives of the saints are an inestimable source of Christian edification in the Eastern church, as well as in that of the West. The church never lacks saints, any more than it lacks the grace of the Holy Spirit, love, and faith. The golden crown of saints, known and unknown to the world, will continue to the end of time. The last great saint glorified in the Russian church in the twentieth century is the venerable Seraphim of Sarov. He radiated the joy of the Holy Spirit. His greeting to visitors was always "Joy, Christ is risen!" There are many servitors of the church and many ascetics of the nineteenth century whom the faithful consider as saints, but who are not yet formally canonized—since this is impossible owing to the present persecution in Russia. This is the case with many *startsy*, spiritual guides of monks and of the people, among others those of the monastery of Optina. It is the case with bishops like Theophan the Recluse (d. 1894), who remained thirty years in complete seclusion in the convent of Vyshensky. This is the case with priests like Father John of Kronstadt. As to martyrs, Russia of our day counts them by thousands. They are "the souls of those who were beheaded for having testified to Jesus and for having believed in the word of God, and the souls of those who have not worshiped the beast" (Rev. 20:4).

First among all the saints, nearest to the throne of God, is John the Baptist, the friend of the Bridegroom, the greatest among those born of woman. This closeness evolves, first of all, from the significance granted to the Baptist at Epiphany and the descent of the Holy Spirit upon the Baptized. This was like a second spiritual birth from the Holy Spirit. The closeness also comes from the special ministry of John the Forerunner himself, whose whole life was devoted to preparing the way for the Other, demonstrating an incomparable spiritual effort of self-denial. "He must increase, but I must decrease" (John 3:30). He was called to reveal the Messiah to the world—"Behold the Lamb of God, who takes away the sin of the world" (John 1:29)—and then, withdrawing into dark shadow, to accept a martyr's death of beheading. Before this he bears witness to and is glorified by his friend. Of him Jesus said, "Yet wisdom is justified by her deeds" (Matt. 11:19). This means that John has achieved the supreme human sanctity and the purpose of creation. The Wisdom which was with God at the creation of the world and whose joy is in the sons of men is justified in John, and still more justified in the Virgin Mary. Both of them, the Theotokos (God-bearer) and the Forerunner, together present to the Word Incarnate the pinnacle and glory of creation, the closest approximation to the angelic world. This belief is expressed iconographically in the *Deisis*, a group depicting the Savior enthroned, with the Virgin and the Forerunner at his right and left hand. This indicates that the Baptist shares with the Mother of God a special nearness to Christ; hence he shares, as well, her special approach to Christ in prayer. The Virgin and the Precursor stand together before the Incarnate Word as representing the summit and the glory of creation; they are nearer to him than is the world of angels. The same idea is expressed in the arrangement of icons on the iconostasis (a screen which hides the sanctuary in Orthodox churches). The icons of Christ, flanked by those of the Virgin and the Precursor, occupy a central place; farther from the center are those of angels and of other saints. The Virgin, it is true, is glorified by the church as being "more honorable than the cherubim and beyond compare more glorious than the seraphim." But the Precursor is also placed higher than the world of angels. Iconography sometimes expresses this by representing the Precursor with wings, like an angel (see Mal. 3:1 and Matt. 11:10). His superhuman, angelic ministry is combined with perfect human sanctity, and by this union he acquires primacy in the angelic world as well, where he is sometimes assigned the place occupied by the morning star before the fall. Also among the saints, the friends of God, the friend of the Bridegroom has primacy, giving way only to the Theotokos, together with whom he represents the human race in prayer before God.

The saints in their totality, headed by the Theotokos and the Forerunner, form the glory of God in human creation. Wisdom is justified in them. This thought is expressed in the prokeimenon (short anthem before Scripture reading) in the service of the saints: "God is wonderful in his saints, the God of Israel." "God has taken his place in the divine council; in the midst of the gods he holds judgment" (Ps. 82:1). The created glory, "the divine council," the crown of creation, corresponds to the glory of God before the ages.

Angels

The glory of God's creation consists not only in the world of humans but also in that of angels, not only in the world, but also in heaven. The Orthodox church has a doctrine concerning the angels, and in practice the veneration of angels approaches that of the saints. Like the saints, angels pray and intercede for the human race, and we address our prayers to them. But this rapprochement does not wipe out the difference that exists between the world of incorporeal powers and the human race. Angels form a special domain of creation, which is nevertheless allied to humanity.[2] Angels, like humans, are formed in the image of God. But the plenitude of that image is inherent only in humans; possessing bodies they participate in the whole terrestrial world and rule over it, according to the divine law. The angels, on the contrary, having no body, have no world and no nature belonging especially to them; but they are always near God and live always in him. The angels are spiritual essences. It is said sometimes that they have transparent bodies, sometimes also—and this corresponds better with the fundamentals—that they have no bodies at all. Nevertheless, even without bodies the holy angels are in a positive relation with the world of humanity.

The church teaches that each human has a guardian angel who stands before the face of the Lord. This guardian angel is a friend and a protector who preserves from evil and who sends good thought. Furthermore, the image of God is reflected in his creatures—angels and humans—in such a way that angels are celestial prototypes of humans. Guardian angels are especially our spiritual kin. Scripture testifies that the guardianship and direction of the elements, of places, of peoples, of societies, are confided to the guardian angels of the cosmos, whose very substance adds something of harmony to the elements they watch over. According to the testimony of Revelation, the angels share, constantly and actively, in the life of the world, as well as in the life of each one of us; by becoming attuned to the spiritual life we can hear these voices of the world beyond and feel that we are in touch with them. The world of angels, which we know at our birth and which is therefore accessible to our remembrance (the anamnesis of Plato), opens to us on the threshold of death, where—according to the belief of the church—the angels greet and guide the soul of the departed.

But side by side with the angels of light there are fallen angels or demons, evil spirits, who strive to influence us, acting upon our sinful inclinations. Evil spirits become visible to those who have attained a certain degree of spiritual experience. The Gospels and the whole of the New Testament give us unshakable testimony on this point. Orthodoxy understands this testimony in a manner wholly realistic; it does not accept an allegorical exegesis and even less refuses to explain these texts as the simple influence of religious syncretism. The spiritual world and the existence of good and evil spirits are evident to all those who live the spiritual life.

2. See Sergius Bulgakov, *Jacob's Ladder: On the Angels* (in Russian) (Paris, 1929).

And the belief in the holy angels is a great joy and a consolation for the Christian. The Orthodox pray to their guardian angels and all the celestial powers, above all to the archangels Michael and Gabriel.

According to Orthodox custom, at baptism one is given a name in honor of a saint who is thereafter called one's angel. The day of commemorating that saint is called the day of one's angel. The saint and the guardian angel are so conjoined in the service of the Christian that they are called by the same name (although they are not identical). Following a spiritual change, such as the taking of monastic vows, which is, one might say, a new birth, the name is changed; whoever bears a new name is henceforth confided to a new saint. The veneration of holy angels and saints creates in Orthodoxy a spiritual family atmosphere full of love and repose. This veneration cannot be separated from the love of Christ and the church—his body.

But the dark spirits, fallen angels, enter into the realm of light; their influence corrupts human life. Against these spirits, heaven and humans and the spiritual world wage a battle in the spirit. These evil powers in humans add to their weakness and sometimes engage in direct and open warfare (the life of the great ascetics and anchorites testifies to this). The church is not far from the demonology professed by the Gospel and the whole of the New Testament. Certainly these conceptions are now complicated by the facts that science reveals to us on the subject of mental maladies, their symptoms, and their treatment. But whatever the discoveries of science about the connection between the life of the soul and that of the body, nothing proves that humans are not open to the influence of demons. It cannot be affirmed that all mental maladies are of a spiritual nature or origin, but neither can it be affirmed that demoniac influences have no connection with mental maladies; what is called hallucination may be considered—at least sometimes—as a vision of the spiritual world, not in its luminous, but in its dark aspect. Aside from this direct vision, which so many occultists are engaged in investigating, the influence of the powers of darkness is exercised in imperceptible, spiritual fashion. Accordingly, the sacrament of baptism is preceded by the prayers of the catechumens, which include four prayers summoning the demoniacal powers to leave the newly baptized.

Part 2
Theology as Tradition:
Councils and Fathers

Doing Theology in an Eastern Orthodox Perspective

John Meyendorff

Born in France in 1926, John Meyendorff received his education in Paris at Saint Sergius Orthodox Theological Institute and the Sorbonne. After becoming ordained as an Orthodox priest, Meyendorff moved to America in 1959 and joined the faculty of St. Vladimir's Orthodox Theological Seminary in New York as professor of patristics and church history. In 1984 he succeeded Alexander Schmemann as dean of St. Vladimir's, a position he held until his death in 1992. In addition, Father Meyendorff taught at Fordham University as professor of Byzantine history (1967–92), Harvard, Columbia, and Union Theological Seminary. A longtime participant in ecumenical affairs, Meyendorff was moderator of the Faith and Order Commission (of the World Council of Churches) from 1967 to 1985. Meyendorff's scholarly works have appeared in at least twelve languages. The chapter which follows originally appeared in a festschrift to honor the evangelical theologian Kenneth Kantzer. In it Meyendorff explains just what it means to "do theology" from an Eastern Orthodox perspective.

Following a lecture I recently gave on the campus of an American university, a student—obviously interested in the content—asked, "Does your denomination have communities in California?" I was taken aback by his question, and it took me a moment to realize that I had been introduced as an "Eastern" Orthodox and that, to average North American ears, this evoked facts of American geography and the history of American religious denominationalism. Was I "Eastern" Orthodox in the same sense as there are "Southern" Baptists?

As I pondered how I could answer the question best, I realized that a purely historical answer—something like "we are Eastern Orthodox because we come from Eastern Europe"—would be insufficient and unfair to the questioner. Of course, his puzzlement clearly showed some lack of historical and geographical information. There was indeed a schism within Christendom, sometime in the high Middle Ages, that opposed the Latin-speaking West to the Greek-speaking East, but the theological issues involved in the schism greatly transcended historical circumstances.[1] When one refers to "Eastern" or "Greek" Orthodoxy, one has in mind a Christian tradition that claims to have preserved the integrity of the apostolic faith (this is implied in the term *orthodoxy*) and the reality of "catholicity," in spite of obvious historical and cultural limitations defined by history and geographics. To North America, this tradition came originally, not from the East with the later waves of immigrants, but from the West, when in the late eighteenth century, monks from the Russian monastery of Valaam (or Valamo) preached Christianity to the indigenous population of Alaska.

Today Orthodox communities are a presence throughout a society that is fundamentally Western in its religious traditions. Some of these communities are still immigrant communities, others are utterly American in language and mentality. Traditions of the Orthodox church are being challenged by the inherent religious pluralism of America, by modern secularism, by the task of preserving an ancient liturgical tradition in an environment accustomed to puritan and individualistic forms of worship. Such are at least some of the conditions under which an Orthodox theologian is "doing theology," with the additional awareness that the great mass of Orthodox faith-

1. Historians agree today that the schism began as a gradual estrangement between East and West and led to a different perception of church authority. The estrangement was a reality as early as the fourth century, without entailing at that time a permanent break of communion. The usual date of 1054, which appears in encyclopedias and textbooks as the date of the schism, corresponds to a relatively minor incident between the churches of Constantinople and Rome. A more permanent state of schism prevailed in the thirteenth century following the Crusades. For good historical information concerning the issue, see, for instance, Francis Dvornik, *Byzantium and the Roman Primacy* (New York: Fordham University Press, 1966).

ful in today's world are living in Eastern Europe and the Middle East, struggling—often quite successfully—against various forms of hostile environments.[2]

The Sources of Theology

Since Christian theology acquired, in the medieval Western universities, the status of a science to be taught and learned with the use of appropriate scientific methodology, it was inevitable that one began also to list the sources of theological discourse. Just as natural sciences begin, according to Aristotle, with an experience of reality reached through the use of the senses, so theology begins with data found in Scripture and tradition. Besides, there is also a natural theology based on the observation of the created world, with human reason—sometimes enlightened by the Holy Spirit—discovering God in created nature.

There is nothing plainly wrong in categorizing the sources of theology in such a neat way, except that the categorization raises more questions than it solves. What is Scripture? What is tradition? What are the guidelines of natural theology, if such a thing exists?

Orthodox theology takes for granted the divine inspiration of the Scriptures. Even a casual acquaintance with the Orthodox liturgical ethos shows the biblical character of the Orthodox religious experience. The divine office, almost entirely, is made up of scriptural texts, particularly Psalms, which are sung or read in the context of the various celebrations. However, if one takes the liturgy as a guide, the Bible is not read as a uniform collection of equally holy texts. There is a certain hierarchy within it: the New Testament, read during the eucharistic liturgy, is the fulfilment of the Old, and within the New Testament itself, the book containing the four Gospels is the object of special and direct veneration not accorded the rest of the New Testament. It is interesting that the Book of Revelation—although it is accepted as part of the scriptural canon—is never read during public worship. It is likely that this omission is rooted in the fact that the church of Antioch—where the lectionary of Constantinople,

2. There are today fifteen autocephalous Orthodox churches, administratively independent of one another, but united in faith, sacraments, and canonical discipline, aware of their being together one church. The ecumenical patriarch of Constantinople (modern Istanbul, Turkey) traditionally enjoys first honorary rank among them. The church of Russia is the largest in numbers. The Orthodox church in America was the last to graduate into autocephaly (1970), although most Orthodox churches in the "old countries" also maintain jurisdiction over groups of American communities parallel to the autocephalous American church. The largest of these—predominantly ethnic—jurisdictions is the Greek archdiocese of America; on the contemporary structure of world Orthodoxy, see John Meyendorff, *The Orthodox Church*, 2d ed. (Crestwood, N.Y.: St. Vladimir's Seminary Press, 1981).

which has been adopted by the church universally, originated—did not include Revelation in the canon until the fifth century, that is, until after the lectionary was formed.

This system of internal priorities *within* the canon of Scriptures is further shown in two facts in the history of the scriptural canon in the Eastern half of the Christian world. The first fact is that the final settlement of the canon did not take place until 692,[3] and that uncertainty as to the boundaries of written revelation was not, for many centuries, considered a major problem in doing theology. The second fact is that, when the settlement took place, a measure of uncertainty remained as to the exact status of the "longer canon" of the Old Testament; books like Wisdom and Ecclesiasticus—which were not a part of the Hebrew canon, but only of the Septuagint, and which are called Apocrypha in the West—were still recognized by some in the eighth century as "admissible," though they were not included in the canon.[4] Even today, Orthodox theologians refer to them as deuterocanonical books. They are considered part of Scripture and are read in church liturgically, but occupy something of a marginal place in the canon.

This rather detached Orthodox attitude toward the problem of the scriptural canon shows clearly that for them the Christian faith and experience can in no way be compatible with the notion of *Scriptura sola*. The issue of tradition arises inevitably, but certainly not in terms of a second source of revelation (fortunately, no one would defend such terms today). Of course there is the famous text by Basil the Great of Caesarea (d. 379) that might at first reading be interpreted as affirming a kind of parallelism between Scripture and oral tradition:

> Among the doctrines and teachings preserved by the Church, we hold some from written sources, and we have collected others transmitted in an inexplicit form (μυστικῶς) from apostolic tradition. They have all the same value. For if we were to try to put aside the unwritten customs as having no great force, we should, unknown to ourselves, be weakening the Gospel in its very essence; furthermore, we should be transforming the *kerygma* into mere words.[5]

What this text in fact implies is that God speaks to humans, as living God to living persons; that he manifested himself in Jesus Christ, who chose a

---

3. Canon 2 of the Quinisext Council; an English text can be found in *Nicene and Post-Nicene Fathers*, 2d series, ed. Philip Schaff et al., 14 vols. (Grand Rapids: Eerdmans, 1982–83), 14:361. The Quinisext Council confirmed the validity of the so-called Apostolic Canon 85, which admitted some books of the "longer canon."

4. John of Damascus *Exposition of the Orthodox Faith* 4.17, in *Patrologia Graeca* (PG), ed. J. P. Migne, 162 vols. (Paris, 1857–66), 94.1180BC.

5. Basil the Great *On the Holy Spirit* 27 (PG 32.188A; Eng. trans., *Nicene and Post-Nicene Fathers*, 2d series, 8:41).

group of *people*—his apostles—to be his witnesses; and that his unique manifestation, death, and resurrection have indeed been witnessed by them and announced to later generations as *apostolic tradition;* and that the essence of this *kerygma* is indeed contained in the books of the New Testament, but that this *kerygma* would be mere human words if it were not delivered in the full context of the living tradition, particularly the sacraments and the liturgy of the church.

In this sense, tradition becomes the initial and fundamental source of Christian theology—not in competition with Scripture, but as Scripture's spiritual context. The ultimate truth was delivered to the saints when Jesus taught them and when the Spirit descended upon them as a community at Pentecost. The church, as eucharistic community, existed before the New Testament books were written, and these books were themselves composed in and for concrete local churches. Their written text is meant to be read and understood by baptized, committed people gathered in the name of the Lord. Theology, therefore, is not simply a science, using Scripture as initial data; it also presupposes living in communion with God and people, in Christ and the Spirit, within the community of the church. Biblical theology is, of course, the best theology, but being truly biblical implies living communion in Christ, without which the Bible is a dead letter.

This approach in no way implies that biblical science does not possess its own proper integrity and methodology, but it does imply a certain understanding of what the Bible is: a collection of writings, composed on various historical occasions, in and for a community. This point has direct implications for a doctrine of inspiration, particularly in its relation to the election of Israel. In the Bible, God speaks to Israel through the mouth of some writers, but he also speaks through Israel, as a people, to the world. So inspiration does not concern only a given individual writer—whose name is often either unknown or conventional—but Israel, chosen as people, whose literature and history are in their entirety the vehicles of divine revelation. Critical historical problems concerning particular books or authors must therefore be solved with proper scientific methodology, because these texts and these authors appeared indeed within the concrete human history of Israel and used various literary genres: history, poetry, parables, and ethical discourse.

Those whom Orthodox theologians call the Fathers of the church—essentially those who in the past have become the recognized defenders of truth against heretical distortions and have therefore become the privileged spokesmen of the authentic Christian tradition—had no difficulty with a purely symbolic interpretation of some Old Testament accounts (consider, e.g., Alexandrian allegorism and the concept of ἀλληγορού-μενα in Gal. 4:24) or with understanding the creation accounts of Genesis in the light of the scientific knowledge of their time (e.g., the homilies on the *Hexaemeron* by Basil the Great).[6] Difficulties with the modern critical approach arise only when it denies the *sacred* character of Israel's history or when *any* form of divine intervention in created reality is deemed to be a myth.

While the collection of books known as the Old Testament reflects the continuous history of a people directed toward the future—the messianic kingdom—the New Testament is entirely concerned with one particular point of history: the passion and resurrection of Jesus, in which the fullness of God's love and wisdom was manifested and to which there is nothing to add. The apostles witnessed the event, and the apostolic tradition preserves its meaning and interprets its significance within the realities of later human history. New writings continued to be added to the Old Testament collection until the time of Christ, but the New Testament was closed with the death of the last witness of the resurrection. There was a continuous revelation to the Old Israel, but nothing of the sort is possible in the new dispensation, because salvation has been accomplished once and for all in Christ. The church can only define the limits of the authentic witness; it cannot add anything to that witness.

This last point is, of course, crucial for our understanding of what tradition is. If, indeed, it is not a series of new revelations, what is the content of the yet unexplicit or mystical teachings which, according to the text of Basil quoted above, are transmitted in the church from generation to generation as the very essence of the gospel, but are not contained in Scripture? Basil himself gives several examples (baptismal immersions, the meaning of the Lord's Day, etc.), all of which refer to sacraments, worship, and the spiritual experience of the Christian community.[7] His point is, therefore, that the Christian faith does not consist only in the rational acceptance of certain propositional truths that can be spelled out in writing, but that it implies a continuous living communion with God in Christ through the Holy Spirit, an experience of new life which is not individual or subjective, but sacramental and common to all the baptized.

It is probably impossible to fully grasp what Eastern Christians have understood by theology without giving full credit to such sayings as the celebrated utterance of Evagrios of Pontus, a major leader of Egyptian monasticism in the fourth century: "If you are a theologian, you truly pray. If you truly pray you are a theologian."[8] Although Evagrios himself—and other monastic writers—may have occasionally fallen into some exaggerated charismatic individualism, it is unquestionable that the whole tradition of the Christian East has attributed to the saints, the spiritual leaders, the

6. PG 29.4–208; Eng. trans., *Nicene and Post-Nicene Fathers*, 2d series, 8:52–107.
7. Basil *On the Holy Spirit* 27 (PG 32.188A).
8. Evagrios of Pontus, *Chapters on Prayer*, trans. J. E. Bamberger (Spencer, Mass.: Cistercian, 1970), 65.

startsy (as such people are called in modern times by Russians and Romanians), a certain particular authority in preserving the truth and guiding the Christian community.[9] It is interesting to note that this particular aspect of the Eastern Christian tradition attracted the attention and admiration of John Wesley, who even translated the writings attributed to Macarius of Egypt into English.[10] However, it was inevitable that in a Protestant ecclesiological context—which is what Wesley adopted in his opposition to the polity of established Anglicanism—his reading of the Eastern tradition would lead to a somewhat emotional "prophetic" subjectivism. The ecclesial and theologically "realistic" context of the Orthodox tradition—which was certainly also that of the Greek fathers, who fought against Arianism and other heresies—does not allow the reduction of truth to subjective, personal experience.[11] In the fourteenth century, there was even a famous doctrinal dispute which ended with the formal endorsement by the church of the theology of Gregory Palamas, whose main point consisted in affirming a real, "uncreated" divine presence in the experience of the saints that was accessible to all the baptized, and not to a few select mystics only.[12]

I mentioned earlier the ecclesial context of tradition. Indeed, the church as eucharistic assembly was the proper locus of teaching. The eucharistic assembly also provided the setting and the models for the exercise of teaching ministries, particularly that of the bishop and the presbyter. What today we call apostolic succession was preserved—as is clearly shown in the writings of the early fathers like Ignatius of Antioch (d. c. A.D. 100) and Irenaeus of Lyons (d. c. 202)—within (not above!) the eucharistic assembly of each local church. The teaching ministry of the apostles, who were chosen personally by Jesus, consisted in witnessing to the resurrection to the entire world. Theirs was a unique traveling ministry unattached to any local church and intransmissible to others because it was limited to the eyewitnesses of the Lord. When the apostles passed from the scene, it was within the framework of the local, eschatological, and sacramental communion of the eucharistic assembly that the apostolic tradition was preserved. Occupying the Lord's own place in the assembly, the bishop possessed a certain "charisma of truth."[13] Without

9. For more detail on this issue see John Meyendorff, *The Byzantine Legacy in the Orthodox Church* (Crestwood, N.Y.: St. Vladimir's Seminary Press, 1982), 197–215.

10. John Wesley, *Christian Library,* vol. 1 (1749; reprint, London, 1819).

11. This is well shown in the classical work of Vladimir Lossky, *The Mystical Theology of the Eastern Church* (Crestwood, N.Y.: St. Vladimir's Seminary Press, 1986).

12. John Meyendorff, *A Study of Gregory Palamas,* 2d ed. (Crestwood, N.Y.: St. Vladimir's Seminary Press, 1969).

13. "*Charisma veritatis certum*"—Irenaeus *Against Heresies* 4.26.2 (in *Sources chrétiennes* 100, ed. A. Rousseau and L. Doutreleau [Paris: Cerf, 1965], 718).

claiming any personal infallibility, he was the guardian of the tradition coming down without interruption from the apostles—a tradition that also had to be justified by the unity of faith, which was maintained by all the members of each church and which bound together all the local churches.[14] The clearest sign of this ecclesial function of the episcopate is the requirement, normal in the early church, for a new bishop to be elected by the clergy and people of a local church and to be solemnly ordained through the laying on of hands by neighboring bishops, who represented the entire episcopate of the world church.

Thus, in doing theology today, an Orthodox theologian is answerable to Scripture and to tradition, as expressed in the reality of communion, which I tried to describe above.[15] But his responsibility is that of a fully free person, entrusted by God to learn the truth and to communicate it to others. This freedom could be restricted only by the truth itself, but divine truth does not restrict human freedom but makes us free (John 8:32). The early church did not know—and the Orthodox does not know today—any automatic, formal, or authoritarian way of discerning truth from falsehood. To quote Irenaeus again: "Where the Church is, there is the Spirit of God; and where the Spirit of God is, there is the Church, and every kind of grace; but the Spirit is truth."[16]

Doctrinal Definitions, Theological Development, and Legitimate Pluralism

One of the most difficult challenges for Orthodox theologians engaged in ecumenical dialogue consists in explaining what is the permanent criterion of truth in Orthodox theology. Their embarrassment before the challenge makes them look like subjectivists or liberals. But on the other hand,

14. Book 3 of Irenaeus's *Against Heresies* is important for the understanding of tradition in the early church. The publicly known succession of bishops in each church is contrasted by the author to secret spiritual genealogies, allegedly supporting the teachings of the Gnostics. He cites particularly the known successions in the churches of Rome, Ephesus, and Smyrna. But the truth of authentic Christianity is also upheld, according to Irenaeus, by the universal consensus of local churches. On modern discussion by Orthodox theologians of what is commonly called eucharistic ecclesiology, see Nicolai Afanasieff, *L'Eglise de Saint-Esprit* (Paris: Cerf, 1975), and particularly John Zizioulas (metropolitan of Pergamos) in "Apostolic Continuity and Orthodox Theology: Towards a Synthesis of Two Perspectives," *St. Vladimir's Theological Quarterly* 19.2 (1975): 75–108; several articles by this author are now gathered in the volume *Being as Communion* (Crestwood, N.Y.: St. Vladimir's Seminary Press, 1985); see also John Meyendorff, *Catholicity and the Church* (Crestwood, N.Y.: St. Vladimir's Seminary Press, 1983), 49–64.

15. For more-detailed discussion of connected problems see John Meyendorff, *Living Tradition* (Crestwood, N.Y.: St. Vladimir's Seminary Press, 1978).

16. Irenaeus *Against Heresies* 3.24.1 (in *Sources chrétiennes* 100.472).

their basic concern for truth and their unwillingness to surrender anything to fashionable doctrinal relativism associate them with extreme conservatism. They themselves, however, refuse to be identified with either.

There are also times and places at which the Orthodox take the offensive and question the usual Western concern for criteria and authority. The very influential nineteenth-century Russian lay theologian Alexei Khomiakov affords a very vivid example:

> The Church is not an authority, just as God is not an authority, and Christ is not an authority, since authority is something external to us. The Church is not authority, I say, but the Truth—and at the same time the inner life of the Christian, since God, Christ, the Church live in him with a life more real than the heart which is beating in his breast and the blood flowing in his veins. But they are alive in him only insofar as he himself is living by the ecumenical life of love and unity; i.e., by the life of the Church.

Khomiakov continues by giving a critique of Western Christianity, where "authority became external power" and "knowledge of religious truths [was] cut off from religious life." Obedience to authority became the content of church life in Roman Catholicism, whereas Scripture as a compendium of written propositional truths replaced church authority in Protestantism. "The premises are identical," Khomiakov concludes.[17]

Unfair as it is, as all sweeping generalizations are, Khomiakov's view is nevertheless illustrative of the way the Orthodox view theology—as *internal* vision, which requires personal, ascetic effort. It does not require an individual effort only, however, but a communal effort, an effort made within the community of saints. The character of knowledge bestowed by the Spirit is indeed a personal knowledge, but one that is accessible in communion of love with the apostles, the Fathers, the saints. The nature of God himself, who is love and triune, can be known only within the categories of loving communion.[18]

This mystical and experiential approach to theology does not mean, however, that the Orthodox church does not possess dogmas that are considered final and therefore authoritative expressions of tradition. Church

---

17. Alexei Khomiakov initially published his writings in French, including the pamphlet entitled *Quelques mots d'un chrétien orthodoxe sur les confessions occidentales* (Paris, 1853); for an English translation by A. E. Morehouse see Alexander Schmemann, ed., *Ultimate Questions* (Crestwood, N.Y.: St. Vladimir's Seminary Press, 1975), 50–51.

18. This approach to theology as internal knowledge and as communion is very well established in Orthodox theology, though it takes a variety of forms and expressions; see particularly Sergy (Stragorodksy, patriarch of Moscow 1943–44), *Pravoslavnoe uchenie o spasenii* (Orthodox doctrine of salvation) (Sergiev Posad, 1894); for more-recent work, see Zizioulas, "Apostolic Continuity," and Dumitru Staniloae, *Theology and the Church* (Crestwood, N.Y.: St. Vladimir's Seminary Press, 1980).

history is a history of doctrinal controversies which usually end with doctrinal definitions that aim at excluding error. Theologians are called to accept such definitions as essential references.

Doctrinal definitions, or dogmas, always result from conciliar agreement. Truth can indeed be expressed by an individual, or a group, or a local church, but such an individual expression by itself does not create a dogma. A dogma always reflects ecclesial consensus along the lines we find expressed by Irenaeus. At the time of the Christian Roman Empire, the most normal way to register a consensus was for the emperor to call an ecumenical council. The Orthodox church recognizes seven of such councils as fully expressing the tradition of the church: Nicea I (325), Constantinople I (381), Ephesus (431), Chalcedon (451), Constantinople II (553), Constantinople III (680), and Nicea II (787). The councils define basic trinitarian and christological issues. But the recognition of those seven councils as ecumenical in no way precludes the existence of an Orthodox consensus reached through means other than an ecumenical council. Local councils have received universal recognition (1341, 1351, 1675, 1872), and, at present, commissions are preparing another great council without being sure whether the adjective *ecumenical* should be used in advance to designate it. Indeed, this adjective has had such a variety of meaning (e.g., in the past it pointed to imperial convocation, and today it is associated with either Roman Catholic universalism or inter-Christian activity) that one wonders whether it remains useful at all in the context of Orthodox ecclesiology.

Be that as it may, for the Orthodox it is the consensus that matters as a sign of truth and unity from God. And yet the knowledge of truth does not depend on consensus either: consensus is not external authority, but a helpful sign, which might be temporarily lacking, leaving the responsibility for the truth to only a few. Historical examples are many: Paul, in his conflict with Judeo-Christians; Athanasius, struggling alone for the Nicene faith in the fourth century, as the episcopates of both East and West seemed to have surrendered to Arianism; Maximus the Confessor, a lonely monk (but also the greatest theologian of the late patristic period), refusing in the seventh century to surrender to Monothelitism, which—as he was told—had been accepted universally; Mark of Ephesus, an equally lonely dissenter, as union with Rome was signed in 1439 at Florence. These and other historical examples stand before the theologian, making him personally responsible for the truth, aware of his obligation to follow Scripture and tradition, but also conscious of the fact that—at the limit—he might have to stand alone—but with God—on the right side of the fence between orthodoxy and heresy.

One of the consequences of the absence in the Orthodox church of a permanently infallible magisterium is that universally accepted formal definitions of faith are brief and rare. The ancient ecumenical councils themselves entered quite reluctantly on the path of issuing doctrinal statements. At the time of the Council of Chalcedon (451) the predominant Eastern opinion was that the common baptismal creed adopted at Nicea (325) and Constantinople (381) was a sufficient guarantee against recurring heresies. The famous definition of Chalcedon (451) begins, therefore, with an apologetic preamble:

> This wise and salutary formula of divine grace (i.e., the Creed of Nicea-Constantinople) *sufficed* for the perfect knowledge and confirmation of religion. . . . But, forasmuch as persons undertaking to make void the preaching of the truth have through their individual heresies given rise to empty babblings . . . this present holy, great, and ecumenical synod, desiring to exclude every device against the truth, and teaching that which is unchanged from the beginning, has decreed. . . .[19]

This text indicates that doctrinal definitions have a primarily negative role—that of preventing the spread of error—and that, in any case, their aim is not to exhaust the truth or freeze the teachings of the church into verbal formulae or systems, but only to indicate the "boundaries" of truth (this is the meaning of the Greek term *horoi*, used to designate conciliar decrees on doctrine). There is no doubt that, once accepted by the church, such ecumenical decrees have a final doctrinal authority, but—by their very nature—they are not to be considered new revelations, but interpretations of the fullness of truth revealed once and for all in Christ. In no way are they to be understood as additions to Scripture. Their very nature is different. The dogma of Chalcedon about the two natures of Christ may have a central and permanent theological importance for understanding Scripture as a whole—it might perhaps be more important than some particular New Testament epistle taken by itself; but still it represents the voice of the apostolic church, guided by the Spirit, and not the witness of the apostles themselves.

These limitations, which are inherent to the Orthodox understanding of the meaning and role of doctrinal definitions, have a direct impact on our topic: What is "doing theology"? Within present-day Orthodoxy there are polarities in the answer given to this question. There exists a "liberal" trend: the definitions are few and brief, some say; therefore theologians have the freedom to say anything that does not contradict the conciliar definitions. Others—conventionally called "conservatives"—would define theology as an exercise in repeating what has been said by the Fathers when they prepared and explained the definitions that were promulgated by the ancient councils. However, there is also a large consensus among

19. The English text is found in *Nicene and Post-Nicene Fathers*, 2d series, 14:263.

modern Orthodox theologians to avoid such artificial polarizations. They would also be reluctant to accept unreservedly the predominant Roman Catholic view about doctrinal development, as found, for instance, in John Henry Newman, and practically implying continuous revelation on issues such as the papal power or the Marian dogmas, which were defined by Rome only in the nineteenth and twentieth centuries. I think I would be faithful to the Orthodox general feeling on the matter if I said that in the Orthodox church formal doctrinal definitions are concerned only with essentials, without which the whole New Testament vision of salvation would not stand. This was certainly the case for the dogmas of the seven ecumenical councils, including the decree of Nicea II (787) on the veneration of icons, which in fact was not so much a decree on religious art as an affirmation of the reality of the incarnation; that is to say, it was a statement that Christ was a historical person—visible, depictable, and representable. On the other hand, particular signs such as the bodily glorification of the Virgin Mary after her death (the dogma of the assumption)—alluded to in some patristic writings and liturgical hymnology, and reflecting a belief in an eschatological anticipation of the general resurrection in her case—are simply not a matter for formal definition, but for reverence and pious respect.

Here one clearly touches on a point that is essential for doing theology in an Orthodox context: the necessary distinction between holy tradition itself and human traditions, which may well carry on precious truths but are not absolute in themselves, and which may furthermore easily become spiritual obstacles for true theology, as were those human traditions that Jesus himself condemned (Mark 7:1–13).[20] The Orthodox often lack the ability to make the necessary distinction in practice. Probably because they lack a formal permanent magisterium that is responsible for the whole life of the church universal, the Orthodox often feel themselves responsible for the integrity of the faith. They tend to identify their Orthodoxy as an integral whole, where doctrinal beliefs are inseparable from worship, customs, language, and cultural attitudes, some of which are fairly recent and quite independent from holy tradition itself. This holistic perception of faith goes back to the times when, early in the Middle Ages, nations of Eastern Europe were converted to Christianity by Greek missionaries whose policy was to translate Scripture and liturgy into the vernacular and thus indigenize Christianity at the very start. The fact that the Orthodox faith has consequently become very much their own explains the remarkable sur-

20. On the issue of tradition and traditions in Orthodoxy, see Vladimir Lossky, *In the Image and Likeness of God* (Crestwood, N.Y.: St. Vladimir's Seminary Press, 1985), 141–68 [chap. 8 in the present volume]; John Meyendorff, "Tradition and Traditions," *St. Vladimir's Theological Quarterly* 6.3 (1962): 118–27; idem, *Living Tradition*, 13–26.

vival of Orthodox communities in the Middle East and in the Balkans during centuries of Muslim rule as well as the survival of the church of Russia under the assault of totalitarian secularism. But the price of this identification of faith and culture is the frequent inability of masses of the faithful to distinguish between tradition and traditions, especially when theological information is lacking. This even leads to schisms, like that of the Old Believers in Russia in the seventeenth century[21] and the present-day Old Calendarists in Greece. Clearly, only a living theological tradition can provide the church with adequate definitions of priorities and issues to solve.

More than in other Christian traditions, the patristic period is accepted by the Orthodox as the preferred model of theological creativity—a model that has not been historically superseded, as it was in the Latin West, by the great medieval scholastic systems, or rejected as a Hellenization of authentic biblical Christianity, as liberal Protestants of the nineteenth century thought it to be. The task pursued and accomplished by the Fathers was to make the gospel acceptable and understandable to a world accustomed to the categories of Greek philosophy. They used Greek philosophical terms to express the teachings of the church about the Trinity and the divine-human being of Christ. Characteristically, however, those trends within patristic thought that surrendered to the metaphysical categories of Platonism, at the expense of the biblical idea of God and creation, were deliberately eliminated by the church, as was the case with Origenism.[22] In spite of this critical attitude to the Greco-Roman civilization, to which they culturally belonged and to which they had to announce the gospel, the Fathers did succeed in their task: Christianity was accepted by the intellectual elite of their time, and the doctrinal controversies of the day were solved not only by condemnations and anathemas, but also through a constructive and creative theological synthesis which is most adequately enshrined not in intellectual systems, but rather in an overall perception of the gospel, in the liturgy, the hymnography, the sacramental actions, and the festal cycles.

The task of theology was, at the time, primarily apologetic. Theological speculation often went wrong when it was used as an end in itself and not as a creative tool to answer the questions posed to the church by the surrounding world. Today this world is no longer the world of Plato or Aris-

21. For a summary history see Frederick C. Conybeare, *Russian Dissenters* (New York: Russell and Russell, 1962).

22. For more-detailed discussion of this problem see John Meyendorff, "Greek Philosophy and Christian Theology in the Early Church," in *Catholicity and the Church*, 31–47. In general, modern historians of Christian thought like George Florovsky and Jaroslav Pelikan are inclined to reject the nineteenth-century idea of a surrender of the patristic tradition to Hellenism.

totle; it is a post-Reformation, post-Enlightenment, postindustrial, and sometimes revolutionary secularized Western world. Historically, Eastern Christianity was spared the crises that shaped this modern Western world. Today, however, coming straight from the Byzantine Middle Ages, so to speak, Orthodoxy is confronting this modern world head-on.

This encounter was late in coming. In the seventeenth century, Roman Catholics and Protestants had looked to the East for support in their struggle against each other. Both sides asked the Orthodox to send their confessions of faith. The results were not very successful; the Orthodox, basically ignoring the implications of the questions they received from their Western colleagues, produced rather unsatisfactory confessions. Some were fundamentally Calvinistic (e.g., the *Confession* of Cyril Lucaris, 1629); others were basically Latin and Tridentine in spirit (e.g., the *Confession* of Peter Mogila, 1640). These episodes showed that the Orthodox tradition could not be adequately expressed in the confessional forms of post-Reformation Europe (neither could Roman Catholicism, for that matter).

The eighteenth century brought to Russia a brutal encounter with the West in the form of the social and educational reforms imposed by Peter I (1682–1725) and Catherine II (1762–96). However, by the nineteenth century what George Florovsky has referred to as the period of Western captivity ended. One of the lasting results of this encounter with the West was solid scientific and creative schools of theology that were adequately equipped to answer issues of the day.

As I tried to show earlier, an Orthodox theologian, although he necessarily defines himself as a consistent follower of the patristic and conciliar tradition of the early church, and although he is inevitably respectful of the present positions of his church as they are expressed in the consensus of the episcopate, is fundamentally free in his expressing the faith. Of course, he is also responsible, since freedom entails the risk of error. Most often he or she belongs to the laity. Lay professors are a majority in the theological faculties in Greece, and they represent a sizable minority in the theological schools of Russia and Serbia. This lack of professional clericalism might, in some cases, denote a certain lack of commitment by academic teachers to the practical and pastoral tasks of the church. On the other hand, men like Khomiakov (1804–60), quoted earlier, were *lay* theologians in a real sense. Their dedication to the church was entirely spontaneous, and they contributed much to establishing links between Orthodox theology and the world of secular intelligentsia.[23]

23. On Khomiakov and other older Slavophiles, including Ivan Kireyevsky and Konstantin Aksakov, see Peter K. Christoff, *An Introduction to Nineteenth-Century Russian Slavophilism*, 3 vols. (New York: Humanities, 1961, 1972; Princeton, N.J.: Princeton University Press, 1982).

If one looks at the world of Orthodox theology in the twentieth century, one can measure a rather wide spectrum of styles, approaches, and schools. Men like John Karmiris, from Athens, are exponents of the tradition of dogmatic systems, propounding the coherence of Greek patristic theology vis-à-vis the Western confessional approach. The Russian school of sophiologists, inspired originally by Vladimir Soloviev (1853–1900) and his vision of the wisdom of God, seen as the *Urgrund* of creation, includes big names like Pavel Florensky and Sergius Bulgakov.[24] Their goal is basically a synthesis of Christianity with the tradition of German philosophical idealism, not very dissimilar to the methodology and the philosophical theology of Paul Tillich. Highly critical of the sophiologists, George Florovsky, Vladimir Lossky, and Justin Popovich initiated a return to the Fathers.[25] Their work is often referred to as a neopatristic synthesis. The truly great Romanian theologian, Dumitru Staniloae, also belongs to the patristic school, but with deliberate openness toward modern existential philosophy. Very creative and challenging, particularly in the fields of ecclesiology and ecumenism, is the trend usually referred to as eucharistic. It includes authors like Nicolai Afanasieff, Alexander Schmemann, and John Zizioulas. In our century a number of Orthodox theologians were drawn to Western Europe and America by political events in their own countries. Others became actively involved in ecumenism. As a result, Orthodox theology began to contribute more actively to Western problematics, and the particular Orthodox way of doing theology became better known within the international theological community.

The observations that I presented earlier, particularly in reference to the Orthodox view of the sources of theology, have clearly shown, I believe, that Orthodox theology does not fit in the category of liberalism or conservatism as developed in Western Christendom. Direct communion with God rather than external authority, sanctification rather than justification, personal experience rather than intellectual proof, consensus rather than passive obedience—these are some important Orthodox intuitions about the nature of the Christian faith. In stressing such contrasts, I do not mean at all that the Orthodox church does not believe in authority, that it rejects the Pauline doctrine of justification by faith, that it does not respect the power of reason, or that dogmas are accepted through democratic referendums. But I do want to emphasize the point that the mystery of the Holy Spirit, present in the church, is the fundamental reality

24. See Robert Slesinski, *Pavel Florensky: A Metaphysics of Love* (Crestwood, N.Y.: St. Vladimir's Seminary Press, 1984); James Pain and Nicolas Zernov, eds., *A Bulgakov Anthology* (Philadelphia: Westminster, 1976).

25. See George Florovsky, *The Ways of Russian Theology*, 2 vols. (Belmont, Mass.: Nordland, 1979; Vaduz, Liech.: Büchervertriebsanstalt, 1987).

of Christian experience, that this experience is a personal and free one, and that authority, reason, and formal hierarchical and conciliar criteria are meant to protect it, not to replace it.[26] In any case, the Spirit guiding the faithful is also the creator of church order, the bestower of the charismata of teaching and governing, as well as the inspirer of the prophets. Thus the personalism of the faith does not result in charismatic subjectivism or individualism; it initiates each person to think and to act as a responsible member of the body, seeking the truth within the communion of the saints.

Conclusion: Doing Theology in America

At the beginning of this century, Christian East and Christian West still lived in practical isolation from each other. It is true that even then—and already in the previous century—Orthodox theologians were generally informed of Western theological trends and used Western theological literature profusely. But their Western colleagues—with the exception of a few specialists—had practically no access to Orthodox theological thought and hardly considered it a potential resource at all. Today an Orthodox presence in ecumenical dialogues is considered a must, and Orthodox theological literature is becoming more and more available. This gives a historically unprecedented responsibility to those Orthodox who are doing theology: making sure they are understood, but also remain faithful to the authentic tradition whose spokesmen they claim to be. It seems to me that their greatest challenge is to preserve the ecclesial character of their theology.

The American religious scene is quite familiar with sectarian theological thinking—relatively small religious groups claim to possess the truth, affirm that salvation has reached their members (and not other groups), and rejoice in their exclusivity and uniqueness. There are Orthodox people who would gladly adopt the psychological attitude of a sect; it would give them a certain (false) security and justify the exotic and unfamiliar sides of historical Eastern Orthodoxy, which frequently seem strange to native Americans. It would free them from the obligation to listen to others and from the effort needed to look at themselves as others look at them. It would make it unnecessary to draw the line between holy tradition and the human traditions inherited from history,

26. Perhaps the greatest witness in the Orthodox tradition to the personal and conscious nature of the Christian experience is the great Byzantine mystic of the eleventh century, Simeon the New Theologian; see Basil Krivocheine, *In the Light of Christ: St. Symeon the New Theologian—Life, Spirituality, Doctrine* (Crestwood, N.Y.: St. Vladimir's Seminary Press, 1986).

and it would reduce theology to straight affirmations, repeating that which was supposedly "always said." Such an attitude, in fact, would not only exclude real theology and renounce the true tradition of the Fathers, whose main achievement was to express and explain the truth to their neighbors and contemporaries, necessarily using their language, but it would also align the Orthodox psychologically with the most extreme forms of Protestant fundamentalism. There would be a denial of history, a temptation that, unfortunately, is familiar to many religious Americans.

But the American religious scene is equally familiar with what is called denominationalism—the belief that doctrinal issues have little real impact within the church of one's choice, or simply of one's neighborhood, and that all (or most) Christian denominations have equal rights within the church universal. As a matter of fact, the mainstream American denominations were formed within the social framework of immigration history.[27] The Orthodox could fit nicely in the scheme, especially if—as is sometimes the case—they identify their ecclesiastical allegiance in purely ethnic terms. The Orthodox church is the church of the Greeks, or of the Russians, and its elaborate rituals have no other significance than the preservation of a cultural heritage. In the perspective of denominationalism, doctrine is largely relativized, and theology easily becomes an interdenominational reflection on social, anthropological, or political issues.

I would like to submit emphatically that authentic Orthodox theology can be neither sectarian nor denominational, but only ecclesial. It presupposes the existence of a catholic church that receives the fullness of divine revelation for the sake of the salvation of all people. This church has existed since Pentecost, preserving the apostolic message and interpreting it in all languages for the sake of all human societies. Therefore the theologian who belongs to it must make sure that his theology is consistent with that of the apostles and the Fathers, but also—precisely because the church is catholic—he is called to rejoice in everything that is true, beautiful, and holy, even beyond the visible limits of the church, because all true and beautiful realities belong to the one church of Christ—the eschatological anticipation of the New Jerusalem. Only that which is false and sinful must be rejected. Thus the Cappadocian Greek fathers of the fourth century admired Origen; Maximus the Confessor was inspired by Evagrios in his spirituality; Nicodemos of Athos (eighteenth

---

27. See the classic and brilliant book of H. Richard Niebuhr, *The Social Sources of Denominationalism* (New York: Meridian, 1957). It is interesting that the Orthodox church is not mentioned in the survey at all—its existence within American society apparently had negligible impact on Niebuhr's scheme.

century) paraphrased the *Invisible Warfare* of Lorenzo Scupoli and the *Spiritual Exercises* of Ignatius Loyola; Tikhon of Zadonsk (eighteenth century) was fond of German pietism. . . .[28]

So today there is clearly no way of doing Orthodox theology in America except the catholic way, hating error and skeptical relativism, but always seeking the best way to be faithful—in agreement with others. Those others include the apostles and the Fathers, the living witnesses of tradition, but also those with whose commitments and allegiances one may disagree, but with whom a constant and intelligent dialogue is necessary if the Orthodox witness today is to have any significance.

---

28. These are well-known examples taken from the history of Orthodox theology and spirituality; for a brief survey see John Meyendorff, *St. Gregory Palamas and Orthodox Spirituality* (Crestwood, N.Y.: St. Vladimir's Seminary Press, 1974).

The Function of Tradition in the Ancient Church

George Florovsky

George Florovsky (1893–1979) was born in Odessa (in present-day Ukraine). At the age of twenty-seven he moved with his family to Bulgaria, and a year later to Prague, where he taught philosophy of law. After marriage in 1922, Florovsky moved to Paris and helped to found the Saint Sergius Orthodox Theological Institute, where he also served as professor of patristics (1926–48). From 1948 to 1955 Florovsky taught at St. Vladimir's Orthodox Theological Seminary in New York, after which he taught at Harvard Divinity School (1954–65) and concurrently at Holy Cross Greek Orthodox School of Theology (1962–65). From 1965 to 1972, and then occasionally until his death in 1979, Florovsky taught at Princeton Theological Seminary. Known for the depth of his piety and defense of Orthodox Christianity as well as for the breadth of his erudition, Florovsky epitomized the Orthodox tradition of the scholar-priest.

Chapters 6 and 7 address the important issues of the criteria and norms of theological authority. Florovsky explores the meaning and extent of the Orthodox commitment to invent nothing new, but instead to restate the tradition, written and unwritten, of the holy fathers, councils, and creeds. Ultimately, contends Florovsky, true theological authority, patristic or modern, is grounded not in any external canonical authority, but in the witness of the Spirit.

From *Greek Orthodox Theological Review* 9.2 (1963): 181–200. Reprinted by permission.

"Ego vero evangelio non crederem, nisi me catholicae ecclesiae commoveret auctoritas" ("Indeed, I should not have believed the gospel, if the authority of the catholic church had not moved me").

Augustine *Contra epistolam Manichaei quam vocant Fundamenti* 6

Vincent of Lérins and Tradition

The famous dictum of Vincent of Lérins was characteristic of the attitude of the ancient church in the matters of faith: *"teneamus quod ubique, quod semper, quod ab omnibus creditum est"* ("we must hold what has been believed everywhere, always, and by all").[1] This was at once the criterion and the norm. The crucial emphasis here was on the permanence of Christian teaching. Vincent was actually appealing to the double ecumenicity of Christian faith—in space and in time. In fact, the same great vision had inspired Irenaeus in his time: the one church, expanded and scattered in the whole world, and yet speaking with one voice, holding the same faith everywhere, as it had been handed down by the blessed apostles and preserved by the succession of the presbyters (*"quae est ab apostolis, quae per successionem presbyterorum in ecclesiis custoditur"*).

These two aspects of faith, or rather these two dimensions, could never be separated from each other. *Universitas* and *antiquitas*, as well as *consensio*, belonged together. Neither was an adequate criterion by itself. Antiquity as such was not yet a sufficient warrant of truth, unless a comprehensive consensus of the ancients could be satisfactorily demonstrated. And *consensio* as such was not conclusive, unless it could be traced back continuously to apostolic origins. Now, suggested Vincent, the true faith could be recognized by a double recourse—to Scripture and tradition, *"duplici modo . . . primum scilicet divinae legis auctoritate, tum deinde ecclesiae catholicae traditione"* ("in two ways . . . first clearly by the authority of the Holy Scriptures, then by the tradition of the catholic church"). This did not imply, however, that there were two sources of Christian doctrine. Indeed, the rule or canon of Scripture was perfect and self-sufficient—*"ad omnia satis superque sufficiat"* ("for all things complete and more than sufficient"). Why then should it be supplemented by any other authority? Why was it imperative to invoke also "the authority of ecclesiastical understanding" (*"ecclesiasticae intelligentiae auctoritas"*)?

The reason was obvious. Scripture was differently interpreted by individuals, *"ut paene quot homines tot illinc sententiae erui posse videantur"* ("so that one might almost gain the impression that it can yield as many different meanings as there are men"). To this variety of private opinions

1. Vincent of Lérins *Commonitorium* 2.

Vincent opposes the common mind of the church, the mind of the church catholic, "*ut propheticae et apostolicae interpretationis linea secundum ecclesiastici et catholici sensus normam dirigatur*" ("so that the trend of the interpretation of the prophets and the apostolic writings be directed in accordance with the rule of the ecclesiastical and catholic meaning"). Tradition was not, according to Vincent, an independent instance, nor was it a complementary source of faith. Ecclesiastical understanding could not add anything to the Scripture. But it was the only means to ascertain and to disclose the true meaning of Scripture. Tradition was, in fact, the authentic interpretation of Scripture. And in this sense it was coextensive with Scripture. Tradition was actually Scripture rightly understood. And Scripture was for Vincent the only, primary and ultimate, canon of Christian truth.[2]

The Hermeneutical Question in the Ancient Church

At this point Vincent was in full agreement with the established tradition. In the admirable phrase of Hilary of Poitiers, "*scripturae enim non in legendo sunt, sed in intelligendo*" ("for Scripture is not in the reading, but in the understanding").[3] The problem of right exegesis was still a burning issue in the fourth century (e.g., in the contest of the church with the Arians), no less than it had been in the second century (e.g., in the struggles against Gnostics and Montanists). All parties in the disputes appealed to Scripture. Heretics, even Gnostics and Manichees, quoted scriptural texts and passages and invoked the authority of the Holy Writ. Moreover, exegesis was at that time the main, and probably the only, theological method, and the authority of the Scripture was sovereign and supreme. The orthodox were bound to raise the crucial hermeneutical question: What is the principle of interpretation? Now in the second century the term *Scriptures* denoted primarily the Old Testament, and the authority of these Scriptures was sharply challenged, and actually repudiated, by the teaching of Marcion. The unity of the Bible had to be proved and vindicated. What were the basis and the warrant of Christian and christological understanding of prophecy, that is, of the Old Testament?

It was in this historical situation that the authority of tradition was first invoked. Scripture belonged to the church, and it was only in the church, within the community of right faith, that Scripture could be adequately understood and correctly interpreted. Heretics, that is, those outside of the church, had no key to the mind of the Scripture. It was not enough

---

2. Ibid.; see also 28.

3. Hilary of Poitiers *Ad Constantium Augustum* 2.9, in *Patrologia Latina* (PL), ed. J. P. Migne, 221 vols. (Paris, 1844–64), 10.570; this sentence is repeated in Jerome *Dialogus contra Luciferianos* 28 (PL 23.190–91).

just to read and to quote scriptural words; the true meaning or intent of Scripture, taken as an integrated whole, had to be elicited. One had to grasp in advance the true pattern of biblical revelation, the great design of God's redemptive providence, and this could be done only by an insight of faith. It was by faith that *Christuszeugnis* could be discerned in the Old Testament. It was by faith that the unity of the tetramorph Gospel could be properly ascertained. But this faith was not an arbitrary and subjective insight of individuals—it was the faith of the church, rooted in the apostolic message or kerygma, and authenticated by it. Those outside of the church were missing precisely this basic and overarching message, the very heart of the gospel. With them Scripture was just a dead letter, or an array of disconnected passages and stories which they endeavored to arrange or rearrange according to their own pattern derived from alien sources. They had another faith. This was the main argument of Tertullian in his passionate treatise *De praescriptione*. He would not discuss the Scripture with heretics—they had no right to use the Scripture, as it did not belong to them. The Scripture was the church's possession. Emphatically did Tertullian insist on the priority of the "rule of faith," *regula fidei*. It was the only key to the meaning of the Scripture. And this rule was apostolic, was rooted in and derived from the apostolic preaching.

C. H. Turner has rightly described the meaning and the intention of the early church's appeal or reference to the rule of faith: "When Christians spoke of the 'Rule of Faith' as 'Apostolic,' they did not mean that the Apostles had met and formulated it. . . . What they meant was that the profession of belief which every catechumen recited before his baptism did embody in summary form the faith which the Apostles had taught and had committed to their disciples to teach after them." This profession was the same everywhere, although the actual phrasing could vary from place to place. It was always intimately related to the baptismal formula.[4] Apart from this rule Scripture would be misinterpreted. Scripture and tradition were indivisibly intertwined for Tertullian. "*Ubi enim apparuerit esse veritatem disciplinae et fidei christianae, illic erit veritas scripturarum et expositionum et omnium traditionum christianarum*" ("For only where the true Christian teaching and faith are evident will the true Scriptures, the true interpretations, and all the true Christian traditions be found").[5] The apostolic tradition of faith was the indispensable guide in the understanding of Scripture and the ulti-

---

4. C. H. Turner, "Apostolic Succession," in *Essays on the Early History of the Church and the Ministry*, ed. H. B. Swete (London, 1918), 101–2. See also Yves M. J. Congar, *La Tradition et les traditions*, vol. 2, *Essai théologique* (Paris, 1963), 21ff.

5. Tertullian *De praescriptione* 19.3.

mate warrant of right interpretation. The church was not an external authority which had to judge the Scripture, but rather the keeper and guardian of that divine truth which was stored and deposited in the Holy Writ.[6]

Irenaeus and the "Canon of Truth"

Denouncing the Gnostic mishandling of Scripture, Irenaeus introduced a picturesque simile. A skillful artist has used many precious jewels in making a beautiful image of a king. Now another man takes this mosaic apart, rearranging the stones so as to produce the image of a dog or of a fox. Then he starts claiming, on the pretext that the gems (the ψηφίδες) are authentic, that this is the original picture by the first master. In fact, however, the original design has been destroyed—λύσας τὴν ὑποκειμένην τοῦ ἀνθρώπου ἰδέαν. This is precisely what the heretics do with the Scripture. They disregard and disrupt the order and connection of the Holy Writ and "dismember the truth"—λύοντες τὰ μέλη τῆς ἀληθείας. Words, expressions, and images—ῥήματα, λέξεις, παραβολαὶ—are genuine; but the design, the ὑπόθεσις, is arbitrary and false.[7]

Irenaeus suggested as well another analogy. There were in circulation at that time certain *Homerocentrones*, genuine verses of Homer that were taken at random and out of context, and rearranged in arbitrary manner. All particular verses were truly Homeric, but the new story, fabricated by the means of rearrangement, was not Homeric at all. Yet one could be easily deceived by the familiar sound of the Homeric idiom.[8] It is worth noticing that Tertullian also refers to these curious *centrones* made of Homeric or Virgilian verses.[9] Apparently they were a common device in the polemical literature of that time. Now the point which Irenaeus endeavored to make is obvious. Scripture has its own pattern or design, its internal structure and harmony. The heretics ignore this pattern, or substitute their own instead. In other words, they rearrange the scriptural evidence into a pattern which is quite alien to the Scripture itself. Now, contended Irenaeus, those who have kept unbending that canon of truth which they received at baptism will have no difficulty in "restoring each expression to its

6. See Ellen Flesseman–van Leer, *Tradition and Scripture in the Early Church* (Assen, 1954), 145–85; Damien van den Eynde, *Les Normes de l'enseignement chrétien dans la littérature patristique des trois premiers siècles* (Paris, 1933), 197–212; J. K. Stirniman, *Die Praescriptio Tertullians im Lichte des römischen Rechts und der Theologie* (Freiburg, West Germany, 1949); and the introduction and notes of R. F. Refoulé, in Tertullian *De praescriptione*, in *Sources chrétiennes* 46 (Paris, 1957).

7. Irenaeus *Adversus omnes haereses* 1.8.1.

8. Ibid., 1.9.4.

9. Tertullian *De praescriptione* 39.

appropriate place" (τῇ ἰδίᾳ τάξει). Then they will be able to behold the true image. The actual phrase used by Irenaeus is peculiar: προσαρμόσας τῷ τῆς ἀληθείας σωματίῳ (which is clumsily rendered in the old Latin translation as *corpusculum veritatis*). But the meaning of the phrase is quite clear. The σωμάτιον is not necessarily a diminutive. It simply denotes a "corporate body." In the phrase of Irenaeus it denotes the *corpus* of truth, the right context, the original design, the true image, the original disposition of gems and verses.[10]

Thus, for Irenaeus, the reading of Scripture must be guided by the rule of faith, to which believers are committed (and into which they are initiated) by their baptismal profession, and by which alone the basic message, or the truth, of the Scripture can be adequately identified and assessed. The favorite phrase of Irenaeus in this regard was "the rule of truth," κανὼν τῆς ἀληθείας, *regula veritatis*. Now this rule was, in fact, nothing else than the witness and preaching of the apostles, their κήρυγμα and *praedicatio* (or *praeconium*), which was deposited in the church and entrusted to her by the apostles, and then was faithfully kept and handed down, with complete unanimity in all places, by the succession of accredited pastors, "*qui cum episcopatus successione charisma veritatis certum acceperunt*" ("those who, together with the succession of the episcopacy, have received the firm charisma of truth").[11]

Whatever the direct and exact connotation of this pregnant phrase may be,[12] there can be no doubt that, in the mind of Irenaeus, this continuous preservation and transmission of the deposited faith was operated and guided by the abiding presence of the Holy Spirit in the church. Irenaeus's conception of the church was at once charismatic and institutional. And tradition was, in his understanding, a *depositum juvenescens*, "a living tradition" entrusted to the church as a new breath of life, just as

10. See F. Kattenbusch, *Das apostolische Symbol*, vol. 2 (Leipzig, 1900), 30ff.; and also his note in *Zeitschrift für neutestamentliche Theologie* 10 (1909): 331–32.

11. Irenaeus *Adversus omnes haereses* 4.26.2.

12. It has been contended that *charisma veritatis* was simply the apostolic doctrine and the truth (of the divine revelation), so that Irenaeus did not imply any special ministerial endowment of the bishops. See Karl Müller, "Kleine Beiträge zur alten Kirchengeschichte 3: Das *Charisma veritatis* und der Episcopat bei Irenaeus," *Zeitschrift für die neutestamentliche Wissenschaft* 23 (1924): 216–22; van den Eynde, *Les Normes*, 183–87; Yves M. J. Congar, *La Tradition et les traditions*, vol. 1, *Etude historique* (Paris, 1960), 97–98; Hans Freiherr von Campenhausen, *Kirchliches Amt und geistliche Vollmacht in den ersten drei Jahrhunderten* (Tübingen, 1953), 185ff.; and also—with special emphasis on the character of succession—Einar Molland, "Irenaeus of Lugdunum and the Apostolic Succession," *Journal of Ecclesiastical History* 1.1 (1950): 12–28; and idem, "Le Développement de l'idée de succession apostolique," *Revue d'histoire et de philosophie religieuses* 34.1 (1954): 1–29. See, on the other hand, the critical remarks of Arnold Ehrhardt, *The Apostolic Succession in the First Two Centuries of the Church* (London, 1953), 207–31, esp. 213–14.

breath was bestowed upon the first man (*"quemadmodum aspiratio plasmationis"*).[13] Bishops or presbyters in the church were accredited guardians and ministers of this once deposited truth:

> Where, therefore, the *charismata* of the Lord have been deposited (*posita sunt*), there is it proper to learn the truth, namely from those who have that succession of the church which is from the apostles (*apud quos est ea quae est ab apostolis ecclesiae successio*), and who display a sound and blameless conduct and an unadulterated and uncorrupt speech. For these also preserve this faith of ours in one God who created all things, and they increase that love for the Son of God, who accomplished such marvelous dispensation for our sake, and they expound the Scriptures to us without danger, neither blaspheming God, nor dishonoring the patriarchs, nor despising the prophets.[14]

The Regula Fidei

Tradition was in the early church, first of all, a hermeneutical principle and method. Scripture could be rightly and fully understood and assessed only in the light and in the context of the living apostolic tradition, which was an integral factor of Christian existence. This was so, of course, not because tradition could add anything to what has been manifested in the Scripture, but because it provided that living context, the comprehensive perspective, in which alone the true intention and the total design of the Holy Writ, of divine revelation itself, could be detected and grasped.

The truth was, according to Irenaeus, a "well-grounded system," a corpus,[15] a "harmonious melody."[16] This harmony could be grasped only by the insight of faith. Indeed, tradition was not just a transmission of inherited doctrines in a Judaic manner, but continuous life in the truth.[17] It was not a fixed core or complex of binding propositions, but an insight into the meaning and impact of the revelatory events, of the revelation of the God who acts. And this was determinative in the field of biblical exegesis. George Prestige has well put it: "The voice of the Bible could be plainly heard only if its text were interpreted broadly and rationally, in accordance with the apostolic creed and the evidence of the historical practice

---

13. Irenaeus *Adversus omnes haereses* 3.24.1.
14. Ibid., 4.26.5.
15. Ibid., 2.27.1.
16. Ibid., 2.38.3.
17. Odo Casel, "Benedict von Nursia als Pneumatiker," in *Heilige Überlieferung* (Münster, 1938), 100–101: *"Die heilige Überlieferung ist daher in der Kirche von Anfang an nicht bloss ein Weitergehen von Doktrinen nach spätjüdischen (nachchristlicher) Art gewesen, sondern ein lebendiges Weiterblühen des göttlichen Lebens."* In a footnote Casel refers the reader to John Adam Möhler.

of Christendom. It was the heretics that relied on isolated texts, and the Catholics who paid more attention on the whole to scriptural principles."[18] Summarizing her careful analysis of the use of tradition in the early church, Ellen Flesseman–van Leer has written: "Scripture without interpretation is not Scripture at all; the moment it is used and becomes alive it is always interpreted Scripture." Now Scripture must be interpreted "according to its own basic purport," which is disclosed in the *regula fidei*. Thus this *regula* becomes, as it were, the controlling factor in the exegesis. "Real interpretation of Scripture is church preaching, is tradition."[19]

Athanasius and the "Scope of Faith"

The situation did not change in the fourth century. The dispute with the Arians, at least in its early phase, was centered in the exegetical field. The Arians and their supporters produced an impressive array of scriptural texts in the defense of their doctrinal position. They wanted to restrict theological discussion to the biblical ground alone. Their claims had to be met precisely on this ground. And their exegetical method, the manner in which they handled the text, was much the same as that of the earlier dissenters. They were operating with selected proof-texts and without much concern for the total context of the revelation.

It was imperative for the orthodox to appeal to the mind of the church, to that faith which had been once delivered and then devoutly kept. This was the main concern and the usual method of Athanasius. The Arians quoted various passages from the Scripture to substantiate their contention that the Savior was a creature. In reply Athanasius invoked the rule of faith. This was his usual argument: "Let us who possess τὸν σκοπὸν τῆς πίστεως (the scope of faith) restore the correct meaning (ὀρθὴν τὴν διάνοιαν) of what they have wrongly interpreted."[20] Athanasius contended that the correct interpretation of particular texts was possible only in the total perspective of faith. "What they now allege from the Gospels they explain in an unsound sense, as we may discover if we take in consideration τὸν σκοπὸν τῆς καθ᾽ ἡμᾶς τοὺς Χριστιανοὺς πίστεως (the scope

18. George L. Prestige, *Fathers and Heretics* (London, 1940), 43.
19. Flesseman–van Leer, *Tradition*, 92–96. On Irenaeus see pp. 100–144; van den Eynde, *Les Normes*, 159–97; B. Reynders, "Paradosis: Le Progrès de l'idée de tradition jusqu'à Saint Irénée," *Recherches de théologie ancienne et médiévale* 5 (1933): 155–91; idem, "La Polemique de Saint Irénée," *Recherches de théologie ancienne et médiévale* 7 (1935): 5–27; Henri Holstein, "La Tradition des apôtres chez Saint Irénée," *Recherches de science religieuse* 36 (1949): 229–70; idem, *La Tradition dans l'église* (Paris, 1960); André Benoit, "Ecriture et tradition chez Saint Irénée," *Revue d'histoire et de philosophie religieuses* 40 (1960): 32–43; idem, *Saint Irénée: Introduction à l'étude de sa théologie* (Paris, 1960).
20. Athanasius *Contra Arianos* 3.35.

of the faith according to us Christians), and read the Scripture using it (τὸν σκοπὸν) as the rule (ὥσπερ κανόνι χρησάμενοι)."[21] On the other hand, close attention must be given also to the immediate context and setting of every particular phrase and expression, and the exact intention of the writer must be carefully identified.[22]

Writing to Bishop Serapion on the topic of the Holy Spirit, Athanasius contends again that the Arians ignored or missed "the scope of the Divine Scripture" (μὴ εἰδόντες τὸν σκοπὸν τῆς Θείας Γραφῆς).[23] The σκοπὸς was, in the language of Athanasius, a close equivalent of what Irenaeus used to denote as ὑπόθεσις—the underlying idea, the true design, the intended meaning.[24] On the other hand, the word σκοπὸς was a habitual term in the exegetical language of certain philosophical schools, especially Neoplatonism. Exegesis played a great role in the philosophical endeavor of that time, and the question of hermeneutical principle had to be raised. Jamblichos was, for one, quite formal on this issue. One had to discover the main point, the basic theme, of the whole treatise under examination, and to keep it in mind at all times.[25] Athanasius could well have been acquainted with the technical use of the term. It was misleading, he contended, to quote isolated texts and passages, disregarding the total intent of the Holy Writ. It is obviously inaccurate to interpret Athanasius's use of the term σκοπὸς as "the general drift" of the Scripture. The "scope" of the faith, or of the Scripture, is precisely the credal core, which is condensed in the rule of faith, as maintained in the church and "transmitted from fathers to fathers"; the Arians by contrast had "no fathers" to support their opinions.[26] As John Henry Newman has rightly observed, Athanasius regarded the rule of faith as an ultimate principle of interpretation, opposing the "ecclesiastical sense" (τὴν ἐκκλησιαστικὴν διάνοιαν) to the private opinions of the heretics.[27]

Time and again in his scrutiny of the Arian arguments, Athanasius would summarize the basic tenets of the Christian faith before going into

21. Ibid., 3.28.
22. Ibid., 1.54.
23. Athanasius *Ad Serapionem* 2.7; cf. *Ad episcopos Aegypti* 4: τὰ λεγόμενα μόνον σκοπῶν, καὶ μὴ τὴν διάνοιαν θεωρῶν).
24. See Guido Müller, *Lexicon Athanasianum*, s.v.: *"id quod quis docendo, scribendo, credendo intendit."*
25. See Karl Prächter, "Richtungen und Schulen im Neuplatonismus," in *Genethliakon* (for Carl Roberts; Berlin, 1910). Prächter translates σκοπός as *Zielpunkt* or *Grundthema* (pp. 128f.). He characterizes the method of Jamblichos as *"universalistische Exegese"* (p. 138). Proclus, in his commentary on *Timaeus*, contrasts Porphyry and Jamblichos. Porphyry interpreted texts μερικώτερον, while Jamblichos did it ἐποπτικώτερον, that is, in a comprehensive or synthetic manner (cited by Prächter, p. 136).
26. Athanasius *De decretis* 27.
27. John Henry Newman, trans., *Select Treatises of St. Athanasius*, 8th impression, vol. 2 (London, 1900), 250–52; Athanasius *Contra Arianos* 1.44.

the actual reexamination of the alleged proof-texts; in this way he restored those texts to their proper perspective. H. E. W. Turner has described this exegetical manner of Athanasius:

> Against the favorite Arian technique of pressing the grammatical meaning of a text without regard either to the immediate context or to the wider frame of reference in the teaching of the Bible as a whole, he urges the need to take the general drift of the Church's Faith as a Canon of interpretation. The Arians are blind to the wide sweep of Biblical theology and therefore fail to take into sufficient account the context in which their proof-texts are set. The sense of Scripture must itself be taken as Scripture. This has been taken as a virtual abandonment of the appeal to Scripture and its replacement by an argument from Tradition. Certainly in less careful hands it might lead to the imposition of a strait-jacket upon the Bible as the dogmatism of Arian and Gnostic had attempted to do. But this was certainly not the intention of Athanasius himself. For him it represents an appeal from exegesis drunk to exegesis sober, from a myopic insistence upon the grammatical letter to the meaning or intention (σκοπός, χαρακτὴρ) of the Bible.[28]

It seems that Professor Turner exaggerated the danger. The argument was still strictly scriptural, and in principle Athanasius admitted the sufficiency of the Scripture, sacred and inspired, for the defense of truth.[29] Scripture had to be interpreted, however, in the context of the living credal tradition under the guidance or control of the rule of faith. This rule was in no sense an extraneous authority which could be imposed on the Holy Writ. It was the same apostolic preaching which was written down in the books of the New Testament, but it was, as it were, this preaching in epitome. Athanasius writes to Bishop Serapion: "Let us look from the beginning at that very tradition, teaching, and faith of the catholic church which the Lord gave (ἔδωκεν), the apostles preached (ἐκήρυξαν), and the Fathers preserved (ἐφύλαξαν). Upon this the church is founded."[30] This passage is highly characteristic of Athanasius. The three nouns actually coincide: παράδοσις (tradition) from Christ himself, διδασκαλία (teaching) by the apostles, and πίστις (faith) of the catholic church. And this is the foundation (θεμέλιον) of the church—a sole and single foundation.[31] Scripture itself seems to be subsumed and included in this tradition, coming, as it does, from the Lord.

28. H. E. W. Turner, *The Pattern of Christian Truth* (London, 1954), 193–94.
29. Athanasius *Contra gentes* 1.
30. Athanasius *Ad Serapionem* 1.28.
31. C. R. B. Shaplund rightly suggested that θεμέλιον in this text meant for Athanasius precisely the threefold name as invoked in holy baptism. In fact, a bit later in the same section of this epistle Athanasius introduces the Great Commission in this way: "The Lord ordered [the Apostles] to lay this foundation for the Church, saying. . . . The Apostles went, and so they taught" (*The Letters of Saint Athanasius concerning the Holy Spirit*, ed. C. R. B. Shaplund [London, 1951], 132 n. 2 [on p. 134]).

In the concluding chapter of his first epistle to Serapion, Athanasius returns once more to the same point: "In accordance with the apostolic faith delivered to us by tradition from the Fathers, I have delivered the tradition, without inventing anything extraneous to it. What I learned, that have I inscribed (ἐνεχάραξα), conformably with the Holy Scripture."[32] On another occasion Athanasius denoted the Scripture itself an apostolic *paradosis*.[33] It is characteristic that in the whole discussion with the Arians no single reference was made to "traditions" in the plural. The only term of reference was always "tradition," indeed, *the* tradition, the apostolic tradition, comprising the total and integral content of the apostolic preaching, and summarized in the rule of faith. The unity and solidarity of this tradition was the main and crucial point in the whole argument.

The Purpose of Exegesis and the "Rule of Worship"

The appeal to tradition was actually an appeal to the mind of the church. It was assumed that the church had the knowledge and the understanding of the truth, that is, the meaning of the revelation. Accordingly, the church had both the competence and the authority to proclaim the gospel and to interpret it. This did not imply that the church was above the Scripture. She stood by the Scripture but, on the other hand, was not bound by its letter. The ultimate purpose of exegesis and interpretation was to elicit the meaning and the intent of the Holy Writ, or rather the meaning of the revelation, of the *Heilsgeschichte*. The church had to preach Christ, and not just the Scripture.

The use of tradition in the ancient church can be adequately understood only in the context of the actual use of the Scripture. The Word was kept alive in the church. It was reflected in her life and structure. Faith and life were organically intertwined.

It would be proper to recall at this point a famous passage from the *Indiculus de gratia Dei*, which was mistakenly attributed to Pope Celestine I but was in fact composed by Prosper of Aquitania: "These are the inviolable decrees of the holy and apostolic see by which our holy fathers slew the baneful innovation. . . . Let us regard the sacred prayers which, in accordance with apostolic tradition, our priests offer uniformly in every catholic church in all the world. Let the rule of worship lay down the rule of faith." It is true, of course, that the phrase "rule of worship" in its immediate context was not a formulation of a general principle, and its direct intention was limited to one particular point: infant baptism as an instance pointing to the reality of an inherited or original sin. Indeed, it was not an author-

32. Athanasius *Ad Serapionem* 1.33.
33. Athanasius *Ad Adelphium* 6.

itative proclamation of a pope, but a private opinion that an individual theologian expressed in the context of a heated controversy.[34] Yet it was not just an accident, and not a misunderstanding, that the phrase was taken out of its immediate context and slightly changed in order to express the principle *"ut legem credendi statuat lex orandi"* ("so that the rule of worship should establish the rule of faith"). "Faith" found its first expression precisely in the liturgical—sacramental rites and formulas—and creeds first emerged as an integral part of the rite of initiation. "Credal summaries of faith, whether interrogatory or declaratory, were a by-product of the liturgy and reflected its fixity or plasticity," says J. N. D. Kelly.[35] "Liturgy," in the wide and comprehensive sense of the word, was the first and initial layer in the tradition of the church, and the argument from the *lex orandi* (rule of worship) was persistently used in discussion already by the end of the second century. The worship of the church was a solemn proclamation of her faith. The baptismal invocation of the name of God was probably the earliest trinitarian formula, as the Eucharist was the primary witness to the mystery of redemption in all its fullness. The New Testament itself came to existence, as a Scripture, in the worshiping church. And Scripture was first read in the context of worship and meditation.

Basil and "Unwritten Tradition"

Already Irenaeus used to refer to "faith" as it had been received at baptism. The liturgical argument was used by Tertullian and Cyprian.[36] Athanasius and the Cappadocians used the same argument. The full development of this argument from the liturgical tradition we find in Basil. In his contest with the later Arians concerning the Holy Spirit, Basil built his major argument on the analysis of doxologies and their use in the churches. The treatise of Basil, *De Spiritu Sancto*, was an occasional tract written in the fire and heat of a desperate struggle, and addressed to a particular historic situation. But Basil was concerned here with the principles and methods of theological investigation.

In his treatise Basil was arguing a particular point—indeed, the crucial point in the sound trinitarian doctrine—the *homotimia* (equal honor) of

34. See M. Capuyns, "L'Origine des Capitula Pseudo-Célestiniens contre les Semi-pélagiens," *Revue bénédictine* 41 (1929): 156–70; and especially Karl Federer, *Liturgie und Glaube: Eine theologiegeschichtliche Untersuchung* (Freiburg, Switz., 1950); see also B. Capelle, "Autorité de la liturgie chez les Pères," *Recherches de théologie ancienne et médiévale* 21 (1954): 5–22.

35. J. N. D. Kelly, *Early Christian Creeds* (London, 1950), 167.

36. See Federer, *Liturgie*, 59ff.; F. De Pauw, "La Justification des traditions non écrites chez Tertullien," *Ephemerides theologicae Lovanienses* 19.1–2 (1942): 5–46. See also Georg Kretschmar, *Studien zur frühchristlichen Trinitätstheologie* (Tübingen, 1956).

the Holy Ghost. His main reference was to a liturgical witness: a doxology with a definite wording ("with the Spirit") which, as he could demonstrate, had been widely used in the churches. The phrase, of course, was not in the Scripture. It was attested only by tradition. But his opponents would not admit any authority but that of the Scripture. It is in this situation that Basil endeavored to prove the legitimacy of an appeal to tradition. He wanted to show that the ὁμοτιμία of the Spirit, that is, his divinity, was always believed in the church and was a part of the baptismal profession of faith. Indeed, as Benoit Pruche has rightly observed, the ὁμότιμος was for Basil an equivalent of the ὁμοούσιος.[37]

There was little new in Basil's concept of tradition, except consistency and precision. His phrasing, however, was rather peculiar: "Of the dogmata and kerygmata which are kept in the church, we have some from the written teaching (ἐκ τῆς ἐγγράφου διδασκαλίας), and some we derive from the apostolic *paradosis*, which has been handed down ἐν μυστηρίῳ. And both have the same strength (τὴν αὐτὴν ἰσχύν) in the matters of piety."[38] At first glance one may get the impression that Basil introduces here a double authority and double standard—Scripture *and* tradition. In fact he was very far from doing so. His use of terms is peculiar. *Kerygmata* were for him what in the later idiom were usually denoted as dogmas or doctrines— formal and authoritative teachings and rulings in the matters of faith, that is, open or public teachings. On the other hand, *dogmata* were for him the total complex of "unwritten habits" (τὰ ἄγραφα τῶν ἐθῶν), or, in fact, the whole structure of liturgical and sacramental life. It must be kept in mind that the term *dogma* was not yet fixed by that time—it was not yet a term with a strict and exact connotation.[39] In any case, one should not be embarrassed by the contention of Basil that *dogmata* were delivered or handed down by the apostles ἐν μυστηρίῳ. It would be a flagrant mistranslation if we render this phrase "in secret." The only accurate rendering is "by the way of mysteries," that is, under the form of rites and liturgical usages or habits. In fact, that is precisely what Basil says himself: "τὰ πλεῖστα τῶν μυστικῶν ἀγράφως ἡμῖν ἐμπολιτεύεται" ("most of the mysteries are communicated to us in an unwritten way"). The term τὰ μυστικά refers here, obviously, to the rites of baptism and Eucharist, which are, for Basil, of apostolic origin. He quotes at this point Paul's own reference to traditions which the faithful have received (εἴτε διὰ λόγου, εἴτε δι᾽ ἐπιστολῆς, 2 Thess. 2:15; cf. 1 Cor. 11:2). The doxology in question is one of these

37. See the introduction to Basil, *De Spiritu Sancto*, ed. Benoit Pruche, in *Sources chré-tiennes* (Paris, 1945), 28ff.

38. Basil *De Spiritu Sancto* 66.

39. See the valuable study by August Deneffe, "Dogma, Wort und Begriff," *Scholastik* 6 (1931): 381–400, 505–38.

unwritten traditions.[40] Indeed, all instances quoted by Basil in this connection are of ritual or liturgical nature: the use of the sign of the cross in the rite of admission of catechumens; the orientation toward the east at prayer; the habit of standing during Sunday worship; the epiclesis in the eucharistic rite; the blessing of water and oil, the renunciation of Satan and his pomp, the triple immersion, in the rite of baptism.

There are many other "unwritten mysteries of the church," says Basil (τὰ ἄγραφα τῆς ἐκκλησίας μυστήρια).[41] They are not mentioned in the Scripture. But they are of great authority and significance. They are indispensable for the preservation of right faith. They are effective means of witness and communication. According to Basil, they come from a silent and private tradition: ἀπὸ τῆς σιωπωμένης καὶ μυστικῆς παραδόσεως ἐκ τῆς ἀδημοσιεύτου ταύτης καὶ ἀπορρήτου διδασκαλίας ("from the silent and mystical tradition, from the unpublic and ineffable teaching"). This silent and mystical tradition which has not been made public is not an esoteric doctrine reserved for some particular elite. The elite was the church. In fact, the tradition to which Basil appeals is the liturgical practice of the church. Basil is referring here to what is now denoted as *disciplina arcani* (the discipline of secrecy). In the fourth century this discipline was in wide use, being formally imposed and advocated in the church. It was related to the institution of the catechumenate and had primarily an educational and didactic purpose. On the other hand, as Basil says himself, certain traditions had to be kept unwritten in order to prevent profanation at the hands of the infidel. This remark obviously refers to rites and usages. It may be recalled at this point that, in the practice of the fourth century, the creed (and also the Dominical Prayer) was a part of this discipline of secrecy and could not be disclosed to the noninitiated. The creed was reserved for the last stage of the instruction of the candidates for baptism, after they had been solemnly enrolled and approved. The creed was communicated ("traditioned") to them by the bishop *orally*, and they had to recite it by memory before him. This was the ceremony of *traditio et redditio symboli* (transmission and repetition [by the initiated] of the creed). The catechumens were strongly urged not to divulge the creed to outsiders and not to commit it to writing; it had to be inscribed in their hearts.[42] In the West Rufinus and Augustine felt that it was

---

40. Basil *De Spiritu Sancto* 71; see also 66: οἱ τὰ περὶ τὰς ἐκκλησίας ἐξαρχῆς διαθεσμοθετήσαντες ἀπόστολοι καὶ πατέρες, ἐν τῷ κεκρυμμένῳ καὶ ἀφθέγκτῳ τὸ σεμνὸν τοῖς μυστηρίοις ἐφύλασσον ("the apostles and Fathers who from the very beginning arranged everything in the churches, preserved the sacred character of the mysteries in silence and secrecy").

41. Ibid., 66–67.

42. Cyril of Jerusalem *Procatechesis* 12, 17.

improper to set the creed down on paper. For that reason Sozomen in his *History* does not quote the text of the Nicene Creed, "which only the initiated and the mystagogues have the right to recite and hear."[43]

It is against this background, and in this historic context, that the argument of Basil must be assessed and interpreted. Basil stresses strongly the importance of the baptismal profession of faith, which included a formal commitment to belief in the Holy Trinity, Father, Son, and Holy Spirit.[44] This was a tradition which had been handed down to the neophytes in mystery and had to be kept in silence. One would be in great danger of shaking "the very foundation of the Christian faith" (τὸ στερέωμα τῆς εἰς Χριστὸν πίστεως) if this unwritten tradition were set aside, ignored, or neglected.[45] The only difference between δόγμα and κήρυγμα is in the manner of their transmission: dogma is kept in silence and kerygmata are publicized (τὸ μὲν γὰρ σιωπᾶται, τὰ δὲ κηρύγματα δημοσιεύονται). But their intent is identical; they convey the same faith, if in different manners. Moreover, the unwritten tradition involved more than just a tradition of the Fathers— such a tradition would not have sufficed (οὐκ ἐξαρκεῖ). In fact, the Fathers derived their principles from the intention of the Scripture—"τῷ βουλή-ματι τῆς Γραφῆς ἠκολούθησαν, ἐκ τῶν μαρτυριῶν . . . τὰς ἀρχὰς λαβόντες" ("they followed the intention of the Scripture, deriving their principles from the scriptural witnesses"). Thus the unwritten tradition in rites and symbols does not actually add anything to the content of the scriptural faith; it only puts this faith in focus.[46]

Basil's appeal to unwritten tradition was actually an appeal to the faith of the church, to her *sensus catholicus*, to the φρόνημα ἐκκλησιαστικόν (ecclesiastical mind). Having to break the deadlock created by the obstinate and narrow-minded pseudobiblicism of his Arian opponents, he pleaded that, apart from this unwritten rule of faith, it was impossible to grasp the true intention and teaching of the Scripture itself. Basil was strictly scriptural in his theology: Scripture was for him the supreme crite-

---

43. Sozomen *Historia ecclesiastica* 1.20.

44. Basil *De Spiritu Sancto* 67, 26.

45. Ibid., 25.

46. See Hermann Dörries, *De Spiritu Sancto: Der Beitrag des Basilius zum Abschluss des trinitarischen Dogmas* (Göttingen, 1956); J. A. Jungmann, *Die Stellung Christi im liturgischen Gebet*, 2d ed. (Münster, 1962), 155ff., 163ff.; David Amand, *L'Ascèse monastique de Saint Basile* (Maredsous, Belgium, 1949), 75–85. The footnotes in the critical editions of *De Spiritu Sancto* that were produced by C. F. H. Johnson (Oxford, 1892) and Benoit Pruche (Paris, 1945) are highly instructive and helpful. On *disciplina arcani* see O. Perler, "Arkandisciplin," in *Reallexikon für Antike und Christentum* (Stuttgart, 1950), 1:671–76. Joachim Jeremias, *Die Abendmahlsworte Jesu* (Göttingen, 1949), 59ff., 78ff., contended that *disciplina arcani* could be detected already in the formation of the text of the Gospels and actually existed also in Judaism; cf. the sharp criticism of this thesis by R. P. C. Hanson, *Tradition in the Early Church* (London, 1962), 27ff.

rion of doctrine.[47] His exegesis was sober and reserved. Yet Scripture itself was a mystery, a mystery of divine economy and of human salvation. There was an inscrutable depth in the Scripture, since it was an inspired book, a book by the Spirit. For that reason true exegesis also had to be spiritual and prophetic. A gift of spiritual discernment was necessary for the right understanding of the Holy Word. "For the judge of the words ought to start with the same preparation as the author. . . . And I see that in the utterances of the Spirit it is also impossible for everyone to undertake the scrutiny of His word; rather, it is possible only for them who have the Spirit that grants the discernment."[48] The Spirit is granted in the sacraments of the church. So Scripture must be read in the light of faith, and also in the community of the faithful. For that reason tradition, the tradition of faith as handed down through generations, was for Basil an indispensable guide and companion in the study and interpretation of the Holy Writ. At this point he was following in the steps of Irenaeus and Athanasius. Augustine used tradition and especially the liturgical witness of the church in a similar way.[49]

The Church as Interpreter of Scripture

The church had the authority to interpret the Scripture, since she was the only authentic depository of apostolic kerygma. This kerygma was unfailingly kept alive in the church, as she was endowed with the Spirit. The church was still teaching *viva voce*, commending and furthering the Word of God. And *viva vox evangelii* (the living voice of the gospel) was indeed not just a recitation of the words of the Scripture. It was a proclamation of the Word of God, as it was heard and preserved in the church by the ever-abiding power of the quickening Spirit.

Apart from the church and her regular ministry that succeeded the apostles, there was no true proclamation of the gospel, no sound preaching, no real understanding of the Word of God. And therefore it would be in vain to look for truth outside of the church catholic and apostolic. This was the common assumption of the ancient church from Irenaeus down to Chalcedon and further. Irenaeus was quite formal at this point. In the church the fullness of truth has been gathered by the apostles: *"plenissime in eam contulerint omnia quae sunt veritatis"* ("lodged in her hands most copiously are all things pertaining to truth").[50] Indeed, Scripture itself was

47. Basil *Epistolae* 189.3.
48. Ibid., 204.
49. See German Mártil, *La tradición en San Agustín a través de la controversia pelagiana* (Madrid, 1942) (originally in *Revista española de teología*, vol. 1, 1940, and vol. 2, 1942); Wunibald Roetzer, *Des heiligen Augustinus Schriften als liturgie-geschichtliche Quelle* (Munich, 1930); see also Federer, *Liturgie*, and Capelle, "Autorité."
50. Irenaeus *Adversus omnes haereses* 3.4.1.

the major part of this apostolic deposit. So was also the church. Scripture and church could not be separated or opposed to each other. Scripture, that is, its true understanding, was only in the church, as she was guided by the Spirit. Origen was stressing this unity between Scripture and church persistently. The task of the interpreter is to disclose the word of the Spirit: *"hoc observare debemus ut non nostras, cum docemus, sed Sancti Spiritus sententias proferamus"* ("we must be careful when we teach to present not our own interpretation but that of the Holy Spirit").[51] And this is simply impossible apart from the apostolic tradition, which is kept in the church. Origen insisted on the *catholic* interpretation of Scripture that is offered in the church: *"audiens in ecclesia verbum Dei catholice tractari"* ("hearing in the church the Word of God presented in the catholic manner").[52] By contrast, heretics in their exegesis ignore precisely the true intention or the *voluntas* of the Scripture. *"Qui enim neque juxta voluntatem Scripturarum neque juxta fidei veritatem profert eloquia Dei, seminat triticum et metit spinas"* ("those who present the words of God, not in conjunction with the intention of the Scriptures, nor in conjunction with the truth of faith, have sown wheat and reaped thorns").[53]

The intention of the Holy Writ and the rule of faith are intimately correlated with and correspond to each other. This was the position of the Fathers in the fourth century and later, in full agreement with the teaching of the ancients. With his usual sharpness and vehemence of expression, Jerome, this great man of Scripture, has voiced the same view:

> Marcion and Basilides and other heretics . . . do not possess the gospel of God, since they have no Holy Spirit, without which the gospel so preached becomes human. We do not think that gospel consists of the words of Scripture but in its meaning, not on the surface but in the marrow, not in the leaves of sermons but in the root of meaning. In this case Scripture is really useful for the hearers when it is not spoken without Christ, nor is presented without the Fathers, and those who are preaching do not introduce it without the Spirit. . . . It is a great danger to speak in the church, lest by a perverse interpretation of the gospel of Christ, a gospel of man is made.[54]

There is the same preoccupation with the true understanding of the Word of God as in the days of Irenaeus, Tertullian, and Origen. Jerome probably was simply paraphrasing Origen. Outside of the church there is no divine gospel, but only human substitutes. The true meaning of Scrip-

---

51. Origen *Commentary on Romans* 1.3.1.
52. Origen *Homilies on Leviticus* 4.5.
53. Origen *Homilies on Jeremiah* 7.3.
54. Jerome *Commentary on Galatians* 1.1.2 (PL 26.386).

ture, the *sensus Scripturae*, that is, the divine message, can be detected only *juxta fidei veritatem* (in conjunction with the truth of faith), under the guidance of the rule of faith. The *veritas fidei* (the truth of faith) is, in this context, the trinitarian confession of faith. This is the same approach as in Basil. Jerome is speaking here primarily of the proclamation of the Word in the church. *"Audientibus utilis est"* ("It is useful to those who hear").

Augustine and Catholic Authority

In the same sense we have to interpret the well-known and justly startling statement of Augustine: *"Ego vero evangelio non crederem, nisi me catholicae ecclesiae commoveret auctoritas"* ("Indeed, I should not have believed the gospel, if the authority of the catholic church had not moved me").[55] This sentence must be read in its context. Augustine did not utter it on his own behalf. He spoke of the attitude which a simple believer has to take when confronted with a heretical claim for authority. In this situation it is proper for a simple believer to appeal to the authority of the church, from which and in which he has received the gospel itself: *"ipsi evangelio catholicis praedicantibus credidi"* ("I believed the gospel itself, being instructed by catholic preachers"). The gospel and the preaching of the *catholici* belong together. Augustine had no intention to subordinate the gospel to the church. He merely wanted to emphasize that the gospel is always received in the context of the church's catholic preaching and simply cannot be separated from the church. Only in this context can it be assessed and properly understood. Indeed, the witness of the Scripture is ultimately self-evident, but only for the faithful, for those who have achieved a certain spiritual maturity; and this is possible only within the church. He contrasted this teaching and preaching *auctoritas* of the church catholic with the pretentious vagaries of Manichean exegesis. The gospel did not belong to the Manicheans. *Catholicae ecclesiae auctoritas* (the authority of the catholic church) was not an independent source of faith. But it was the indispensable principle of sound interpretation. Actually, the sentence could be converted: one should not believe the church, unless one is moved by the gospel. The relationship is strictly reciprocal.[56]

55. Augustine *Contra epistolam Manichaei quam vocant Fundamenti* 6.
56. See Louis de Montadon, "Bible et église dans l'apologétique de Saint Augustin," *Recherches de science religieuse* 2 (1911): 233–38; Pierre Batiffol, *Le Catholicisme de Saint Augustin*, 5th ed. (Paris, 1929), 25–27 (see the whole of chap. 1, "L'Eglise règle de foi"); and especially A. D. R. Polman, *The Word of God according to St. Augustine* (Grand Rapids, 1961), 198–208 (this is a revised translation of *De theologie van Augustinus: Het Woord Gods bij Augustinus* [1955]); see also W. F. Dankbaar, "Schriftgezag en kerkgezag bij Augustinus," *Nederlands theologisch tijdschrift* 11 (1956–57): 37–59 (this article was written in connection with the Dutch edition of Polman's book).

The Authority
of the Ancient Councils
and the Tradition of the Fathers
George Florovsky

The Councils in the Early Church

The scope of this essay is limited and restricted. It is no more than an introduction. Both subjects—the role of the councils in the history of the church and the function of tradition—have been intensively studied in recent years. The purpose of the present essay is to offer some suggestions which may prove helpful in the further scrutiny of documentary evidence and in its theological assessment and interpretation. In dealing with these subjects it should be kept in mind that the church historian is inevitably also a theologian. He is bound to bring in his personal options and commitments. On the other hand, it is imperative that theologians also should be aware of that wide historical perspective in which matters of faith and doctrine have been continuously discussed and comprehended. Anachronistic language must be carefully avoided. Each age must be discussed on its own terms.

Instead of attempting any overarching definition in advance, the student of the ancient church must begin with the study of particular councils taken in their concrete historical setting and against their specific existential background. Indeed, this is precisely what historians are doing. There was no conciliar theory in the ancient church, no elaborate theology of the

From *Glaube, Geist, Geschichte: Festschrift für Ernst Benz* (Leiden: Brill, 1967), 177–88. Reprinted by permission.

councils, and even no fixed canonical regulations. The councils of the early church, in the first three centuries, were occasional meetings convened for special purposes, usually in the situation of urgency to discuss particular items of common concern. They were *events* rather than an institution. Or, to use the phrase of the late Gregory Dix, "in the pre-Nicene times Councils were an occasional device, with no certain place in the scheme of church government."[1] Of course, it was commonly assumed and agreed, already at that time, that meeting and consultation of bishops representing or, rather, personifying their respective local churches or communities was a proper and normal method to manifest and to achieve unity and consent in matters of faith and discipline.

The sense of the unity of the church was strong in early times, although it had not yet been reflected on the organizational level. The collegiality of the bishops was assumed in principle, and the concept of the *episcopatus unus* was already in the process of formation. Bishops of a particular area used to meet for the election and consecration of new bishops. Foundations had been laid for the future provincial or metropolitan system. But all this was rather a spontaneous movement. It seems that councils came into existence first in Asia Minor by the end of the second century, in the period of intensive defense against the spread of the new prophecy, that is, of the Montanist enthusiastic explosion. In this situation it was but natural that the main emphasis should be put on the apostolic tradition, of which bishops were guardians and witnesses in their respective *paroikiai*. It was in North Africa that a kind of conciliar system was established in the third century. It was found that councils were the best device for witnessing, articulating, and proclaiming the common mind of the church and the accord and unanimity of local churches. Professor Georg Kretschmar has rightly said, in his study on the councils of the ancient church, that the basic concern of the early councils was precisely with the unity of the church: "*Schon von ihrem Ursprung her ist ihr eigentliches Thema aber das Ringen um die rechte, geistliche Einheit der Kirche Gottes.*"[2] Yet this unity was based on the identity of tradition and the unanimity in faith rather than on any institutional pattern.

The Imperial or Ecumenical Council

The situation changed with the conversion of the empire. Since Constantine, or rather since Theodosius, it was commonly assumed and acknowledged that church was coextensive with commonwealth, that is,

---

1. Gregory Dix, "Jurisdiction, Episcopal and Papal, in the Early Church," *Laudate* 16 (June 1938): 108.
2. Georg Kretschmar, "Die Konzile der alten Kirche," in *Die ökumenischen Konzile der Christenheit*, ed. H. J. Margull (Stuttgart, 1961), 1.

with the universal empire which had been christened. The conversion of the empire made the universality of the church more visible than ever before. Of course, it did not add anything to the essential and intrinsic universality of the Christian church. But the new opportunity provided for its visible manifestation.

It was in this situation that the first general council was convened, the great Council of Nicea. It was to become the model for the later councils. "The new established position of the Church necessitated *ecumenical* action, precisely because Christian life was now lived in the world which was no longer organized on a basis of localism, but of the Empire as a whole. . . . Because the Church had come out into the world the local churches had to learn to live no longer as self-contained units (as in practice, though not in theory, they had largely lived in the past), but as parts of a vast spiritual government."[3] In a certain sense the general councils as inaugurated at Nicea may be described as imperial councils, *die Reichskonzile*, and this was probably the first and original meaning of the term *ecumenical* as applied to the councils.[4]

It would be out of place now to discuss at any length the vexed and controversial problem of the nature or character of that peculiar structure which was the new Christian commonwealth, the theocratic *res publica Christiana*, in which the church was strangely wedded with the empire.[5] For our immediate purpose it is actually irrelevant. The councils of the fourth century were still occasional meetings or individual events, and their ultimate authority was still grounded in their conformity with the apostolic tradition. It is significant that no attempt to develop a legal or canonical theory of general council as a seat of ultimate authority with specific competence and models of procedure was made in the fourth century or later, although they were de facto acknowledged as a proper channel for dealing with the questions of faith and doctrine and as an authority on these matters. It will be no exaggeration to suggest that councils were never regarded as a canonical institution, but rather as occasional charismatic events. Councils were not regarded as periodical gatherings which had to be convened at certain fixed dates. And no council was accepted as valid in advance; indeed, many councils were actually disavowed in spite of their formal regularity. It is enough to mention the notorious Robber Council of 449. Indeed, those councils which were actually recognized as ecumenical, in the sense of their binding and infallible authority, were

3. Dix, "Jurisdiction," 113.

4. See Eduard Schwartz, "Über die Reichskonzilien von Theodosius bis Justinian" (1921), reprinted in *Gesammelte Schriften*, vol. 4 (Berlin, 1960), 111–58.

5. See George Florovsky, "Empire and Desert: Antinomies of Christian History," *Greek Orthodox Theological Review* 3.2 (1957): 133–59.

recognized, immediately or after a delay, not because of their formal canonical competence, but because of their charismatic character. That is, under the guidance of the Holy Spirit they witnessed to the truth in conformity with the Scripture as handed down in the apostolic tradition.[6]

There is no space now to discuss the theory of conciliar authority. In fact, as we have suggested, there was no theory. The councils simply had an insight into the matters of faith. Hans Küng in his *Strukturen der Kirche* has suggested a helpful avenue of approach to this very problem. Indeed, Küng is not a historian, but his theological scheme can be fruitfully applied by historians. Küng suggests that we should regard the church herself as a council, an assembly convened by God himself, *aus göttlicher Berufung*, and the historic councils, that is, the ecumenical or general councils, as councils *aus menschlicher Berufung*, as a representation of the church— indeed, a true representation, but yet no more than a representation.[7] It is interesting to note that a similar conception had been made already many years ago by the great Russian church historian, V. V. Bolotov, in his *Lectures on the History of the Ancient Church*. The church is *ecclesia*, an assembly which is never adjourned.[8] In other words, the ultimate authority— and the ability to discern the truth in faith—is vested in the church, which is indeed a "divine institution" in the proper and strict sense of the word, whereas no council, and no conciliar institution, is *de jure divino*, except insofar as it happens to be a true image or manifestation of the church herself.

We may seem to be involved here in a vicious circle. Indeed, we may actually be involved in it, if we insist on formal guarantees in doctrinal matters. But, obviously, such guarantees do not exist and cannot be produced, especially in advance. Certain councils were actually failures, no more than *conciliabula*, and did err. And for that reason they were subsequently disavowed. The story of the councils in the fourth century is, in this respect, very instructive.[9] The claims of the councils were accepted or rejected in the church not on formal or canonical ground. And the verdict of the church has been highly selective. *The council is not above the church:* this was the attitude of the ancient church. The council is precisely a representation. This explains why the ancient church never appealed to conciliar authority in general or *in abstracto*, but always to particular councils,

6. See V. V. Bolotov, *Lectures on the History of the Ancient Church* (in Russian), vol. 3 (1913), 320ff.; idem, *Letters to A. A. Kireev* (in Russian), ed. D. N. Jakshich (1931), 31ff.; A. P. Dobroklonsky, "The Ecumenical Councils of the Orthodox Church: Their Structure" (in Serbian), *Bogoslovlje* 11.2–3 (1936): 163–72, 276–87.

7. Hans Küng, *Strukturen der Kirche* (Freiburg, 1962), 11–74.

8. Bolotov, *Lectures*, vol. 1 (1907), 9–14.

9. See Monald Goemans, *Het algemeene concilie in de vierde eeuw* (Nijmegen, 1945).

or rather to their faith and witness. Yves Congar has published an excellent article on the "Primacy of the First Four Ecumenical Councils," and the evidence he has collected is highly instructive.[10] In fact, the dogmatic rulings of Nicea, Ephesus, and Chalcedon were afforded normative priority precisely because they were felt to be a faithful and adequate expression of the perennial commitment of faith as once delivered unto the church. Again the stress was not so much on canonical authority, but on the truth. This leads us to the most intricate and crucial problem—what are the ultimate criteria of the Christian truth?

Christ: The Criterion of Truth

There is no easy answer to this query, even though there is a very simple answer—*Christ is the Truth*. The source and the criterion of the Christian truth is the divine revelation in its twofold structure, in its two dispensations. The source of the truth is the Word of God. Now this simple answer was readily given and commonly accepted in the ancient church, as it may be also gratefully accepted in the divided Christendom of our own days. Yet this answer does not solve the problem. In fact, it has been variously assessed and interpreted to the point of most radical divergence. As a result, the problem was actually shifted a step further. A new question came to be asked: How is revelation to be understood?

The early church had no doubt about the sufficiency of the Scriptures, and never tried to go beyond, and always claimed not to have gone beyond. But already in the Apostolic Age itself the problem of interpretation arose in all its challenging sharpness. What was the guiding hermeneutical principle? At this point there was no other answer than the appeal to the faith of the church, the faith and kerygma of the apostles, the apostolic *paradosis*. The Scripture could be understood only within the church, as Origen strongly insisted, and as Irenaeus and Tertullian insisted before him. The appeal to tradition was actually an appeal to the mind of the church, her *phronema*. The method was to discover and ascertain the faith as it had been always held (*semper creditum*) from the very beginning. The permanence of Christian belief was the most conspicuous sign and token of its truth; there were no innovations.[11] And this permanence of the holy church's faith

10. Yves M. J. Congar, "Primauté des quatre premiers conciles oecuméniques," in *Le Concile et les conciles: Contribution à l'histoire de la vie conciliaire de l'église* (1960), 75–109.

11. For further discussion of this topic see George Florovsky, "The Function of Tradition in the Ancient Church," *Greek Orthodox Theological Review* 9.2 (1963–64): 181–200; idem, "Scripture and Tradition: An Orthodox Point of View," *Dialog* 2.4 (1963): 288–93. See also idem, "Revelation and Interpretation," in *Biblical Authority for Today*, ed. Alan Richardson and W. Schweitzer (Philadelphia, 1951), 163–80.

could be appropriately demonstrated by the witnesses from the past. It was for that reason, and for that purpose, that the ancients—οἱ παλαιοί—were usually invoked and quoted in theological discussions.

This argument from antiquity, however, had to be used with certain caution. Occasional references to old times and casual quotations from old authors could often be ambiguous and even misleading. This was well understood already at the time of the great baptismal controversy in the third century, when the question about the validity or authority of ancient customs was formally raised. Already Tertullian contended that *consuetudines* (customs) in the church had to be examined in the light of truth: *"Dominus noster Christus veritatem se, non consuetudinem, cognominavit"* ("Our Lord Christ designated himself not as custom but as truth").[12] This phrase was taken up by Cyprian and was adopted by the council at Carthage in 256. In fact, antiquity as such might happen to be no more than an inveterate error: *"nam antiquitas sine veritate vetustas erroris est"* ("for antiquity without truth is age-old error").[13] Augustine also used the same phrase: *"In Evangelio Dominus, Ego sum, inquit, veritas. Non dixit, Ego sum consuetudo"* ("In the Gospel the Lord says, 'I am the truth.' He did not say, 'I am custom'").[14] Antiquity as such was not necessarily a truth, although the Christian truth was intrinsically an ancient truth, and innovations in the church had to be resisted. On the other hand, the argument from tradition was first used by the heretics, by Gnostics, and it was this usage of theirs that prompted Irenaeus to elaborate his own conception of tradition—in opposition to the false traditions of the heretics which were alien to the mind of the church.[15]

The appeal to antiquity or traditions had to be selective and discriminative. Certain alleged traditions were simply wrong and false. One had to detect and to identify the true tradition, the authentic tradition which could be traced back to the authority of the apostles and be attested and confirmed by a universal *consensio* of the churches. In fact, however, this *consensio* could not be so easily discovered. Certain questions were still open. The main criterion of Irenaeus was valid: tradition—apostolic and catholic (or universal). Origen, in the preface to his *De principiis*, tried to describe the scope of the existing agreement, which was to his mind binding and restrictive, and then he quoted a series of important topics which had to be further explored.

12. Tertullian *De virginibus velandis* 1.1.
13. Cyprian *Epistolae* 74.9.
14. Augustine *De baptismo* 3.6.9.
15. See B. Reynders, "Paradosis: Le Progrès de l'idée de tradition jusqu'à Saint Irénée," *Recherches de théologie ancienne et médiévale* 5 (1933): 155–91; idem, "La Polemique de Saint Irénée," *Recherches de théologie et médiévale* 7 (1935): 5–27.

There was in language and discipline a considerable variety of local traditions, even within the unbroken communion in faith and *in sacris*. It suffices to recall at this point the paschal controversy between Rome and the East, in which the whole question of the authority of ancient habits came to the fore. One should also recall the conflicts between Carthage and Rome, and also between Rome and Alexandria, in the third century, and the increasing tension between Alexandria and Antioch which came to its tragic climax and impasse in the fifth century. Now, in this age of intense theological controversy, all participating groups used to appeal to tradition and antiquity. Chains of ancient testimonies were compiled on all sides in the dispute. These testimonies had to be carefully scrutinized and examined on a basis more comprehensive than antiquity alone. Certain local traditions, liturgical and theological, were finally discarded and disavowed by the overarching authority of an ecumenical consensus.

A sharp confrontation of diverse theological traditions took place already at the Council of Ephesus. The council was actually split in twain—the ecumenical council of Cyril and Rome and the *conciliabulum* of the Orient. Although reconciliation was achieved, there was still a tension. The most spectacular instance of condemnation of a theological tradition of long standing and of considerable, if rather local, renown was, of course, the dramatic affair of the Three Chapters. At this point a question of principle was raised: to what extent was it fair and legitimate to disavow the faith of those who had died in peace and in communion with the church? There was a violent debate on this matter, especially in the West, and strong arguments were produced against such retrospective discrimination. Nevertheless, the chapters were condemned by the fifth ecumenical council. Antiquity was overruled by ecumenical *consensio*, as strained as it probably was.

The Meaning of the Appeal to the Fathers

It has been rightly observed that the appeal to antiquity changed its function and character with the course of time. The apostolic past was still at hand, and within the reach of human memory, in the times of Irenaeus or Tertullian. Indeed, Irenaeus had heard in his youth the oral instruction of Polycarp, the immediate disciple of John the Divine. It was only the third generation since Christ! The memory of the Apostolic Age was still fresh. The scope of Christian history was brief and limited. The main concern in this early age was with the apostolic foundations, with the initial delivery of the kerygma. Accordingly, tradition meant at that time, primarily, the original delivery or deposition. The question of accurate transmission, over a bit more than one century, was comparatively simple, especially in the churches founded by the apostles themselves. Full attention was given, of course, to the lists of episcopal succession (e.g., in Irenaeus or Hegesippus), which were not difficult to compile.

The question of succession, however, appeared to be much more complicated for the subsequent generations, which were more removed from the apostolic time. It was but natural, under these new conditions, that emphasis should shift from the question of initial apostolicity to the problem of the preservation of the deposit. Tradition came to mean transmission rather than delivery. The question of the intermediate links of the "succession"—in the wide and comprehensive sense of the word—became especially urgent. The issue here was faithful witnesses. It was in this situation that the authority of the Fathers was for the first time formally invoked; they were witnesses of the permanence or identity of the kerygma as transmitted from generation to generation.[16] Apostles *and* Fathers—these two terms were generally and commonly coupled together in the argument from tradition, as it was used in the third and fourth centuries. It was this double reference, both to the origin and to the unfailing and continuous preservation, that assured authenticity and warranted belief. On the other hand, Scripture was formally acknowledged and recognized as the ground and foundation of faith, as the Word of God and the Writ of the Spirit. Yet there was still the problem of right and adequate interpretation. Scripture and Fathers were usually quoted together, that is, kerygma and exegesis— ἡ γραφὴ καὶ οἱ πατέρες.

Reference or even direct appeal to the Fathers was a distinctive and salient note of theological research and discussion in the period of the great general or ecumenical councils, beginning with that of Nicea. The term *Fathers* has never been formally defined. It was used, occasionally and sporadically, already by early ecclesiastical writers. Often it simply denoted Christian teachers and leaders of previous generations. It was gradually becoming a title for the bishops, insofar as they were appointed teachers and witnesses of faith. Later the title was applied specifically to bishops in the councils. The common element in all these cases was the teaching office or task. "Fathers" were those who transmitted and propagated the right doctrine, the teaching of the apostles; they were guides and masters in Christian instruction and catechesis. In this sense the term was emphatically applied to great Christian writers. It must be kept in mind that the main, if not also the only, manual of faith and doctrine

16. See P. Smulders, "Le Mot et le concept de tradition chez les Pères," *Recherches de science religieuse* 40 (1952): 41–62; and Yves M. J. Congar, *La Tradition et les traditions*, vol. 1, *Etude historique* (Paris, 1960), 57ff.

was, in the ancient church, precisely the Holy Writ. And for that reason the renowned interpreters of Scripture were regarded as Fathers in an eminent sense.[17]

The Fathers were teachers first of all—doctores, διδάσκαλοι. And they were teachers insofar as they were witnesses, testes. These two functions must be distinguished, and yet they are most intimately intertwined. Teaching was an apostolic task: Christ commissioned the apostles to "teach all nations." And it was in this commission that their authority, which was in fact the authority to bear witness, was rooted. Two major points must be made in this connection.

First, the phrase "the Fathers of the church" has an obvious restrictive accent: they were acting not just as individuals, but rather as viri ecclesiastici (a favorite expression of Origen), on behalf and in the name of the church. They were spokesmen for the church, expositors of her faith, keepers of her tradition, witnesses of truth and faith—magistri probabiles, in the phrase of Vincent of Lérins. And in that was their authority grounded.[18] This leads us back to the concept of representation. George Prestige has rightly observed:

> The creeds of the church grew out of the teaching of the church: the general effect of heresy was rather to force old creeds to be tightened up than to cause fresh creeds to be constructed. Thus the most famous and most crucial of all creeds, that of Nicea, was only a new edition of an existing Palestinian confession. And a further important fact always ought to be remembered. *The real intellectual work, the vital interpretative thought, was not contributed by the Councils that promulgated the creeds, but by the theological teachers who supplied and explained the formulae which the Councils adopted. The teaching of Nicea, which finally commended itself, represented the views of intellectual giants working for a hundred years before and for fifty years after the actual meeting of the Council.*[19]

The Fathers were true inspirers of the councils, whether they were present or in absentia, and often even after they had gone to eternal rest. For that reason, and in this sense, the councils used to emphasize that they were "following the Holy Fathers" (ἑπόμενοι τοῖς ἁγίοις πατράσιν), as Chalcedon has said.

17. See J. Fessler, Institutiones Patrologiae, ed. B. Jungmann, vol. 1 (Innsbruck, 1890), 15–57; E. Amann, "Pères de l'église," in Dictionnaire de théologie catholique 12.1192–1215; Basilius Steidle, "Heilige Vaterschaft," Benediktinische Monatsschrift 14 (1932): 215–26; idem, "Unsere Kirchenväter," Benediktinische Monatsschrift 14 (1932): 387–98, 454–66.

18. See Basilius Steidle, Patrologia (Freiburg, Germany, 1937), 9: "qui saltem aliquo tempore per vinculum fidei et caritatis Ecclesiae adhaeserunt testesque sunt veritatis catholicae."

19. George L. Prestige, Fathers and Heretics (London, 1940), 8 (italics added).

Secondly, it was precisely the *consensus patrum* which was authoritative and binding, and not their private opinions or views, although even they should not be hastily dismissed. Again, this consensus was much more than just an empirical agreement of individuals. The true and authentic consensus was that which reflected the mind of the catholic and universal church (τὸ ἐκκλησιαστικὸν φρόνημα).[20] It was that kind of consensus to which Irenaeus was referring when he contended that neither a special ability nor a deficiency in the speech of individual leaders in the churches could affect the identicalness of their witness, since the "power of tradition" (*virtus traditionis*) was always and everywhere the same.[21] The preaching of the church is always identical, "*constans et aequaliter persever-ans.*"[22] The true consensus manifests and discloses this perennial identity of the church's faith (*aequaliter perseverans*).[23]

The teaching authority of the ecumenical councils is grounded in the infallibility of the church. The ultimate authority is vested in the church, which is forever the pillar and the foundation of truth. This is not primarily a *canonical* authority, in the formal and specific sense of the term, although canonical strictures or sanctions may be appended to conciliar decisions on matters of faith. It is a *charismatic* authority, grounded in the assistance of the Spirit ("for it seemed good to the Holy Spirit and to us").

20. See Eusebius *Historia ecclesiastica* 5.28.6, quoting an anonymous third-century treatise, *Against the Heresy of Artemon*. The attribution of this treatise to Hippolytus is doubtful.

21. Irenaeus *Adversus omnes haereses* 1.10.2.

22. Ibid., 3.24.1.

23. See George Florovsky, "Offenbarung, Philosophie und Theologie," *Zwischen den Zeiten* 9 (1931): 463–80. Cf. Karl Adam, *Christus unser Bruder* (1926), 116f.: "*Der konservative Traditionsgeist der Kirche fliesst unmittelbar aus ihrer christozentrischen Grundhaltung. Von dieser Grundstellung aus wandte sich die Kirche von jeher gegen die Tyrannie von Führerpersönlichkeiten, von Schulen und Richtungen. Da, wo durch diese Schulen das christliche Bewusstsein, die überlieferte Botschaft von Christus, getrübt oder bedroht schien, da zögerte sie nicht, selbst über ihre grössten Söhne hinwegzuschreiten, über einen Origenes, Augustin, ja—hier und dort—selbst über einen Thomas von Aquin. Und überall da, wo grundsätzlich nicht die Überlieferung, nicht das Feststehen auf dem Boden der Geschichte, der urchristlichen Gegebenheit, der lebendigen fortdauernden Gemeinschaft, sondern die eigene Spekulation und das eigene kleine Erlebnis und das eigene arme Ich zum Träger der Christusbotschaft gemacht werden sollte, da sprach sie umgehend ihr Anathema aus. . . . Die Geschichte der kirchlichen Verkündigung ist nichts anderes als ein zähes Festhalten an Christus, eine folgestrenge Durchführung des Gebotes Christi: Nur einer sei eurer Lehrer, Christus.*" Actually, this moving passage is almost a paraphrase of the last chapter (27) of the (first) *Commonitorium* of Vincent of Lérins, in which he sharply discriminates between the common, universal mind of the church and the *privatae opiniunculae* of individuals: "*quidquid vero, quamvis ille sanctus et doctus, quamvis episcopus, quamvis confessor et martyr, praeter omnes aut etiam contra omnes senserit.*"

8

Tradition and Traditions

Vladimir Lossky

*Vladimir Lossky (1903–58), son of the famous Russian philosopher Ni-
kolai Lossky (1870–1965), was exiled from Russia in 1922. Subsequently
he lived and worked in Paris among the Russian émigré community until
his death. Although several works have been published posthumously,
Lossky published only one book in his lifetime, his justly famous classic*
Mystical Theology of the Eastern Church. *John Meyendorff once observed that it was the genius of Lossky, a scholar not only in Byzantine theology but in the Latin Middle Ages (his doctoral dissertation on Meister
Eckhart was published in Paris), to maintain "the double intention of preserving the integrity of Orthodoxy while maintaining a dialogue with the
Christian West."*

Orthodoxy often appeals to the consensus patrum, *or to the threefold
criteria expounded by Vincent of Lerins's* Commonitorium *(434) that the
church adhere to what has been believed "everywhere, always, by all." But
as church history shows, sometimes the Fathers, creeds, and councils have
disagreed with one another, or even fallen into heresy. How does one distinguish between the essential tradition to which we are to adhere, and the
many various nonessential traditions which claim our allegiance? Like Florovsky, Lossky ultimately points us to the dynamic witness of the Incarnate
Word and the Holy Spirit as the "twofold condition of the fullness of the
revelation."*

From Vladimir Lossky, *In the Image and Likeness of God* (Crestwood, N.Y.: St. Vladimir's
Seminary Press, 1985), 141–68. Reprinted by permission.

The Pure Notion of Tradition

Tradition (παράδοσις, *traditio*) is one of those terms which, through being too rich in meanings, runs the risk of finally having none. Part of the reason is the secularization which has depreciated so many words of the theological vocabulary—"spirituality," "mystic," "communion"—detaching them from their Christian context in order to make of them the current coin of profane language. If the word *tradition* has suffered the same fate, this has happened all the more easily because even in the language of theology itself this term sometimes remains somewhat vague. In fact, if one tries to avoid mutilation of the idea of tradition by attempting to keep all of the meanings which it can comprise, one is reduced to definitions which embrace too many things at a time and which no longer capture what constitutes the real meaning of tradition.

As soon as precision is desired, the overabundant content has to be broken up and a group of narrow concepts created, the sum of which is far from expressing that living reality called the tradition of the church. A reading of the erudite work of August Deneffe, *Der Traditionsbegriff*,[1] raises the question of whether tradition is capable of being expressed in concepts, or indeed whether, as with all that is life, it overflows the intelligence and has to be described rather than defined. There are, in fact, in the works of some theologians of the romantic epoch, such as Johann Möhler in Germany or Alexei Khomiakov in Russia, beautiful pages of description in which tradition appears as a catholic plenitude and cannot be distinguished from the unity, the catholicity (Khomiakov's *sobornost'*), the apostolicity, or the consciousness of the church, which possesses the immediate certitude of revealed truth.

Faced with these descriptions, faithful in their general outline to the image of tradition in the patristic writings of the first centuries, one is anxious to recognize the quality of pleroma which belongs to the tradition of the church, but all the same one cannot renounce the necessity of drawing distinctions which is imposed on all dogmatic theology. To distinguish does not always mean to separate, nor even to oppose. In opposing tradition to Holy Scripture as two sources of revelation, the polemicists of the Counter Reformation put themselves from the start on the same ground as their Protestant adversaries in that they tacitly recognized in tradition a reality other than that of Scripture. Instead of being the very ὑπόθεσις[2] of the sacred books—their fundamental coherence due to the living breath passing through them, transforming their letter into a unique body

1. August Deneffe, *Der Traditionsbegriff*, in *Münsterische Beiträge zur Theologie* 18 (Münster, 1931).
2. The expression is from Irenaeus *Adversus omnes haereses* 1.1.15–20.

of truth—tradition would appear as something added, as an external principle in relation to Scripture. Henceforth, patristic texts which attributed a character of pleroma to the Holy Scripture[3] became incomprehensible, while the Protestant doctrine of the sufficiency of Scripture received a negative meaning by the exclusion of all that is tradition. The defenders of tradition saw themselves obliged to prove the necessity of uniting two juxtaposed realities, each of which remained insufficient alone. Hence a series of false problems, like that of the primacy of Scripture or of tradition, of their respective authority, of the total or partial difference of their content. How is the necessity of knowing Scripture through the tradition to be proved? How is their unity, which was ignored in separating them, to be found again? If the two are "fullness," there can be no question of two pleromas opposed to one another, but of two modalities of one and the same fullness of revelation communicated to the church.

A distinction which separates or divides is never perfect nor sufficiently radical: it does not allow one to discern, in its purity, the difference that the unknown term opposes to the term that is supposed to be known. Separation is at the same time more and less than a distinction: it juxtaposes two objects detached from one another, but in order to do this it must first of all lend to one the characteristics of the other. In the present case, in seeking to juxtapose Scripture and tradition as two independent sources of revelation, tradition is inevitably endowed with qualities which belong to Scripture: it becomes the ensemble of other writings or of unwritten "other words," that is, all that the church can add to the Scripture on the horizontal plane of her history. Thus we find on the one hand Scripture or the scriptural canon and on the other hand the tradition of the church, which in its turn can be divided into several sources of revelation or *loci theologici* of unequal value: acts of ecumenical or local councils, writings of the Fathers, canonical prescriptions, liturgy, iconography, devotional practices, and so on. But can this still be called "tradition"? Would it not be more exact to say, with the theologians of the Council of Trent, "the traditions"? This plural well expresses what is meant when, having separated Scripture and tradition instead of distinguishing them, one projects the latter onto the written or oral testimonies which are added to the Holy Scripture, accompanying or following it. Just as time projected in space presents an obstacle to the intuition of Bergsonian duration, so too this projection of the qualitative notion of tradition into the quantitative domain of traditions disguises rather than reveals its real character, for tradition is free of all determinations which, in situating it historically, limit it.

3. See L. Bouyer, "The Fathers of the Church on Tradition and Scripture," *Eastern Churches Quarterly* 7 (1947), special issue on Scripture and tradition.

An advance is made toward a purer notion of tradition if this term is reserved to designate solely the oral transmission of the truths of faith. The separation between tradition and Scripture still subsists, but instead of isolating two sources of revelation, one opposes two modes of transmitting it: oral preaching and writing. It is then necessary to put in one category the preaching of the apostles and of their successors, as well as all preaching of the faith performed by a living teaching authority, and in another category the Holy Scripture and all other written expressions of the revealed truth (these latter differing in the degree of their authority recognized by the church). This approach affirms the primacy of tradition over Scripture, since the oral transmission of the apostles' preaching preceded its recording in written form in the canon of the New Testament. It even might be said that the church could dispense with the Scriptures, but she could not exist without tradition.

This attempt at a pure definition of tradition is right only up to a certain point. It is true that the church always possesses the revealed truth, which she makes manifest by preaching, and which equally well could have remained oral and passed from mouth to mouth without ever having been fixed by writing.[4] But however much the separability of Scripture and tradition is affirmed, they have not yet been radically distinguished. We remain, on the surface, opposing books written with ink to discourses uttered with the living voice. Both cases are a matter of the word that is preached. The preaching of the faith here serves as a common foundation which qualifies the opposition between the two. But is not that to attribute to tradition something which still makes it akin to Scripture? Is it not possible to go further in search of the pure notion of tradition?

Among the variety of meanings that can be noted in the Fathers of the first centuries, tradition sometimes receives that of a teaching kept secret, not divulged, lest the mystery be profaned by the uninitiate.[5] This is clearly expressed by Basil in the distinction which he makes between δόγμα and κήρυγμα.[6] "Dogma" here has a sense contrary to that given to this term today; far from being a doctrinal definition loudly proclaimed by the church, it is a "teaching (διδασκαλία), unpublished and secret, that our fathers kept in silence, free from disquiet and curiosity, well knowing that in being silent one safeguards the sacred character of the mysteries."[7] On the other hand, the κήρυγμα (which means "preaching"

4. Irenaeus *Adversus omnes haereses* 3.4.1 envisages this possibility.
5. Clement of Alexandria *Stromata* 6.61.
6. Basil *De Spiritu Sancto* 27, in *Patrologia Graeca* (PG), ed. J. P. Migne, 162 vols. (Paris, 1857–66), 32.188A–93A.
7. Ibid., 188C–89A.

in the language of the New Testament) is always an open proclamation, whether it be a doctrinal definition,[8] the official prescription of an observance,[9] a canonical act,[10] or public prayers of the church.[11]

Although they call to mind the *doctrina arcana* of the Gnostics, who also laid claim to a hidden apostolic tradition,[12] the unwritten and secret traditions of which Basil speaks differ from it notably. First, the examples that he gives in the passage that we have mentioned show that Basil's expressions relating to the mysteries do not concern an esoteric circle of a few perfect men in the interior of the Christian community, but rather the ensemble of the faithful participating in the sacramental life of the church, who are here opposed to the uninitiate—those whom a progressive catechism must prepare for the sacraments of initiation. Secondly, the secret tradition (δόγμα) can be declared publicly and thus become preaching (κήρυγμα) when a necessity (for example, the struggle against a heresy) obliges the church to make a pronouncement.[13] So, if the traditions received from the apostles remain unwritten and subject to the discipline of secrecy, if the faithful do not always know their mysterious meaning,[14] this is due to the wise economy of the church, which surrenders its mysteries only to the extent that their open declaration becomes indispensable. One is here faced with one of the antinomies of the gospel. On the one hand, one must not give what is holy to the dogs, nor cast pearls before swine (Matt. 7:6). On the other hand, "nothing is covered that will not be revealed, or hidden that will not be known" (Matt. 10:26; Luke 12:2). The traditions guarded in silence and in mystery, which Basil opposes to oral preaching in public, make one think of the words that were told "in the dark," "whispered," but that will be spoken "in the light," "upon the housetops" (Matt. 10:27; Luke 12:3).

This is no longer an opposition between the ἄγραφα and the ἔγγραφα, oral preaching and written preaching. The distinction between tradition and Scripture here penetrates further into the heart of the matter, placing on one side that which is kept in secret and which, for this reason, must not be recorded in writing, and on the other all that which is the subject of

---

8. Basil *Epistolae* 51 (PG 32.392C) calls ὁμοούσιος "the great declaration of piety (τὸ μέγα τῆς εὐσεβείας κήρυγμα) which has made manifest the doctrine (δόγμα) of salvation" (see also *Epistolae* 125 [PG 32.548B]).

9. Basil *Homilia de ieiunio* (PG 31.185C).

10. Basil *Epistolae* 251 (PG 32.933B).

11. Basil *Epistolae* 155 (PG 32.612C).

12. Ptolemy *Letter to Flora* 7.9.

13. The example of ὁμοούσιος is typical in this sense. The economy of Basil on the subject of the divinity of the Holy Spirit is explained not only by a pedagogue's care, but also by this conception of the secret tradition.

14. Basil *De Spiritu Sancto* 27 (PG 32.189C–92A).

preaching and which, once having been publicly declared, can henceforth be ranged on the side of the Scriptures (Γραφαί). Did not Basil himself judge it opportune to reveal in writing the secret of several traditions, thus transforming them into κηρύγματα?[15] This new distinction puts the accent on the secret character of tradition by thus opposing a hidden fund of oral teachings, received from the apostles, to that which the church offers for the knowledge of all; hence it immerses preaching in a sea of apostolic traditions that cannot be set aside or underestimated without injury to the gospel. Even more, if one did this, "one would transform the teaching that is preached (τὸ κήρυγμα) into a simple name" devoid of meaning.[16] The several examples of these traditions offered by Basil all relate to the sacramental and liturgical life of the church (sign of the cross, baptismal rites, blessing of oil, eucharistic epiclesis, the custom of turning toward the east during prayer, and that of remaining standing on Sunday and during the period of Pentecost, etc.). If these unwritten customs (τὰ ἄγραφα τῶν ἐθῶν), these mysteries of the church (ἄγραφα τῆς ἐκκλησίας μυστήρια), so numerous that one could not expound them in the course of a whole day,[17] are necessary for understanding the truth of the Scripture (and in general the true meaning of all preaching), it is clear that the secret traditions point to the "mysterial character" of Christian knowledge. In fact, the revealed truth is not a dead letter but a living Word; it can be attained only in the church through the "mysteries" or "sacraments"[18] that initiate believers into the "mystery hidden for ages and generations but now made manifest to his saints" (Col. 1:26).

The unwritten traditions or mysteries of the church that are mentioned by Basil constitute then the boundary with tradition proper, and they give glimpses of some of its features. In effect, there is participation in the revealed mystery through the fact of sacramental initiation. This is a new knowledge, a gnosis of God (γνῶσις Θεοῦ) that one receives as grace; and this gift of gnosis is conferred in a tradition which is, for Basil, the confession of the Trinity at the time of baptism, a sacred formula which leads us into light.[19] Here the horizontal line of the traditions received from the mouth of the Lord and transmitted by the apostles and their successors crosses with the vertical, with *tradition*—the communication of the Holy Spirit, which opens to members of the church an infinite perspective of

15. Ibid., 192A–93A.

16. Ibid., 188AB.

17. Ibid., 188A, 192C–93A.

18. On the identification of these two terms and on the "mysterial" meaning of the sacraments in the writings of the first centuries, see Odo Casel, *Das christliche Kultusmysterium* (Regensburg, 1932), 105ff.

19. Basil *De Spiritu Sancto* 10 (*PG* 32.113B).

mystery in each word of the revealed truth. Thus, starting from traditions such as Basil presents to us, it is necessary to go further and admit tradition, which is distinguished from them.

If we were to stop our inquiry with the unwritten and secret traditions, without making a last distinction, we would still remain on the horizontal plane of the παραδόσεις, where tradition appears to us as projected into the realm of the Scriptures. It is true that, while it would be impossible to separate these secret traditions from the Scriptures or, more generally, from preaching, we could always oppose them, as words spoken in secret or guarded in silence, to words declared publicly. The fact is, however, that the final distinction has not yet been made so long as there remains a last element which links tradition with Scripture, with the *word*—and which serves as a basis for opposing hidden traditions to open preaching. In order to isolate the pure notion of tradition, in order to strip it of all that is its projection on the horizontal line of the church, it is necessary to go beyond the opposition of secret words and words preached aloud, placing the traditions and preaching together rather than in opposition. For the two have this in common, that, secret or not, they are nonetheless expressed by word. They always imply a verbal expression, whether words proper, pronounced or written, or the dumb language which is addressed to the understanding by visual manifestation (iconography, ritual gestures, etc.). Taken in this general sense, word is not uniquely an external sign used to designate a concept, but above all a content which is defined intelligibly and declared in assuming a body, in being incorporated in articulate discourse or in any other form of external expression.

If such is the nature of word, nothing of what is revealed and makes itself known can remain foreign to it. Whether it be the Scriptures, preaching, or the apostles' traditions guarded in silence, the same word λόγος or λόγια can be applied equally to all that constitutes expression of the revealed truth. In fact, this word ceaselessly recurs in patristic literature to designate equally the Holy Scripture and the symbols of faith. Thus John Cassian says on the subject of the symbol of Antioch: "It is the abridged word (*breviatum verbum*) that the Lord has given . . . contracting into a few words the faith of his two Testaments, in order for it to contain in a brief way the meaning of all the Scriptures."[20]

20. John Cassian *De incarnatione* 6.3, in *Patrologia Latina* (*PL*), ed. J. P. Migne, 221 vols. (Paris, 1844–64), 50.149A: "*Hoc est ergo breviatum verbum quod fecit Dominus . . . fidem scilicet duplicis Testamenti sui in pauca colligens, et sensum omnium Scripturarum in brevia concludens.*" The *breviatum verbum* is an allusion to Rom. 9:27, which in its turn quotes Isa. 10:22. See also Augustine *De symbolo* 1 (*PL* 40.628), and Cyril of Jerusalem *Catechesis* 5.12 (*PG* 33.521AB).

If one next considers that the Scriptures are not a collection of words about God, but the Word of God (λόγος τοῦ Θεοῦ), one will understand why, above all since Origen, there has been a desire to identify the presence of the divine Logos in the writings of the two Testaments with the incarnation of the Word by which the Scriptures were "accomplished." Well before Origen, Ignatius of Antioch refused to see in the Scriptures merely a historical document—"archives"—and to justify the gospel by the texts of the Old Testament, declaring: "For me, my archives are Jesus Christ; my inviolable archives are his cross and his death and his resurrection, and the faith which comes from him. . . . He is the door of the Father, by which enter in Abraham, Isaac, and Jacob, and the prophets, and the apostles, and the church."[21] If the incarnation of the Word means that the Scriptures are not archives of the truth but its living body, the Scriptures can be possessed only within the church, which is the unique body of Christ.

Once again one returns to the idea of the sufficiency of Scripture. But here there is nothing negative; it does not exclude, but assumes the church, with its sacraments, institutions, and teachings transmitted by the apostles. Nor does this sufficiency, this pleroma of the Scripture, exclude any other expressions of the same truth which the church could produce (just as the fullness of Christ, the head of the church, does not exclude the church, the complement of his glorious humanity). One knows that the defenders of the holy images founded the possibility of Christian iconography on the fact of the incarnation of the Word; icons, just as well as the Scriptures, are expressions of the inexpressible, and have become possible thanks to the revelation of God which was accomplished in the incarnation of the Son. The same holds good for the dogmatic definitions, the exegesis, the liturgy—for all in the church of Christ that participates in the same fullness of the Word as is contained in the Scriptures. In this totalitarian quality of the Incarnate Word, all that expresses the revealed truth is thus related to Scripture. Moreover, if all were in fact to become "scripture," the world itself could not contain the books that would be written (John 21:25).

Now since expression of the transcendent mystery has become possible by the fact of the incarnation of the Word, and since all that expresses it becomes in some way scripture alongside the Holy Scripture, the question arises as to where finally is that tradition which we have sought by detaching progressively its pure notion from all that can relate it to scriptural reality. As we have said, it is not to be sought on the horizontal lines of the traditions which, just as much as the Scripture, are determined by the

21. Ignatius of Antioch *To the Philadelphians* 8.2; 9.1.

Word. If again we wished to oppose it to all that belongs to the reality of
the Word, it would be necessary to say that the tradition is silence. "He
who possesses in truth the word of Jesus can hear even its silence (τῆς
ἡσυχίας αὐτοῦ ἀκούειν)," says Ignatius of Antioch.[22] As far as I know,
this text has never been used in the numerous studies which quote patristic passages on tradition in abundance, always the same passages known
by everyone, but with never a suggestion that texts in which the word *tradition* is not expressly mentioned can be more eloquent than many others.

The faculty of hearing the silence of Jesus, attributed by Ignatius to
those who in truth possess his word, echoes the reiterated appeal of Christ
to his hearers: "He who has ears to hear, let him hear." The words of revelation have then a margin of silence which cannot be picked up by the
ears of those who are outside. Basil moves in the same direction when he
says, in his passage on the traditions, "There is also a form of silence,
namely the obscurity used by the Scripture, which, for the profit of readers,
is intended to make it difficult to gain understanding of the teachings."[23]
This quality of silence cannot be detached from the Scriptures; it is transmitted by the church with the words of revelation as the very condition of
their reception. If it could be opposed to words (always on the horizontal
plane, where they express the revealed truth), this silence which accompanies words would imply no kind of insufficiency or lack of fullness of revelation, nor the necessity of adding to it anything whatever. It signifies
that the revealed mystery, to be truly received as fullness, demands a conversion toward the vertical plane, in order that one may be able to com-
prehend with all the saints not only the breadth and length of revelation,
but also its depth and its height (Eph. 3:18).

At the point which we have reached, we can no longer oppose Scripture to tradition, nor juxtapose them as two distinct realities. We must,
however, distinguish them, the better to seize their indivisible unity,
which lends to the revelation given to the church its character of fullness.
Whereas the Scriptures and all that the church can produce in words written or pronounced, in images or in symbols liturgical or otherwise, represent the differing modes of expression of the truth, tradition is the *unique
mode* of receiving it. We say specifically *unique mode* and not *uniform mode*,
for to tradition in its pure notion there belongs nothing formal. It does not
impose on human consciousness formal guarantees of the truths of faith,
but gives access to the discovery of their inner evidence. Tradition is not
the content of revelation, but the light that reveals it; it is not the word,
but the living breath which makes the words heard at the same time as the

22. Ignatius of Antioch *To the Ephesians* 15.2.
23. Basil *De Spiritu Sancto* 27 (PG 32.189BC).

silence from which it came;[24] it is not the truth, but a communication of the Spirit of truth, outside which the truth cannot be received. "No one can say 'Jesus is Lord' except by the Holy Spirit" (1 Cor. 12:3).

The pure notion of tradition can then be defined by saying that it is the life of the Holy Spirit in the church, communicating to each member of the body of Christ the faculty of hearing, of receiving, of knowing the truth in the light which belongs to it, and not according to the natural light of human reason. This is true gnosis, owed to an action of the divine light (φωτισμὸς τῆς γνώσεως τῆς δόξης τοῦ Θεοῦ, 2 Cor. 4:6), the unique tradition, independent of all philosophy, independent of all that lives "according to human tradition, according to the elemental spirits of the universe, and not according to Christ" (Col. 2:8). This freedom from every condition of nature, every contingency of history, is the first characteristic of the vertical line of tradition; it is inherent in Christian gnosis: "You will know the truth, and the truth will make you free" (John 8:32). One cannot know the truth nor understand the words of revelation without having received the Holy Spirit, "and where the Spirit of the Lord is, there is freedom" (2 Cor. 3:17).[25] This freedom of the children of God, opposed to the slavery of the sons of this world, is expressed by the "freeness" (παρρησία) with which those who know God can address him whom they worship, for they worship the Father "in spirit and truth" (John 4:23–24).

Wishing to distinguish tradition from Scripture, we have sought to strip the notion of all that could make it akin to scriptural reality. We have had to distinguish it from the traditions, ranking these latter, together with the Scriptures and all expressions of the truth, on the same horizontal line, where we have found no other name for designating tradition than that of silence. When tradition has been detached from all that can receive its projection on the horizontal plane, it is necessary to enter another dimension in order to reach the conclusion of our analysis. Contrary to philosophical analyses since Plato and Aristotle, which end in dissolving the concrete by resolving it into general ideas or conceptions, our analysis leads us finally toward the Truth and the Spirit, the Word and the Holy Spirit, two persons distinct but indissolubly united, whose twofold economy, while founding the church, conditions at the same time the indissoluble and distinct character of Scripture and of tradition.

The Concrete Role of Tradition in Ecclesiastical Life

The culmination of our analysis—Incarnate Word and Holy Spirit in the church as the twofold condition of the fullness of the revelation—will

24. Ignatius of Antioch *To the Magnesians* 8.2.
25. See Basil's interpretation of this text, *De Spiritu Sancto* 20 (PG 32.164C–65C).

serve us as a turntable from which to set forth now on the way of synthesis and to assign to tradition the place which belongs to it in the concrete realities of ecclesiastical life. It will first of all be necessary to establish a double reciprocity in the economy of the two divine persons sent by the Father. On the one hand, it is by the Holy Spirit that the Word is made incarnate of the Virgin Mary. On the other hand, it is by the Word, following his incarnation and work of redemption, that the Holy Spirit descends on the members of the church at Pentecost. In the first case, the Holy Spirit comes first, but with a view to the incarnation, in order that the Virgin may be able to conceive the Son of God, come to be made man. The role of the Holy Spirit here, then, is functional. He is the power of the incarnation, the virtual condition of the reception of the Word. In the second case, it is the Son who comes first, for he sends the Holy Spirit who comes from the Father; but it is the Holy Spirit who plays the principal role. It is he who is the aim, for he is communicated to the members of the body of Christ in order to deify them by grace. So here the role of the Incarnate Word is, in its turn, functional in relation to the Spirit. It is the form, so to speak, the canon of sanctification, a formal condition of the reception of the Holy Spirit.

The true and holy tradition, according to Philaret of Moscow, "does not consist uniquely in visible and verbal transmission of teachings, rules, institutions and rites: it is at the same time an invisible and actual communication of grace and of sanctification."[26] If it is necessary to distinguish what is transmitted (the oral and written traditions) and the unique mode according to which this transmission is received in the Holy Spirit (tradition as the principle of Christian knowledge), it will nonetheless be impossible to separate these two points. Hence the ambivalence of the term *tradition*, which designates simultaneously the horizontal line and the vertical line of the truth possessed by the church. Every transmission of a truth of faith implies, then, a communication of the grace of the Holy Spirit. In fact, outside of the Spirit "who spoke by the prophets," that which is transmitted cannot be recognized by the church as word of truth—word akin to the sacred books inspired by God and, together with the Holy Scriptures, "recapitulated" by the Incarnate Word. This wind of pentecostal fire, communication of the Spirit of truth proceeding from the Father and sent by the Son, actualizes the supreme faculty of the church: the consciousness of revealed truth, the possibility of judging and of discerning between true and false in the light of the Holy Spirit ("It has seemed good to the Holy Spirit and to us" [Acts 15:28]). If the Paraclete

26. Quoted by George Florovsky, *The Ways of Russian Theology* (in Russian) (Paris, 1937), 178.

is the unique criterion of the truth revealed by the Incarnate Word, he is also the principle of the incarnation, for the same Holy Spirit by whom the Virgin Mary received the faculty of becoming Mother of God, acts as a function of the Word, that is, as a power for expressing the truth in intelligible definitions or sensible images and symbols—documents of the faith which the church will have to judge as to whether or not they belong to its tradition.

These considerations are necessary to enable us to find again, in concrete cases, the relationship between tradition and the revealed truth received and expressed by the church. As we have seen, tradition in its primary notion is not the revealed content, but the unique mode of receiving revelation, a faculty owed to the Holy Spirit, who renders the church capable of knowing the Incarnate Word in his relationship with the Father (this knowledge is supreme gnosis and, for the Fathers of the first centuries, "theology" in the proper meaning of the word) as well as the mysteries of the divine economy, from the creation of the heaven and earth of Genesis to the new heaven and new earth of the Apocalypse. Recapitulated by the incarnation of the Word, the history of the divine economy makes itself known through the Scriptures in the recapitulation of the two Testaments by the same Word. But this unity of the Scriptures can be recognized only in the tradition, in the light of the Holy Spirit communicated to the members of the unique body of Christ. The books of the Old Testament, composed over a period of several centuries, written by different authors who often brought together and fused different religious traditions, have only an accidental, mechanical unity for the eyes of the historian of religions. Their unity with the writings of the New Testament will appear to him factitious and artificial. But a son of the church will be able to recognize the unity of inspiration and the unique object of faith in these heteroclitic writings, woven by the same Spirit who, after having spoken by the prophets, preceded the Word in rendering the Virgin Mary apt to serve as means for the incarnation of God.

It is only in the church that one is able to recognize in full consciousness the unity of inspiration of the sacred books, because the church alone possesses the tradition—the knowledge in the Holy Spirit of the Incarnate Word. The fact that the canon of the writings of the New Testament was formed relatively late, with some hesitations, shows us that the tradition is in no way automatic. It is the condition of the church's having an infallible consciousness, but it is not a mechanism which will infallibly make known the truth outside and above the consciousness of individuals, outside all deliberation and all judgment. In fact, if tradition is a faculty of judging in the light of the Holy Spirit, it obliges those who wish to know the truth in the tradition to make incessant efforts. One does not remain in the tradition by a certain historical inertia, by keeping as a tradition received from the Fathers all that which, by force of habit, flatters a certain devout sensibility. On the contrary, it is by substituting this sort of "traditions" for the tradition of the Holy Spirit living in the church that one runs the most risk of finding oneself finally outside the body of Christ. It must not be thought that the conservative attitude alone is salutary, nor that heretics are always innovators. While the church, after having established the canon of Scripture, preserves it in the tradition, this preservation is not static and inert, but dynamic and conscious—in the Holy Spirit, who purifies anew "the words of the LORD . . . words that are pure, silver refined in a furnace on the ground, purified seven times" (Ps. 12:6). If that were lacking, the church would have conserved only a dead text, witness of an ended epoch, and not the living and vivifying Word, perfect expression of the revelation which it possesses independently of the existence of old discordant manuscripts or of new critical editions of the Bible.

One can say that tradition represents the critical spirit of the church. But, contrary to the critical spirit of human science, the critical judgment of the church is made acute by the Holy Spirit. It has then quite a different principle, namely, the undiminished fullness of revelation. Thus the church, which will have to correct the inevitable alterations of the sacred texts (alterations which certain traditionalists wish to preserve at any price, sometimes attributing a mystical meaning to stupid mistakes of copyists), will be able at the same time to recognize in some late interpolations (for example, the "three that bear record in heaven . . ." in 1 John 5:7) an authentic expression of the revealed truth. Naturally authenticity here has a meaning quite other than it has in the historical disciplines.[27]

Not only the Scriptures, but also the oral traditions received from the apostles have been conserved only by virtue of the tradition—the light which reveals their true meaning and their significance, essential for the church. Here more than elsewhere tradition exercises its critical action, showing above all its negative and exclusive aspect. It rejects the "godless and silly myths" (1 Tim. 4:7) piously received by all those whose traditionalism consists in accepting with unlimited credulity all that is insinuated into the life of the church to remain there by force of habit.[28] In the epoch

27. Origen, in his homilies on the Epistle to the Hebrews, after having expressed his views on the source of this epistle, of which the teaching is Pauline but the style and composition denote an author other than Paul, adds this: "If, then, some church considers this epistle as written by Paul, let it be honored also for that. For it is not by chance that the ancients have transmitted it under the name of Paul. But who wrote the epistle? God knows the truth"—quoted by Eusebius *Historia ecclesiastica* 6.25 (PG 20.584C).

28. In our days still, the literature of the *Synaxaria* and the *Leimonaria* offer similar examples, not to mention liturgical monstrosities which, for certain people, also carry a traditional and sacred character.

in which the oral traditions coming from the apostles began to be fixed in writing, the true and the false traditions crystalized together in numerous apocrypha, several of which circulated under the names of the apostles or other saints. "We are not ignorant," says Origen,

> that many of these secret writings have been composed by impious men, from among those who make their iniquity sound loudest, and that some of these fictions are used by the Hypythiani, others by the disciples of Basilides. We must therefore pay attention, in order not to receive all the apocrypha which circulate under the names of saints, for some have been composed by the Jews, perhaps to destroy the truth of our Scriptures and to establish false teachings. But on the other hand we must not reject as a whole all that is useful for throwing light on our Scriptures. It is a mark of greatness of spirit to hear and to apply these words of the Scripture: "Test everything; hold fast what is good" (1 Thess. 5:21).[29]

Since some of the deeds and the words that the memory of the church has kept since apostolic times "in silence, free from disquiet and curiosity,"[30] have been divulged in writings of heterodox origin, these apocrypha, though separated from the scriptural canon, should nonetheless not be totally rejected. The church knows how to extract from them some elements suitable for completing or for illustrating events on which the Scriptures are silent, but which tradition recognizes as true. Further, amplifications having an apocryphal source serve to color the liturgical texts and the iconography of some feasts. Thus one uses apocryphal sources, with judgment and moderation, to the extent to which they may represent apostolic traditions. Re-created by the tradition, these elements, purified and made legitimate, return to the church as its own property. Such judgment will be necessary each time that the church has to deal with writings claiming to belong to the apostolic tradition. She will reject them, or she will receive them, without necessarily posing the question of their authenticity on the historical plane, but considering above all their content in the light of tradition.

Sometimes a considerable labor of clarification and adaptation will be necessary in order that a pseudepigraphic work finally may be utilized by the church as a witness of her tradition. Thus Maximus the Confessor wrote his commentary on the *Corpus Dionysiacum* in order to uncover the orthodox meaning of these theological writings, which were circulating in Monophysite circles under the pseudonym of Dionysius the Areopagite, which had been adopted by their author or compiler. With-

29. Origen *Commentary on Matthew* 28 (PG 13.1637).
30. Basil *De Spiritu Sancto* 27 (PG 32.188).

out belonging to the apostolic tradition proper, the Dionysian corpus belongs to the patristic tradition, which continues that of the apostles and of their disciples.[31] The same could be said of some other writings of this kind. As for the oral traditions claiming apostolic authority, above all insofar as concerns customs and institutions, the judgment of the church will take into account not only their meaning but also the universality of their usage.

Let us note that the formal criterion of traditions which was expressed by Vincent of Lérins—*"quod semper, quod ubique, quod ab omnibus"*—can be applied in full only to those apostolic traditions which were orally transmitted during two or three centuries. The New Testament Scriptures already escape from this rule, for they were neither "always," nor "everywhere," nor "received by all," before the definitive establishment of the scriptural canon. Whatever may be said by those who forget the primary significance of tradition, wishing to substitute for it a rule of faith, the formula of Vincent is even less applicable to the dogmatic definitions of the church. It is enough to recall that the term ὁμοούσιος was anything but traditional. With a few exceptions, it was never used anywhere or by anyone except by the Valentinian Gnostics and the heretic Paul of Samosata.[32] The church has transformed it into "words that are pure, silver refined in a furnace on the ground, purified seven times" in the crucible of the Holy Spirit and of the free consciousness of those who judge within the tradition, allowing themselves to be seduced by no habitual form, by no natural inclination of flesh and blood, which often takes the form of an unconsidered and obscure devotion.

31. It would be as false to deny the traditional character of the work of Pseudo-Dionysius, by basing oneself on the fact of its nonapostolic origin, as to wish to attribute it to the convert of Paul, on the pretext that these writings were received by the church under the title of Dionysius the Areopagite. Both these attitudes would equally reveal a lack of true consciousness of the tradition.

32. Before Nicea, the term ὁμοούσιος is found in a fragment of the commentary of Origen on the Epistle to the Hebrews, quoted by Pamphilus the Martyr (*PG* 14.1308); in the *Apology for Origen* of the same Pamphilus, translated by Rufinus (*PG* 17.580–81); and in the anonymous dialogue *On True Faith in God* falsely attributed to Origen (ed. W. H. van de Sande Bakhuyzen [Leipzig, 1901]). According to Athanasius, Dionysius of Alexandria was accused, about 259–61, of not recognizing that Christ is consubstantial with God; Dionysius is said to have replied that he avoided the word ὁμοούσιος, which is not in Scripture, but he recognized the orthodox meaning of this expression (Athanasius *De sententia Dionysii* 18 [*PG* 25.505]). The treatise *On Faith*, where one finds the expression in the Nicene sense (*PG* 10.1128), does not belong to Gregory of Neocaesarea; it is a post-Nicene writing, probably of the end of the fourth century. Thus, the examples of the term among orthodox writers before Nicea are for the most part uncertain; one cannot trust the translation of Rufinus. In any case the use of this term is very restricted and has an accidental character.

The dynamism of tradition allows of no inertia either in the habitual forms of piety or in the dogmatic expressions that are repeated mechanically like magic recipes of truth, guaranteed by the authority of the church. To preserve the dogmatic tradition does not mean to be attached to doctrinal formulas. To be within the tradition is to keep the living truth in the light of the Holy Spirit; or rather, it is to be kept in the truth by the vivifying power of tradition. But this power, like all that comes from the Spirit, preserves by a ceaseless renewing.

Tradition and "Dogmatic Development"

"To renew" does not mean to replace ancient expressions of the truth by new ones, more explicit and theologically better elaborated. If that were so, we should have to recognize that the erudite Christianity of theology professors represents a considerable progress in relation to the primitive faith of the disciples and the apostles. In our days there is much talk of "theological development," often without taking account of the extent to which this expression (which has become almost a commonplace) can be ambiguous. In fact, it implies, among some modern authors, an evolutionary conception of the history of Christian dogma. Attempts are made to interpret in the sense of dogmatic progress this passage of Gregory of Nazianzus: "The Old Testament manifested clearly the Father and obscurely the Son. The New Testament manifested the Son, but gave only indications of the divinity of the Holy Spirit. Nowadays, the Spirit is among us and shows himself in all his splendor. It would not have been prudent, before recognizing the divinity of the Father, openly to preach the divinity of the Son, and as long as that of the Son had not been accepted, to impose the Holy Spirit, if I dare so express myself."[33] But "the Spirit is among us" since the day of Pentecost and, with him, the light of tradition, that is, not only what has been transmitted (as a sacred and inert deposit would have been), but also the very force of transmission that is conferred on the church and that accompanies, as the unique mode of receiving and possessing the revelation, all that is transmitted. However, the unique mode of having the revelation in the Holy Spirit is to have it in fullness, and it is thus that the church knows the truth in the tradition. If there was an increase in knowledge of the divine mysteries, a progressive revelation, light coming little by little before the coming of the Holy Spirit, it is otherwise for the church. If one can still speak of development, it is not knowledge of revelation in the church which progresses or is developed with each dogmatic definition. If one were to embrace the

33. Gregory of Nazianzus *Orationes* 31.26 (PG 36.161C).

whole account of doctrinal history from its beginnings down to our own day by reading the *Enchiridion* of Heinrich Denzinger or the fifty in-folio volumes of Giovanni Mansi, the knowledge that one would thus have of the mystery of the Trinity would be no more perfect than was that of a Father of the fourth century who spoke of the ὁμοούσιος, nor than that of an ante-Nicene father who did not yet speak of it, nor than that of a Paul, to whom even the term *Trinity* remained as yet foreign. At every moment of its history the church gives to its members the faculty of knowing the truth in a fullness that the world cannot contain. It is this mode of knowing the living truth in the tradition that the church defends in creating new dogmatic definitions.

"To know in fullness" does not mean "to have the fullness of knowledge"; this belongs only to the world to come. If Paul says that he now knows "in part" (1 Cor. 13:12), this ἐκ μέρους does not exclude the fullness *in which* he knows. It is not later dogmatic development that will suppress the "knowledge in part" of Paul, but the eschatological actualization of the fullness in which, confusedly but surely, Christians here below know the mysteries of revelation. The knowledge ἐκ μέρους will not be suppressed because it was false, but because its role was merely to make us adhere to the fullness which surpasses every human faculty of knowledge. Hence it is in the light of the fullness that one knows "in part," and it is always through this fullness that the church judges whether or not the partial knowledge expressed in this or that doctrine belongs to tradition. Any theological doctrine which pretends to be a perfect explanation of the revealed mystery will inevitably appear to be false: by the very fact of pretending to the fullness of knowledge it will set itself in opposition to the fullness in which the truth is known in part. A doctrine is traitor to tradition when it seeks to take its place; Gnosticism offers a striking example of an attempt to substitute, for the dynamic fullness that is given to the church as the condition of true knowledge, a kind of static fullness of a revealed doctrine. On the other hand, a dogma defined by the church in the form of partial knowledge each time opens anew an access toward the fullness outside of which the revealed truth can be neither known nor confessed. As an expression of truth, a dogma of faith belongs to tradition without all the same constituting one of its "parts." It is a means, an intelligible instrument, which makes for adherence to the tradition of the church. It is a witness of tradition, its external limit or, rather, the narrow door which leads to knowledge of truth in the tradition.

Within the circle of dogma, the knowledge of the revealed mystery that a member of the church will be able to attain—the degree of Christian gnosis—will vary in proportion to the spiritual measure of each. This knowledge of the truth in the tradition thus will be able to increase in a person in company with his increase in sanctification (Col. 1:10). A Christian will be more perfect in knowledge at the age of his spiritual maturity. But would one dare to speak, against all the evidence, of a collective progress in the knowledge of the Christian mystery, a progress which would be due to a dogmatic development of the church? Would this development have started in gospel infancy to end today—after a patristic youth and a scholastic maturity—in the sad senility of the manuals of theology? Or indeed should this metaphor (false, like so many others) give place to a vision of the church like that which is to be found in the Shepherd of Hermas, where the church appears in the features of a woman young and old at the same time, bringing together all ages in the "measure of the stature of the fullness of Christ" (Eph. 4:13)?

Returning to the text of Gregory of Nazianzus, so often misinterpreted, we shall see that the dogmatic development in question is in no way determined by an inner necessity which would effect a progressive increase in the church's knowledge of revealed truth. Far from being a kind of organic evolution, the history of dogma depends above all on the conscious attitude of the church in face of the historical reality in which she has to work for the salvation of humans. If Gregory spoke of a progressive revelation of the Trinity before Pentecost, it was in order to insist on the fact that the church, in her economy in relation to the external world, must follow the example of the divine pedagogy. In formulating these dogmas (cf. κήρυγμα in Basil; see pp. 128–29 above), it must conform to the necessities of a given moment, "not unveiling all things without delay and without discernment, and nonetheless keeping nothing hidden until the end. For the one would be imprudent and the other impious. The one would risk wounding those without, and the other separating us from our own brothers."[34]

In replying to the lack of understanding of the external world, incapable of receiving revelation—in resisting the attempts of the "debater of this age" (1 Cor. 1:20) who, in the womb of the church itself, seeks to understand the truth "according to human tradition, according to the elemental spirits of the universe, and not according to Christ" (Col. 2:8)—the church finds herself obliged to express her faith in the form of dogmatic definitions, in order to defend it against the thrust of heresies. Imposed by the necessity of the struggle, dogmas once formulated by the church become for the faithful a rule of faith which remains firm forever, setting the boundary between orthodoxy and heresy, between knowledge

---

34. Ibid., 31.27 (PG 36.164B). It is known that Gregory of Nazianzus reproached his friend Basil for excess of prudence with regard to the open proclamation of the divinity of the Holy Spirit, a truth which had the character of traditional evidence for members of the church, but which exacted a moderation in economy with regard to the *pneumatomachoi*, whom it was necessary to bring into the unity of the faith.

within the tradition and knowledge determined by natural factors. Always confronted with new difficulties to overcome, with new obstacles of thought to remove, the church will always have to defend her dogmas. Her theologians will have the constant task of expounding and interpreting them anew according to the intellectual demands of the milieu or of the epoch. In critical moments of the struggle for the integrity of the faith, the church will have to proclaim new dogmatic definitions which will mark new stages in this struggle, which will last until all arrive at "the unity of the faith, and of the knowledge of the Son of God" (Eph. 4:13). Having to struggle against new heresies, the church never abandons her ancient dogmatic positions in order to replace them by new definitions. These stages are never surpassed by an evolution; and, far from being relegated to the archives of history, they preserve the quality of an ever actual present in the living light of the tradition.

Thus one can speak of dogmatic development only in a very limited sense. In formulating a new dogma the church takes as her point of departure already existing dogmas, which constitute a rule of faith that she has in common with her adversaries. Thus the dogma of Chalcedon, making use of that of Nicea and speaking of the Son as consubstantial with the Father in his divinity, said afterwards that he is also consubstantial with us in his humanity. Against the Monothelites, who in principle admitted the dogma of Chalcedon, the fathers of the sixth ecumenical council again took up its formulae on the two natures in order to affirm the two wills and the two energies of Christ. The Byzantine councils of the fourteenth century, in proclaiming the dogma on the divine energies, referred, among other things, to the definitions of the sixth council, and so on. In each case one can speak of a dogmatic development to the extent that the church extends the rule of faith while remaining, in her new definitions, in conformity with the dogmas already received by all.

If the rule of faith develops as the teaching authority of the church adds to it new acts having dogmatic authority, this development, which is subject to an economy and presupposes a knowledge of truth in the tradition, is not an augmentation of tradition. This is clear if one is willing to take into account all that has been said concerning the primordial notion of tradition. It is the abuse of the term *tradition* (in the singular and without an adjective to qualify it and determine it) by authors who see only its projection on the horizontal plane of the church—the plane of the *traditions* (in the plural or with a qualification which defines them)—and above all a vexatious habit of designating by this term the church's ordinary teaching authority which have allowed such frequent talk to be heard about a development or an enriching of tradition. The theologians of the seventh ecumenical council distinguish clearly between the "tradition of the Holy

Spirit" and the divinely inspired "teaching (διδασκαλία) of our holy fathers."[35] They were able to define the new dogma "with all rigor and justice" because they considered themselves to be in the same tradition which allowed the Fathers of past centuries to produce new expressions of the truth whenever they had to reply to the necessities of the moment.

There exists an interdependence between the tradition of the catholic church (= the faculty of knowing the truth in the Holy Spirit) and the teaching of the Fathers (= the rule of faith kept by the church). One cannot belong to the tradition while contradicting the dogmas, just as one cannot make use of the dogmatic formulas received in order to oppose a formal "orthodoxy" to every new expression of the truth that the life of the church may produce. The first attitude is that of revolutionary innovators, of false prophets who sin against the expressed truth, against the Incarnate Word, in the name of the Spirit to which they lay claim. The second is that of the conservative formalists, pharisees of the church who, in the name of the habitual expressions of truth, run the risk of sinning against the Spirit of truth.

In distinguishing the tradition in which the church knows the truth from the dogmatic tradition which she establishes by her teaching authority and which she preserves, we find again the same relationship as we have been able to establish between tradition and Scripture. One can neither confound them nor separate them without depriving them of the character of fullness that they possess together. Like Scripture, dogmas *live* in the tradition, with this difference, that the scriptural canon forms a determinate body which excludes all possibility of further increase, while the dogmatic tradition, though keeping its stability as the rule of faith from which nothing can be cut off, can be increased by receiving, to the extent that may be necessary, new expressions of revealed truth formulated by the church. The ensemble of the dogmas which the church possesses and transmits is not a body constituted once and for all, but neither has it the incomplete character of a doctrine in process of becoming. At every moment of its historical existence, the church formulates the truth of the faith in its dogmas, which always express a fullness to which one adheres intellectually in the light of the tradition, while never being able to make it definitively explicit. A truth which would allow itself to be

35. Heinrich Denzinger, *Enchiridion symbolorum* 302: Τὴν βασιλικὴν ὥσπερ ἐρχόμενοι τρίβον, ἐπακολουθοῦντες τῇ θεηγόρῳ διδασκαλίᾳ τῶν ἁγίων πατέρων ἡμῶν, καὶ τῇ παραδόσει τῆς καθολικῆς ἐκκλησίας. Τοῦ γὰρ ἐν αὐτῇ οἰκήσαντος ἁγίου πνεύματος εἶναι ταύτην γινώσκομεν. Ὁρίζομεν σὺν ἀκριβείᾳ πάσῃ καὶ ἐμμελείᾳ ... ("walking, so to speak, on the royal road, following the divinely inspired teaching of our holy fathers as well as the tradition of the catholic church [for we know that it belongs to the Holy Spirit, who dwells in the church], we define in all rigor and justice . . .").

made fully explicit would not have the quality of living fullness which belongs to revelation. Fullness and rational explicitness mutually exclude one another. However, if the mystery revealed by Christ and known in the Holy Spirit cannot be made explicit, it does not remain inexpressible. Since "the whole fullness of deity dwells bodily" in Christ (Col. 2:9), this fullness of the divine Word Incarnate will be expressed as much in the Scriptures as in the "abridged word" of the symbols of faith[36] or of other dogmatic definitions. This fullness of the truth that they express without making explicit allows the dogmas of the church to be akin to the Holy Scriptures. It is for this reason that Pope Gregory the Great brought together in the same veneration the dogmas of the first four councils and the four Gospels.[37]

All that we have said of the dogmatic tradition can be applied to other expressions of the Christian mystery that the church produces in the tradition, conferring on them equally the presence of the "fullness of him who fills all in all" (Eph. 1:23). Just like the divinely inspired *didascalia* of the church, the iconographic tradition also receives its full meaning and its intimate coherence with other documents of the faith (Scripture, dogmas, liturgy) in the tradition of the Holy Spirit. Just as much as dogmatic definitions, it has been possible for the icons of Christ to be compared to Holy Scriptures, to receive the same veneration, since iconography sets forth in colors what the Word announces in written letters.[38] Dogmas are addressed to the intelligence; they are intelligible expressions of the reality which surpasses our mode of understanding. Icons impinge on our consciousness by means of the outer senses, presenting to us the same suprasensible reality in "esthetic" expressions (in the proper sense of the word αἰσθητικός: that which can be perceived by the senses). But the intelligible element does not remain foreign to iconography. In looking at an icon one discovers in it a logical structure, a dogmatic content which has

36. See above at n. 20.

37. Gregory the Great *Epistolarum liber* 1.25 (*PL* 77.613).

38. "We prescribe the veneration of the holy icon of our Lord Jesus Christ, rendering to it the same honor as to the books of the Holy Gospels. For just as by the letters of these latter we all come to salvation, so by the action of the colors in images, all—learned as well as ignorant—equally find their profit in what is within reach of all. In effect, just as the word is set forth by letters, painting sets forth and represents the same things by colors. Hence, if someone does not venerate the icon of Christ the Savior, he may be unable to see his face at the second coming . . ." (Denzinger, *Enchiridion symbolorum* 337). The third canon of the anti-Photian synod (869–70), whose acts have been rejected by the church (not only in the East but also in the West, as shown by Francis Dvornik, *The Photian Schism* [London, 1948], 176–77), is cited here because this text gives a beautiful example of the rapprochement current between the Holy Scriptures and iconography, which are united in the same tradition of the church. The sequel to the text quoted deals similarly with icons of the Mother of God, of angels, and of the saints.

determined its composition. This does not mean that icons are a kind of hieroglyph or sacred rebus translating dogmas into a language of conventional signs. If the intelligibility which penetrates these sensible images is identical with that of the dogmas of the church, it is that the two traditions—dogmatic and iconographic—coincide insofar as they express, each by its proper means, the same revealed reality. Although it transcends the intelligence and the senses, Christian revelation does not exclude them. On the contrary, it assumes them and transforms them by the light of the Holy Spirit in the tradition which is the unique mode of receiving the revealed truth, of recognizing it in its scriptural, dogmatic, iconographic, and other expressions, and also of expressing it anew.

Part 3
Theology as Encounter: God, Christ, and Humanity

9

Apophasis
and Trinitarian Theology

Vladimir Lossky

In this essay on apophaticism Lossky explores one of the most salient charac-
teristics of all of Orthodox theology—its insistence that the hidden God is abso-
lutely transcendent, that only negative language befits our speech about him, and
that, on the other hand, this mysterious God can be mystically known and expe-
rienced, if not in his essence, then most certainly in his energies.

The negative way of the knowledge of God is an ascendant undertaking of
the mind that progressively eliminates all positive attributes of the object it
wishes to attain, in order to culminate finally in a kind of apprehension by
supreme ignorance of him who cannot be an object of knowledge. We can say
that the negative way of the knowledge of God is an intellectual experience
of the mind's failure when confronted with something beyond the conceiv-
able. In fact, consciousness of the failure of human understanding constitutes
an element common to all that we can call *apophasis*, or negative theology,
whether this apophasis remains within the limits of intellection, simply
declaring the radical lack of correspondence between our mind and the reality it wishes to attain, or whether it wishes to surpass the limits of understanding, imparting to the ignorance of what God is in his inaccessible nature the
value of a mystical knowledge superior to the intellect, ὑπὲρ νοῦν.

From Vladimir Lossky, *In the Image and Likeness of God* (Crestwood, N.Y.: St. Vladimir's
Seminary Press, 1985), 13–29. Reprinted by permission.

The apophatic element, as the consciousness of intellectual failure, is present in various forms in most Christian theologians (exceptions are rare). We can say as well that it is not foreign to sacred art, where failure of artistic means of expression, deliberately conspicuous in the very art of the iconographer, corresponds to the learned ignorance of the theologian. However, just as iconographic "antinaturalistic" apophaticism is not iconoclasm, so also the antirationalistic negative way is not gnosimachian. It does not so suppress theological thought as to do detriment to the essential fact of Christianity: the incarnation of the Word, the central event of revelation, which makes iconography as well as theology possible.

The apophasis of the Old Testament, which expressed itself in the prohibition of all images, was suppressed by the fact that the image of the substance of the Father revealed himself, having assumed human nature. But at the same time a new negative element entered into the canon of the art of icons, whose sacred schematism is a call to detachment, to purification of the senses, in order to contemplate the divine person who has come in the flesh. So also for New Testament thought, that which was negative and exclusive in Judaic monotheism vanished before the necessity of recognizing in Christ a divine person consubstantial with the Father. But at the same time, in order for trinitarian theology to become possible, it was necessary for apophasis to preside at a divesting of the mind—for the mind to raise itself to the notion of a God who transcends all relation with created being and is absolutely independent, in what he is, of the existence of creatures.

Despite the undeniable fact that the negative elements of a progressive divesting of the mind among Christian theologians are in general linked, in their elaboration, with the speculative technique of Middle and Neo-Platonism, it would be unfair necessarily to see in Christian apophasis a sign of the Hellenization of Christian thought. The existence of an apophatic attitude—of a going beyond everything that has a connection with created finitude—is implied in the paradox of the Christian revelation: the transcendent God becomes immanent in the world, but in the very immanence of his economy, which leads to the incarnation and to death on the cross, he reveals himself as transcendent, as ontologically independent of all created being. This is a condition without which one could not imagine the voluntary and absolutely gratuitous character of Christ's redemptive work and, in general, of all that is the divine "economy" beginning with the creation of the world, where the expression *ex nihilo* must indicate precisely the absence of all necessity *ex parte Dei*—a certain divine contingency, if one dares to put it so, in the act of the creative will. Economy is the work of the will, while trinitarian being belongs to the transcendent nature of God.

This is the basis of the distinction between οἰκονομία and θεολογία, which goes back to the fourth and perhaps even to the third century and

which remains common to most of the Greek fathers and to all of the Byzantine tradition. Θεολογία—which was for Origen a knowledge, a *gnosis*
of God in the λόγος—means, in the fourth century, everything which
concerns trinitarian doctrine, everything which can be said of God considered in himself outside of his creative and redemptive economy. In
order to reach this "theology" proper, one therefore must go beyond the
aspect under which we know God as Creator of the universe, in order to
be able to extricate the notion of the Trinity from the cosmological implications proper to the "economy." To the economy in which God reveals
himself in creating the world and in becoming incarnate, we must respond
by theology, confessing the transcendent nature of the Trinity in an ascent
of thought which necessarily has an apophatic thrust.

Now we cannot know God outside of the economy in which he reveals
himself. The Father reveals himself through the Son in the Holy Spirit;
and this revelation of the Trinity always remains "economic," inasmuch as
outside of the grace received in the Holy Spirit no one could recognize in
Christ the Son of God and in this way be elevated to knowledge of the
Father. This is the classical *via* of theognosis traced by Basil. "The way of
knowing God goes from the one Spirit, through the one Son, to the one
Father; and inversely, essential goodness, natural sanctity, and royal dignity flow from the Father, through the Only-Begotten, to the Spirit," he
says in his *Treatise on the Holy Spirit*.[1] So also, every act of the divine economy follows this descending line: from the Father, through the Son, in the
Holy Spirit. Accordingly, the way of the knowledge of God, contrary to
that of the manifestation of God, will be not a katabasis, a descent, but an
anabasis, an ascent—an ascent toward the source of all manifesting
energy, toward the "thearchy," according to the vocabulary of Pseudo-
Dionysius, or toward the monarchy of the Father, according to the expression of Basil and other Greek fathers of the fourth century.

But on this level one must abandon the descending line of revelation
of the nature of the Father through the Son in the Spirit, in order to be
able to recognize the consubstantiality of the three hypostases beyond all
manifesting economy. It is an exclusive attachment to the economic
aspect of the Trinity, with stress on the cosmological significance of the
Logos, which renders ante-Nicene trinitarian theology suspect of subordinationism. To speak of God in himself, outside of any cosmological link,
outside of any engagement in the οἰκονομία vis-à-vis the created world, it
is necessary for theology—the knowledge which one can have of the consubstantial Trinity—to be the result of a way of abstraction, of an

---

1. Basil the Great *On the Holy Spirit*, in *Patrologia Graeca*, ed. J. P. Migne, 162 vols.
(Paris, 1857–66), 32.153B.

apophatic decanting by negation of all the attributes (goodness, wisdom, life, love, etc.) which in the plane of economy can be attached to notions of the divine hypostases[2]—of all the attributes which manifest the divine nature in creation. What will subsist beyond all negating or positing is the notion of the absolute hypostatic difference and of the equally absolute essential identity of the Father, the Son, and the Holy Spirit. And at the same time triadological terms and distinctions—nature, essence, person, hypostasis—still will remain inaccurate, despite their mathematical purity (or perhaps because of this purity), expressing above all the deficiency of language and the failure of the mind before the mystery of the personal God who reveals himself as transcending every relation with the created.

Every trinitarian theology which wishes to be disengaged from cosmological implications in order to be able to ascribe some of its notions to the beyond, to God-in-himself, ought to have recourse to apophasis. But one could ask by the same token whether all the apophasis which can be found in Christian thinkers necessarily results in a trinitarian theology. To reply to this question, it would be necessary to examine a number of cases of the use of the negative method in theology, classifying them according to different types of Christian apophasis. I hope to be able to do this one day, but for the moment I must limit myself to two cases of the use of the negative way by Christian theologians: I shall speak here of Clement of Alexandria and of Pseudo-Dionysius.

The former, who died at the beginning of the third century (215 A.D.), professed an economic trinitarian doctrine despite some efforts which he made to go beyond it. By his philosophical formation he was very close to the intellectual circles of Middle Platonism. As we shall see, the *via remotionis* of Clement remains in the framework of a trinitarian theology of the ante-Nicene type.

As to the second theologian—the mysterious author of the "Areopagite writings," who surely lived after Nicea and after the great Cappadocians (probably toward the end of the fifth or at the beginning of the sixth century)—the question of the trinitarian result of his apophasis is less clear. In fact, Dionysius's technique of apophasis, borrowed from the Plotinian tradition, seems to be necessarily linked to a conception of the One, transcendent to everything which can be named, and thus transcendent to the trinitarian notions of Christian theology as well. This is all the more serious because it is precisely the author of the Dionysian corpus who, under cover of the authority of Paul's disciple, introduces the negative way in its most elaborate form into the theological and mystical tradition of the East and of the West.

---

2. For example, when we say "the Son is Wisdom" or "the Spirit is Love."

The question concerning Dionysius which we shall have to pose, after having taken note of the triadic apophasis of Clement, can be formulated in this way: since apophasis or negative theology ought to prevail, according to Dionysius, over cataphasis or the way of affirmations, the personal characteristics affirmed by trinitarian theology ought to be denied, just as other affirmations relative to the attributes common to the three hypostases have been. If this is the case, one can ask whether Dionysius's apophasis, which seems to go beyond the Trinity, does not imply an aspect of the divinity which would be superior to the personal God of the Judeo-Christian tradition. And since apophasis is the common property of religious thought—since one finds it in India as well as among the Greek Neo-Platonists or later in Islamic mysticism—one would have a right to see in the Dionysian negative method the sanction of a primacy of natural mysticism over revealed theology. A mystical syncretism would then superimpose itself upon the faith of the church, and the pagan altar of the Θεὸς ἄγνωστος would remain superior to the Christian altar of a revealed God, of him who was preached by Paul on the Areopagus. Would the self-styled disciple of the apostle of the Gentiles reverse things in this way, Hellenizing the God of Christian theology? Before approaching this troubling question, let us say a few words about the use of apophasis by Clement of Alexandria.

The Apophasis of Clement of Alexandria

As the author of the *Areopagitica* does later, Clement reserves the negative way for those who have been initiated into the Christian mysteries. It is a contemplation of God which one reaches by way of intellectual abstractions—a contemplation which, according to Clement, ought to correspond to the ἐποπτεία, the highest degree of the mysteries of Eleusis. The use of the language of the mysteries and the effort to establish parallels between the stages of Christian gnosis and those of the Hellenic mysteries are explained by Clement of Alexandria's attitude toward Greek wisdom: it profited in large measure by the revelation given to Israel, whether by simply plagiarizing Moses and the prophets or by receiving a partial revelation through the deceit of an angel, similar to the deceit of Prometheus, who stole the fire of Olympus in order to communicate it to mortals. This being said, one understands the ease with which Clement established a concordance between the Holy Scriptures and the philosophers, and especially with Plato, "the friend of Truth."

As for apophasis, it is thus implied, as we have said, in the Christian ἐποπτεία, which is the "fourth part"—the "theological" part—of Moses' "philosophy." Therefore it follows the part which Clement calls "natural contemplation" (φυσικὴ θεωρία) and corresponds to what Plato himself would class among the "great mysteries of true being" (τῶν μεγάλων ὄντως εἶναι μυστηρίων), to what Aristotle calls μετὰ τὰ φυσικά.[3]

The negative way by which one sets out toward contemplation is described in the fifth book of the *Stromata*. It is presented at first as a "geometric analysis." Beginning with a body, by abstraction one eliminates volume, surface, and length in order to obtain a punctual unity. Eliminating next the situation of the point in space—its τόπος—one reaches the notion of an intelligible monad, which one will strip of everything which can be attributed to intelligible beings in order to approach a certain notion of God.

The first movement of apophasis, which Clement calls analysis, is found under the same name among the representatives of Middle Platonism in the second century. Celsus, that adversary of the Christians, in the *True Discourse* (Ἀληθὴς λόγος), which we know only by Origen's citations, places analysis, or the way of successive abstractions, among the three rational ways of the knowledge of God. Albinus spoke of it before him in the *Didaskalikos*. But the Platonizing philosophers combined the negative way (analysis) with the positive way (synthesis, or knowledge of the First Cause in its effects), thus obtaining a third way, that of analogy or eminence, in order to render "intelligible," as Celsus says, "in a certain inexpressible quality, the God who is beyond everything."[4] On the other hand, Clement of Alexandria holds to analysis and keeps for the negative way its independent value. But the analysis which leads to the notion of an intelligible monad cannot suffice for him. As he says elsewhere, "God is One and beyond the One, and superior to the monad itself (ἓν δὲ ὁ Θεός, καὶ ἐπέκεινα τοῦ ἑνὸς καὶ ὑπὲρ αὐτὴν μονάδα)."[5] Let us note that well before Clement, Philo—who had seen in the monad the Logos, the perfect image of God—declared that God is beyond the monad.[6] For the Jewish philosopher and for the Christian theologian, the living God of Scripture transcended the intelligible monad, and the apophatic search had to pursue what lies beyond, in the dark of Sinai. This biblical image is common to Philo and to Clement.

Here begins the second apophatic movement and, at the same time, a trinitarian theognosis, which Clement sketches briefly in this way: "We fling ourselves (ἀπορρίψωμεν) upon the majesty (μέγεθος) of Christ. If we then advance through holiness towards the abyss (βάθος), we shall have a kind of knowledge of God-who-contains-everything (παντοκράτωρ), knowing not

3. Clement of Alexandria *Stromata* 1.28.
4. Quoted in Origen *Contra Celsum* 7.44–45.
5. Clement of Alexandria *Pedagogus* 1.8.
6. Philo *Legum allegoriae* 2.3; *De vita contemplativa* 1.2.

what he is, but what he is not (οὐχ ὅ ἐστιν, ὅ δὲ μὴ ἐστιν γνωρίσαντες)."[7] Nonetheless, it seems that Clement remains on the level of speculation when he proposes to know God in what he is not. His apophasis has nothing ecstatic about it. It is not a way of mystical union.

Reaching the summit of things intelligible—ἐπὶ τὴν κορυφὴν τῶν νοητῶν—one notices with Plato that, if it is difficult to find God, it is impossible to express him.[8] Having been informed of Moses' ascent of Sinai, Plato knew that "holy theory" had permitted the legislator of the Jews to reach the intelligible summits which are the "region of God" (χώρα τοῦ Θεοῦ), difficult to find. Plato also called it the "region of the Ideas" (plagiarizing a little from Moses, according to Clement), having learned from Moses that God is a region, because he contains everything (ὡς τῶν ἁπάντων καὶ τῶν ὅλων περιεκτικόν). Evidently this is a Plato somewhat Aristotelianized, the Plato of Middle Platonism. As with Albinus, the Ideas are the thoughts of God and do not subsist outside of him, even though they constitute, so to speak, the divine second principle. For Clement of Alexandria, this second principle is the majesty or grandeur of Christ, of Christ-the-Logos, the place of the Ideas. It is necessary to surpass it in order to go "by Sanctity" toward the abyss of the Father. Sanctity means, without any doubt, the Holy Spirit; for further on Clement makes it clear that the Father cannot be recognized except by divine grace and by the Word who is near to him,[9] and that all intellectual investigation remains formless and blind without the grace of the knowledge which comes from the Father through the Son.

We would expect Plato to give way to Moses—that the philosopher, after having spoken of transcendent Good and of the region of the Ideas, would be silent at last before the revelation of the living God, who through the Son confers the grace of knowledge, the gift of Christian gnosis. Indeed Plato is silent for a moment and permits John to speak. John, who according to Clement is one of the greatest Gnostics (along with James, Peter, and Paul), would say that no one has ever seen God, except the only Son who is in the bosom of the Father. It is he who manifests God to us. Clement would explain that the bosom (κόλπος) is the abyss, "the invisible and inexpressible" (τὸ ἀόρατον καὶ ἄρρητον) which had enveloped Moses in the shadow beyond the majesty of Christ; for the Father-Pantokrator contains all, he himself being contained by nothing. He is therefore inaccessible and unlimited (ἀνέφικτος καὶ ἀπέραντος). This is the reason for the transcendence and the unknowability of the Father, who, in contrast to the Son, is called the Unbegotten. Since there is

7. Clement of Alexandria Stromata 5.11.
8. Plato Timaeus 28c.
9. Clement of Alexandria Stromata 5.12.

nothing in the order of knowledge which can be anterior to the notion of the unbegotten God, demonstrative science which proceeds from anterior and more evident truths is not of any assistance here and must give way to the unfruitful and unformed apophasis of a despairing agnosticism.

But here Plato again picks up the conversation in order to help the Christian theologian out of a difficulty, by reminding him discreetly that, if it is impossible to know God through our own powers, there is always the resource of grace, that "God-given virtue" of which he had spoken in the *Meno*—virtue which is sent by divine fate, by the Θεῖα μοῖρα. Grace, for Clement, is above all a new aptitude for knowing, a ἕξις γνωστικὴ which obtains for the perfect Christian, for the Gnostic (today one would say for the spiritual or contemplative), eternal contemplation (ἀΐδιος θεωρία), that is, the capacity for seeing God-Pantokrator face to face.[10] This is the limit of apophasis for Clement of Alexandria. Its object is the transcendence of the Father. After having conducted the intelligence toward a complete aporia before the transcendent abyss, negative investigation is suppressed by the grace which the Father sends through the Son in "Sanctity."

If Clement's apophasis is triadic to the extent that it implies the notion of three persons who are not suppressed by the *via remotionis*, nonetheless it is determined only by the hypostasis of the Father, the only truly transcendent hypostasis in this view of the "economic Trinity," so close to the schemes of Middle Platonism. The notion of the hypostasis of the Father is so close to that of the divine essence that it is almost impossible to dissociate them. The Father is limitless (ἀπέραντος), and the expression "abyss of the Father" proclaims without a doubt the infinity of essence which belongs to him, which is of the essence of the "unbegotten God" as opposed to the Logos. For while the Logos becomes the "begotten" Son in identity (ἐν ταὐτότητι—without doubt, in essential identity), he acquires his personal character "by delimitation and not by essence (κατὰ περιγραφὴν καὶ οὐ κατ' οὐσίαν)."[11] There is a manifest effort here to go beyond the economic aspect in order to express the essential identity of the Son with the transcendent and infinite Father, which without doubt excludes from Clement's thought all trinitarian subordinationism. But, in the order of theognosis, the opposition between the knowable hypostasis of the Son and the unknowability of the Father always subsists. It is conditioned by the triadological ambiguity which results from opposing the limitless Unbegotten to the "limited" person of the begotten Son. After its first movement, that of analysis, Clement's apophasis aims solely at the unknowability of the Father: the two other hypostases—the Son and

10. Ibid., 5.11.
11. *Excerpta ex Theodoto* 19.

"Sanctity" (the Holy Spirit, not distinguished from grace and rather eclipsed)—play the role of mystagogues, suppressing natural ignorance by the gnosis which they give of the transcendent being of the Father. This apophasis can be called triadic, since it does not go beyond the notion of the personal God in three hypostases, but it is not triadological, for, having as its object the transcendence of the Father-Pantokrator, this negative way does nothing to transpose trinitarian notions into the beyond. Clement's trinitarian thought has nothing of θεολογία, in the sense which the Fathers of the fourth century will impart to the term. Rather, all its merits lie in the economic perspective which is its own.

The Apophasis of Pseudo-Dionysius the Areopagite

The author of *Mystical Theology* belongs to a totally different epoch subsequent to the great trinitarian century. The ambiguities of Clement of Alexandria and even the imprecisions of Athanasius have been ousted from the language of theology by the terminological labors of the three Cappadocians. The "abyss of the Father" has become, in the terminology of Gregory of Nazianzus, "the ocean of undefined and undetermined essence"[12]—an expression which will be taken up again and propagated by John of Damascus, from whom it will later pass into Scholastic Latin (*pelagus essentiae infinitae*) and will be cited by Thomas Aquinas and other theologians. The three hypostases extend to the infinity of essence, and Gregory of Nazianzus himself speaks of "the infinite connaturality of the Infinite Three."[13] Thus infinity, which for Clement of Alexandria was the reason for the transcendence and the unknowability of the Father, becomes an attribute of the common nature of the Three. The three hypostases, decanted, stripped of all economic attribution, maintain only the relative properties of paternity, filiation, and procession, necessary only to make theological discourse possible. But then, in order to be liberated from the logical category of relation, which permits of limitation due to opposition, trinitarian theology comes to be expressed antinomically. "They are One distinctly and distinct conjointly, somewhat paradoxical as that formula may be," Gregory of Nazianzus says;[14] and Basil strives to show that the Trinity is not a matter of arithmetic numbers.[15] A movement of apophasis therefore accompanies the trinitarian theology of the Cappadocians and, in the last analysis, deconceptualizes the concepts which are ascribed to the mystery of a personal God in his transcendent nature.

12. Gregory of Nazianzus *Orationes* 38 (*In theophaniam*).
13. Gregory of Nazianzus *Orationes* 40 (*In sanctum baptisma*).
14. Gregory of Nazianzus *Orationes* 23.8 (*De pace*).
15. Basil the Great *On the Holy Spirit* 18.

It is time to ask whether Dionysius's apophasis can be considered a supreme θεολογία—whether it transfers beyond the knowable the Trinity of divine persons, or whether it goes beyond this in its negative rush toward a superessential identity which, at the same time, would be a suprapersonal Unity. If this is the case, the author of *Mystical Theology* was a docile instrument in an offensive return of Platonism, which he introduced in its Plotinian form at the very heart of Christian theology.

Certainly there is much in common between the mystical theology of Dionysius and Plotinian apophasis, such as is described in the sixth *Ennead*. The same progressive stripping away is pursued on the way to mystical union. I am prepared here to recognize the appropriateness of the reproach that has been made against me: that I have somewhat hardened the difference between Plotinus and Dionysius in that which concerns the properly mystical element of their apophasis, that is, the unitive way as such.[16] Certainly the unitive way in Dionysius is dominated by the notion of Unity—of the One who is contrary to all otherness from which we must be liberated in order to enter into union with "him who is beyond everything."[17] But we might ask if the notion of him to whom we are united does not surpass the notion of the Unity to which the mystical ascent of the human subjects aspires. It is difficult to dissociate the mystical and unitive aspect of Dionysian apophasis from its dialectical structure. Nevertheless, we are going to examine only this last aspect, the properly intellectual side of the *via remotionis*, in order to be able to reply to the question: in what measure does the apophasis of Pseudo-Dionysius remain faithful to the exigencies of a trinitarian theology?

The Περὶ μυστικῆς θεολογίας is a treatise on the negative way. It also occupies first place in the plan which Dionysius himself gives to the ensemble of his treatises on the knowledge of God. Among these works, he cites two unknown treatises; one may ask whether these have been lost, or whether they are simply a fiction. With the treatise on *Divine Names*, which has come down to us, they ought to form the cataphatic or affirmative group of studies. The most voluminous of the three would have been the study of *Symbolic Theology*, which was supposed to have examined the application of sensible images to God and to have interpreted biblical anthropomorphisms. The treatise on *Divine Names*, which must precede it, is more concise, for it has as its object the intelligible attributions of God, such as goodness, being, life, wisdom, and power, which are less numerous than the sensible images. Finally, the briefest of the cataphatic treatises, the first of the three (for the affirmative way descends from superior

---

16. Maurice de Gandillac, *La Sagesse de Plotin* (Paris, 1952), xvii n. 3.
17. Pseudo–Dionysius the Areopagite *De mystica theologia* 1.1.

notions), bears the title *On Hypotyposes* or *Outlines of Theology*. In this treatise, says Dionysius, "we have celebrated the principal affirmations of affirmative theology, showing in what sense the excellent nature of God is called one, in what sense it is called trine, what in it can be called paternity and filiation, what theology means when it speaks of the Spirit."[18] There is no doubt that the *Theological Hypotyposes* (if this treatise ever existed) would have had as its object trinitarian properties, since the following treatises were devoted principally to the study of the attributes of the nature common to the three persons. The treatise on *Mystical Theology* goes beyond the *Theological Hypotyposes* in its supreme concision and inclines toward the cessation of all speech and all thought in order to celebrate by silence him who cannot be known except by unknowing. It seems, therefore, that the bounds of trinitarian theology ought finally to be swept away by apophasis, rather than be found again in the beyond, toward which the negative way makes us progressively ascend.

In fact, after enumerating—while denying them—the intelligible attributes, the apophatic ascent in Dionysius's mystical theology does not stop at the properties-relations of the divine persons: transcendent Divinity is neither filiation nor paternity nor anything which is accessible to our understanding.[19] However, one should not rush to draw conclusions about the supratrinitarian consequences of Dionysian apophasis. This would be to misunderstand the dialectic which governs the game of negations and affirmations. One can define it as an intellectual discipline of the non-opposition of opposites—a discipline which is proper for all discourse about true transcendence, the transcendence which remains unimaginable for non-Christians.[20] This is not the way of eminence, whose outlines can be found in Middle Platonism—the way toward which Thomas Aquinas wished to channel the Areopagite's apophasis in order to restore an affirmed signification to God, denying merely the human mode of signifying him. Dionysius's negations triumph over affirmations; and, if the author of *Divine Names* allows the formation of superlatives in ὑπερ-, these names do not signify the transcendent nature in itself, but its processions *ad extra* (πρόοδοι) or "virtues" (δυνάμεις), in the measure that these transcend all created participations and remain united to the Superessence, from which they are ineffably distinguished. The nonopposition of negative and positive in theology proper thus implies, in the doctrine of attributes, the idea of unity of the transcendent nature which prevails over distinctions, over the διακρίσεις of manifesting energies, without suppressing, for all that, their real character. The principle of preeminence of

18. Ibid., 5.
19. Ibid.
20. Ibid., 1.5.

negations over affirmations therefore remains confirmed at the level of *Divine Names*. The transcendent God of θεολογία becomes more and more immanent, so to speak, in his economy, by which "the energies descend to us," according to the expression of the great Cappadocians that has been Platonized by Dionysius, who speaks of δυνάμεις. But in order to speak of the Superessence, it is necessary, by means of apophasis, to go beyond economic manifestations and to enter trinitarian theology, which is the summit of cataphasis according to the plan of Dionysian theognosis.

The few bits of information which one finds in the corpus about what Dionysius's triadological treatise (*Theological Hypotyposes*) should be like allow us to affirm that the rule of nonopposition, which presides over utilization of apophasis, excludes every attempt to reduce the Trinity of hypostases to a primordial, transpersonal Unity. In the last chapter of *Divine Names*, devoted to the name of the One, Dionysius declares that "the transcendent Deity is celebrated at the same time both as Unity and as Trinity. In fact, he is not knowable either by us or by any other kind of being, whether as Unity or as Trinity."[21] Denied in their opposition, the two terms must be understood together, in a sort of σύνοψις or simultaneous vision which identifies by distinguishing. And Dionysius continues: "In order to celebrate in all truth that which in [the transcendent Deity] is more than united, as well as the divine fecundity, we attribute by faith the name of Unity and that of Trinity to him who is above all names and who transcends superessentially all that exists."[22] The principle of divine fecundity (τὸ θεόγονον) is upheld at the same level as superunity; this suggests the distinction between nature and hypostases without submitting the Trinity to Unity, contrary to what has been said of processions *ad extra*, where the διακρίσεις were submitted to the ἕνωσις.

At the beginning of this same treatise, after having reproduced almost literally the negative conclusion of the first hypothesis of the *Parmenides*, Dionysius asks himself how one can speak of divine names in the face of this radical unknowability.[23] Then, referring to his triadological treatise (perhaps fictitious), he adds: "As I have already said in my *Hypotyposes*, the Unknowable, the Superessential, the Good-in-itself, he who is—I mean the *triadic Henad* [or Unitrinity][24]—cannot be attained either in words or in thought." Thus true transcendence, which Christians alone can confess, belongs to the "Unitrinity," and this contradictory term must express the "synopsis" of the One and the Three, the object of *Mystical Theology*.

21. Pseudo–Dionysius the Areopagite *De divinis nominibus* 13.3.
22. Ibid.
23. Ibid., 1.5; Plato *Parmenides* 142a.
24. Τὴν τριαδικὴν ἑνάδα; de Gandillac, *Sagesse*, 73, has translated this term most felicitously as "Unitrinity."

One cannot attain the transcendent Trinity of θεολογία through the notion of opposed relation. Let us not forget that, if the God of the philosophers is not the living God, the God of the theologians is such only by halves, as long as the last step has not been taken. That is why we have seen the terms of paternity and filiation denied by the apophasis of *Mystical Theology*—denied by virtue of the principle of nonopposition, which dominates this supreme stage of Dionysian theognosis. How can the two, the Father and the Son, be opposed, when one would need to find an opposition impossible for human logic, the opposition of the Three, in order truly to explain the mystery of a personal God? Since we cannot oppose the Three, absolutely different in their absolute identity, the logic of opposition as well as use of arithmetic numbers must remain on this side of the consubstantial Trinity. Is the Triad not an exclusion of the Dyad, a surpassing of the principle of the opposition of two relative terms? In fact, it suggests to us a distinction more radical than that of two opposites: an *absolute* difference, which can only be personal, proper to the three divine hypostases, "united by distinction and distinct by union."[25] The author of the corpus here seems to be strictly dependent on the Cappadocians' handling of the trinitarian problem.[26]

The same principle of triadic nonopposition was formulated hermetically by Gregory of Nazianzus with the image of the Monad which is set in motion in order to surpass the Dyad and to come to rest at the Triad.[27] Dionysius finds at the end of his theognosis, a tributary of the same trinitarian conceptions, the principle of personal nonopposition, the root of the unknowability of the transcendent God-Trinity, the object of theology proper, which can only be mystical.

In concluding our study of the negative method and trinitarian theology, we can state that in the two cases briefly examined here, apophasis has a very different character. Determined by the transcendence of the Father-Pantokrator, Clement of Alexandria's apophasis does not succeed in liberating trinitarian theology from the cosmological implications of economy. What the Alexandrian *didaskalos* was not able to express was later accomplished by "the capable unknown," who, after the Cappadocians, delivered the final blow to the triadic schemes of the Platonic tradition by identifying the unknowable God of the negative way with the Unitrinity of Christian transcendence.

The apophasis of *Mystical Theology* is not determined by the principle of absolute identity of the transcendent One with Being. The dialectic of affir-

25. Pseudo–Dionysius the Areopagite *De divinis nominibus* 2.4.
26. Ceslas Péra, "Denys le Mystique et la Théomachia," *Revue des sciences philosophiques et théologiques* 25 (1936): 47–50.
27. Gregory of Nazianzus *Orationes* 23.8, 29.2.

mations and nonopposed negations, applied to trinitarian dogma, makes it necessary to go beyond the One opposed to the Other. It is not the impersonal Monad, but the "superessential and more-than-divine Triad" that the author of *Mystical Theology* invokes at the beginning of his treatise. The plea here is that the theologian in search of the God of Christian revelation, who transcends the opposition between the transcendent and the immanent, since he is beyond all affirmation and all negation, be directed "even beyond unknowing" and toward the way of union with triune Divinity.

The Procession
of the Holy Spirit
in Orthodox Trinitarian Theology

Vladimir Lossky

While Western Christians tend to think of the fundamental division of Christendom as having occurred between Catholics and Protestants in the sixteenth-century Reformation, the Orthodox consciousness is conditioned by what it considers a much more serious and fundamental division, in 1054, caused by the debate over the term filioque *that the West adopted and the East rejected as a later interpolation that threatened trinitarian orthodoxy. Did the Holy Spirit proceed from the Father alone, as Orthodoxy insists and the Nicene Creed reads, or from the Father "and from the Son (*filioque*)"? This matter is, as Lossky notes in the first sentence of this essay, "the sole dogmatic grounds for the separation of East and West."*

Whether we like it or not, the question of the procession of the Holy Spirit has been the sole dogmatic grounds for the separation of East and West. All the other divergences which, historically, accompanied or followed the first dogmatic controversy about the term *filioque*, in the measure in which they too had some dogmatic importance, were more or less dependent upon that original issue. This is only too easy to understand, when we take into account the importance of the mystery of the Trinity and its place in the whole body of Christian teaching. Thus the polemical battle between

From Vladimir Lossky, *In the Image and Likeness of God* (Crestwood, N.Y.: St. Vladimir's Seminary Press, 1985), 71–96. Reprinted by permission.

163

the Greeks and the Latins was fought principally about the question of the Holy Spirit. If other questions have arisen and taken the first place in more recent interconfessional debates, that is chiefly because the dogmatic plane on which the thought of theologians operates is no longer the same as it was in the medieval period. Ecclesiological problems increasingly determine the preoccupations of modern Christian thought. This is as it should be. However, the tendency which may be noticed among certain modern Orthodox theologians (and especially among Russians, who are too often ungrateful to Byzantium) to underestimate and even to despise the pneumatological debates of the past suggests that these theologians, so ready to renounce their fathers, lack both dogmatic sense and reverence for the living tradition.

True, it is always necessary to revalue the truths which the church affirmed in the past in order to meet the needs of the present. But this revaluation is never a devaluation. It is the restatement of the value of that which was said in a different epoch under different historical circumstances. It is the duty of the historian to inform us about the circumstances in which a dogma was first required and to state the historical implications of dogma. But it is not his duty, as a historian, to judge dogmatic values as such. If this is not remembered, there is a danger that historical theology will become a gray eminence, or rather a lay eminence, in the church, seeking to establish by the methods of secular science a new canon of tradition. This is a sort of Caesaropapism of the scholars, which might succeed in imposing its authority over the church, if tradition were not, for her, a living reality of revelation in the Holy Spirit.

Thus, for example, the learned Russian theologian, V. Bolotov, an eminent historian of theology, on the occasion of the Bonn conversations with the Old Catholics, considered himself able to declare, on the basis of an analysis of patristic texts, that the term *filioque* hardly constitutes an *impedimentum dirimens* in the path of dogmatic reconciliation.[1] According to Bolotov, the question concerned two theologoumena expressing in two different formulas—a Filio and διὰ Υἱοῦ—the doctrine of the procession of the Holy Spirit. Bolotov was too good a historian of theology to conclude that the doctrine on both sides was identical. But he lacked the dogmatic sense to perceive the true place of these two formulas in two different triadologies. Even historically, he made a mistake in treating *a Filio* as the opposite of διὰ Υἱοῦ, as if these were the two formulas which express the doctrine of the hypostatic procession of the Holy Spirit. It was *a Patre Filioque* and ἐκ μόνου τοῦ Πατρὸς which, as formulas about the procession,

---

1. V. Bolotov, "Thesen über das Filioque (von einem russischen Theologe)," *Revue internationale de théologie* (published at Berne by the Old Catholics) 6 (1898): 681–712.

came into conflict and thus exposed a divergence in the theology of the Trinity.[2] The formula διὰ Υἱοῦ, interpreted in the sense of a mediation of the Son in the hypostatic procession of the Holy Spirit, was a formula of concord adopted by partisans of union in the thirteenth century precisely because their triadology was not the same as that of the adversaries of *filioque*. By adopting the interpretation of διὰ Υἱοῦ proper to the Latinizing Greeks, Bolotov minimized the doctrinal divergence between the two triadologies; hence he could write about two tolerable "theological opinions."

Our task here will not be that of a historian. We shall leave aside questions concerning the origins of the two different formulas. We shall even admit the possibility of an Orthodox interpretation of *filioque*, as it first appeared at Toledo for example.[3] We are not dealing with verbal formulas here, but with two established theological doctrines. We shall try to show the outlines of the trinitarian theology which Orthodox theologians regard themselves as obliged to defend when they are confronted with the doctrine of the eternal personal procession of the Holy Spirit from the Father and the Son as from a single principle. We shall confine ourselves to setting forth certain general theological principles about the formulas ἐκ μόνου τοῦ Πατρὸς and διὰ Υἱοῦ. We shall not enter into the controversies of the past in detail. Our sole aim will be to make Orthodox triadology better understood.

Imprecision in the Description of the Holy Spirit

Roman Catholic and Orthodox theologians agree in recognizing that a certain anonymity characterizes the Third Person of the Holy Trinity. While the names *Father* and *Son* denote very clear personal distinctions, are in no sense interchangeable, and cannot in any case refer to the common nature of the two hypostases, the name *Holy Spirit* has not that advantage. Indeed, we say that God is spirit, meaning by that the common nature as much as any one of the persons. We say that he is holy: The triple *Sanctus* of the canon of the mass alludes to three holy persons having the common holiness of the same Godhead. Taken in itself, the term *Holy Spirit* thus might be applied, not to a personal distinction, but to the com-

2. Bolotov must have recognized, implicitly, the radical character of the divergences, since, after all, he categorically denied the *causal character* of the mediation of the Son in the procession of the Holy Spirit: "Aber wenn auch in den innersten geheimnisvollsten Beziehungen des trinitarischen Lebens begründet, ist das 'durch den Sohn' frei von dem leisesten Anstrich einer *Kausalitäts*-Bedeutung" ("Thesen," 700).

3. A study of the Filioquism of the Spanish councils of the fifth, sixth, and seventh centuries would be of capital importance, so that a dogmatic appreciation of these formulas might be made. Here the disinterested work of historical theology could be really useful to the church.

mon nature of the three. In that sense, Thomas Aquinas is right in saying that the Third Person of the Trinity has no name of his own and that the name *Holy Spirit* has been given to him on the basis of scriptural usage (*accommodatum ex usu Scripturae*).[4]

We meet the same difficulty when we wish to define the mode of origin of the Holy Spirit, contrasting his "procession" with the "generation" of the Son. Even more than the name *Holy Spirit*, the term *procession* cannot be considered to be, in itself, an expression which exclusively envisages the Third Person. It is a general term that could be applied, *in abstracto*, to the Son; Latin theology even speaks of *duae processiones*. We leave aside, for the moment, the question of the extent to which such an abstract way of dealing with the mystery of the Trinity is legitimate. The one point which we stress here is that the term *procession* has not the precision of the term *generation*. The latter term, while preserving the mysterious character of the divine Fatherhood and Sonship, states a definite relationship between two persons. That is not the case with the term *procession*—an indefinite expression which confronts us with the mystery of an anonymous person whose hypostatic origin is presented to us negatively: it is not generation, it is other than that of the Son.[5] If we seek to treat these expressions positively, we find an image of the economy of the Third Person rather than an image of his hypostatic character: we find the procession of a divine force or spirit which accomplishes sanctification. We reach a paradoxical conclusion: all that we know of the Holy Spirit refers to his economy; all that we do not know makes us venerate his person, as we venerate the ineffable diversity of the consubstantial three.

In the fourth century the question of the Trinity was examined in a christological context and was raised in connection with the *nature* of the Logos. The term ὁμοούσιος, while assuming the diversity of the three persons, was meant to express the identity in the Trinity by stressing the unity of the common nature against all subordinationism. In the ninth century the pneumatological controversy between the Latins and the Greeks raised the question of the Trinity in connection with the *hypostasis* of the Holy Spirit. Both contending parties, while assuming the natural identity of the three, intended to express hypostatic diversity in the Trinity. The former party strove to establish personal diversity on the basis of the term ὁμοούσιος, starting from natural identity. The latter party, more conscious of the trinitarian antinomy of οὐσία and ὑπόστασις, while taking into account consubstantiality, stressed the monarchy of the

---

4. Thomas Aquinas *Summa theologica* 1, q. 36, a. 1.

5. Gregory of Nazianzus *Orationes* 20.11, 31.8, in *Patrologia Graeca* (PG), ed. J. P. Migne, 162 vols. (Paris, 1857–66), 35.1077C, 36.141B.

Father as a safeguard against all danger of a new Sabellianism.[6] Two doctrines of the hypostatic procession of the Holy Spirit, *a Patre Filioque tanquam ab uno principio* and ἐκ μόνου τοῦ Πατρός, represent two different solutions of the question of personal diversity in the Trinity, two different triadologies. It is important that we should describe the general outlines of these triadologies.

The Latin and Greek Conceptions of the Trinity

Starting from the fact that the hypostatic character of the Holy Spirit remains undefined and anonymous, Latin theology seeks to draw a positive conclusion as to his mode of origin. Since the term *Holy Spirit* is, in some sense, common to the Father and the Son (both are holy and both are spirit), it should denote a person related to the Father and the Son in respect of what they have in common.[7] Even when the matter at hand is the procession, taken as the mode of origin of the Third Person, the term *procession*—which in itself does not signify any mode of origin distinguishable from generation—should denote a relation to the Father and the Son together to serve as the basis for a Third Person distinct from the other two. Since a "relation of opposition"[8] can be established only between two terms, the Holy Spirit should proceed from the Father and the Son, inasmuch as they represent a unity. This is the meaning of the formula according to which the Holy Spirit is said to proceed from the Father and the Son as from one principle of spiration.[9]

One cannot deny the logical clarity of this process of reasoning, which seeks to base hypostatic diversity on the principle of relations of opposition. This triadological principle, formulated by Thomas Aquinas, becomes unavoidable the moment that the doctrine of the procession of the Holy Spirit *ab utroque* is admitted. It presupposes the following conditions: (1) Relations are the basis of the hypostases,[10] which define them-

6. The expression comes from Photius *Mystagogia* 9 (PG 102.289B): καὶ ἀναβλαστήσει πάλιν ἡμῖν ὁ Σαβέλλιος, μᾶλλον δέ τι τέρας ἕτερον ἡμισαβέλλειον.

7. Thomas Aquinas *Summa theologica* 1, q. 36, a. 1, with a reference to Augustine *De Trinitate* 1.11.

8. Thomas uses the expressions *relativa oppositio, oppositio relationis* (this above all with reference to the essence), *relatio* (or *respectus) ad suum oppositum*, and *relationes oppositae* to signify what we here have called "relation of opposition." In using this expression, we do not in any way misrepresent Thomas's thought, for the idea of opposition is implied in his very definition of relation: "De ratione autem relationis est respectus unius ad alterum, secundum quem aliquid alteri opponitur relative" (*Summa theologica* 1, q. 28, a. 3).

9. Thomas Aquinas *Summa theologica* 1, q. 36, a. 2, 4.

10. Thomas Aquinas goes further: for him the persons of the Trinity *are* relations (*persona est relatio* [*Summa theologica* 1, q. 40, a. 2]).

selves by their mutual opposition, the first to the second, and these two together to the third. (2) Two persons represent a nonpersonal unity, in that they give rise to a further relation of opposition. (3) In general the origin of the persons of the Trinity therefore is impersonal, having its real basis in the one essence, which is differentiated by its internal relations. The general character of this triadology may be described as a preeminence of natural unity over personal trinity, as an ontological primacy of the essence over the hypostases.

The attitude of Orthodox thought, when confronted with the mysterious name of the Holy Spirit, denoting a divine economy rather than a hypostatic mark of distinction, is far from being simply a refusal to define his personal diversity. On the contrary, because that diversity, or (to speak more generally) the diversity of the three persons, is presented as something absolute, we refuse to admit a relation of origin which opposes the Holy Spirit to the Father and the Son, the latter two being taken as a single principle. If this were admitted, personal diversity in the Trinity in effect would be relativized: Inasmuch as the Holy Spirit is one hypostasis, the Holy Spirit would represent only the unity of the two in their identical nature. Here the logical impossibility of any opposition between *three* terms intervenes, and the clarity of this triadological system shows itself to be extremely superficial. Indeed, on these lines, we cannot reach a mode of distinguishing the three hypostases from each other without confounding them in one way or another with the essence. In fact, the absolute diversity of the three cannot be based on their relations of opposition without admitting, implicitly or explicitly, the primacy of the essence over the hypostases by assuming, in contrast to natural identity, a relative (and therefore secondary) basis for personal diversity.[11] But that is exactly what Orthodox theology cannot admit.

Against the doctrine of procession *ab utroque* the Orthodox have affirmed that the Holy Spirit proceeds from the Father alone—ἐκ μόνου τοῦ Πατρός. This formula, while verbally it may seem novel, represents in its doctrinal tenor nothing more than a very plain affirmation of the traditional teaching about the monarchy of the Father as the unique source of the divine hypostases. It may be objected that this formula for the pro-

11. T. de Régnon, inquiring why filioquist considerations were never developed in the rich works of the Greek fathers, asks: "Is this not proof that [such considerations] never occurred to them in their conception of the Trinity?" And he replies with a significant avowal: "In fact all these [filioquist considerations] presuppose that, in the order of concepts, nature is anterior to person and that the latter represents a kind of efflorescence of the former" (*Etudes de théologie positive sur la Sainte Trinité* [Paris, 1892], 1.309). He also writes: "Latin philosophy envisages first the nature in itself and then proceeds to the expression; Greek philosophy envisages first the expression and then penetrates it to find the nature. The Latin considers personality as a mode of nature, the Greek considers nature as the content of the person" (p. 433).

cession of the Holy Spirit from the Father alone provides no place for any relation of opposition between the Second Person of the Trinity and the Third Person. But those who say this overlook the fact that the very principle of relations of opposition is unacceptable to Orthodox triadology— that the expression "relations of origin" has a different sense in Orthodox theology than it has among defenders of *filioque*.

When we state that the eternal procession of the Holy Spirit from the Father alone is distinguished in an ineffable manner from the eternal generation of the Son, who is begotten of the Father alone, no attempt is being made to establish a relation of opposition between the Son and the Holy Spirit. This is so not merely because the procession is ineffable (the generation of the Son is no less ineffable),[12] but also because relations of origin in the Trinity—filiation, procession—cannot be considered as the basis for the hypostases, as that which determines their absolute diversity.[13] When we say that the procession of the Holy Spirit is a relation which differs absolutely from the generation of the Son, we indicate the difference between them as to mode of origin (τρόπος ὑπάρξεως)[14] from that common source in order to affirm that community of origin in no way affects the absolute diversity between the Son and the Spirit.

Here it may be stated that the relations serve only to *express* the hypostatic diversity of the three; they are not the basis of it. It is the absolute diversity of the three hypostases which determines their differing relations to one another, not vice versa. Here thought stands still, confronted by the impossibility of defining a personal existence in its absolute difference from any other, and must adopt a negative approach to proclaim that the Father—he who is without beginning (ἄναρχος)—is not the Son or the Holy Spirit, that the begotten Son is neither the Holy Spirit nor the Father, that the Holy Spirit, "who proceeds from the Father," is neither the Father nor the Son.[15] Here

---

12. John of Damascus *De fide orthodoxa* 1.8 (PG 94.820–24A).

13. Gregory of Nazianzus *Orationes* 20.11, 31.8 (PG 35.1077C, 36.141B).

14. More exactly, "mode of subsistence." This expression is found, first of all, in Basil the Great *De Spiritu Sancto* 18 (PG 32.152B); and later, e.g., in John of Damascus *De fide orthodoxa* 1.8, 10 (PG 94.828D, 837C). It is heavily used by George of Cyprus *Apologia* (PG 142.254A et passim).

15. "To be unbegotten, to be begotten, to proceed—these are the features which characterize the Father, the Son, and him whom we call the Holy Spirit, in such a way as to safeguard the distinction of the three hypostases in the one nature and majesty of the Divinity; for the Son is not the Father, because there is only one Father, but he is what the Father is; the Holy Spirit, although he proceeds from God, is not the Son, because there is only one only begotten Son, but he is what the Son is. The three are one in divinity and the one is three in persons. Thus we avoid the unity of Sabellius and the triplicity of the odious present-day heresy" (Gregory of Nazianzus *Orationes* 30.9 [PG 36.141D–44A]).

we cannot speak of relations of opposition but only of relations of diversity.[16] To follow here the positive approach, and to envisage the relations of origin otherwise than as signs of the inexpressible diversity of the persons, is to suppress the absolute quality of this personal diversity, that is, to relativize the Trinity and in some sense to depersonalize it.

The positive approach employed by filioquist triadology brings about a certain rationalization of the dogma of the Trinity, insofar as it suppresses the fundamental antinomy between the essence and the hypostases. One has the impression that the heights of theology have been deserted in order to descend to the level of religious philosophy. On the other hand, the negative approach, which places us face to face with the primordial antinomy of absolute identity and no less absolute diversity in God, does not seek to conceal this antinomy but to express it fittingly, so that the mystery of the Trinity might make us transcend the philosophical mode of thinking and that the truth might make us free from our human limitations by altering our means of understanding. If in the former approach faith seeks understanding in order to transpose revelation onto the plane of philosophy, in the latter approach understanding seeks the realities of faith, in order to be transformed by becoming more and more open to the mysteries of revelation. Since the dogma of the Trinity is the keystone of the arch of all theological thought and belongs to the region which the Greek fathers called θεολογία par excellence, it is understandable that a divergence in this culminating point, insignificant as it may seem at first sight, should have a decisive importance. The difference between the two conceptions of the Trinity determines, on both sides, the whole character of theological thought. This is so to such an extent that it becomes difficult to apply, without equivocation, the same name of theology to these two different ways of dealing with divine realities.

The Father as the Cause of the Other Hypostases

If personal diversity in God presents itself as a primordial fact, not to be deduced from any other principle or based on any other idea, that does not mean that the essential identity of the three is ontologically posterior to their hypostatic diversity. Orthodox triadology is not a counterblast to Filioquism; it does not run to the other extreme. As we already have said, relations of origin signify the personal diversity of the three, but they indi-

16. In his polemic against the Latins, Mark of Ephesus, in affirming the principle of the *diversity* of the persons, criticizes the Thomist principle of *opposition* of the persons (*Capita syllogistica contra Latinos* 24 [PG 161.189–93]).

cate no less their essential identity. In that the Son and the Holy Spirit are distinguished from the Father, we venerate three persons; in that they are one with him, we confess their consubstantiality.[17] Thus the monarchy of the Father maintains the perfect equilibrium between the nature and the persons, without coming down too heavily on either side.[18] There is neither an impersonal substance nor nonconsubstantial persons. The one nature and the three hypostases are presented simultaneously to our understanding, with neither prior to the other. The origin of the hypostases is not impersonal, since it is referred to the person of the Father; but it is unthinkable apart from their common possession of the same essence, the "divinity in division undivided."[19] Otherwise we should have three divine individuals, three Gods bound together by an abstract idea of Godhead. On the other hand, since consubstantiality is the non-hypostatic identity of the three, in that they have (or rather *are*) a common essence, the unity of the three hypostases is inconceivable apart from the monarchy of the Father, who is the *principle* of the common possession of the same one essence. Otherwise we should be concerned with a simple essence differentiated by relationships.[20]

It may be asked whether, in seeking to avoid the semi-Sabellianism of the Latins, their Greek adversaries did not fall into subordinationism because of their emphasis on the monarchy of the Father. This might perhaps seem all the more likely to happen, because in Greek patristic literature one often finds the idea of causality applied to the person of the Father. The Father is called the cause (αἰτία) of the hypostases of the Son and the Holy Spirit, or even the "Godhead-source" (πηγαῖα Θεότης). Sometimes he is designated simply as "God," with the definite article ὁ Θεός, or even as αὐτόθεος.

It is worthwhile to recall here what we have said before about the negative approach characteristic of Orthodox thought—an approach which radically changes the value of philosophical terms applied to God. Not only the image of "cause," but also such terms as "production," "proces-

17. "For us there is one God, for the Godhead is one, and the three in whom we believe proceed from and are referred to the One. . . . Thus when we look at the Godhead, the First Cause, and the monarchy, the One appears to us; but when we look at the persons in whom the Godhead is, who timelessly and with equal glory come forth from the First Cause, we adore the three" (Gregory of Nazianzus *Orationes* 31.14 [PG 36.148D–49A]).

18. Photius compares the Trinity to a pair of scales in which the needle represents the Father, and the two platforms represent the Son and the Holy Spirit (*Amphilochia* q. 181 [PG 101.896]).

19. Gregory of Nazianzus *Orationes* 31.14 (PG 36.148D).

20. "The one nature in the three is God; but the union (ἕνωσις) is the Father, from whom the others proceed and to whom they refer, not so as to be confounded but rather to have all in common with him, without distinction of time, will, or power" (Gregory of Nazianzus *Orationes* 42 [PG 36.476B]).

sion," and "origin" ought to be seen as inadequate expressions of a reality which is foreign to all becoming, to all process, to all beginning. Just as relations of origin mean something different from relations of opposition, so causality is nothing but a somewhat defective image which tries to express the personal unity which determines the origins of the Son and the Holy Spirit. This unique cause is not prior to his effects, for in the Trinity there is no priority and posteriority. He is not superior to his effects, for the perfect cause cannot produce inferior effects. He is thus the cause of their equality with himself.[21] The causality ascribed to the person of the Father, who eternally begets the Son and eternally causes the Holy Spirit to proceed, expresses the same idea as the monarchy of the Father: the Father is the personal principle of unity of the three, the source of their common possession of the same content, of the same essence.

The expressions "Godhead-source" and "source of the Godhead" do not mean that the divine essence is subject to the person of the Father, but only that the person of the Father is the basis of common possession of the same essence, because the person of the Father, not being the sole person of the Godhead, is not to be identified with the essence. In a certain sense it can be said that the Father *is* this possession of the divine essence in common with the Son and the Holy Spirit, and that he would not be a divine person if he were only a monad; he would then be identified with the divine essence. Here it may be useful to recall that Cyril of Alexandria regarded the name *Father* as superior to the name *God*, because the name *God* is given to God in respect of his relations with beings of a different nature.[22]

If the Father is sometimes called simply God—ὁ Θεὸς or even αὐτόθεος—nevertheless we cannot find in Orthodox writers expressions which treat consubstantiality as participation by the Son and the Holy Spirit in the essence of the Father.[23] Each person is God by nature, not by participation in the nature of another.

The Father is the cause of the other hypostases in that he is not his essence, that is, in that he does not have his essence for himself alone. What the image of causality wishes to express is the idea that the Father, being not merely an essence but a person, is by that very fact the cause of the other consubstantial persons, who have the same essence as he has.

21. "For he would be the origin (ἀρχή) of petty and unworthy things, or rather the term *origin* would be used in a petty and unworthy sense, if he were not the origin of the God-head (τῆς Θεότητος ἀρχή) and of the goodness contemplated in the Son and in the Spirit: in the former as Son and Word, in the latter as Spirit which proceeds without separation" (Gregory of Nazianzus *Orationes* 2.39 [PG 35.445]).

22. Cyril of Alexandria *Thesaurus*, assertio 5 (PG 75.65, 68).

23. Such a concept may be found in the works of Origen, e.g., *Commentary on John* 2.2 (PG 14.109). On this subject the excellent work of Th. Lieske, *Theologie der Logosmystik bei Origen* (Münster, 1938), may be usefully consulted.

God as Monad and Triad beyond the Dyad

With reference to the Father, causality expresses the idea that he is God-person in that he is the cause of other divine persons—the idea that he could not be fully and absolutely person unless the Son and the Holy Spirit are equal to him in possession of the same nature and *are* that same nature. This might lead to the idea that each person of the Trinity could be regarded as the cause of the other two, in that each person is not the common essence; this would amount to a new relativization of the hypostases, transforming them into conventional and interchangeable signs of three diversities. Roman Catholic theology avoids this personal relativism by professing belief in the procession of the Holy Spirit *ab utroque*, that is, by falling into an impersonal relativism, that of relations of opposition, which are regarded as the basis of the three persons in the unity of a simple essence. Orthodox theology, while taking as its starting point the initial antinomy of essence and hypostasis, avoids personal relativism by attributing causality to the Father alone. The monarchy of the Father thus sets up irreversible relationships which enable us to distinguish the two other hypostases from the Father, and yet to relate them to the Father as a concrete principle of unity in the Trinity. There is not only unity of the same one nature in the three, but also unity of the three persons of the same one nature. Gregory of Nazianzus expresses this neatly: "Each considered in himself is wholly God, as the Father so the Son, as the Son so the Holy Spirit, but each preserves his own properties; considered together the three are God; each (considered in himself is) God because of the consubstantiality, the three (considered together are) God because of the monarchy."[24]

According to Maximus the Confessor, God is "identically a monad and a triad."[25] He is not merely one and three; he is $1 = 3$ and $3 = 1$. That is to say, here we are not concerned with number as signifying quantity: absolute diversities cannot be made the subjects of sums of addition; they have not even opposition in common. If, as we have said, a personal God cannot be a monad—if he must be more than a single person—neither can he be a dyad. The dyad is always an opposition of two terms, and, in that sense, it cannot signify an absolute diversity. When we say that God is Trinity, we are emerging from the series of countable or calculable numbers.[26] The procession of the Holy Spirit is an infinite passage beyond the

---

24. Gregory of Nazianzus *Orationes* 40.41 (*In sanctum baptisma*) (PG 36.417B).

25. Maximus the Confessor *Capita theologica et oeconomica* 2.13 (PG 90.1125A).

26. Basil appears to express this idea well: "For we do not count by way of addition, gradually making increase from unity to plurality, saying 'one, two, three' or 'first, second, third.' 'I am the first and I am the last,' says God (Isa. 44:6). And we have never, even unto our own days, heard of a second God. For in worshiping 'God of God' we both confess the distinction of persons and abide by the monarchy" (*De Spiritu Sancto* 18 [PG 32.149B]).

dyad, which consecrates the absolute (as opposed to relative) diversity of the persons. This passage beyond the dyad is not an infinite series of persons but the infinity of the procession of the Third Person. The Triad suffices to denote the living God of revelation.[27] If God is a monad equal to a triad, there is no place in him for a dyad. Thus the seemingly necessary opposition between the Father and the Son, which gives rise to a dyad, is purely artificial, the result of an illicit abstraction. Where the Trinity is concerned, we are in the presence of the One or of the three, but never of two.

The procession of the Holy Spirit *ab utroque* does not signify passage beyond the dyad but rather reabsorption of the dyad in the monad, the return of the monad upon itself. It is a dialectic of the monad opening out into the dyad and closing again into its simplicity.[28] On the other hand, procession of the Holy Spirit from the Father alone, by emphasizing the monarchy of the Father as the concrete principle of the unity of the three, passes beyond the dyad without a return to primordial unity, without the necessity of God retiring into the simplicity of the essence. For this reason the procession of the Holy Spirit from the Father alone confronts us with the mystery of the "Tri-Unity." We have here not a simple, self-enclosed essence upon which relations of opposition have been superimposed in order to masquerade a god of philosophy as the God of Christian revelation. We say "the simple Trinity," and this antinomic expression, characteristic of Orthodox hymnography,[29] points out a simplicity which the absolute diversity of the three persons can in no way relativize.

The Trinity as Primordial Reality

When we speak of the personal God, who cannot be a monad, and when, bearing in mind the celebrated Plotinian passage in the works of Gregory of Nazianzus, we say that the Trinity is a passage beyond the dyad and beyond its pair of opposed terms,[30] this in no sense implies the Neo-Platonist idea of *bonum diffusivum sui* or any kind of moral basis for the doctrine of the Trinity, for example, the idea of love seeking to share its

27. Gregory of Nazianzus *Orationes* 23.10 (*De pace* 3) (PG 35.1161); *Orationes* 45 (*In sanctum pascha*) (PG 36.628C).

28. The idea of the Holy Spirit as the mutual love of the Father and the Son is characteristic, in this sense, of filioquist triadology.

29. Andrew of Crete *Great Canon of Repentance*, odes 3, 6, 7.

30. "The monad is set in motion on account of its richness; the dyad is surpassed, because the Divinity is beyond matter and form; perfection is reached in the triad, the first to surpass the composite quality of the dyad, so that the Divinity neither remains constrained nor expands to infinity" (Gregory of Nazianzus *Orationes* 23.8 [*De pace* 3] [PG 35.1160C]; see also *Orationes* 29.2 [*Theologica* 3] [PG 36.76B]).

own plenitude with others. If the Father shares his one essence with the Son and the Holy Spirit and in that sharing remains undivided, this is neither an act of will nor an act of internal necessity. In more general terms, it is not an act at all, but the eternal mode of trinitarian existence in itself. It is a primordial reality which cannot be based on any notion other than itself, for the Trinity is prior to all the qualities—goodness, intelligence, love, power, infinity—in which God manifests himself and in which he can be known.

When Roman Catholic theology presents the relations of origin as notional acts and speaks of two processions *per modum intellectus* and *per modum voluntatis*, it commits—from the point of view of Orthodox triadology—an inadmissible error of confusion concerning the Trinity. In effect, the external qualities of God—intellect, will, or love—are introduced into the interior of the Trinity to designate the relations between the three hypostases. This line of thought gives us a divine individuality rather than a Trinity of persons—an individuality which in thought is conscious of its own essential content (generation of the Word *per modum intellectus*) and which, in knowing himself, loves himself (the procession of the Holy Spirit *ab utroque, per modum voluntatis* or *per modum amoris*). We are here confronted with a philosophical anthropomorphism having nothing in common with biblical anthropomorphism; for the biblical theophanies, while showing us in human guise the acts and manifestations of a personal God in the history of the world, also place us face to face with the mystery of his unknowable being, which Christians nevertheless dare to venerate and to invoke as the unique being in three persons, Father, Son, and Holy Spirit, who live and reign in the inaccessible light of their essence.

For us the Trinity remains the *Deus absconditus*, the Holy of Holies of the divine existence, where no "strange fire" may be introduced. Theology will be faithful to tradition insofar as its technical terms—οὐσία, ὑπόστασις, consubstantiality, relations of origin, causality, monarchy— serve to present more and more clearly the initial mystery of God the Trinity, without obscuring it with trinitarian deductions derived from another starting point. By defending the hypostatic procession of the Holy Spirit from the Father alone, Orthodoxy professes its faith in the simple Trinity, wherein relations of origin denote the absolute diversity of the three while at the same time indicating their unity, as represented by the Father, who is not simply a monad but—in that he is the Father—the principle of the Tri-Unity. This means, if God is truly the living God of revelation and not the simple essence of the philosophers, he can only be God the Trinity. This is a primordial truth, incapable of being based on any process of reasoning whatever, because all reasoning, all truth, and all thought prove to be posterior to the Trinity, the basis of all being and all knowledge.

As we have seen, all triadology depends on the question of the procession of the Holy Spirit:

(1) If the Holy Spirit proceeds from the Father alone, this ineffable procession confronts us with the absolute diversity of the three hypostases, excluding all relations of opposition. If he proceeds from the Father and the Son, the relations of origin, instead of being signs of absolute diversity, become determinants of the persons, which emanate from an impersonal principle.

(2) If the Holy Spirit proceeds from the Father alone, this procession presents us with a Trinity which escapes the laws of quantitative number, since it goes beyond the dyad of opposed terms, not by means of a synthesis or a new series of numbers, but by an absolutely new diversity which we call the Third Person. If the Holy Spirit proceeds *ab utroque*, we get a relativized Trinity, submitted to the laws of number and of relations of opposition—laws which cannot serve as a basis for the diversity of the three persons without confusing them either with each other or with their common nature.

(3) If the Holy Spirit proceeds from the Father alone, as the hypostatic cause of the consubstantial hypostases, we find the simple Trinity, where the monarchy of the Father conditions the personal diversity of the three while at the same time expressing their essential unity. The balance between the hypostases and the οὐσία is safeguarded. If the Holy Spirit proceeds from the Father and the Son as from one single principle, essential unity takes precedence over personal diversity, and the persons become relations of the essence, differentiating themselves from one another by mutual opposition. This is no longer the simple Trinity, but an absolute simplicity of essence, which is treated as an ontological basis at a point where there can be no basis except the primordial Tri-Unity itself.

Essence and Energies

By the filioquist dogma the god of the philosophers and savants is introduced into the heart of the living God, taking the place of the *Deus absconditus, qui posuit tenebras latibulum suum*. The unknowable essence of the Father, Son, and Holy Spirit receives positive qualifications. It becomes the object of natural theology: we get "God in general," who could be the god of Descartes, or the god of Leibniz, or even perhaps, to some extent, the god of Voltaire and of the dechristianized deists of the eighteenth century. Manuals of theology begin with a demonstration of his existence, thence to deduce, from the simplicity of his essence, the mode in which the perfections found among creatures are to be attributed to this eminently simple essence. From his attributes they go on to a discussion of what he can or cannot do, if he is not to contradict himself and is to remain true to his essential perfection. Finally a chapter about the relations of the essence—which do not at all abolish its simplicity—serves as a fragile bridge between the god of the philosophers and the God of revelation.

By the dogma of the procession of the Holy Spirit from the Father alone, the god of the philosophers is forever banished from "the Holy of Holies, which is hid from the gaze of the seraphim and glorified through the Three Holinesses who are united into a single Sovereignty and Divinity."[31] The ineffable essence of the Trinity escapes all positive qualification, including that of simplicity. If we speak of the simple Trinity, this self-contradictory expression means that distinctions between the three hypostases and between them and the essence do not introduce into the Tri-Unity any division into constituent elements. Where the idea of the monarchy of the Father remains unshakable, no distinction postulated by faith can introduce composition into the Godhead. Precisely because God is unknowable in that which he is, Orthodox theology distinguishes between the essence of God and his energies, between the inaccessible nature of the Holy Trinity and its "natural processions."[32]

When we speak of the Trinity in itself, we are confessing, in our poor and always defective human language, the mode of existence of the Father, Son, and Holy Spirit, one sole God who cannot but be Trinity, because he is the living God of revelation, who, though unknowable, has made himself known, through the incarnation of the Son, to all who have received the Holy Spirit, who proceeds from the Father and is sent into the world in the name of the incarnate Son.

Every name except those of Father, Son, and Holy Spirit—even the names of "Word" and "Paraclete"—is inappropriate for designating the special characteristics of the hypostases in the inaccessible existence of the Trinity, and refers rather to the external aspect of God, to his manifestation,[33] or even to his economy. The dogma of the Trinity marks the summit of theology, where our thought stands still before the primordial mystery of the existence of the personal God. Apart from the names denoting the three hypostases and the common name of the Trinity, the innumerable names which we apply to God—the divine names which textbook the-

31. Gregory of Nazianzus Orationes 38.8 (In theophaniam) (PG 36.320BC).

32. See the acts of the councils of Constantinople in 1341, 1347, and 1350, in Sacrorum Conciliorum Nova et Amplissima Collectio, ed. G. D. Mansi, 31 vols. (Florence, 1759–98), 25.1147–50; 26.105–10, 127–212; Gregory Palamas Theophanes (PG 150.909–60).

33. It is thus that the Logos of the prologue to John's Gospel signifies the Son, in that he manifests the nature of the Father—the common nature of the Trinity. In this sense, the Logos also includes the manifesting role of the Holy Spirit: "In him was life, and the life was the light of men."

ology calls his attributes—denote God not in his inaccessible being, but in "that which surrounds the essence" (τὰ περὶ τῆς οὐσίας).[34] This is the eternal radiance of the common content of the three persons, who reveal their incommunicable nature in energies. This technical term of Byzantine theology, denoting a mode of divine existence besides essence, introduces no new philosophical notion alien to revelation. The Bible, in its concrete language, speaks of nothing other than energies when it tells us of the "glory of God"—a glory with innumerable names which surrounds the inaccessible being of God, making him known outside himself, while concealing what he is in himself. This is the eternal glory which belongs to the three persons and which the Son had before the world was. And when we speak of the divine energies in relation to the human beings to whom they are communicated and given and by whom they are appropriated, this divine and uncreated reality within is called grace.

External Manifestation of the Common Nature of the Trinity

The manifesting energies of God—which signify a mode of divine existence other than that of the Trinity in itself, in its incommunicable nature—do not make a breach in its unity; they do not abolish the simple Trinity. The same monarchy of the Father, who is the cause of the consubstantial hypostases of the Son and the Holy Spirit, also presides over the external manifestation of the unity of the Trinity. Here the term *causality*, applied to the person of the Father in that he is the principle of the absolute diversities of the three consubstantial persons (a term implying the hypostatic procession of the Holy Spirit from the Father alone), must be clearly distinguished from the revelation or manifestation of the Father by the Son in the Holy Spirit. Causality, with all its defects as a term, expresses what it stands for quite well: the hypostatic distinction of the three which arises from the person of the Father—a distinction between absolute diversities, brought about by the fact that the Father is not uniquely the essence. It is not possible to replace the conventional term *causality* by that of *manifestation* of the Father—as Sergius Bulgakov has tried to do[35]—without confounding the two planes of thought: that of the existence of the Trinity in itself, and that of existence *ad extra*, in the radiance of the essential glory of God.

If the Father is the personal cause of the hypostases, he is also, for that very reason, the principle of their common possession of one and the same nature; and in that sense, he is the source of the common divinity of the

34. Gregory of Nazianzus *Orationes* 38.7 (*In theophaniam*) (PG 36.317B).
35. Sergius Bulgakov, *Le Paraclet* (Paris: Aubier, 1946), 69–75.

three. The revelation of this nature, the externalization of the unknowable essence of the three, is not a reality foreign to the three hypostases. Every energy, every manifestation, comes from the Father, is expressed in the Son, and goes forth in the Holy Spirit.[36] This procession—natural, "energetic," manifesting—must be clearly distinguished from hypostatic procession, which is personal, internal, from the Father alone. The same monarchy of the Father conditions both the hypostatic procession of the Holy Spirit—his personal existence ἐκ μόνου τοῦ Πατρὸς—and the manifesting, natural procession of the common Godhead *ad extra* in the Holy Spirit through the Son—διὰ Υἱοῦ.

If, as we have already said, the name *Holy Spirit* expresses more a divine economy than a personal quality, this is because the third hypostasis is par excellence the hypostasis of manifestation, the person in whom we know God the Trinity. His person is hidden from us by the very profusion of the divinity which he manifests. It is this personal kenosis of the Holy Spirit on the plane of manifestation and economy which makes it hard to grasp his hypostatic existence.

The same plane of natural manifestation gives to the name *Logos*, as applied to the Son, all its significance. The Logos is "a concise declaration of the nature of the Father," as Gregory of Nazianzus says.[37] When Basil speaks to us of the Son who "shows in himself the whole of the Father, shining with all his glory in resplendence,"[38] he also is concerned with the manifesting and energetic aspect of the Trinity. Likewise all the patristic passages in which the Son is called "the image of the Father" and the Holy Spirit is called "the image of the Son"[39] refer to the energetic manifestation of the content common to the three; for the Son is not the Father, but he is what the Father is; the Holy Spirit is not the Son, but he is what the Son is.[40] In the order of divine manifestation, the hypostases are not the respective images of the personal diversities but of the common nature: the Father reveals his nature through the Son, and the divinity of the Son is manifested in the Holy Spirit. This is why, in the realm of divine manifestation, it is possible to establish an order of persons (τάξις) which, strictly speaking, should not be attributed to trinitarian existence

---

36. Thus all the divine names, denoting as they do the common nature, can be applied to each of the persons, but only in the *energetic* order—the order of the manifestation of the Divinity. See, for example, Gregory of Nyssa *Adversus Macedonianos* 13 (PG 45.1317): "The source of power is the Father; the power is the Son; the spirit of power is the Holy Spirit"; Gregory of Nazianzus *Orationes* 23.11 (PG 35.1164A): "The True, the Truth, the Spirit of Truth."

37. Gregory of Nazianzus *Orationes* 30.20 (*Theologica* 4) (PG 36.129A).

38. Basil the Great *Adversus Eunomium* 2.17 (PG 24.605B).

39. Cyril of Alexandria *Thesaurus*, assertio 33 (PG 75.572); John of Damascus *De imaginibus* 3.18 (PG 94.1337D–40B); *De fide orthodoxa* 1.13 (PG 94.856B).

40. Gregory of Nazianzus *Orationes* 31.9 (*Theologica* 5) (PG 36.144A).

in itself, despite the monarchy and causality of the Father. These confer upon him no hypostatic primacy over the other two hypostases, since he is a person only because the Son and the Holy Spirit are also.

Procession of the Holy Spirit through the Son

Confusion between trinitarian existence and energetic radiance, between personal causality and natural manifestation, can arise in two different and, in a certain sense, opposite ways: (1) The Trinity may be conceived as an internal revelation of the divine nature in notional acts: the Father expresses his nature in the Word, and the two cause the Holy Spirit to proceed as a mutual bond of love. This is the triadology of Latin Filioquism. (2) The Trinity may be conceived as an internal revelation of the hypostases or of the "Tri-hypostatic subject" in the common nature. This is the triadology of Russian sophiology, particularly of Bulgakov. In both cases, the equilibrium between essence and hypostases is broken. The trinitarian antinomy is suppressed, with the former in favor of the essence, and the latter in favor of the hypostases.

The distinction between the unknowable essence of the Trinity and its energetic processions, clearly defined by the great councils of the fourteenth century, allows Orthodox theology to maintain firmly the difference between tri-hypostatic existence in itself and tri-hypostatic existence in the common manifestation outside the essence. In his hypostatic existence, the Holy Spirit proceeds from the Father alone; and this ineffable procession enables us to confess the absolute diversity of the three persons, that is, our faith in the Tri-Unity. In the order of natural manifestation the Holy Spirit, after the Word, proceeds from the Father through the Son (διὰ Υἱοῦ); and this procession reveals to us the common glory of the three, the eternal splendor of the divine nature.

It is curious to notice that the distinction between the hypostatic existence of the Holy Spirit, proceeding from the Father alone, and his eternal radiance—εἰς ἀΐδιον ἔκφανσιν—through the Son, was formulated in the course of discussions which took place in Constantinople toward the end of the thirteenth century, after the Council of Lyons.[41] The doctrinal continuity can be recognized here: defense of the doctrine of the procession of the Holy Spirit from the Father alone necessitates a decision as to the import of the phrase διὰ Υἱοῦ; this in turn opens the way for the distinction between essence and energies. This is not a dogmatic development. Rather, one and the same tradition is defended, at different points, by the Orthodox from Photius to George of Cyprus and Gregory Palamas.

41. See the expression εἰς ἀΐδιον ἔκφανσιν in the works of George of Cyprus: *Expositio fidei* (PG 142.241A); *Confessio* (PG 142.250); *Apologia* (PG 142.266–67); *De processione Spiritus Sancti* (PG 142.290C, 300B).

It would not be exact to say, as some Orthodox polemicists have, that the procession διὰ Ὑιοῦ signifies solely the temporal mission of the Holy Spirit. In the case of the temporal mission of the persons of the Son and the Holy Spirit, a new factor is involved: that of will. This will, as we know, can only be the common will of the Trinity. The temporal mission is a specific case of divine manifestation *in the economy*, that is, in relation to created being. In general, the divine economy in time expresses the eternal manifestation; but the eternal manifestation is not necessarily in relation to created beings, which could have not existed. Independently of the existence of creatures, the Trinity is manifested in the radiance of its glory. From all eternity, the Father is "the Father of glory" (Eph. 1:17); the Word is "the brightness of his glory" (Heb. 1:3); and the Holy Spirit is "the Spirit of glory" (1 Peter 4:14).

Poverty of vocabulary sometimes makes it hard to recognize whether it is the hypostatic procession of the Holy Spirit or the procession of manifestation to which a writer is alluding: both are eternal, though having a different point of reference. Very often the Fathers simultaneously employed expressions referring to the hypostatic existence of the Holy Spirit and to the eternal manifestation of the divine nature in the Holy Spirit, even when defining his personal qualities or distinguishing his person from the other two. Nevertheless, they well distinguished between the two different modes of hypostatic subsistence and of manifestation. In evidence, we can cite this passage from Basil: "From the Father proceeds the Son, through whom are all things, and with whom the Holy Spirit is ever inseparably known, for none can think of the Son without being enlightened by the Spirit. Thus on one hand the Holy Spirit, the source of all good things distributed to created beings, is linked to the Son, with whom he is inseparably conceived; on the other hand his being is dependent on the Father, from whom he proceeds. Therefore the characteristic mark of his personal quality is *to be manifested* after the Son and with him, and *to subsist* in proceeding from the Father."[42] Many other patristic texts could be cited in which the writer is "concerned simultaneously with the eternal manifestation of the Divinity in the Holy Spirit and with his personal existence.[43] It was on the basis of these texts that Latinizing Greeks sought to defend the hypostatic procession of the Holy Spirit "through the Son" in order to reconcile two such different triadologies.

42. Basil the Great *Epistolae* 38.4 (PG 32.329C–32A). See also two passages in Gregory of Nyssa *Adversus Eunomium* 1 (PG 45.369A, 416C).
43. For example, the pneumatological formula of the *Synodicon* of Tarasius, read at the seventh ecumenical council, in which the distinction between the plane of subsistence and that of eternal manifestation is not noticed (*Collectio*, ed. Mansi, 12.1122).

The Condition for Reconciliation

It is easy to conceive the difficulties which the distinction between hypostatic existence of the Holy Spirit and eternal manifestation of the divine nature in his person presented to the theologically rude and uneducated minds of Western Christians of the Carolingian period. It may well be supposed that it was the truth of the eternal manifestation which the first filioquist formulas, in Spain and elsewhere before the ninth century, were intended to express. It is possible that the Filioquism of Augustine can also be interpreted in the same sense, although here the problem is more difficult and a theological analysis of the treatise *De Trinitate* is needed—something which has not yet been done by the Orthodox. Filioquism as a doctrine of the hypostatic procession of the Holy Spirit from the Father and the Son as from a single principle reached its clear and definitively explicit form in the great centuries of scholasticism. After the councils of Lyons and Florence, it was no longer possible to interpret the Latin formula for the procession of the Holy Spirit in the sense of eternal manifestation of the Divinity. At the same time it also became impossible for Roman Catholic theologians to admit the energetic manifestation of the Trinity as something not contradicting the truth of the divine simplicity. No longer was there any place for the concept of the energies of the Trinity; nothing was admitted to exist outside the divine essence except created effects, acts of will analogous to the act of creation. Western theologians had to profess the created character of glory and of sanctifying grace, to renounce the concept of deification; and in doing this they were quite consistent with the premises of their triadology.

Reconciliation will be possible and *filioque* will no longer be an *impedimentum dirimens* at that moment when the West, which has been frozen for so long in dogmatic isolation, ceases to consider Byzantine theology as an absurd innovation and recognizes that it only expressed the truths of tradition, which can be found in a less explicit form in the Fathers of the first centuries of the church. Then it will be recognized that what may seem absurd for a theology in which faith seeks understanding is not so absurd for an understanding open to the full reception of revelation— open to the acquisition of the sense of the Scriptures, whose sacred words long ago were foolishness to the Greek philosophers. The Greeks have ceased to be Greeks in becoming sons of the church. That is why they have been able to give to the Christian faith its imperishable theological armory. May the Latins in their turn cease to be solely Latins in their theology! Then together we shall confess our catholic faith in the Holy Trinity, who lives and reigns in the eternal light of his glory.

Partakers of Divine Nature

Christoforos Stavropoulos

Born in Greece in 1929, Christoforos Stavropoulos graduated from the University of Athens with a degree in theology. After ordination to the priesthood, he served for nine years as preacher for the Royal Greek Navy and teacher of religion at two naval schools. After serving two parishes, Stavropoulos undertook doctoral studies at the Catholic University of Louvain, Belgium, in the areas of catechetics and pastoral theology.

The following text is but a portion of the short book entitled Partakers of Divine Nature, *which explores the theme so characteristic of Orthodoxy, but alien to Protestants, that people are called to divinization or theosis. Stavropoulos summarizes what this important doctrine does and does not mean, offers its biblical basis, and, in part, explains how one attains theosis.*

Our Calling

Have we paid any attention to our calling? Not our human daily work, but our divine calling? We speak here not of our natural and physical purposes, but of our spiritual calling. Which is more important? Has the sense of our spiritual calling reached the depths of our souls? Has it entered into our very being? Has our heart been fired by the calling directed to us by the only Lord of life, our only true Father, God himself?

From Christoforos Stavropoulos, *Partakers of Divine Nature* (Minneapolis: Light and Life, 1976), 17–38. Reprinted by permission.

In the Holy Scriptures, where God himself speaks, we read of a unique call directed to us. God speaks to us human beings clearly and directly: "I said, 'You are gods, sons of the Most High—all of you'" (Ps. 82:6; John 10:34). Do we hear that voice? Do we understand the meaning of this calling? Do we accept that we should in fact be on a journey, a road which leads to theosis? As human beings we each have this one, unique calling, to achieve theosis. In other words, we are each destined to become a god, to be like God himself, to be united with him. The apostle Peter describes with total clarity the purpose of life: we are to become partakers of divine nature (2 Peter 1:4). This is the purpose of life: that we be participants, sharers in the nature of God and in the life of Christ, communicants of divine grace and energy—to become just like God, true gods. Man, according to Basil the Great, is a creature that has received the command to become a god. "He has been ordered to become God," says Gregory of Nazianzus.[1] God is not united except with gods, Simeon the New Theologian noted epigrammatically.

Theosis! What does this deep and profound word mean? It means the elevation of the human being to the divine sphere, to the atmosphere of God. It means the union of the human with the divine. That, in its essence, is the meaning of theosis. Thus, human nature ought to be moving toward spiritualization, and in the process, its heavy materialism is to be broken down and dissolved. The human soul is to be polished so that it may be transformed from its present dullness to a shining spirituality. That is how the union of the human with the divine becomes a reality. We are transformed into his likeness. However, this union is not absolute. It is relative, for it is not the transformation of our essence. Rather, it is natural, ethical, and in accordance with grace. It is the union of the whole person with God as unrestricted happiness in the divine kingdom. Human nature becomes the outgrowth of divine nature. It is remade into its original beauty. It is reborn to a new life. It is re-created through divine adoption. Consider Anastasius of Sinai's wonderful definition of theosis: "Theosis is elevation to what is better, but not the reduction of our nature to something less, nor is it an essential change of our human nature. A divine plan, it is the willing condescension of tremendous dimension by God, which he did for the salvation of others. That which is of God is that which has been lifted up to a greater glory, without its own nature being changed."[2]

The Holy Scriptures Concerning Theosis

In the very first book of the Old Testament, the Book of Genesis, we find the divine descent of humanity and their relationship to God. "God

---

1. Gregory of Nazianzus *Funeral Oration for St. Basil*, in *Patrologia Graeca* (PG), ed. J. P. Migne, 162 vols. (Paris, 1857–66), 36.560A.
2. Anastasius of Sinai *Concerning the Word* (PG 89.77BC).

said, 'Let us make man in our image, after our likeness. . . .' So God created man in his own image, in the image of God he created him" (Gen. 1:26–27). Human beings were created in the image and likeness of their Creator. This relationship with God is truly impressive. Humanity was created in the image of God, and each and every human being is called to become like God. We are called to become divine, not only before our fall into sin, but afterwards as well. After the fall of mankind through sin, the realization of this purpose began to be seen in the Israelite people, whom God selected to be his chosen people. This divine adoption had a group character. Later on, it took on an individual character in the persons of the pious kings David and Solomon, and before them in the judges, who were called "sons of God" as well as "gods," in spite of the fact that as human beings they had to die. This divine adoption is nothing other than the call to all persons to become divine—a call to theosis. The Old Testament is full of these teachings in which men and women are seen as sons and daughters of God, with a unique call to theosis, that is, to union with God.

The New Testament in a quite special and magnificent way teaches about the theosis of human beings. The fact that God himself becomes man and takes on human nature, making it divine by uniting it with his own divine nature and raising it up to the throne of God, cries out in the most eloquent manner the truth which Athanasius formulated: "God became man, so that we might be made gods."[3] The Son of God repeatedly speaks to us, calling us to theosis. And his refrain is "Love your enemies . . . so that you may be sons of your Father who is in heaven" (Matt. 5:44–45).

Paul writes on this topic with great clarity in his Letter to the Galatians: "But when the time had fully come, God sent forth his Son, born of a woman, born under the law, to redeem those who were under the law, so that we might receive adoption as sons. And because you are sons, God has sent the Spirit of his Son into our hearts, crying, 'Abba, Father!' So through God you are no longer a slave but a son, and if a son then an heir" (Gal. 4:4–7). He is our Father. We are his children, his inheritors through Jesus Christ. This is our calling—theosis. The meaning of theosis in the New Testament is the adoption of man, his participation in the incorruptibility of God, and his mixture with the divine nature in indescribable glory and blessedness. This whole situation of divine adoption and theosis is summarized in Athanasius's phrase, "God becomes a man, so that he may make Adam into a god."

"He Created Man in His Own Image"

The fact that our original and unique call is theosis is evident from the meaning of human creation "in the image of God." God "created man in his

---

3. Athanasius *Concerning the Incarnation of the Word* 54 (PG 25.192B).

own image." What does "in his own image" mean? The Fathers of the Eastern church present different dimensions of the answer to this question, each supplementing the other. Sometimes the Fathers attribute the character of the image of God to the kingly office of mankind, that is, to our superiority and authority over the material world. Sometimes the Fathers see the image in the spiritual aspect of human nature, in the soul, or in the governing aspect of our nature. They have seen it in the mind, the higher powers, such as the intellect or human self-determination, a characteristic according to which we internally make free decisions, which are the main cause of our actions. Occasionally, the image of God in man is compared with one of the characteristics of the soul, such as its simplicity, its immortality, as well as the possibility of a true communion with God by means of the presence of the Holy Spirit in the soul.[4]

Other Fathers emphasize that not only the soul was created in the image of God, but also the human body shares in the image of God. In the teaching of Gregory Palamas we read: "We are not able to call human just the soul or just the body, but rather, both together, of which it is said that they were created by God in his own image."[5] It follows that when Holy Scripture speaks of the image, it speaks of the whole human being. Thus, in general, the image of God does not refer to any one specific element of our complex human nature (body or soul). Rather, it refers to the totality of human nature in its completeness. As Gregory of Nyssa says, "For this reason, the Word of God in saying that man was made in the image of God included everything in a comprehensive phrase. It was the same as saying that he created human nature to be a participant in every good."[6]

Thus, human beings, created as they are of matter and spirit, are called to share in all the good things of God. Within each human being, God sows all those seedlike gifts which make us his image and lead us toward his likeness, insomuch as we cultivate these gifts. This is our calling—theosis. Theosis is achieved little by little, through the step-by-step spiritualization of our human nature. In this manner we achieve incorruption and the vision of God. The life of the first human beings in paradise was a life of joy, which was to have found unlimited fulfilment with the complete realization of the image of God. John of Damascus notes: "With his body, the first human being lived in a most divine and beautiful place. With his soul, however, he resided in an even higher and more beautiful place. For there he had God as both house and resident and as a delightful garden surrounding him. He was wrapped about with God's grace; and feeding, so to speak, as another sort of angel, he continuously enjoyed the vision of God as his only deliciously sweet fruit."[7]

4. Vladimir Lossky, The Mystical Theology of the Eastern Church (Crestwood, N.Y.: St. Vladimir's Seminary Press, 1976), 115.

5. Gregory Palamas Prosopopoiea (PG 150.1361C).

6. Gregory of Nyssa Concerning the Creation of Man (PG 44.184B).

7. John of Damascus Concerning Paradise (PG 94.916BC).

Theosis after the Fall

Man sinned freely. His sin consisted fundamentally in his disobedience, in the violation of the divine command. Adam ignored the command of God. He took an ungrateful stance before his unique and eternal benefactor, God. He took not the divine, but the demonic road. The immediate consequence of this apostasy was the fall, that is, separation from the living God. Humanity loses the divine gift. Human nature becomes distorted. Death comes. Our subjugation to the tyranny of the devil follows. And thus, we human beings ourselves stand in the way of the divine grace which is poured out upon us. The image of God within us is weakened. We ourselves preclude the possibility of our union with God. We deny the human characteristic and possibility of divinization. The potential of becoming like God disappears and becomes impossible.

But if Adam did not respond to his calling, and if it be the case that he did not succeed in being united with God, and if his sin divided him and separated him from the living God, this does not mean that the divine plan for the theosis of humankind was destroyed. In spite of the fall, there remains a possibility which may lead to divinization. No power and no sin is able to overcome the love of God for humanity. In spite of human sin, God's love for all of mankind stands firm. And this is true because man did not conceive of sin by himself. He did not invent it. He was deceived by the father of deceit and sin, the devil. Divine mercy does not overlook the fact that mankind sinned because of deceit, and because of deceit they disobeyed the divine command. Human beings are not the source of sin; they are, however, those who put it into practice.

The fact that human beings are not only spirit, but also flesh is one more reason which gives them the possibility of returning to God. For if people were only spirit and consequently sinned as spirits, they could not be redeemed since the spirit cannot change, but remains unchangeable because of its simplicity. But human beings also have bodies. And they are changeable and can be transformed because they are complex. That is, they have the ability to change direction and to return whence they came. The divine image of the first creation which exists in the whole of human nature, including both body and spirit, was not totally destroyed by that first sin; it was weakened, it was darkened, but it was not lost. This is the basis upon which the re-creation of humanity and their return to the road of theosis will take place. This re-creation was to be realized only with the incarnation of the Divine Logos. "'The vocation of the first Adam was fulfilled by Christ, the second Adam. God became man that man might become god,' to use the words of Irenaeus and Athanasius, echoed by the Fathers and theologians of every age."[8] Thus, the work of the Incarnate

8. Lossky, *Mystical Theology*, 133–34.

Word once again opens the way for us human beings to the achievement of theosis, which is the ultimate purpose of our life. The divine incarnation brings us again to the Father and presents us with the potential of realizing the likeness of God in our lives. Incarnation-crucifixion-resurrection-ascension bridge the gap which separates us from God. That chasm is death, sin, and fallen nature. The chasm which our fallen nature creates is bridged over by the incarnation of the Divine Word. The chasm which is created by our sin is bridged over by his crucifixion. And the third chasm, death, is filled in by his resurrection. "The last enemy to be destroyed is death" (1 Cor. 15:26). And with his holy ascension, Christ unites the earth with the heavens and unites the two into one; he has made both into one (see Eph. 2:14).

Our union with God, the theosis which is objectively offered to us by the incarnate, crucified, resurrected, and ascended God, can be realized only in the Holy Spirit. Only with the Holy Spirit will we be able to receive and taste redemption and theosis. Only in the Holy Spirit will we reach the point of becoming gods, the likenesses of God. Only the Holy Spirit will transmit to us that which the Son and Word of God has offered to us. Our call remains only one: theosis through our Lord Jesus Christ in the Holy Spirit.

"Divine and Divinizing"

The theosis of man, his perfect union with God made possible by grace, will be realized completely in the future age after the resurrection of the dead. However, beginning in this life, this union which divinizes people can be made more and more real. Our corrupt and weakened nature ought to be transformed little by little and adapted to eternal life.

God has given us this good in the church. In the church he has given us all of the objective presuppositions and all the necessary means to achieve our goal. On the other hand, the necessary subjective presuppositions have to be created on our part. The work of our theosis, our union with God, is not transmitted to us in some kind of mechanical fashion. Our weakened human nature will not be transformed magically. The change will happen in conjunction with our own efforts. It will be realized with the cooperation of man and God. This subjective aspect of our union with God provides the way of theosis which we must follow. This way is none other than the life in Christ. The true purpose of the life in Christ is the receiving of the Holy Spirit.

The Holy Spirit is the great resident of the church. It is there that the Holy Spirit exercises all of his sanctifying and deifying power. The work of our theosis, which our Lord Jesus Christ accomplished objectively, is completed by the Holy Spirit, adapting it to the life of every faithful Christian. The Holy Spirit is the main and essential beginning of sanctification. The

Fathers of the church specifically teach that the theosis of human beings is attributable to the Holy Spirit. The essential place of the Incarnate Word of God is matched by that of the Holy Spirit. The divine Spirit that proceeds from the Father divinizes us. The Spirit is "divine and divinizing." The Holy Spirit is a divine bond which harmonizes and draws the mystical body of Christ, that is, the church, together with its Lord. It is the Holy Spirit who makes the faithful into other Christs, and thus creates the church. Our incorporation in the mystical body of Christ and our theosis are not exclusively the work of the incarnation of Christ. They are also the work of the creative Holy Spirit, who creates the church with his spiritual gifts.

Through the Holy Spirit the faithful become sharers of divine nature. They are formed in the new life. They put off corruption. They return to the original beauty of their nature. They become participants of God and children of God. They take on the shape of God. They reflect the light of Christ and inherit incorruptibility. Thus, the contribution of the Holy Spirit is always a finalizing action. God the Father, before all ages, conceives of the work of salvation and theosis. He realizes it in time, in the Son. The Holy Spirit completes and perfects and adapts this work to people. In the sphere of the church, the Holy Spirit mystically sanctifies and unites the faithful with Christ, thus creating and giving life to the mystical body of the Lord. Here, in this mystical body, the Holy Spirit's sanctifying energy shines forth. These divine energies and the variety of graces of the Holy Spirit and the gifts which he mystically transmits to the soul of the believer, all shape and form the new Godlike human nature. The Holy Spirit consequently has a power which re-creates, renews, and causes a rebirth. Basil writes, "From the Holy Spirit there are the foreknowledge of the future, the comprehension of mysteries, the understanding of hidden things, the distribution of graces, the heavenly way of life, association with angels, unending happiness, residence in God, the likeness of God, and the highest of all things to be desired, to become God." This re-creative power of the Holy Spirit is what is known as divine grace. It comes and meets people. It does not force. It strengthens them in a spiritual way to walk the road leading to theosis. However, it is absolutely necessary that people receive divine grace willingly and without coercion. It is absolutely necessary for individuals to freely cooperate with divine grace in order to be able to travel the blessed road of union with God.

Divine Grace and Free Will

Theosis. Union with God. Reception of the Holy Spirit. How is it possible for us to make this a reality? Which is the road that leads there? The answer remains one: the Christian life. The Christian life comes into being with the sacraments and with holy works, those virtuous works which are done with a pure and holy motive in the name of Christ.

At this point there is the need for special attention, because many Christians believe that good works and virtues are what save us and unite us with God. We must understand this point very well. The purpose of our struggles, our efforts, the purpose of the Christian life is not good works and virtues. This is so because they do not of themselves grant us theosis. The true purpose of the Christian life is that we receive the Holy Spirit as our own, which in turn divinizes our existence. Prayer, fasting, and all those other Christian practices and exercises are, of course, very good things. But alone, they do not represent the purpose of the Christian life. They are only necessary means for the achievement of the purpose. Fastings, vigils, prayers, alms, and other good works which are done in the name of Christ are means which help us reach that goal which always remains the same: the reception of the Holy Spirit and the making him our own, that is, theosis. Good works are able to grant us the fruits of the Holy Spirit only when they are done in the name of Jesus Christ. Those good works which are not done in the name of Jesus Christ (which may be done either by non-Christians or by Christians who suppose that there is some kind of independent Good separate from Christ) are not able to help us receive a reward in the life to come. Nor are they able to offer the grace of God to us in the present life. There is no independent Good for the Christian. A work is good insofar as it is a means for a purpose, insofar as it serves to unite us with God, and insofar as it leads us to the reception and personal acceptance of divine grace. Let us note this point once more. Virtues, good works, the Christian struggle are necessary for every Christian. They themselves, however, are not the goal. They are the means, or rather the signs—the external expressions of the Christian life. There is only one purpose: the reception of the grace of the Holy Spirit and making it one's own.

But here there is a problem. When do we obtain the Holy Spirit? Do we first do good works, become virtuous, and then receive the grace of the Holy Spirit as a reward? Or are we first visited by the Holy Spirit, thus being moved to become virtuous? Theological thought has spent much time with this problem, for we are at the very heart of the topic of grace and self-determination (or free will). Self-determination is the ability and activity of human beings to make free choices. Grace is the spiritual gift of the Holy Spirit to human beings.

According to the tradition and teaching of the Eastern Orthodox Church, grace and human freedom are expressed concurrently and may not be understood the one without the other. There are not two separate moments. At the same time that a person freely makes the decision from within for the good and for the Christian life, at the very same moment divine grace comes and strengthens him. Just as this grace is given to the individual, the individual makes a free choice. Gregory of Nyssa says: "The grace of God is not able to visit those who flee salvation. Nor is human virtue of such power as to be adequate of itself to raise up to authentic life those souls who are untouched by grace. . . . *But when righteousness of works and the grace of the Spirit come together at the same time* in the same soul, together they are able to fill it with blessed life."[9]

Consequently, grace is not a reward for the virtues of our human will. Nor is it, on the other hand, the cause of the so-called virtuous acts of our free will. The issue here is not one of virtues but of cooperation. What we are discussing is the cooperation of two wills: the divine will, which is divine grace, and the human will, which is our self-determination. Inasmuch as there is concurrence by our free will, divine grace is able to increase within us. It occupies the human personality, strengthening it and building it up so as to make the good a reality. The more freely each human being receives the divine gift of grace, so much more does the Christian life become in fact grace-filled and complete; and in the same measure do the Christian's good works increase and does progress in virtue grow. What this means is that the Christian increasingly practices good works and virtues—strengthened by grace—on the way toward the realization of theosis. Let us understand this well. Each human being realizes the work of salvation in his or her life with the help of divine grace, which must be freely received. And just as the yeast must be thoroughly mixed with flour in order to make the dough rise, in the same way grace becomes one with each person, like one essence, elevating and raising the individual Godward. Maximus the Confessor, in a classical and epigrammatic fashion, expresses the church's teaching on this topic: "God made his willingness and his purpose clear by means of his loving condescension toward mankind, making divine through grace those who consciously travel upwards with it."[10]

Here we see the irreplaceable value of divine grace in the work of our unification with God. Equally irreplaceable are our free will and the cooperation of each human being with divine grace in the whole task of theosis.

In order, therefore, for the individual to walk the road to unity with God and to become divine, he or she must totally, freely, and wholeheartedly say yes to God. The turning to God has to be real. God must be truly accepted, and the world must be denied. The world is evil passions. Evil passions and desires constitute the road which leads away from God. The world is a foreign wandering of the human spirit; it is the betrayal of the nature of our soul. The denial of the world is a return of our soul to itself, a bringing together of the self, restoration of our spiritual existence, which

---

9. Gregory of Nyssa *Peri tou kata Theon skopou* (PG 46.289C).
10. Maximus the Confessor *Pros Georgion presbyteron* (PG 91.57A).

returns again to be united with God. And for this reason there is need for zeal, flame, warmth, and fire. Daily, until death and without pause, the Christian must never cease to turn toward God as "fire in fire, as heat in heat, as attentiveness in attentiveness, as desire in desire" (John Climacus).

All of these things emphasize the need for attention to our heart. Our heart is the workshop of righteousness as well as unrighteousness. It is the vessel which contains every sin. However, at the same time "God is found there; there the angels; there the life and the kingdom; there the light and the apostles; there the treasures of grace" (Macarius of Egypt). When grace conquers all of the springs, desires, and expressions of the heart, then it reigns in each of our members and in every thought, because the mind and thoughts of the soul are found there, in the heart. When the grace of God passes through the heart, it penetrates the whole of human nature. Consequently, the descent of the grace of the Holy Spirit must take place in our heart. And the Holy Spirit must guard over our heart. Equally necessary, however, on our part are decision and zeal. When zeal is lessened, when decision is weakened, then grace remains inactive. We must continuously enforce the evangelical command to be vigilant and not to be drugged by sleep, as we travel our life's road which leads to theosis.[11]

It is, however, necessary to underline with emphasis the truth that all of these things cannot be made real through theory alone, that is, by simply thinking and studying about them. There must also be action. Maximus says that theory without action, that is, theory which is not founded on activity, is no different from mere fantasy. The same is true of our action if it is not inspired by theory; it is sterile and inanimate like a statue.

The road toward our theosis, our union with God, can be formulated in the following short statement: divine grace and human freedom; theory and action; enthusiastic zeal and decision; abandonment of the world and return to God; good works as means toward theosis; a warm heart and vigilant eye. Only then, the open road. We *are* able to walk that road. We will be accompanied and strengthened by divine grace. The holy mysteries (sacraments) are what transmit this grace of the All-Holy Spirit. His sanctifying and deifying energy is actualized in the holy services of the church, especially in holy baptism, repentance, and the divine Eucharist. It is fulfilled and completed with prayer and love.

11. Lossky, *Mystical Theology*, 200–204.

Part 4
Theology as Mission:
Orthodoxy and the West

The Missionary Imperative in the Orthodox Tradition

Alexander Schmemann

Born in Estonia, Alexander Schmemann (1921–83) was educated in France, first at the University of Paris, and later at the Saint Sergius Orthodox Theological Institute. After graduation in 1945 he taught for six years at Saint Sergius. In 1951 Schmemann moved to the United States to join St. Vladimir's Orthodox Theological Seminary as professor of church history and liturgical theology, where he was later appointed dean (1962–83). In addition, Schmemann taught as an adjunct professor in Columbia University's Slavic Department. The best known among his many works include Introduction to Liturgical Theology *and* Historical Road of Eastern Orthodoxy.

Although the following two essays are somewhat dated, they both address the important issue of the relationship of the Orthodox East to the Catholic and Protestant West. The first explores Orthodoxy's self-identity as the one true church of Christ on earth and its concept of mission, while the second outlines Orthodoxy's historically ambivalent relationship with Western confessions, especially as that has found expression in ecumenical circles, and, more important still, the conditions that must be met for true healing and communion to occur between East and West.

Until quite recently the Eastern Orthodox Church was regarded in the West as a nonmissionary church. It was an opinion commonly held that the great missionary movement which marked so deeply the Christian West during the last centuries bypassed somehow the static Christianity of

From Gerald H. Anderson, ed., *The Theology of the Christian Mission* (New York: McGraw-Hill, 1961), 250–57.

the East. Today this view seems to have lost some of its strength: new historical research has made it quite clear that the Orthodox achievements in the field of mission, although somewhat different from those of the West, are nonetheless important and impressive.[1] Our purpose in this brief essay, however, is not to present a historical or statistical survey of the Orthodox missionary expansion. It is much more important to try to understand and to analyze—be it only tentatively and partially—the missionary imperative in the Orthodox tradition, or, in other terms, the relation in it between mission, on the one hand, and the faith, the life, and the whole spiritual vision of Orthodoxy on the other hand.

A theology of mission is always the fruit of the total being of the church and not a mere speciality for those who receive a particular missionary calling. But for the Orthodox church there is a special need to reflect upon its basic missionary motivations, because its presumably nonmissionary character has been too often explained by, and ascribed to, the very essence, the "holy of holies" of Orthodoxy: its sacramental, liturgical, mystical ethos. Even now, as the study of Orthodox missions seems to correct the traditional view, there remains the temptation to explain these missions as a marginal epiphenomenon in the history of Orthodoxy, as something that happened in spite of its general tendencies and trends. This is why a theological clarification is necessary. Can a church whose life is centered almost exclusively on the liturgy and the sacraments, whose spirituality is primarily mystical and ascetical, be truly missionary? And if it is, where in its faith are the deepest motivations of the missionary zeal to be found? In somewhat simplified terms this is the question addressed, explicitly or implicitly, to the Orthodox church by all those for whom "ecumenical" means necessarily and unescapably "missionary."

Obstacles to Understanding the Orthodox Approach to Missions

It is without any doubt in Orthodox ecclesiology, that is, in the doctrine and experience of the church, that we find the basic elements of an answer. To formulate them, however, is not an easy task. It must be kept in mind that the Orthodox church has never been challenged by an ecclesiological or doctrinal crisis comparable to the Reformation or Counter-Reformation. And because of this it had no compelling reason to reflect upon itself, upon the traditional structures of its life and doctrine. There was no theological elaboration of the doctrine of the church, this doctrine having been never questioned or opposed.

1. Josef Glazik, *Die Russisch-Orthodoxe Heidenmission seit Peter dem Grossen: Ein missionsgeschichtlicher Versuch nach russischen Quellen und Darstellungen* (Münster: Aschendorff, 1954); idem, *Die Islammission der Russisch-Orthodoxen Kirche* (Münster: Aschendorff, 1959).

It was in the ecumenical encounter with the West, an encounter whose beginnings must be traced back to the twenties (Stockholm, 1925, and Lausanne, 1927), that for the first time the Orthodox were requested not only to state their ecclesiological beliefs, but also to explain them, that is, to express them in consistent theological terms. But at this point there appeared an additional difficulty which has remained ever since as the major difficulty of the Orthodox participation in the ecumenical movement. A dialogue presupposes necessarily an agreement on the terms that are being used, a common language. Yet from the Orthodox point of view it was precisely the rupture in theological understanding, the theological alienation of the West from the East, that, first, made the schism so deep and, then, all attempts to heal it—from 1054 to the Council of Florence in 1438–39—so hopelessly inadequate. Therefore, in the ecumenical encounter, the Orthodox church had to face a Christian world with several centuries of autonomous theological and spiritual development behind it, with a mind and thought forms radically different from those of the East. The questions asked of the Orthodox were formulated in Western terms, were conditioned very often by specifically Western experience and developments. The Orthodox answers were classified according to Western patterns, reduced to categories familiar to the West, but hardly adequate to Orthodoxy. This situation, although years of contacts and conversations have no doubt improved it, is still far from being overcome completely. The catholic language has not yet been recovered. All this, in addition to basic dogmatical differences, explains the agony of Orthodox participation in the ecumenical movement and constitutes a very real obstacle not only to an agreement, but to a simple understanding. One must remember this when trying to grasp the Orthodox approach to missions.

Orthodox Doctrine and Experience of the Church

"Heaven on earth": this formula familiar to every Orthodox expresses rather well the fundamental Orthodox experience of the church. The church is first of all and before everything else a God-created and God-given reality, the presence of Christ's new life, the manifestation of the new eon of the Holy Spirit. An Orthodox in his contemplation of the church sees it as the divine gift before he thinks of the church as human response to this gift. One can rightly describe the church as an eschatological reality, for its essential function is to manifest and to actualize in this world the eschaton, the ultimate reality of salvation and redemption. In and through the church the kingdom of God is made already present, is communicated to men. And it is this eschatological, God-given fullness of the church (not any juridical theory of mediation) that constitutes the root of the ecclesiological absolutism of Eastern Orthodoxy, absolutism which is so often misunderstood and misinterpreted by the Protestants.

The church as a whole is a means of grace, the sacrament of the kingdom. Therefore its structure—hierarchical, sacramental, liturgical—has
no other function but of making the church ever capable of fulfilling itself
as the body of Christ, as the temple of the Holy Spirit, to actualize its very
nature as grace. For the God-given fullness of the church, or rather the
church as fullness—and this is an essential aspect of Orthodox ecclesiology—cannot be manifested outside these ecclesiastical structures. There
is no separation, no division, between the church invisible (*in statu
patriae*) and the visible church (*in statu viae*), the latter being the expression and the actualization of the former, the sacramental sign of its reality.
Hence the unique, the central ecclesiological significance of the Eucharist, which is the all-embracing sacrament of the church. In the Eucharist
"the church becomes what it is," fulfils itself as the body of Christ, as the
divine parousia—the presence and the communication of Christ and of
his kingdom. Orthodox ecclesiology is indeed eucharistic ecclesiology. For
in the Eucharist the church accomplishes the passage from this world into
the world to come, into the eschaton; participates in the ascension of its
Lord and in his messianic banquet; tastes of the joy and peace of the kingdom. "And thou didst not cease to do all things until thou hadst brought
us back to heaven, and hadst endowed us with thy kingdom . . ." (eucharistic prayer in the Liturgy of John Chrysostom). Thus the whole life of the
church is rooted in the Eucharist, is the fruition of this eucharistic fullness
in the time of this world whose "image passeth by. . . ." This is indeed the
mission of the church.

The church is also *human response* to the divine gift, its acceptance and
appropriation by humanity. If the order of the church is shaped and conditioned by the eschatological fullness of the gift, is its sacramental sign,
it is the acceptance of the gift and the growth into its fullness that are the
purpose of the Christian community. The church is fullness, and the
church is also increase and growth in faith and love, knowledge and koi-
nonia. This response has two aspects, neither of which can be separated
from the other, because they condition each other and together constitute
the dynamics of Christian life and action.

The first aspect of the church as response is *God-centered:* it is the sanctification, the growth in holiness, of both the Christian individual and the
Christian community, the "acquisition by them of the Holy Spirit," as the
ultimate goal of Christian life was defined by one of the last and the greatest Orthodox saints, Seraphim of Sarov (d. 1833). It is the slow transformation of the old Adam in us into the new one, the restoration of the pris-
tine beauty, which was lost in sin, the illumination with the noncreated
light of Mount Tabor. It is also the slow victory over the demonic powers
of the cosmos, the joy and peace which *hinc et nunc* make us partakers of
the kingdom and of life eternal. The Orthodox spiritual tradition has

always stressed the mystical nature of Christian life, as life hidden with Christ in God. And the great monastic movement which started in the fourth century after the church was officially recognized by the Roman Empire, and given a status in this world, was nothing else but a new expression of the early Christian eschatologism, the affirmation of Christianity as belonging ontologically to the life of the world to come, the negation of any permanent home and identification in this world.

The second aspect of the church as response is *man- or world-centered*. It is the understanding of the church as being left in this world, in its time, space, and history, with a specific task or mission: "to walk in the same way in which he walked" (1 John 2:6). The church is fullness and its home is in heaven. But this fullness is given to the world, sent into the world as its salvation and redemption. The eschatological nature of the church is not the negation of the world, but, on the contrary, its affirmation and acceptance as the object of divine love. Or, in other terms, the whole otherworldliness of the church is nothing but the sign and the reality of the love of God for this world, the very condition of the church's mission to the world. The church thus is not a self-centered community but precisely a missionary community, salvation not from, but of, the world. In the Orthodox experience and faith it is the church-sacrament that makes possible the church-mission.

The Missionary Imperative

We can try now to formulate with more precision the various aspects of the missionary imperative as implied in the Orthodox experience of the church. This imperative is the essential expression of the church as gift and fullness, its projection in time and space of this world. For if, on the one hand, nothing can be added to the church—its fullness is that of Christ himself—the manifestation and the communication of this fullness constitute, on the other hand, the very life of the church in this eon. On the day of Pentecost, when the fullness of the church was realized once for all, began the time of the church, the last and the crucial segment of the history of salvation. Ontologically the only newness and, therefore, the only soteriological content of this segment is precisely *mission*: the proclamation and the communication of the eschaton, which is already the being of the church and indeed its only being. It is the church as mission that gives to this time its real significance and to history its meaning. And it is mission that gives to the human response in the church its validity, makes us real co-workers in the work of Christ.

Nothing reveals better the relation between the church as fullness and the church as mission than the Eucharist, the central act of the church's *leiturgia*, the sacrament of the church itself. There are two complementary movements in the eucharistic rite: the movement of ascension and the movement of return. The Eucharist begins as an ascension toward the throne of God, toward the kingdom. "Let us put aside all earthly care," says the hymn of offertory, and we prepare ourselves to ascend into heaven with Christ and in Christ, and to offer in him his Eucharist. This first movement, which finds its fulfilment in the consecration of the elements, the sign of the acceptance by God of our Eucharist, is, to be sure, already an act of mission. The Eucharist is offered "on behalf of all and for all"; it is the fulfilment by the church of its priestly function: the reconciliation of the whole creation with God, the sacrifice of the whole world to God, the intercession for the whole world before God. All this in Christ, the God-man, the unique priest of the new creation, the "one who offers and the one who is offered. . . ." This is accomplished by a total separation of the church from the world ("The doors, the doors!" proclaims the deacon as the eucharistic prayer begins), by its ascension to heaven, its entrance into the new eon.

And then, precisely at the moment when this state of fullness has been reached and consummated at the table of the Lord in his kingdom, when "we have seen the true Light and partaken of the Holy Spirit," the second movement begins—that of the return into the world. "Let us depart in peace," says the celebrant as he leaves the altar and leads the congregation outside the temple—and this is the last, the ultimate, commandment. The Eucharist is always the end, the sacrament of the parousia; and yet it is always the beginning, the starting point: now the mission begins. "We have seen the true Light, we have enjoyed life eternal," but this life, this Light, are given us in order to transform us into Christ's witnesses in this world. Without this ascension into the kingdom we would have had nothing to witness to; now, having once more become his people and his inheritance, we can do what Christ wants us to do: "you are witnesses of these things" (Luke 24:48). The Eucharist, transforming the church into what it is, transforms it into mission.

The Objects of Mission

What are the objects, the goals, of mission? The Orthodox church answers without hesitation: these objects are man and world. Not man alone in an artificially religious isolation from the world, and not world as an entity of which man would be nothing but a part. Man not only comes first, but is indeed the essential object of mission. And yet the Orthodox idea of evangelism is free from individualistic and spiritualistic connotations. The church, the sacrament of Christ, is not a religious society of converts, an organization to satisfy the religious needs of man. It is new life and redeems therefore the whole life, the total being of man. And this whole life of man is precisely the world in which and by which he lives. Through man the church saves and redeems the world. One can say that this world is saved and redeemed every time a man responds to the divine gift, accepts it, and lives by it. This does not transform the world into the kingdom or the society into the church. The ontological abyss between the old and the new remains unchanged and cannot be filled in this eon. The kingdom is yet to come and the church is not of this world. And yet this kingdom to come is already present and the church is fulfilled in this world. They are present not only as proclamation, but in their very reality; and through the divine *agapē*, which is their fruit, they perform all the time the same sacramental transformation of the old into the new; they make possible a real action, a real "doing" in this world.

All this gives the mission of the church a cosmical and a historical dimension that in the Orthodox tradition and experience are essential. State, society, culture, nature itself, are real objects of mission and not a neutral milieu in which the only task of the church is to preserve its own inner freedom, to maintain its religious life. It would require a whole volume to tell the story of the Orthodox church from this point of view: of its concrete participation in societies and cultures of whose whole existence Orthodoxy became the total expression; of its identification with nations and peoples, yet without betrayal of its otherworldliness, of the eschatological communion with the heavenly Jerusalem. It would require a long theological analysis to express adequately the Orthodox idea of the sanctification of matter, or precisely the cosmical aspect of its sacramental vision. Here we can state only that all this is the object of Christian mission, because all this is assumed and offered to God in the sacrament. In the world of incarnation nothing neutral remains, nothing can be taken away from the Son of man.

Moment of Truth
for Orthodoxy

Alexander Schmemann

If the participation of the Orthodox churches in the ecumenical movement or, more precisely, in the World Council of Churches, were to be evaluated on the sole basis of official reports, declarations, and statistics, there would be no doubts as to the positive and optimistic character of such an evaluation. Officially this participation has been indeed steadily growing since the pioneering days of Stockholm and Lausanne, and by now virtually all Orthodox churches have joined the World Council. The image and place of Orthodoxy in the council are symbolized by the traditional election of an Orthodox hierarch as one of the council's five presidents. The significance of this symbol seems to be that Orthodoxy is not only *in*, but, given actual leadership, is to become one of the guiding forces of the whole ecumenical movement. Officially the Orthodox participation in the WCC looks like a well-established tradition, raising no question or doubts.

But does this official optimism correspond to the real situation? To this question I must quite honestly give a negative answer, and my purpose in this brief essay is to substantiate it, that is, to show, first, that there exists a discrepancy between the official Orthodox position in the WCC and the real Orthodoxy, and, second, that this discrepancy constitutes an urgent issue for the WCC which, if it is not understood on time, may sooner or later lead to a major ecumenical crisis.

No one who has followed ecumenical developments from within the Orthodox church would deny that, in spite of all official pronouncements, affirmations, and actions, the Orthodox participation in the WCC not only remains an ever open question, but encounters a deeply rooted suspicion and even hostility that cannot be simply ascribed to dead conservatism, lack of interest, or mere provincialism. The suspicion is widely spread not only among laity but also among hierarchy and theologians. There exists, to be sure, an official position endorsed by Orthodox leadership. But a Western reader should be warned immediately that in the Orthodox church "officialdom" cannot be simply identified with the voice of the church. History is here to remind us that no official pronouncement is of any binding effect unless it is accepted by the whole body of the church, though it is very difficult, if not impossible, to give a clear-cut definition of how such acceptance is to be achieved and expressed. What, for example, could have been more official than the unions with Rome signed at Florence in 1438 and in Brest-Litovsk in 1596? Yet neither was accepted by the church, and these failures only increased the number of tragic misunderstandings that make our present relations with Rome so difficult.

Today—as was the case then—the official position seems to me to be dangerously cut off from not so much the feelings or reactions of the average Orthodox, but from Orthodox reality itself, that is, the totality of spiritual, theological, and liturgical experience which alone can give life and authenticity to the acts of ecclesiastical policy. The Orthodox participation in the WCC remains precisely on the level of ecclesiastical policy despite the fruitful work performed by Orthodox theologians. For if participation means, above all, a real sense of involvement and responsibility, an irrevocable certitude of belonging, a kind of self-identification with the ecumenical movement in all its complexity, achievements, and difficulties, then one must openly admit that although Orthodox representatives may be in, the Orthodox church as a whole is certainly out. Representation here has not yet been transformed into participation. The question is—why?

The Lack of Encounter between East and West

The ecumenical movement is by its very nature an encounter, a conversation, an accepted partnership in the search for Christian unity and wholeness. The encounter, however, is fruitful and meaningful only when it is founded on some degree of mutual understanding, on a common language, even if this language serves as a means of a sharp controversy.

The tragedy of Orthodoxy is that from the very beginning of its ecumenical participation no such common language, no theological continuity existed between her and her Western partners within, at least, the organized and institutionally structured ecumenical movement. *There*

was no real encounter. For, as I will try to show, even the seemingly successful participation of Orthodox theologians and ecumenists was limited by an artificial theological framework imposed on it, and this not
because of any bad will but by the very nature of the early ecumenical
movement.

The Isolation of the Eastern Church

To explain this initial failure, two facts are of paramount importance. One
is the isolation of the Orthodox church from the Christian West, the other
a specifically Western character and ethos of the ecumenical movement.

It is indeed impossible to understand the uniqueness of the Orthodox
ecumenical situation without realizing that for many centuries the Orthodox East was virtually absent from the life of the West, took no role in it,
and, what is equally important, was not considered a part of it. This means
that the crucial events in the Western spiritual and theological history—
the Reformation and the Counter-Reformation, events which precisely
shaped and conditioned the religious situation and the theological mentality of the contemporary Christian West—had minimal impact on the
Orthodox church and were not significant events of her own history and
life. Isolated from the West and its religious effervescence, on the one
hand, she was, on the other hand, forced into a kind of defensive
immobility by the external conditions of her own existence: the Turkish
domination and its various consequences. And thus she remained basically unaltered in her structure, spirituality, liturgy, in the whole of her tradition. The only notable exception was the rather deep Westernization of
Orthodox theology, but it was an exception confirming the rule. For, precisely because of its alienation from the traditional sources and methods,
this Westernizing theology, failing to have any significant impact on the
life of the church, was not really accepted.

This Eastern isolation of the Orthodox church and her very real identity with tradition as formulated and accepted before the Western schism
explain those basic presuppositions which conditioned the initial Orthodox attitudes and reactions in the ecumenical movement and determined
the subsequent development of Orthodox participation. To understand
them in all their implications is of the greatest importance for all those
preoccupied with the ecumenical future.

The first of these presuppositions concerns the very orientation of the
ecumenical movement. If for a Western Christian, because of his historical
background, the central ecumenical problem of unity, division, reunion is
formulated mainly in terms of the Catholic-Protestant dichotomy and opposition, for the Orthodox church the fundamental opposition is that between
the East and the West, understood as two spiritual and theological trends or

worlds; it is this opposition that, in the Orthodox mind, should determine the initial framework of the ecumenical encounter. We must not forget that the only division or schism which the Orthodox church remembers to speak of existentially as an event of her own past is precisely the alienation from her of the whole West. For at the time of the fateful rupture between Constantinople and Rome (1054), the latter represented both institutionally and theologically the whole Christian West, and it was as a whole that the West broke its communion with the East. This, according to the Orthodox point of view, was owing to an initial deviation from the common tradition, a deviation that blinded the West and made it accept doctrines incompatible with the teachings of the undivided church. Reformation, in this Orthodox perspective, was understood as a crisis within the more general Western distortion of Orthodoxy, as a specifically Western development attributable to Western conditions and presuppositions. Therefore, the first ecumenical question, the starting point of the whole ecumenical movement from the Orthodox standpoint, was, What happened between the East and the West, when and how did this alienation begin, what is its real scope and content? There had to be, in other terms, a revaluation of the past, of that history which at a certain moment ceased to be the common history for both halves of the original Christendom. The ecumenical movement, to be fruitful and meaningful, had to accept as its first item of investigation that initial and determining tragedy of the universal church.

The second presupposition is the logical consequence of the first one. It concerns the basic terms of reference of the ecumenical encounter and conversation. From the Orthodox point of view the only really common language, the only workable set of references in such a conversation, would be supplied by that tradition which at one time was accepted by all Christians as the common and universal teaching of the church; that tradition was precisely the tradition represented by Orthodoxy. For again it is to be remembered that at the time of the Western schism the Eastern tradition—that of the Fathers, ecumenical councils, and the *lex orandi*—still formed the common basis and was thought of as not the Eastern expression of the Christian faith, as something specifically Eastern and, therefore, particular, but as indeed the universal tradition of the church. It could therefore—if such was the Orthodox ecumenical thinking—give the ecumenical encounter a real framework of common references, a possibility to clarify the fundamental issues. Alien to the acute Western controversies and frustrations, the Orthodox church could contribute, at least in her own eyes, a *tertium datum*, not as her tradition, but as a common heritage in which everyone could discover the starting point of his own spiritual and theological development.

Hence, and this is the third presupposition, the only adequate ecumenical method from the Orthodox point of view was that of a total and direct doctrinal confrontation, with, as its inescapable and logical conclusion, the acceptance of truth and the rejection of error. Throughout all its history Orthodoxy knew only those two categories: the right belief (orthodoxy) and the heresy, without any possibility of compromise between them. Heresy was looked at not so much as intellectual distortion, but as a deficient faith, endangering salvation itself. It was, therefore, truth, and not unity, which in the Orthodox opinion and experience had to be the real goal of the ecumenical movement, unity in this experience being nothing else but the natural consequence of truth, its fruit and blessing.

The Western Orientation of the Ecumenical Movement

None of these presuppositions had been accepted or even understood in the ecumenical movement when the Orthodox church made its appearance in it. This means that from its very beginning the ecumenical movement was heavily dominated by Western religious and theological problems.

Thus, if the Orthodox understood the ecumenical phenomenon as encounter between the East and the West considered as the two halves of the original Christian world, the very sting of being just a half was almost completely alien to the West, Protestant as well as Roman. The long isolation of Orthodoxy and the dramatic dynamics of its own religious history developed in the West a sense of self-sufficiency which hardly left any room for the archaic and static Easterners, who, only a few decades before, were an object of Western missionary proselytism. For the Christian West the ever-present and ever-burning tragedy was not its alienation from the East, but the collapse of its own religious unity in the crisis of Reformation and Counter-Reformation.

The Orthodox idea of an early and universal tradition as a common heritage and, therefore, a possible common ground for the ecumenical encounter was ignored, for there developed in the West another tradition: that of a polemical defensive and offensive theology in which the very concept of tradition was radically altered. For the Orthodox church, tradition is the living experience of the church, existing prior to its formulation and definitions and independently of them. But the West reduced tradition progressively to an almost juridical category of authority, so that it was no longer the content, but the very existence of tradition that became the ecumenical problem and preoccupation.

And, finally, the central Orthodox affirmation that truth and truth alone is to constitute the formal object of the ecumenical movement, that is, truth is to be both the content and the form of unity, was also to be misunderstood and practically ignored because, in the Western experience, truth is understood primarily as again a formal authority and is therefore opposed not to error, but to freedom. The very categories of "orthodoxy" and "heresy" had here a connotation very different from the one they had in the Orthodox mind. And if in the Orthodox understanding the ecumenical movement was to be centered on an ultimate choice between truth and heresy, the Western presupposition of it was that ultimately all choices are to be integrated into one synthesis in which all are mutually enriching and complementary one to another. *The word heresy, in fact, is absent even today from the ecumenical vocabulary, and does not exist even as a possibility.*

The False Position of Orthodoxy in the WCC

The Theological Level

The initial misunderstanding which I have briefly analyzed results, in my opinion, in a fundamentally false position of the Orthodox church in the WCC. It is false both theologically and institutionally, and this false-hood explains the constant Orthodox agony in the ecumenical move-ment, the anxiety and the doubts it raises in Orthodox consciousness.

On the theological level the Orthodox church, because she failed to impose her own vision on the ecumenical movement, her own ecumenical presuppositions, had to accept and, in fact, accepted the formulation of the movement in terms of the Catholic-Protestant dichotomy. This meant not only that she was somehow forced to identify herself with one of the two opposing Western positions, but also that she had to make her own all the derived dichotomies—word and sacrament, vertical and horizontal, authority and freedom, and so on—typical of the Western theological sit-uation, but fundamentally alien to the real Orthodox tradition. In the absence of Rome, she was assigned the role of the ecumenically acceptable Catholicism at the extreme right wing of the whole spectrum of Protestant denominations. It is indeed tragic that the Orthodox theologians and rep-resentatives, with a very few exceptions, so easily accepted this assign-ment; they accepted, perhaps without realizing it, a part in a Western con-troversy, whereas their real contribution might have been the overcoming of the Western impasses and wrong dichotomies!

It is here, probably, that the long Westernization of the Orthodox pro-fessional theology produced its negative fruit. For while it is true that the Orthodox church is hierarchical, sacramental, traditional, horizontal, dogmatical, Catholic, and so forth, neither the affirmation and defense of these characteristics by the Roman Catholics nor their negation and crit-icism by the Protestants coincide with the Eastern approach. Orthodoxy cannot be simply reduced to the Orthodox doctrine of apostolic succes-sion, seven sacraments, three degrees of hierarchy; and it is even doubtful whether such doctrines exist in a clearly defined form. Many of these terms themselves have been borrowed directly from Western manuals and are to be still evaluated in the light of the total and genuine Orthodox tradition. Yet it was precisely as a "position" on this or that question that Orthodoxy was always presented and represented in the ecumenical conversation, but virtually never as a totality, as a living spiritual reality which alone gives life and meaning to its external forms. And then this position itself was usually identified with an existing Western category which only enforced the accepted theological framework. The "separate Orthodox statements" attached to the reports of virtually all major ecumenical conferences is a good, if too often a helpless, illustration of the feeling of being in a false position, which was almost always the feeling of the Orthodox delegates.

The Institutional Level

But it is on the institutional level that the falsehood of the Orthodox position within the WCC is the most apparent. Because of the Western religious situation, the structure of the council is based on the denominational principle. Since no common definition of the "church" is to be found, any group with some degree of organizational autonomy must be accepted as "church" even if this term does not belong to its self-determination. This principle adequately reflects the Protestant view of the ecumenical movement, but is radically incompatible with the views of the Roman and the Orthodox churches. What is involved here is not a question of prestige (the Orthodox church being equal in importance with some minor denomination), but a question of ecumenical truth and reality. For the division between Protestant denominations is radically different in its very nature from the division between Orthodoxy and Protestantism on the one hand, and Orthodoxy and Roman Catholicism on the other hand. In the first case there are disagreements within a basic agreement, in the second there may be partial agreement but within a radical disagreement made painfully obvious by the impossibility of intercommunion.

The ecumenical reality is threefold: Catholic, Protestant, Orthodox—but this is not expressed in the institutional forms of the ecumenical movement. Here again the blame is not with the Protestant architects of the WCC, who in their own way tried their best to incorporate in the structure of the WCC the basic ecumenical tensions (cf. the Toronto document), but with the Orthodox themselves who by accepting the denominational principle and applying it to themselves betrayed once more their own ecumenical mission and function, namely, representing the wholly different pole of the experience of the church or, in other terms, the church herself in all her reality and unity. This, however, is to be achieved not by the routine repetition of her claim to be the true church, but by the firm affirmation of the simple fact that in any ecumenical encounter the Orthodox church is always and by her very nature the other half standing together with, and yet always against, the totality of the Protestants. And as long as this real opposition is not expressed in the very structure of the WCC, the position of Orthodoxy in it will be misleading and confusing for both the Orthodox themselves and their Protestant brothers.

It is my hope that these remarks, sharp and disappointing as they may seem, will be understood as coming from a very real concern for the future of the ecumenical movement and the Orthodox participation in it. We have reached, it seems to me, the moment of truth, and there is a great need for clarity and responsibility. So much has been given to us in the ecumenical encounter, so many wonderful possibilities open. We have no right to betray them.

14

Eastern Orthodoxy and Evangelicalism
The Status of an Emerging Global Dialogue
Bradley Nassif

Bradley Nassif is professor of historical and systematic theology in the Antiochian House of Studies, Orthodox patriarchate of Antioch (in St. John of Damascus Seminary, Balamand University, Lebanon/U.S.A.) and founder of the Society for the Study of Eastern Orthodoxy and Evangelicalism. After studies at St. Vladimir's Orthodox Seminary (M.Div.), Denver Seminary (M.A., New Testament), and Wichita State University (European History), he earned his Ph.D. at Fordham University in patristics under the late Fr. John Meyendorff. Nassif also served as director of academic programs at Fuller Theological Seminary, Orange County extension in California. He also has been a featured television commentator for the documentary series "Christianity: The First Thousand Years" and "The Jesus Experience—Jesus Among the Slavs." In the following chapter, Nassif

Adapted from Bradley Nassif, "Eastern Orthodoxy and Evangelicalism: The Status of an Emerging Dialogue," *Scottish Bulletin of Evangelical Theology* 18.1 (Spring 2000): 21–55. Reprinted by permission. Dr. Nassif has updated the material for this book through A.D. 2003 with several significant changes. He writes, "In general, from 2000–2003 the Orthodox posture towards evangelicals has been the same: closed and uninterested for the most part, though cracks in the cocoon are discernable and significant, coming as they do from individual Orthodox scholars. Evangelicalism was more open to Orthodoxy during the decade of the 1990s than at any previous time. In the past five years, however, evangelicals have decisively closed ranks against the Orthodox with a kind of fortress mentality, especially in its educational institutions as described below."

summarizes the history of Eastern Orthodox and evangelical relations from 1990 to the present. The article concludes that the Orthodox and evangelical traditions now stand at a crossroad: either return to the isolationism of the Communist era or change the course of history. The author strongly encourages both sides not to give up on each other but to renew their conversations regarding this potentially powerful spiritual alliance.

Introduction

In November of 1999 the American Academy of Religion hosted its first Joint Dialogue between the "Eastern Orthodox Studies Group" and the "Evangelical Theology Group." The respondent, Robert Jenson from Princeton University, summarized their relations by declaring, "I know of no two groups of Christians who pose a greater challenge to ecumenical unity than the dialogue between Eastern Orthodox and Evangelical Christians. It boggles the mind to conceive just how two such different groups can ever bridge their differences. They have both a remarkable unity and remarkable divergences. But as Jesus said, 'With God, all things are possible!'"

The purpose of this article is to identify and describe the most important dialogues and scholarly exchanges that have emerged around the world over the past decade between the Eastern Orthodox and Protestant evangelical traditions. These include the work of academic societies, individual scholars, ecumenical agencies, seminaries, and mission organizations. The previous two hundred years of Orthodox-evangelical history before 1990, and the increasing number of personal pilgrimages to Orthodoxy by evangelical believers in recent days, will be touched upon in a general way below but are too numerous and complex to trace in any detail here. As a result of this survey from 1990 to the present, readers hopefully will be given fresh and vitally important information on a potentially momentous turning point in Orthodox and evangelical relations in modern church history.

Past Relations

The history of relations between the Eastern Orthodox and Protestant evangelical traditions has never been written. One does not have to search very far, however, to see that their past relationships have been predominantly characterized by a long negative history of proselytism, persecution, mutual suspicion, hostility, fear, and ignorance. Throughout the nineteenth and early twentieth centuries in the Middle East, Orthodox Christians were viewed as objects of conversion during a period of Presbyterian missions to the Arab lands. Thousands of Arab Christians left the

Orthodox, Melkite, and Syrian Jacobite churches and took up residence in newly founded Presbyterian communities. Less successful were Protestant missions to Russia and Greece. In Russia, prior to the Communist Revolution in 1917, "Orthodoxy, nationalism, and autocracy" were the Slavic slogans of Orthodox nationalism, which socially disadvantaged and oppressed Russian Protestants in the name of "Holy Russia." In Greece civil laws were passed outlawing "proselytism" by Protestant missionaries, the violation of which was punishable by fines and/or imprisonment. Throughout the twentieth century, hundreds of Protestant missionaries suffered sporadic persecution and disgrace under the hands of Greek Orthodox law.

In the United States, thousands of Orthodox peoples arrived on American shores from Syria, Lebanon, Russia, Greece, and parts of Europe during the immigration period of the late nineteenth and early twentieth centuries. Unlike the national unity some Orthodox once enjoyed in their homelands, America now presented a new external challenge of religious pluralism. During this time the church did not fare well. Second and third generation Orthodox immigrant children hemorrhaged out the doors of the church in large numbers due to the church's apparent irrelevance to their lives and their inability to pray the liturgy in the English language. A number of those parishioners (difficult to quantify) joined Protestant churches after being (re)converted to Christ through evangelical outreach via the Billy Graham Crusades, Young Life, Campus Crusade for Christ, and other parachurch organizations, as well as through the personal witness of individual believers. In some cases, former Orthodox believers became socially ostracized by their families after leaving the church. Such were the general conditions between Orthodox and evangelical Christians.

Emerging Global Dialogue

In approximately the last thirteen years, a new paradigm of ecumenical relations has begun to emerge between Orthodox and evangelical Christians on the popular and professional levels. On the popular level, more evangelicals have begun to join the Orthodox Church in America than ever before. The same has been true to a lesser extent in the United Kingdom. Though no formal study has been done to document the exact reasons for these conversions, the growing number of defections has clearly caught the attention of both Orthodox and evangelical leaders. From a cursory survey, the most important reasons why evangelicals are leaving their churches appear to be a growing hunger for liturgical worship, a desire for connectedness to historic Christianity, and the search for a historic consensus of truth. One source estimates that approximately 80 percent of the people who are joining the Orthodox church today come from evangelical and charismatic backgrounds such as Campus Crusade for Christ, Young Life, Youth for Christ, Vineyard fellowships, the Evangelical Free Church, Baptist denominations, the Christian and Missionary Alliance, and other independent churches. The remaining 20 percent come from high churches such as Anglicanism, Episcopalianism, Lutheranism, Methodism, and Presbyterianism.[1] Millard Erickson, a leading American evangelical theologian, describes this phenomenon as a small but significant movement that has the potential of greatly impacting the future of evangelicalism.

An increasing number of persons, especially college students, are turning to denominations emphasizing tradition, historical connection, and liturgy. I have in mind the movement of people like Robert Webber and Walter Dunnett into the Episcopal and Anglican Churches. An even more radical step is the movement of evangelicals into the Eastern Orthodox Church. Peter Gillquist, a major leader in this movement, has described the journey of two thousand evangelical Protestants toward Eastern Orthodoxy. One issue of his magazine *Again* featured the testimonies of recent evangelical converts to Eastern Orthodoxy. Among the more conspicuous is Franky Schaeffer, son of the late Francis Schaeffer. A few, such as Thomas Howard, have even been attracted to Roman Catholicism.

> This movement is small, but it is real and of potentially great influence because it includes young people who could be the leaders of the evangelical movement in the years ahead. Unless mainstream evangelicalism finds ways to meet the needs of young people desiring some tie with the historic faith and with more formal worship, more of them will leave for denominations that offer real alternatives to popular experience-centered worship.[2]

Erickson's reference to Peter Gillquist describes the former Campus Crusade for Christ leader who led approximately 1,700 followers into the Antiochian Orthodox Church in 1987.[3] The remaining 500 of his followers broke ranks with the group and remained a separate denomination called "The Evangelical Orthodox Church." A few years later, Franky Schaeffer, son of the late Francis Schaeffer, joined the Greek Orthodox

1. Telephone conversation with Peter Gillquist, chairman of the Department of Missions and Evangelism, Antiochian Orthodox Archdiocese of North America, July 1999.

2. Millard Erickson, *Where Is Theology Going?* (Grand Rapids: Baker, 1994), 41–42.

3. "Evangelical Denomination Gains Official Acceptance into the Orthodox Church," *Christianity Today* (Feb. 6, 1987): 40.

Church. Though Gillquist and Schaeffer are quite serious in their call for discipleship,[4] by their own admission neither possesses a substantial theological education, as reflected in their educational histories and often oversimplified interpretations of church history and theology. It is also worth noting that in the United Kingdom, Michael Harper recently converted to Orthodoxy in response to the doctrinal erosion of the Anglican Church.[5]

Alongside these popular trends, there are a variety of professional forums through which evangelicals and Orthodox have begun to engage each other over the past decade. Most are aimed at establishing friendly relations with each other while only a few have engaged in substantive discussions of theology. In the following paragraphs I will attempt to document and assess the work of academic societies and mission organizations, individual scholars, and seminaries and universities. In so doing I am certain that I will leave out important people and projects due to the weaknesses of my own limitations. What follows is my best effort to locate all the major players, insofar as I am able to see them.

Academic Societies and Mission Organizations

Over the past thirteen years, there have been three leading organizations that have been working on Orthodox-evangelical dialogue from different angles. There are no formal relations between the organizations since each was formed with its own purpose independently from the others. At times, however, each *de facto* complements or overlaps the work of the others. As a primary focus the first organization deals with theological subjects, the second with church life, and the third with attitudes and practical relationships between the two groups. In addition to these orga-

---

4. See Peter Gillquist, *Becoming Orthodox: A Journey to the Ancient Christian Faith* (Brentwood, Tenn.: Wolgemuth & Hyatt, 1989); Frank Schaeffer, *Dancing Alone: The Quest for Orthodox Faith in the Age of False Religions* (Brookline, Mass.: Holy Cross Orthodox Press, 1994). However, Father Eusebius Stephanou, a reform-minded cradle Orthodox who has promoted evangelical renewal long before Gillquist entered the church, has criticized Gillquist and Schaeffer for preaching Orthodoxy rather than Christ, viewing "everything in the Orthodox Church through rose-colored glasses" ("Converts to Orthodoxy: A Grave Concern," *The Logos* 25 [November/December, 1992]: 1–2, 4). A historical evaluation of Gillquist and his followers' move into the Antiochian Orthodox Church in 1987 has been done by Timothy Weber ("Looking for Home: Evangelical Orthodoxy and the Search for the Original Church," in Bradley Nassif, ed., *New Perspectives on Historical Theology: Essays in Memory of John Meyendorff* [Grand Rapids: Eerdmans, 1996], 95–121). Gillquist's criticism of the way the Greek Archdiocese handled his group's trip to Constantinople (Weber, 113) should be balanced by the oral history of Fr. Gregory Wingenbach, a priest of the Greek Archdiocese who oversaw their visit.

5. Michael Harper and Peter Gillquist, eds., *A Faith Fulfilled: Why Are Christians across Great Britain Embracing Orthodoxy?* (Ben Lomond, Calif.: Conciliar Press, 1998).

nizations, I will also comment on situational dialogues that have been created for only a limited duration and purpose, as well as the work in Romania, where the second largest population of Orthodox reside.

The most serious and sustained effort to understand the areas of theological convergence and divergence between the Orthodox and evangelical traditions that is being undertaken today comes from the *Society for
the Study of Eastern Orthodoxy and Evangelicalism* (SSEOE). This is a
learned group that was founded in the United States in 1990 by the
present author along with six other Orthodox and evangelical scholars
(James Stamoolis, Fr. George Liacopoulos, Andrea Sterk, Barbara Nassif,
and Dale Allison). All had personal experience and academic training in
both traditions in varying degrees. Through its annual meetings and
unpublished papers,[6] the SSEOE seeks to make the two traditions known
and understood in relation to each other's history, doctrine, worship, and
spirituality. It thus serves both the academy and the church. Until 1999,
the organization met annually at the Billy Graham Center on the campus
of Wheaton College and now meets in different regions of the United
States. Past themes of the annual meetings have been: "Proselytism or
Conversion? An Orthodox and Evangelical Exchange" (1991), "Scrip-
ture, Tradition and Authority" (1992), "Salvation by Grace" (1993), "The
Kingdom of God and the Role of the Church in Salvation" (1994), "The
Role of Theology in the Spiritual Life" (1995), and "'Outside the Church
There Is No Salvation': An Orthodox and Evangelical Exchange" (1999).
Keynote speakers from North America have included, among others,
Orthodox theologians Stanley Harakas, Leonid Kishkovsky, Theodore
Stylianopoulos, Emmanuel Clapsis, George Liacopoulos, Michael Proku-
rat, and Edward Rommen; evangelical theologians have been J. I. Packer,
Thomas Oden, Gerald Bray, Donald Bloesch, Grant Osborne, James Stamoolis, Kent Hill, Thomas Finger, Harold O. J. Brown, Craig Blaising,
and Dale Allison. The format consists of a single annual theme that is
addressed by two keynote speakers from each side, followed by audience
participation and a summary of the conclusions that have been reached at
the end of the conference. The purpose of the SSEOE is not to convert
people from one side to the other, though most members would view theological conversion as a legitimate consequence of the dialogue. Its main
purpose is to enrich participants by removing false barriers that have
divided them while also identifying continuing differences. In the words
of the constitution, the SSEOE seeks "to promote fellowship and mutual
enrichment among scholars engaged in these activities, and to coordinate

6. Fr. Edward Rommen has recently put together a website for learning more about the
SSEOE.

the work of such theologians in North America and abroad." Membership includes a wide cross section of evangelical denominations and Orthodox jurisdictions. Institutions represented by students and faculty include Trinity Evangelical Divinity School (Illinois), Wheaton College, Eastern Nazarene College, Eastern Mennonite Seminary, Southern Baptist Seminary (Kentucky), Dallas Seminary, Fuller Seminary, St. Vladimir's Orthodox Seminary, Holy Cross Greek Orthodox Seminary, and others. Evangelical and Orthodox endorsements of the SSEOE have been conferred by Kenneth Kantzer, J. I. Packer, Ward Gasque, Kent Hill, Bill Bright, Bishop Timothy (Kallistos) Ware, Father Stanley Harakas, the late Father John Meyendorff, and Metropolitan Philip Saliba of the Antiochian Orthodox Church of North America.[7]

The second organization that is dedicated to Orthodox-evangelical dialogue is *Evangelicals for Middle East Understanding* (EMEU) based at North Park University in Chicago, Illinois. According to its mission statement, "Evangelicals for Middle East Understanding is an informal fellowship of North American Evangelical Christians committed to dialogue which seeks mutual understanding, respect and friendship between Middle Eastern and Western Christians."[8] Much of their work seeks to raise the level of consciousness among evangelicals of North America and to foster a sense of solidarity with Arab Christians of the Middle East. The churches that are involved in EMEU include Presbyterians and other Protestants in their relations with the Orthodox and Oriental Orthodox Churches of Egypt, Lebanon, Syria, Palestine, Jordan, Iraq, Southern Sudan, and neighboring Arab countries. By organizing educational travels for American evangelicals to the Middle East, and hosting consultations in the Middle East and North America, EMEU is forging a vital link between East and West. Unlike the SSEOE, which centers primarily on theological issues, EMEU focuses on the practical, pastoral, and regional realities of the Orthodox churches in Islamic lands. The SSEOE and EMEU nevertheless complement each other's ministries by exploring both the doctrinal and practical realities of contemporary church life.

The third organization is the *World Council of Churches* (WCC). It is widely known that the WCC has been in existence since the turn of the century, but only since 1993 has it made a concerted effort to create a

7. For media accounts of the SSEOE, see "Peering Over the Orthodox-Evangelical Crevasse," *Christianity Today* (Oct. 9, 1992); "Scholars Hope for Thaw in Evangelical-Orthodox Relations," *Christianity Today* (Oct. 25, 1993); "A True Meaning of Church Service," *Chicago Tribune* (Oct. 1, 1993); "Orthodox and Evangelical Scholars Meet," *The Word* (Antiochian Archdiocese) (February 1995); "Orthodox, Evangelical Scholars Meet," *The Orthodox Observer* 60 (April 1995).

8. *EMEU Journal* 6 (Spring 1999): 1.

series of dialogues between the Eastern Orthodox and evangelical communities. There were two historic events that prompted this new ecumenical venue by the WCC. First, in 1991 at the WCC's Canberra Assembly, heretical trinitarian prayers were offered during one of the plenary sessions in which a pagan female "spirit-goddess" was evoked rather than the Holy Spirit of the Triune God. Similar syncretistic religious expressions occurred during the Assembly, and this caused the Orthodox to voice their objections. Evangelical "observers" responded similarly, which, in turn, prompted the Orthodox and evangelicals to take notice of each other for a potential defensive alliance. Two years later a small handful of evangelical leaders and church representatives from the Ecumenical patriarchate (i.e., the Orthodox Church of Constantinople) convened in Stuttgart, Germany to discuss the possibility of holding a joint conference. The impetus for an Orthodox-evangelical dialogue included the mutual reactionary discovery of each other in the Canberra Assembly of the WCC, but also the recent fall of communism and the ensuing flood of Western missionaries to the formerly Orthodox lands of Russia and Eastern Europe. Tensions and hostilities had been rapidly rising in those parts of the world between Orthodox nationalists and Protestant missionaries, who had operated on the assumption that there were few true believers in those lands and thus set as part of their missionary task the conversion of Orthodox Christians. After Stuttgart, discussions and contacts continued, especially within the framework of the Central Committee of the WCC. Eventually, the WCC sponsored two international Orthodox-evangelical dialogues. The first was hosted by the Coptic Orthodox Church in Alexandria, Egypt from July 10–15, 1995, where forty participants gathered from around the globe. Its proceedings were published in the book *Proclaiming Christ Today*.[9] The second dialogue was convened at the Missionsakademie an der Universitat Hamburg, Germany, March 30–April 4, 1998 with proceedings published in the book *Turn to God, Rejoice in Hope! Orthodox-Evangelical Consultation*.[10] The international composition of the meeting included representatives from Greece, Syria, Lebanon, Egypt, Romania, Russia, Bulgaria, Albania, Sweden, United Kingdom, United States, and other countries. Neither of the consultations, however, engaged in what could be described as "substantial theological dialogues." Instead, they would more accurately be characterized as "relational meetings" that were primarily designed to break the ice and foster goodwill between the two communities.

9. Huibert van Beek and George Lemopoulos, eds., *Proclaiming Christ Today* (Geneva: WCC, 1997).

10. Huibert van Beek and George Lemopoulos, eds., *Turn to God, Rejoice in Hope! Orthodox-Evangelical Consultation, Hamburg, Germany, 1998* (Geneva: WCC, 1998).

In addition to these efforts by organizations, other attempts at dialogue have been more occasional in nature. In the United Kingdom, dialogue between evangelicals and Orthodox is currently being carried out by a study group under the aegis of ACUTE, the theological commission of the UK Evangelical Alliance (with input from other evangelical bodies). ACUTE sponsors a number of such groups dealing with pertinent theological issues. The study group on Orthodoxy sought to elucidate the extent of shared convictions and differences, with special reference to the concerns of evangelical and Orthodox constituencies in the United Kingdom. The group met during 1999–2000 for discussion of papers dealing with matters of doctrine and spirituality, which were recently collected and edited as a published report titled, *Evangelicalism and the Orthodox Church* (Cumbria: ACUTE, an imprint of Paternoster Publishing, 2001). This report should serve as a stimulus to further contact between evangelicals and Orthodox in the United Kingdom and elsewhere. The group's aim is to introduce evangelicals and Orthodox to each other and to clear away some of the misunderstanding and lack of awareness of one another's beliefs and practices. While they are aware that fundamental disagreements between each other will remain, they are convinced that the two constituencies have much to learn from each other.[11]

Elsewhere in the world, a conference in Prague on "Baptists and Orthodoxy" took place August 2–8, 2002. It was sponsored by the International Baptist Theological Seminary, a postgraduate institution under the wing of the European Baptist Fellowship. It brought together Baptists from several European countries and one lone Orthodox (though they tried to get many more, they were unable to attend). Also, the Church Mission Society (CMS), the main missionary arm of the Church of England, was involved in a conference that took place in Moscow at the invitation of Metropolitan Kyril April 24–30, 2001. It was one of a series arranged by CMS with partner churches around the world with representatives from twelve Orthodox churches (Chalcedonian and non-Chalcedonian) from Europe, the Middle East, and India. The papers were published by CMS and are available in Russian and English.[12] The patriarch's foreword indicates that, for the Russians, a major concern was the issue of proselytism.

---

11. Members of the group are Drs. Tim Grass (Baptist and convenor of the group), John Brigs (Baptist), David Wright (Church of Scotland), Kevin Ellis (Anglican), David Hilborn (United Reformed Church), Fr. John Jillions (Russian Orthodox), Mr. Nigel Pocock (Ichthus, a U.K. "House Church" movement), Dr. Nick Needham (Baptist), and Professor Andrew Walker (Russian Orthodox). For more information contact Tim Grass at grass@tesco.net. I am grateful to him for the updated information I obtained on the most recent developments in the U.K.

12. For more information contact info@cms-uk.org.

A repeated concern such as this from the Moscow patriarchate causes us to wonder whether the Russians see dialogue more as a means of dealing with proselytism than genuine dialogue. It is also worth noting that Eastern and Western participants in dialogue (even from the same tradition) often have quite different concerns.

In 1999 in the United States, the American Academy of Religion (AAR) held its first joint session between the *Eastern Orthodox Theology Group* (EOTG) and the *Evangelical Theology Group* (ETG). Serving as the cochair of the EOTG with Anna Williams of Cambridge University, I proposed in 1998 that such a dialogue take place within the AAR at the next annual meeting. Dr. Williams and the Steering Committee of the EOTG accepted the proposal and extended an invitation to the ETG, which enthusiastically accepted. The joint session was titled, "Eastern Orthodoxy and Evangelicalism in Dialogue." The topics for discussion centered on charismatic and Orthodox understandings of the spirit of tradition, evangelical and Orthodox worship, and the sacramental notion of "participation" in Karl Barth and St. Gregory Palamas. A sizeable turnout of one hundred scholars attended the session. Students and professors from Duke Divinity School and Loyola University of Chicago presented papers, followed by a response from Professor Robert Jensen of Princeton University. The very existence of such a session in the halls of the AAR demonstrates the growing relevance of Orthodox-evangelical studies in North America and abroad and adds further testimony to the fact that the subject has now grown to the point of being affirmed by religion scholars as a legitimate object of academic inquiry.

The country of Romania deserves special attention in this article given its religious history and strategic place among the Orthodox churches.[13] Romania contains the largest population of Orthodox Christians in the world today second only to Russia. Although historic difficulties remain in the areas of communication and religious freedom between Orthodox and evangelical believers in Romania, small steps of progress are slowly being made in the wake of the post-communist era. The country holds much promise for constructive relations. At present, however, the "dialogue" in Romania remains weak and indirect, consisting mostly of a growing awareness of the need to explore the points of contact between each other. Academically speaking, there are more evangelical students of Romanian Orthodoxy than there are Orthodox students of Romanian

13. Russia would also certainly qualify for special treatment, but there is little information readily available to report at this time beyond the remarks later made in this report. Readers of this chapter are invited to send me such information at blnassif@yahoo.com. The Keston Institute in the U.K. offers the most up-to-date reports on religion in Russia, as does the East/West Institute at Samford University in Alabama.

evangelicalism. Some of the leading proponents on the evangelical side of the Romanian dialogue include Silviu Eugen Rogobete, who heads the *Areopagus Centre for Christian Studies and Contemporary Culture* located in Timisoara. Part of the centre's mission is to build bridges with the local Romanian Orthodox Church through cultural and religious dialogue. The centre is housed in a relatively small building with a library, classroom, and office space.[14] Other evangelical leaders who are attempting dialogue include Paul Negrut (principal of Emanuel Bible Institute in Oradea), Emil Bartos (the dean), and Danut Manastireanu (World Vision; Dr. Manastireanu has had a formative influence on opening doors with the Orthodox for World Vision over the past four years though there is much work yet to be done). On the Orthodox side are Fr. Ion Bria (now retired but an active participant in the WCC's Orthodox-evangelical dialogues), Vasile Mihoc (professor of New Testament at Sibi University and director of World Vision Romania), and Stelian Tofana (professor of New Testament at Cluj University). A truly exciting theological renaissance of theses and doctoral dissertations on Orthodox theology is now underway among Romanian evangelical students of the Orthodox church. The writings of the great Romanian Orthodox theologian, Fr. Dumitru Staniloae, have become a special object of evangelical interest due to Staniloae's popularity and enduring influence in Romania and abroad. Beyond Staniloae, wider evangelical interests have begun to explore Orthodox approaches to Scripture, authority, and soteriology.[15] Although evangelicals are in a distinct minority in Romania, the new and creative interest in Orthodoxy that is on the rise among the younger generation of scholars—coupled with the changing attitudes toward evangelical theology by a small group of Orthodox leaders—makes Romania the most fertile soil in Eastern Europe for the growth of an emerging global dialogue. What it

14. E-mail areopag@mail.dnttm.ro for further information.

15. A nearly exhaustive list of recent theses and dissertations is as follows: Paul Negrut, "The Development of the Concept of 'Authority' Within the Romanian Orthodox Church in the Twentieth Century" (Ph.D. diss., London Bible College/Brunel University, 1994), parts of which were recently published as *Revelation, Scripture, Communion: An Investigation of 'Authority' in Theological Knowledge* (Oradea, 1996); Silviu Eugen Rogobete, "Subject and Supreme Personal Reality in the Theological Thought of Fr. Dumitru Staniloae: An Ontology of Love" (Ph.D. diss., London Bible College/Brunel University, 1998); Emil Bartos, "The Concept of Deification in Eastern Orthodox Theology with Detailed Reference to Dumitru Staniloae" (Ph.D. diss., University of Wales, 1997), revised as *The Concept of 'Theosis' in the Theology of Dumitru Staniloae* (Oradea, 1999); Gheorghe Verzea, "Salvation in the Church in the Theology of Dumitru Staniloae" (Ph.D. diss., Queen's University, 1996); and Danut Manastireanu, "The Place of Scripture in the Orthodox Tradition" (M.A. thesis, London Bible College/Brunel University, 1994). Credit belongs to Mr. Danut Manastireanu for most of the information provided in this footnote and the above paragraph.

needs to succeed and flourish is for the Orthodox to initiate a stronger public stance in reaching out to evangelical institutions and churches at all levels—from the ecumenical department of the Romanian patriarchate down to the grassroots levels of local Orthodox priests and laypeople. These initiatives may include setting up special ecumenical dialogue commissions, creating faculty exchanges in which Orthodox and evangelical history and theology may be taught in each other's schools, the creation of theological journals in which both sides can participate in a shared forum, and personal visits to each other's local churches in an atmosphere of Christian love. Clearly the Orthodox are in a stronger position of influence than are evangelicals, and therefore they bear the heavier weight of responsibility for achieving Christian unity in Romania. Nothing less than courageous initiatives by Orthodox leaders, lay and ordained, can break the decades of hatred, fear, and ignorance toward evangelical Christianity, which continue to dominate the perceptions of the Romanian Orthodox peoples. Similarly, nothing less than bold initiatives by evangelical leaders, lay and ordained, that may risk offending their Protestant constituency will be able to move evangelicals beyond their doctrinal misconceptions of Orthodoxy and the offensive behavior tied to popular abuses of the Orthodox faith by the Orthodox themselves.

Scholars

There is a small but growing number of individual scholars who are slowly beginning to publish works on Orthodox and evangelical theology. It appears that there is more activity on the side of evangelical interest in Orthodoxy rather than vice versa.[16] A surprising number of evangelical converts to Orthodoxy in America over the past fifteen years has caught the evangelical community off guard and recently prompted a few well-known conservative writers to respond to the growing losses within their ranks. Representatives of this group would be R. C. Sproul,[17] a theologian at Reformed Theological Seminary in Florida, and Hank Hanegraaff,[18]

16. An exception can be found in the popular apologetic books and tracts against evangelicals written by Orthodox priests and lay workers in America. Peter Gillquist and Frank Schaeffer would fall into this category. Much less apologetic literature has been published by evangelicals against Orthodoxy, with the exception of older mission agencies such as Spiros Zodhiates' former "American Mission to the Greeks."

17. R. C. Sproul's Ligonier Ministry magazine, *Tabletalk* (June 1999), with several articles devoted to attacking the "heretical" teachings and practices of the Eastern Orthodox Church.

18. Hanegraaff's Christian Research Institute journal, *Christian Research Journal*, published Paul Negrut, "Searching for the True Apostolic Church: What Evangelicals Should Know about Eastern Orthodoxy," *Christian Research Journal* 20 (Jan.–March, 1998).

also known as "The Bible Answer Man," a popular radio apologist and cult-watcher who succeeded the late Walter Martin.

Beyond these reactions from the evangelical right, more informed and balanced evangelical theologians are aggressively widening their perspectives on Orthodoxy through a study of ancient and modern writers of the Christian East. Their motivation appears to be rooted in a healthy self-awareness of the deficiencies and gaps that are currently present in modern theology and the laudable desire for growth. Some proceed in their studies with an awareness that patristic and Byzantine theology are not only foundational to historic Christianity in both East and West, but also are especially formative to the contemporary identity of the Eastern Orthodox Church. A brief survey of selected scholars and their works will show the direction in which evangelicals are charting their studies of the Christian East.

Gerald Bray, a British evangelical now working in America, is one of the most knowledgeable and linguistically competent researchers in Eastern Orthodoxy today. The breadth of his linguistic skills puts Bray at the forefront of evangelical scholarship. He is fluent not only in the biblical languages of Hebrew and Greek, but also in Latin, Byzantine Greek, modern Greek, and Russian. A specialist in historical theology and Anglican canon law, Bray teaches courses (among many others) in Greek and Latin patristics and has written on theological topics that are central to Orthodoxy in the ancient and modern worlds. A selection of his writings include "Eastern Orthodox Theology,"[19] "Justification and the Eastern Orthodox Churches,"[20] "The *Filioque* Clause in History and Theology"[21] and the books *The Doctrine of God*[22] (which deals extensively with Orthodoxy as well as early Christian thought), *Biblical Interpretation: Past and Present*,[23] and his patristic commentaries in the *Ancient Christian Commentary on Scripture*[24] (Romans, 1, 2 Corinthians, and James to Jude, to be discussed below under the work of Thomas Oden). Bray characterizes his stance toward Orthodoxy as follows:

19. Gerald Bray, "Eastern Orthodox Theology," in Sinclair B. Ferguson, David F. Wright, J. I. Packer, eds., *New Dictionary of Theology* (Downers Grove, Ill.: Inter-Varsity, 1998), 215–18.

20. Gerald Bray, "Justification and the Eastern Orthodox Churches," in J. I. Packer, ed., *Here We Stand* (Downers Grove, Ill.: Inter-Varsity, 1993), 83ff.

21. Gerald Bray, "The *Filioque* Clause in History and Theology," *Tyndale Bulletin* 34 (1983): 91–144.

22. Gerald Bray, *The Doctrine of God* (Downers Grove, Ill.: Inter-Varsity, 1993).

23. Gerald Bray, *Biblical Interpretation: Past and Present* (Downers Grove, Ill.: Inter-Varsity, 1998).

24. Gerald Bray, ed., *Romans* (Downers Grove, Ill.: Inter-Varsity, 1998); idem, ed., *1–2 Corinthians* (Downers Grove, Ill.: Inter-Varsity, 1999); idem, ed., *James, 1–2 Peter, 1–3 John, Jude* (Downers Grove, Ill.: Inter-Varsity, 2000).

My stance vis-à-vis Orthodoxy is sympathetic but not uncritical. I do not share the fascination with Orthodoxy which characterizes some people in the West (after living in both Greece and Russia it is hard to romanticize the Orthodox Church) but I am very sympathetic to the underlying theological concerns of Orthodoxy and believe that there is a lot of common ground with Evangelical Protestants (and others, of course) which we need to explore. I suppose you could say that I am in the C. S. Lewis tradition of 'mere Christianity'—looking for what unites us across the cultural and historical differences, and concentrating on that.[25]

What sets Bray apart from other evangelicals in the "C. S. Lewis tradition," however, is his concentration on the Orthodox faith as vitally central to that tradition. While others, such as Lewis and G. K. Chesterton, have explored "orthodoxy" through the Fathers, creeds, and councils of "historic Christianity," Bray has linked much of that "historic Christianity" to the ongoing institutional and spiritual life of the Orthodox Church. In this way, Bray does not deal with a *disembodied* orthodoxy but an orthodoxy that has largely been the achievement of the *Byzantine Orthodox Church* and the theological legacy it has bequeathed for much of Protestant and Catholic orthodoxy today.

Donald Fairbairn's recent book titled, *Eastern Orthodoxy through Western Eyes*[26] deserves special notation. Dr. Fairbairn served as a Baptist missionary who worked in Russia and Eastern Europe during the early 1990s. He is also a patristics scholar with a Ph.D. from Cambridge University, where he centered on the Christology of St. Cyril of Alexandria. He has written several important essays on missionary work among the Orthodox and the place of evangelicalism in that context.[27] Of all the books and articles I have read on Orthodoxy and the West, none surpasses *Eastern Orthodoxy through Western Eyes*. It is balanced, judicious, and extremely well informed on the fine points of patristic theology as well as on the practical, grassroots level of Russian Orthodox life and thought. (Readers should note that there are regional differences between Orthodox churches. The Orthodox in Russia and Eastern Europe are often more rigid than Orthodox in the Middle East and America, where attitudes are generally more open and flexible.) I believe it should be required reading not only for missionaries preparing for evangelistic work in Orthodox countries, but also in theology classes in Orthodox and evangelical seminaries. His critiques and affirmations of the Orthodox Church will help Orthodox and evangelicals to better understand the genuine areas of com-

25. E-mail from Gerald Bray to the author, July 23, 1999.
26. Donald Fairbairn, *Eastern Orthodoxy through Western Eyes* (Louisville: Westminster John Knox Press, 2002).
27. Ibid., 199 for a complete list of references.

mon agreement and disagreement. The Orthodox especially need to hear what Fairbairn has said about us because he helps keep our eyes on what is truly central to Orthodox identity. He shows us how our own faith is deeply evangelical at heart and thus largely compatible with the core of Protestant evangelical identity, if properly defined. In only a few theological topics would I have interpreted them differently than Fairbairn. The book is, by definition, provincial since it is limited to the Russian and Eastern European contexts. The Arab Orthodox communities of the Middle East are quite understudied and are noticeably different than the Russian Orthodox Church. So some of his conclusions are not applicable to the pan-Orthodox community. For instance, his treatment of "The Orthodox Vision and Its Distortions" contains excellent material coming from Russian folk religion. Some of the religious distortions do, of course, apply to other Orthodox communities, but readers must be careful not to transpose the Russian experience on all Orthodox churches. Nevertheless, the book is absolutely first-class reading for anyone interested in the relationship between Orthodox and evangelical theology. In fact, Orthodox readers should read it if for no other reason than to have a better understanding of their own faith and the dangers of doctrinal distortions that have resulted from the influence of popular folk religion.

Another important scholar working between the traditions is Thomas Oden. According to Oden,

> In *Agenda for Theology* (1979) I proposed a program of post-modern paleo-orthodoxy which would seek to reground contemporary theology in the consensual classic Christian sources. Everything I have done since has sought to develop that premise. The three volumes of *Systematic Theology*, of course, have constant reference to patristic sources, as do *Pastoral Theology* and the four volume work on *Classical Pastoral Care*.[28]

Oden utilizes a theological method that proceeds from the conviction that the consensus of the church fathers during the first millennium of Christian history constitutes a normative status for defining Christian orthodoxy. This doctrinal history includes the decisions of the ecumenical councils (A.D. 325–787), the *consensus patrum*, the church's *lex orandi*, pastoral theology, and other expressions of "catholic" Christianity. In addition to the works cited above, a recent project that reveals Oden's premise most decisively is his editorial work on a new twenty-seven-volume collection of patristic commentaries on the entire Bible. Titled the *Ancient Christian Commentary on Scripture*, this series is the first modern patristic commentary of its kind from the pen of a leading evangelical theologian and leading

28. E-mail from Thomas Oden to the author, July 21, 1999.

evangelical publishing house (Inter-Varsity Press). Oden describes the nature and purpose of the project in the "General Introduction."

> The Ancient Christian Commentary on Scripture has as its goal the revitalization of Christian teaching based on classical Christian exegesis . . . This series provides the pastor, exegete, student and lay reader with convenient means to see what Athanasius or John Chrysostom or the desert fathers and mothers had to say about a particular text for preaching, for study and for meditation. There is an emerging awareness among Catholic, Protestant and Orthodox laity that vital biblical preaching and spiritual formation need deeper grounding beyond the scope of the historical-critical orientations that have governed biblical studies in our day. Hence this work is directed toward a much broader audience than the highly technical and specialized scholarly field of patristic studies.[29]

Clearly this is an intentionally ecumenical project whose team of volume editors originates from Catholic, Protestant, and Orthodox scholars and who, under Oden, designed the project to edify those audiences. The fact that the series is not being manufactured and sold by a Roman Catholic or Orthodox publishing house, but by Inter-Varsity Press, shows how remarkable a renaissance of patristic studies is now underway among evangelicals the world over. The impact that this series will very likely have on future Orthodox and evangelical dialogue is potentially enormous. Since the church fathers played a formative role in shaping the identity of the Eastern Orthodox Church, the series will naturally encourage readers to think beyond the ancient Christian commentators themselves to the church that has most deeply appropriated those sources. Inevitably, it will prompt evangelicals to explore in much greater depth the christological, trinitarian, ecclesiological, and sacramental themes of the early church fathers and that of the Orthodox church, the Fathers' heir apparent. This does not mean that the Fathers gave us a single authoritative interpretation of every verse of the Bible. As the series makes evident, there are varied patristic interpretations on any given text of Scripture. Oden is under no illusion of concocting a uniform exegetical tradition by all the Fathers on any given text of Scripture. He recognizes that there are many varieties of interpretations within almost every pericope. Yet it is also evident that there are central exegetical motifs that correspond to the great themes of Eastern Orthodox theology. By letting the Fathers speak for themselves, the ACCS series reflects the Fathers' wide differences in cultural expression and theological creativity while at the same time yielding a remarkable consensus on central themes of divine revelation. Such a discovery can only lead evangelicals into a deeper appreciation of

---

29. Bray, *Romans*.

Orthodoxy while at the same time accentuating its similarities and differences with the Catholic and Protestant traditions.

By virtually all accounts, J. I. Packer is one of this century's greatest evangelical statesmen. As he reaches the golden years of his career, we notice that he has begun to take a serious interest in conservative Christian dialogue with the hopes of forming a common agenda for the church's unified witness in the modern world. His work in "evangelical ecumenics" (to coin a phrase) began most visibly in his dialogue with Catholics in 1995, which led to his signing the document "Evangelicals and Catholics Together." Although his interest in Orthodoxy began much earlier, it was not until 1995 that it took concrete expression at a conservative ecumenical gathering of Catholics, Orthodox, and evangelicals called the "Rose Hill" conference. It was there that Dr. Packer and the present author worked as formal dialogue partners. At Rose Hill, Packer delivered a paper titled, "On from Orr: Cultural Crisis, Rational Realism and Incarnational Ontology," to which I responded with "An Eastern Orthodox Response to J. I. Packer."[30] The dialogue was followed up in 1997 when Packer and the author team-taught a course at Regent College titled, "Eastern Orthodoxy and Evangelicalism in Dialogue."[31] This dialogical course was a historic first of its kind among evangelical seminaries in North America. Given Packer's distinguished stature and the constructive theological purpose of the course, the class proved that such a dialogue between Orthodox and evangelicals was not only possible, but that it could actually achieve a common witness without requiring either to compromise the doctrinal integrity of their positions. Then in September 1999 Dr. Packer advanced the Orthodox-evangelical dialogue in America by being the featured evangelical speaker at the annual meeting of the Society for the Study of Eastern Orthodoxy and Evangelicalism.[32] The theme for the conference was, "'Outside the Church There Is No Salvation': An Orthodox and Evangelical Exchange." The conference turned out to be the largest gathering of Orthodox and evangelical Christians to date with approximately two hundred people in attendance.

In addition to Bray, Oden, and Packer, the work of other scholars should also be mentioned, if ever so briefly. They come from Calvinist,

---

30. James Cutsinger, ed., *Reclaiming the Great Tradition: Evangelicals, Catholics and Orthodox in Dialogue* (Downers Grove, Ill.: Inter-Varsity, 1997), 155–84. See also J. I. Packer's "Christian Morality Adrift," delivered to the Faith and Renewal Conference with an Orthodox response by Fr. Stanley Harakas in Kevin Perrota and John Blattner, eds., *A Society in Peril* (Ann Arbor, Mich.: Servant Publications, 1989).

31. Available on audiotape through the Regent College bookstore.

32. Dr. Edward Rommen was the lead Orthodox speaker. Rommen is a former tenured professor in the missions department at Trinity Evangelical Divinity School, Deerfield, Illinois. His conversion to the Orthodox church was reported in *Christianity Today* (Aug. 11, 1998).

Anglican, Anabaptist, Free Church, Nazarene, Mennonite, Wesleyan, Pentecostal, and other denominations. Included in this list would be Miroslav Volf,[33] Grant Osborne,[34] Harold O. J. Brown,[35] Daniel Clendenin,[36] James Stamoolis,[37] Donald Bloesch,[38] Kent Hill,[39] Mark Noll,[40]

33. Volf offers the most penetrating Free Church critique of modern Orthodox and Catholic "communion" ecclesiologies as developed by John Zizioulas and Cardinal Ratzinger respectively (Miroslav Volf, *After Our Likeness: The Church as the Image of the Trinity* [Grand Rapids: Eerdmans, 1998]). Volf is a Croatian Pentecostal formerly at Fuller Seminary and now at Yale. The trajectory of his career and theological interests witness to the growth of evangelical scholarship in the direction of an "ecumenical orthodoxy" that envisions the collegial model of "communion" ecclesiology in Orthodoxy to be more compatible with evangelical theology than the papal model of "communion" ecclesiology in Roman Catholicism.

34. Osborne offers the finest hermeneutical comparison to date in "The Many and the One: The Interface Between Eastern Orthodox and Protestant Evangelical Hermeneutics," *St. Vladimir's Theological Quarterly* 3 (1995): 281–304. The paper was originally delivered to the SSEOE, where Osborne is an active dialogue partner. He is professor of New Testament at Trinity Evangelical Divinity School, Deerfield, Illinois.

35. Brown is one of the few evangelical students who did their doctoral work under the late Orthodox theologian George Florovsky at Princeton. Brown has been an effective interpreter of Florovsky for the evangelical community, though at times he squeezes Florovsky into an uncomfortably tight pair of evangelical shoes, e.g., "On Method and Means in Theology," in John D. Woodbridge and Thomas E. McComiskey, eds., *Doing Theology in Today's World: Essays in Honor of Kenneth S. Kantzer* (Grand Rapids: Zondervan, 1991), 147–69.

36. Clendenin's exposure to Orthodoxy came while living in Moscow for several years as a religion professor at Moscow State University. A widely read two-volume work introducing Orthodoxy to Western readers resulted: *Eastern Orthodox Christianity: A Western Perspective* (Grand Rapids: Baker, 1994); ibid., ed., *Eastern Orthodox Theology: A Contemporary Reader* (Grand Rapids: Baker, 1995). Clendenin's chief contribution is his synthesis of the essential points of Orthodox writers in the secondary literature and focused interpretation of those facts for a Protestant evangelical audience.

37. Stamoolis was one of the founding members of the SSEOE. He is a Baptist with a Greek Orthodox upbringing and formerly the dean of the Wheaton Graduate School. Sympathetic, yet also constructively critical of the Eastern Church, his contribution to the dialogue to date has mainly been in the area of Orthodox missions. See James Stamoolis, *Eastern Orthodox Mission Theology* (Maryknoll, N.Y.: Orbis Books, 1986). For his reflections on why he became an evangelical, see "Reflections on Becoming Evangelical" in the *Occasional Bulletin* of the Evangelical Missiological Society, 11.1 (Spring 1999): 3–4.

38. A participant in the SSEOE, where he delivered a paper titled, "Salvation in Protestant Evangelicalism" (1993), from his monumental series on *Christian Foundations*, vol. 2 (Downers Grove, Ill.: Inter-Varsity, 1997).

39. Kent Hill, *The Soviet Union on the Brink: An Inside Look at Christianity and Glasnost* (Portland, Ore.: Multnomah, 1991). Hill has also been an active participant and supporter of the SSEOE.

40. Although he has not written much in the field, he is a member of the SSEOE, personal friend, and faithful encourager of Orthodox-evangelical dialogue. His use of the late Fr. George Florovsky's views on the task of the Christian historian remains fundamental to his class lectures in the History of Western Civilization course at Wheaton College.

Kenneth Kantzer,[41] Randy Maddox,[42] Thomas Finger,[43] T. F. Torrance,[44] Elaine Storkey,[45] Vinay Samuel,[46] David Dockery,[47] and others[48] whom no doubt I have missed. It would be claiming too much to say that all of these individuals are experts on the Christian East, but each in his or her own way has begun to lead the evangelical community into a more advanced level of academic dialogue than ever before. In fact, Zondervan, a leading evangelical publishing house, has very recently acknowledged the study of Orthodoxy as a lacuna that needs to be filled in evangelical scholarship today. In July 1999 the academic editors commissioned the publication of a new book in their "Counterpoint Series" that will be devoted exclusively

41. Expressed in his involvement with and endorsement of the SSEOE: "Nothing but good could come from serious conversations between Eastern Orthodox thinkers and conservative Evangelicals. This society provides just such a forum."

42. Randy Maddox, *Responsible Grace: John Wesley's Practical Theology* (Nashville: Kingswood Books, 1994). One of Maddox's goals is to find in Wesley an instructive integration of theological emphases that have traditionally separated Eastern and Western Christianity.

43. Thomas Finger, "Anabaptism and Eastern Orthodoxy: Some Unexpected Similarities," *Journal of Ecumenical Studies* (Fall 1995), originally delivered to the SSEOE.

44. Torrance pleads for space in the evangelical establishment of North America, but less so in Europe. Concerns of North American evangelicals have been partly due to his theological epistemology and deemphasizing of propositional revelation. Nevertheless his rare mastery of the language and literature of the Eastern Church (ancient and modern), coupled with his relatively conservative ecumenism from a Calvinist platform, makes it impossible to overlook his contributions. Evangelicals should interact with his proposals more thoroughly than they have to date. Among his writings, too numerous to list, see his recent work on the Reformed-Eastern Orthodox dialogue in *Trinitarian Perspectives: Toward Doctrinal Agreement* (Edinburgh: T & T Clark, 1994).

45. Elaine Storkey, "The WCC Statement on Mission: A Paper for Discussion" in van Beek and Lemopoulos, eds., *Turn to God, Rejoice in Hope!*, 75–79. Storkey has been John Stott's assistant for the Institute for Contemporary Christianity, London.

46. Notable more for his participation in the WCC's Orthodox-evangelical consultation, Hamburg, Germany, 1998 than for his academic writing on the topic. He is executive director for the Oxford Center for Mission Studies.

47. David Dockery, *Biblical Interpretation Then and Now: Contemporary Hermeneutics in the Light of the Early Church* (Grand Rapids: Baker, 1992). It demonstrates the recovery of the ancient exegetical tradition by a Baptist New Testament scholar. The Baptists Glen Hinson and Charles Scalese do similarly in the areas of evangelism, patristic ecclesiology, sacramental theology, and theological hermeneutics.

48. Craig Blaising, "Scripture, Tradition and Authority: A Response to Emmanuel Clapsis," unpublished paper delivered to the SSEOE (1995); Blaising also served as secretary-treasurer of the SSEOE (1995–97); Robert Rakestraw, "Becoming Like God: An Evangelical Doctrine of *Theosis*," *Journal of the Evangelical Theological Society* 2 (1994); Gabriel Fackre, *The Christian Story*, 3d ed., 3 vols. (Grand Rapids: Eerdmans, 1996–). Fackre grew up with a father from a Middle Eastern, Orthodox home. Walter Sawatsky, a Mennonite, has published numerous books and articles on evangelicals in Russia. Cecil Robeck, a Pentecostal, has also worked in Cyprian's ecclesiology in light of contemporary ecumenical Catholic and Orthodox discussions.

to this subject. It is tentatively titled, *Three Views on Eastern Orthodoxy and Evangelicalism*, edited by James Stamoolis (forthcoming).

Theology is not the only field of evangelical scholarship that is engaging the Orthodox church today. Evangelical psychologists are also appropriating insights from the monastic fathers of the Byzantine, Syrian, and Coptic Orthodox Churches. Without minimizing the essential role that theology must play in healing the wounds between Orthodox and evangelical believers, there is also great practical value in enlisting the resources of Orthodox anthropology into the service of Christian psychology. One scholar who has been working specially in this area is Dr. Janice Strength, a professor of family therapy at Fuller Seminary's School of Psychology.[49] She is also the cofounder of a graduate school of Christian psychology in Moscow, whose leadership and student body is overwhelmingly Orthodox. More recently, however, the school's American board has discontinued their relationship with the school in Russia due to some very different values regarding marriage. Nevertheless the school continues under Christian auspices with both Orthodox and Protestant professors teaching there.[50] In a chapter titled "From Conflict to Love: Suggestions for Healing the Christian Family," Strength offers the Orthodox and evangelical communities a very sensitive analysis of the dynamics of human nature and conflict resolution, along with guidelines for Orthodox-evangelical dialogue in Russia from a family therapist's point of view.[51]

When turning to the Orthodox side of the dialogue, we regret to report that with but a few notable exceptions,[52] theologians in Russia and Greece have little or no contact with evangelicals and are even disdainful of them, mainly because of evangelical missions—which are frequently successful in Russia but often unsuccessful in Greece.

Outside of Russia and Greece, Orthodox theologians are working to build bridges with evangelicals at a variety of levels. I am reluctant to speak about myself, but I have been honored to devote a portion of my scholar-

49. She currently serves as assistant to the president, but health problems may require her to resign soon.

50. E-mail from Janice Strength, February 12, 2003.

51. Janice Strength, "From Conflict to Love: Suggestions for Healing the Christian Family," in S. Linzey and K. Kaisch, eds., *God in Russia: The Challenge of Freedom* (Lanham, Md.: University Press of America, 1999).

52. Such as the St. Petersburg Evangelical Theological Academy, which includes Russian Orthodox professors on its faculty (see further under "Seminaries and Universities"). Other exceptions would be Russian Orthodox leaders Frs. Alexander Borisov, the late Alexander Menn, and Metropolitan Kyrill. I know of no such counterparts in Greece, though Archbishop Demetrios Trakatellis would have qualified as a friend of evangelicals in Athens before leaving Greece in 1999 to become the new Archbishop of the Greek Orthodox Archdiocese in North America.

ship to this area as an Orthodox theologian. I have already noted three contributions in the above paragraphs: the SSEOE, the rejoinder chapter "An Eastern Orthodox Response to J. I. Packer," and a team-taught course at Regent College with Dr. Packer on "Eastern Orthodoxy and Evangelicalism in Dialogue." In addition are the following chapters and essays: An introductory guide to the study of Eastern Orthodoxy written especially for evangelical students of theology can be found in my chapter "New Dimensions in Eastern Orthodox Theology."[53] Though intended for a North American audience with little familiarity with European languages, it serves as an introduction to the principal features of Orthodox theology and the methodological pitfalls to avoid when studying it. A suggested missiological strategy for evangelicals who are ministering in Orthodox lands such as Russia and Eastern Europe is outlined in the essay "Evangelical Missions in Eastern Orthodox Lands."[54] Also in the field of missiology, see the brief article on "Orthodox Mission Movements" in the *Evangelical Dictionary of World Missions*, edited by A. Scott Moreau et al. (Baker, 2000). See also "What Orthodox Christians Can Learn from Evangelical Christians" in the *Global Missions Report* (2003) of the East/West Institute of Samford University under Dr. Mark Elliot. In the area of comparative spirituality, the author delivered a public lecture at Regent College on "Eastern Orthodox and Evangelical Spirituality: The Core of a Common Agenda."[55] On the international scene, I was privileged to serve as a featured speaker for the Orthodox-evangelical consultations sponsored by the World Council of Churches in Alexandria, Egypt and Hamburg, Germany,[56] as noted above. I am also preparing a chapter for the forthcoming book *Three Views on Eastern Orthodoxy and Evangelicalism*, edited by James Stamoolis (Zondervan, as noted earlier) and titled "The Evangelical Theology of the Eastern Orthodox Church." There I hope to set forth my past thirty years of theological study and experience in Orthodox and evangelical theology by arguing why I believe they are compatible in key areas yet incompatible in others. These works are supplemented by several graduate courses on Orthodox history, theology, and missions, which I teach in both Orthodox and Protestant evangelical seminaries throughout North America (to be discussed below under "Seminaries").

53. David Dockery, ed., *New Dimensions in Evangelical Thought* (Downers Grove, Ill.: Inter-Varsity, 1998), 92–117.

54. *Trinity World Forum* (Winter, 1996), published by Trinity Evangelical Divinity School, Deerfield, Illinois.

55. Available on audiocassette at the Regent College bookstore.

56. "Eastern Orthodoxy and Evangelicalism in Dialogue," in van Beek and Lemopoulos, eds., *Turn to God, Rejoice in Hope!*, 69–74.

Other Orthodox theologians have contributed occasional papers offering specific direction on the Orthodox church's relationship to evangelical scholarship. Such publications are by no means abundant, but the
scholars themselves and what they are calling for is highly significant due
to their strategic ecclesiastical positions within the Orthodox church.
These theologians are Frs. Stanley Harakas,[57] Theodore Stylianopoulos,[58]
Emmanuel Clapsis,[59] Bishop Timothy (Kallistos) Ware,[60] Archbishop Philip
Saliba,[61] Edward Rommen,[62] Eusebius Stephanou,[63] and a small but growing
number of local Orthodox priests[64] across North America. A sample of
Orthodox endorsements of the SSEOE will indicate the strength of pan-
Orthodox interest in evangelical dialogue:

We are happy to endorse the good work you and your organization are doing
to promote fellowship and mutual enrichment among those engaged in your
activities. We hope that you will be fruitful and multiply in membership so

57. Stanley Harakas, "On Theological Method," unpublished paper delivered to the
SSEOE (1996).
58. Featured speaker on Orthodox spirituality at the SSEOE meeting, Billy Graham
Center, Wheaton College, 1995. See his further comments below.
59. Emmanuel Clapsis, "Scripture, Tradition and Authority: An Eastern Orthodox
View" delivered to the SSEOE, 1995.
60. Unpublished paper on "The Holy Spirit in the Eastern Church Fathers" given at a
Pentecostal-Orthodox dialogue in Prague, 1998.
61. Primate of the Antiochian Orthodox Archdiocese of North America who admitted
members of the Evangelical Orthodox Church into the Antiochian church in 1987.
62. An evangelical convert to Orthodoxy in 1997. See "Reflections on Becoming
Orthodox" in *The Occasional Bulletin* of the Evangelical Missiological Society, 11.1 (Spring
1999): 1–3.
63. Stephanou is a cradle Greek Orthodox with five graduate degrees in theology from
Greece and the United States. He has promoted Orthodox renewal along evangelical lines
for over three decades. Once highly controversial in the Greek Archdiocese—for perceptions of spiritual imbalance along charismatic lines, not dogmatic heresy—he was perse-
cuted by church authorities but never excommunicated. He now enjoys the blessing of the
church heirarchy on his organization, "The Brotherhood of St. Symeon the New Theologian." The brotherhood is a spiritual renewal group that holds quarterly renewal conferences at its headquarters in Destin, Florida and publishes a bimonthly periodical, *The
Orthodox Evangelist* (formerly *The Logos*). Much of his current work is devoted to Orthodox
evangelism and physical and emotional healing of individuals and families. He has also
been instrumental in promoting the ministry of a dynamic young Orthodox evangelist,
Charles Omuroka, from Kenya, East Africa.
64. The local Orthodox parishes have been the least affected by the dialogue. As so
often happens in ecumenical discussions, the conclusions reached often get stuck at the top
and seldom filter down to practical church life. A notable exception, however, can be
found at St. Paul's Greek Orthodox Church, Irvine, California. The pastor, Fr. Steve
Tschilis, hosted the annual SSEOE meeting at the church in September 1999, where Drs.
J. I. Packer and Edward Rommen spoke to a record audience. Fr. Steve is a solid cradle
Orthodox man who is also open to constructive dialogue with evangelicals in the Southern

that the message of Jesus Christ according to the biblical and apostolic teachings will be known to all.—Archbishop Philip Saliba, primate of the Antiochian Archdiocese of North America

The SSEOE is fulfilling a vital role. . . . How much we have to gain from listening to each other! May Jesus Christ, our common Lord and Saviour, bless your work.—Bishop Timothy (Kallistos) Ware, Oxford University

In the post-Soviet world, with the opening of traditionally Orthodox nations to the potential for open proselytism, Evangelical and Orthodox relations can go in one of two directions: either return to the dangers of a pre-ecumenical era, or change the course of history. The SSEOE has already begun addressing this important theological and practical missiological question. Much good can come of such a scholarly dialogue.—Fr. Stanley Harakas, professor of theology and ethics, emeritus, Holy Cross Greek Orthodox Seminary

Of special importance are the remarks by Fr. Theodore Stylianopoulos, a seasoned professor of New Testament at Holy Cross Greek Orthodox Seminary (Brookline, Massachusetts). As Stylianopoulos has matured over the years, he has become openly bold and forthright in his desire to interface with evangelical scholarship in the area of theology and biblical studies. Apparently this has been the result of years of interaction with evangelicals in the Boston area, including cooperative work with Gordon-Conwell Theological Seminary (an evangelical consortium school of Holy Cross), visits to Gordon McDonald's church in the Boston area, active participation in the Society for the Study of Eastern Orthodoxy and Evangelicalism, and similar Orthodox-evangelical contacts. He states,

Many Evangelical scholars such as Donald G. Bloesch, Gordon D. Fee, and James I. Packer, appear to have the closest affinities to Orthodox scholars, at least pertaining to Scripture. These and other Evangelicals form a kind of 'golden mean' between fundamentalism and liberal Protestantism, working out their own kind of 'neo-patristic synthesis' within the diverse world of Protestantism. To be sure, such Evangelicals need to rethink the 'ecclesial principle' as expressed by the Orthodox tradition, and some are doing so.

California area. The church is a model pan-Orthodox parish with an outstanding Sunday school program headed by Eve Tibbs, an Orthodox graduate student at Fuller Seminary, and consisting of a curriculum of Bible training, Orthodox history, liturgy, and spirituality. There are other Orthodox graduate students from evangelical seminaries that have not been mentioned in this article. Notably, Tatiana Glebova, a Russian Orthodox from Moscow who just graduated from Fuller's School of Psychology and is now working with a Russian Orthodox priest to develop a screening process for Russian Orthodox priests, as well as Fr. Martin Ritsi, a graduate from Fuller's School of World Mission, who is now serving as the Director for the Orthodox Christian Mission Center in St. Augustine, Florida.

However, pertaining to the 'scripture principle' . . . these Evangelical scholars . . . appear to be even more 'patristic' than many Orthodox who think of
the patristic heritage as their own inheritance.

Again I would stress that, if the 'ecclesial principle' as well is brought into
play, Orthodox and Evangelical scholars can support each other in substantive terms on the basis of their unanimity on classic Christian doctrine as a
summary of abiding biblical truth. Their theological commitments and contemporary circumstances drive them together to work toward a common
witness and common biblical hermeneutics. . . .

those who affirm the authority of Scripture and seek to live and work with
some balance between faith and reason, will continue to gravitate toward a
consensus that is called either 'evangelical catholicity' or 'catholic evangelicalism' as the enduring Christian option of the third millennium.[65]

These comments by a scholar of Stylianopoulos's stature should not be
glossed over as ecumenical rhetoric. His call for mutual support is clear,
specific, and authoritative. If Stylianopoulos is correct, then Orthodox
and evangelical biblical scholars and churchmen have no other option but
to take this invitation seriously and respond to it with specific and decisive
action. Such action might include creating joint biblical consultations,
exploring faculty exchange programs (which can break down caricatures
and stereotypes), initiating collaborative writing projects in the areas of
ecclesiology, canon formation, tradition, and scriptural hermeneutics, and
other projects.

From the perspective of the big picture, then, if one were to ask
where, geographically, the Orthodox-evangelical dialogue is being most
fruitfully nurtured in the world, the answer would be found in the
United States. This should come as no surprise to readers since North
America is saturated with evangelical Christianity, and it is precisely
because evangelicals enjoy a position of religious dominance in American culture that the American Orthodox have been forced to respond to
its influence. That response has contributed in part to the rise of what
may be termed an "American Orthodox theology." By that I mean that
Orthodox theologians in America have been forced to draw upon the
rich theological resources of their own tradition in order to respond cre-
atively to the challenges of American religion—including American
evangelicalism. Just as there are characteristic theological emphases in
Greece, Romania, Bulgaria, and elsewhere due to the political, histori-

65. Theodore G. Stylianopoulos, *The New Testament: An Orthodox Perspective*, vol. 1
(Brookline, Mass.: Holy Cross Orthodox Press, 1997), 212, 227–28, 232. This last quotation refers not only to Protestant evangelicals but also to Roman Catholics and Orthodox.

cal, geographical, and religious questions that have faced the Orthodox church and required it to address itself to the special challenges of those given contexts, so also have the Orthodox in America begun to slowly offer theological responses that are culturally and theologically relevant to them. But here lies an interesting irony. Whereas in places like Russia and Eastern Europe, the Orthodox church has occupied a position of religious dominance over evangelical churches, in America the evangelical community enjoys the position of dominance over the minority of Orthodox churches. These simple facts bear significantly on the question of why the Orthodox-evangelical dialogue is faring better in the United States than anywhere else in the world. One could offer several explanations to account for it, but perhaps the most significant reason is due to the American tolerance of religious pluralism. In America Christians enjoy the constitutional privilege of "freedom of religion." Orthodox leaders in Russia and Eastern Europe should take note of this fact because it contradicts the cherished assumption that only a legally imposed protection of Orthodoxy can ensure the spiritual health of the Orthodox people. In fact, just the opposite has been true in America. It is precisely because of our religious freedoms that an increasing number of evangelicals want to explore the Orthodox church independently from the cultural imposition of an offending legislation. Put simply, the only Orthodoxy worth joining is the one that has been freely explored and understood. Likewise, the few influential Orthodox theologians in America who have an informed knowledge of evangelical scholarship understand that these believers are not at all to be lumped together with cults and sects as if they were part of one great sea of undifferentiated darkness. On the contrary, they see its followers as true believers who live in dynamic Christian communities that possess a respectable intellectual heritage of scholarship.

What is happening in the American dialogue thus brings exciting possibilities for realignment and renewal in the mother Orthodox countries. This should not be construed, however, as a demeaning of the mother Orthodox churches outside America, since they will always remain highly valued by the American Orthodox people. Nevertheless it seems hardly debatable that the mantle is falling to their spiritual children in the United States to achieve the kind of constructive approach to evangelicalism that the older lands have not been able to accomplish as effectively thus far. That being said, however, it would be quite misleading to paint an overly optimistic portrait of Orthodox-evangelical relations in America. To be sure, not all is rosy in the United States. Major challenges and obstacles remain for both the academy and the church, challenges to which we shall now turn.

Seminaries and Universities

On the missiological front, walls of tension and hostility between Orthodox and evangelicals have been rising in pockets of Russia and Eastern Europe since the fall of communism. A staggering number of approximately seven hundred Western missionary agencies have been documented as presently at work in these countries.[66] Very few missionaries, however, are prepared to operate with even a basic grasp of the countries' history, culture, or language. There is almost a total lack of missionary preparation being given to evangelical students who minister in those countries. It is no wonder why Orthodox believers are insulted that some Protestant missionaries have come into their country on the assumption that Russia (or other Eastern European bloc countries) is a heathen nation with no presence or history of the gospel. Some hold evangelistic meetings with only a superficial concern for discipling new believers. As a result Orthodox leaders have shown increasingly strong resentment toward missionaries who have attempted to convert or proselytize their parishioners. Yet Western evangelicals are equally offended that some Russian Orthodox churchmen have confused them with a cult or sect. They are astonished and angry that the Orthodox would take such extreme measures as to outlaw their ministries in the country. They are bewildered by the behavior of right-wing nationalists who have burned the bridges for dialogue by doing such things as holding a literal bond fire to destroy the theological books of ecumenists John Meyendorff, Alexander Schmemann, and George Florovsky, who by nearly all accounts are ranked among this century's greatest Orthodox theologians.

I am only skimming the surface of these problems, which I trust are well known to the reader. For those on the mission field, they are lively issues that sometimes impinge upon their very survival. What all this underscores is the fact that if Orthodox and evangelicals want to "preserve the unity of the Spirit in the bond of peace" (Eph. 4:3 NASB) they must begin by widening their comprehension of each other's theological history. This means that there are no shortcuts, no easy ways out, no painless paths to follow, but only the cross of Christ. Each must study at each other's seminaries (or at least make friends with each other's faculties so a conversation can begin), share bibliographies, visit each other's churches, and spend time together in worship and fellowship. Two traditions that are so vastly different in some ways, yet so closely alike in others, cannot be

66. Sharon Linzey, Holt Ruffin, and Mark Elliot, eds., *East-West Christian Organizations: A Directory of Western Christian Organizations Working in East Central Europe and the Newly Independent States Formerly Part of the Soviet Union* (Evanston, Ill.: Berry Pub. Services, 1993).

understood from the inside apart from the sacrificial gifts of time and respect each can give to the other. The dialogue must be that important to people before any real progress can be made to heal the wounds of Christian division.

Given these pressing realities, both sides must ask themselves the hard question, "What is being done in our seminaries and Christian universities to address these vital issues in modern theology and missiology?" The answer is not very heartening. In general, evangelical seminaries are doing more than the Orthodox seminaries to rectify the imbalance. But while some evangelical seminaries are beginning to offer a small number of courses on the Orthodox church, almost no Christian colleges or universities offer even a single introductory class in their history or religion departments. A survey of specific schools will document these general conclusions and give an up-to-date assessment of the current state of the field.

In American evangelical seminaries, we can happily report that over the past thirteen years a small number of courses on the Orthodox church have been introduced as a new part of the curricula. All such courses are noteworthy since, historically, evangelical seminaries previously offered them on an "on demand" basis only. A study of actual course offerings shows that at least one class on the Orthodox tradition has been taught at Fuller Seminary, Southern Baptist Seminary, Gordon-Conwell Seminary, and Trinity Evangelical Divinity School[67] to name only a few of the better known in the United States. Until recently, other Orthodox adjuncts and myself had offered several elective courses at Fuller Seminary on such topics as "Eastern Orthodox Theology," "Eastern Church Fathers," "Theology and Spirituality of Icons," and others. In fact, Fuller hired Samuel Gantt, who became a full-time Orthodox faculty member for many years. Fr. Sam is an Antiochian priest who served as Fuller's director of biblical language instruction and instructor in biblical languages. He was one of the most revered professors among students for over twenty years. The present author also served as a full-time administrator at Fuller Seminary for two years (1997–99) as the director of academic programs for the Orange County extension site. The position itself was surprisingly eliminated in 1999 under the protest of national Christian leaders such as J. I. Packer, Thomas Oden, Robert Webber, Richard John Neuhaus, and others. There are now no Orthodox faculty or administrators left at Fuller Seminary. Trinity Divinity School has also offered occasional elective courses in

67. The missions department at Trinity, notably John Nyquist and Paul Hiebert, has been very gracious in extending to me several opportunities to teach Orthodox subjects to their students. Other faculty have been equally gracious in their fellowship and support, such as the late Kenneth Kantzer, Murray Harris (now in New Zealand), Grant Osborne, Walter Liefeld, and Keith Wells.

their missions department on "Evangelical Missions in Orthodox Lands," "Eastern Orthodox Theology and Practice" and "Introduction to the Orthodox Church." In the United Kingdom, London Bible College has offered occasional courses in the field, as does a newly formed evangelical college in Odessa in the Ukraine under President Sergei Sannikov. In general, schools in the United Kingdom have not closed ranks against the Orthodox as they have here in the United States (see below). This is simply because they have never yet opened the doors. This creates a hopeful situation because it does not come from any settled opposition. On the contrary, there appear to be a number of Baptist theologians who are willing to interact with Orthodox theology, and that is creating an increasing openness to dialogue. What is most needed in the United Kingdom and elsewhere is a substantive encouragement from the Orthodox. Part of the problem, however, is created by the decentralized nature of evangelicalism. With whom do the Orthodox communicate in such a diverse group? How do they know which individuals/organizations to contact? Here the SSEOE has been helpful because it is both pan-Orthodox and pan-evangelical. Perhaps readers of this chapter will wish to start a chapter in their own respective countries. Still, the bishops need to be more aggressive in enlisting the help of others who can offer informed guidance on how to proceed with the dialogue.

Fuller Seminary has been regarded by some as the "flagship" school of evangelicalism as it traveled into the stormy winds of controversy throughout its history, so its relationship with the Orthodox church deserves special attention for the purpose of this article. To contextualize this relationship, a historical summary of key turning points in Fuller's history is in order. Fuller was born out of a controversy that centered in part on the relationship between the gospel and culture. The school was founded with the intention of engaging the culture at all levels with the gospel of Christ, as opposed to the cultural isolationism of separatist fundamentalists of the 1940s. The next major debate came in the 1970s concerning the inerrancy of the Bible, with Fuller taking an essentially errantist position. Then in the 1980s Fuller entered into controversy over the role of women in the church and ended up concluding that the school would actively support the full inclusion of women in ministry. In the 1990s one of the key issues before Fuller was its attitude toward ecumenism. To what extent would Fuller join itself with other Christian bodies in advancing the gospel of Jesus Christ? Over the course of Fuller's fifty-year history, the school was already practicing a *de facto* type of ecumenism by openly welcoming students from all historic branches of the Christian church. It is this openness that has made it one of the largest interdenominational seminaries in the world today. But what was to be its posture toward the Orthodox? Could it embrace the full inclusion of Orthodox students and professors into its ranks as part of the evangelical family?

There are three educational alliances that Fuller has attempted to achieve with the Orthodox over the past thirteen years with varying degrees of success and commitment. First, in Fuller's School of Psychology, as noted earlier, family therapist Dr. Janice Strength founded a counseling school in Russia, which is named the Moscow Christian School of Psychology. Most of its student body consists of Russian Orthodox Christians, and its faculty permits both Orthodox and evangelical professors.

A second educational ministry is Fuller's extension-type program based in St. Petersburg, Russia. I have not been able to update recent developments for this chapter, so things may have changed over the past few years. Dr. James Bradley, the faculty coordinator for the program, describes its work as of 1998.

> St. Petersburg Theological Academy was founded in 1990 by Dr. Sergei Nikolaev with the support of Dr. Arthur DeKruyter, pastor of Christ Church of Oak Brook, Illinois and Trustee of Fuller Seminary. In consultation with the President and Dean of Fuller Seminary, it was agreed that Fuller would serve in an advisory capacity to the new institution, and that we would send four professors each year to teach intensive, two week courses. From the Spring of 1990 through September 1998, the School of Theology at Fuller has involved fourteen of its own faculty persons (one-third of the School of Theology Faculty) and three graduate students in this project and together they have taught a total of fifty-six courses. Professors normally teach two courses over a period of two weeks with thirty contact hours with students per week.

> The experience for the Fuller faculty involved in this endeavor has been uniformly positive and enriching. Participation has enabled School of Theology faculty to experience the church in a cross cultural context. . . . While our faculty are used to the rich cultural and ethnic diversity of students in Los Angeles, the diversity of backgrounds represented by students from the Russian republics is, of course, even greater. *Good ecumenical relations with the Russian Orthodox Church have been maintained; currently two Orthodox priests serve as adjunct faculty and teach specialized courses at the academy.* (emphasis mine)[68]

Under Dr. Bradley's leadership, the St. Petersburg project is a model for similar cooperative ventures between Orthodox and evangelical faculties. One cannot help but think that if it can be done successfully in Russia, there is every reason to believe that it should be able to be done success-

68. Taken from a report by Bradley addressed to Judith A. Berling, director, Incarnating Globization, The Association of Theological Schools, October 3, 1998, 1.

fully anywhere else in the world. But such was not the case in Fuller's own home in America, where a third and largest educational alliance with Orthodox regrettably failed.

Fuller's third venture with the Orthodox tested the seriousness of the school's stated mission of church renewal, but it proved to require more from Fuller than it was willing or able to give. It was a landmark proposal in the history of Orthodox-evangelical relations. In 1995 the Antiochian Orthodox Church in North America (perhaps the most progressive of all Orthodox churches) initiated contact with Fuller Seminary to propose a joint educational alliance for Orthodox and evangelical seminarians. Never before in either the history of evangelicalism or in the history of Orthodoxy had an ecumenical proposal of such magnitude ever been discussed, let alone proposed, by an Orthodox church, especially one of such great historical distinction as the ancient patriarchate of Antioch. Fr. Michel Najim (a Syriac scholar, dean of St. Nicholas Orthodox Cathedral in Los Angeles and former dean of St. John of Damascus Seminary in Beirut, Lebanon) and I were appointed as official representatives of the Antiochian Church to Fuller. We worked with and under the direction of Fr. Joseph Allen, chair of the theological commission, which was overseen by Archbishop Philip Saliba and Bishop Demetri Khouri. The proposal sought to provide a pan-Orthodox program of studies leading to the Master of Divinity (M.Div.) degree granted by Fuller Seminary in conjunction with the Antiochian House of Studies (an American graduate program of St. John of Damascus Seminary in Balamand University, Beirut, Lebanon). It was intended to be an ecumenical program with an Orthodox emphasis that would be based in Pasadena but made available to Orthodox and evangelical students in America and throughout the world by using classical and contemporary methods of theological education (including media technologies over the Internet and individualized distance learning courses). Greek and Russian bishops from the Greek Orthodox Church and Orthodox Church in America agreed to participate as Orthodox professors in the program, and the Coptic Orthodox Church in Los Angeles was in the early stages of discussing their involvement with the Antiochians as well.

As the engineer for the curriculum, I performed several revisions in consultations with both parties involved while seeking to achieve a balance between the theological demands of an authentically Orthodox curriculum and the evangelical distinctives of Fuller Seminary. The final curriculum appeared to be a unique ecumenical achievement that created an authentic synthesis between our theological traditions without resulting in doctrinal compromise or a theological hybrid. It also offered Fuller's own students the opportunity to study with Orthodox professors at one of the world's largest and most progressive interdenominational evangelical seminaries. Eastern Orthodox students would have been asked to grapple with the theological emphases of the Reformation, and evangelical students would have been asked to do the same with Orthodox theology. Both would have found Fuller a safe place to learn each other's history and theology while actually witnessing Christian unity in action for the good of the body of Christ. In this way the joint program would fulfill Fuller's own stated "Mission Beyond the Mission," a goal dedicated to the renewal of the entire Christian church, including the historic "catholic" traditions such as "the Orthodox Church" among others.

Despite the numerous prior contacts with Fuller administrators, Fuller's faculty had been given only one introductory opportunity to listen to our proposal and respond. Fr. Michel Najim and I presented a general overview of the reasons and goals of the program without reference to the specifics in the curriculum. A few did not feel they could do a responsible job in the area of Orthodox-evangelical cooperation since they were already overcommitted to other projects. However, others (notably Miroslav Volf who has since moved to Yale) felt the proposal was of enormous significance, were eager to support it, and felt honored to be involved in such a historic ecumenical moment. Afterwards the dean (William Dyrness) and faculty felt they should turn it over to the higher levels of Fuller's administration to move the process forward. A very ambiguous stage in the dialogue ensued after that between the faculty and administration over whether and how to go ahead with the proposal. Despite many of the faculty's readiness to move ahead with advanced union negotiations, the dean later provided a written statement to me in which he explained that the administration/board of trustees (i.e., President Richard Mouw, Provost Russell Spittler, and the board) failed to provide the faculty with a clear signal to proceed. Thus a historic program of enormous ecumenical import tragically died.[69] Should George Marsden's book on the history of Fuller Seminary (*Reforming Evangelicalism*) ever be revised in the future, it ought to include a detailed narrative of this missed opportunity in modern church history.

When turning to an evaluation of Orthodox seminaries that offer courses on evangelicalism, it is obvious that they are behind their evangelical counterparts. Nevertheless, Holy Cross Greek Orthodox Seminary makes evangelical courses available to its students through its sister consortium school Gordon-Conwell Seminary. In 1980 a dialogue on preaching was held at the campus of Holy Cross between its faculty and Gordon-

---

69. Union negotiations between Fuller and the Antiochian Archdiocese was noted briefly in "Universities Question Orthodox Conversions," *Christianity Today* (August 11, 1998).

Conwell's. The papers were published in the book *God's Living Word: Orthodox and Evangelical Essays on Preaching*.[70] Several of its faculty members have also been featured speakers at the annual SSEOE conferences (Frs. Stanley Harakas, Emmanuel Clapsis, and Theodore Stylianopoulos). St. Vladimir's Orthodox Seminary (Crestwood, New York) has shown verbal signs of interest in Orthodoxy's relationship with evangelicalism among several of its faculty and students, but so far no concrete action has been taken to implement such courses or to engage evangelicals in academic conversation. Saint Nersus, its sister school from the Armenian Orthodox Church, invited an Armenian evangelical, Joseph Alexanian from Trinity International University (Deerfield, Illinois) to teach a course on evangelism in the book of Acts in the summer of 1994. In August 1995 Metropolitan Philip Saliba of the Antiochian Orthodox Archdiocese took a bold step forward to raise seminarians' level of knowledge by offering an annual comparative theology course for his Antiochian students on "Orthodoxy and American Evangelicalism" in the Antiochian House of Studies (Ligonier, Pennsylvania) taught by the present author.

Many of these attempts can be regarded as progressive. Still one must be honest enough to view them only as a good beginning and that not nearly enough is being done to fill in the gaps in our respective curricula. Nevertheless, for over a decade evangelical schools were doing more to rectify the situation than were the Orthodox seminaries. Now, however, neither side appears to be reaching out to the other.

Clearly of late evangelical schools in the United States have not had a very constructive relationship with the Orthodox church. In the past four years, two schools in particular have gone through some very difficult times when trying to determine what to do with their Orthodox faculty. They are Biola University (La Mirada, California) and Columbia International University (Columbia, South Carolina).

Biola University is a very conservative evangelical school with a denominationally diverse student body. In 1997–98 three Orthodox employees of the school endured the possibility of termination as a result of a vocal minority of students who portrayed the Orthodox faculty as members of a heretical sect. One professor occupied the chair of a highly successful R. A. Torrey Honors Program, another professor was head of the Art Department, and the third an ordained Orthodox priest who served as the dean of students. By all accounts, including Biola's students and administration, all three performed their jobs with honorable distinction.

---

70. *God's Living Word: Orthodox and Evangelical Essays on Preaching*, ed. Theodore Stylianopoulos (Brookline, Mass.: Holy Cross Orthodox Press, 1983).

In the name of academic freedom, the vocal student minority were allowed to express their views but took advantage of their privileges and soon became disruptive to the professors and the institutional life of the school. The students increased the tension by posting anti-Orthodox messages throughout the school and, to put it lightly, generally demeaned the Orthodox church. As a result, a theological commission of three was set up from the school's adjacent Talbot School of Theology to write a report on Eastern Orthodox theology and its compatibility with Biola's statement of faith. If the two were compatible, the professors could remain at the school; if not, they would have to be let go. To help facilitate the dialogue, two outside Orthodox theologians were invited to Biola for an evening's discussion with the members of Talbot's theological commission. After meeting for several hours, the provost, Sherwood Lingenfelter (who, ironically, is now the provost at Fuller Seminary), concluded that there were no major breaches with Biola's statement of faith and that the Orthodox professors could remain in their jobs.[71] The face-to-face dialogue between Orthodox and evangelical theologians that occurred at Biola University was originally constructive. As time passed, however, the school reaffirmed that it is indeed a Protestant evangelical school and therefore any faculty member outside that branch of Christianity is to be excluded. Currently, the university suggests that there is no blacklisting of church affiliation and that it is possible for sincere Christians of whatever affiliation to be employed. But all such Christians are required to sign the school's premillennial statement of faith. In the past few years, one original Orthodox employee resigned, one part-time faculty member in the communication department who became Orthodox was let go, and a senior Orthodox faculty member overseeing the R. A. Torrey section was told he would not qualify for tenure because of his church affiliation. The latter's wife also sought to take classes at Talbot School of Theology but was denied admittance because of her Orthodoxy.

A similar incident of an evangelical backlash against Orthodoxy occurred at another conservative school with the same negative results. One of the mission professors at Columbia International University, Dr. Edward Rommen, joined the faculty after serving as a tenured professor at Trinity Evangelical Divinity School. Rommen grew up in the Evangelical Free Church and spent fourteen years as a missionary and seminary professor of that denomination in Germany. He possesses a doctorate in theology and missions and studied with Wolfhart Pannenberg at Munich, Germany. His most recent book was coauthored with David Hesselgrave and titled, *Contextualization: Meanings, Methods and Models*. After many years

71. Reported in "Universities Question Orthodox Conversions," 21–23.

of studying and searching for a deeper church life, in 1997 Rommen left the Evangelical Free Church denomination and joined the Orthodox Church. As a result of his conversion, he was almost immediately asked to resign from his new teaching post at Columbia International University in 1998. While the majority of professors and administrators seemed to support Rommen, two or three top administrators appear to have engineered a quiet dismissal. He is now an ordained Orthodox priest and new president of the SSEOE.[72]

Another example of a more quiet form of an evangelical reaction against Orthodoxy can be seen in the case of Wheaton College.[73] Here one needs to distinguish between Wheaton's *public* statement of faith and its *private* stance against the Orthodox. There is nothing in Wheaton's statement of faith that any Orthodox theologian could not sign. What Wheaton hopes for, however, is that such theologians would object to what is not contained in it (e.g., the "real presence" of Christ in the Eucharist). According to Robert Webber, Wheaton operates on a rule of thumb that only Protestants can speak in chapel or be hired as faculty members. However, this is only an "oral" tradition among most (not all) of the faculty, not a "written" prohibition.[74] Such a posture, however, is curious in light of the fact that Webber himself is an Episcopalian, which is nearly identical with the Orthodox tradition, barring differences over the *filioque* clause in the Nicene Creed and a few other similar technicalities that are not vital for faculty signatures at Wheaton. Also there are more Episcopal students attending Wheaton College than at any other time in the school's history. Another irony lies in the contradictory message one hears when a renowned Orthodox speaker was asked to grace the christening of one of evangelicalism's most distinguished institutions. During the 1980s the renowned Orthodox philosopher, educator, and theologian, Charles Malik, was invited to give the prestigious dedication speech for the new Billy Graham Center, which is located on the campus of Wheaton College. The late Charles Malik was a theologian of the Antiochian Orthodox Church in Lebanon and the United States, a founding member in the United Nations, a member of the board of trustees of Harvard University, and personal friend of Carl Henry and Bill

72. Ibid.

73. Similarly, Westmont College in Santa Barbara, California has implemented an official policy to exclude the hiring of Orthodox or Catholic faculty members in all of its departments, not just in Religious Studies (E-mail from Tremper Longman to the author, November 2002).

74. Phone conversation with Robert Webber, December 21, 1999. Webber referred me to Wheaton's president, Duane Litfin, for confirmation, but he was "unavailable for comment." Mark Noll takes exception to this policy along with Webber.

Bright. Though the Billy Graham Center is functionally distinct from Wheaton College, Wheaton wholeheartedly embraced the honor of Malik's presence.

In sum, there have been a number of well-qualified Orthodox candidates and faculty members who have suffered persecution of one kind or another in evangelical schools in the United States. The presence or potential of Orthodox faculty in evangelical schools has begun to challenge the adequacy of public evangelical statements of faith and privately held faculty opinions. The statements of faith were often forged as a historical reaction against Tridentine Roman Catholicism and the once rising tide of Protestant liberalism. Orthodoxy was not even on the radar screen of evangelical schools at the time of drafting their statements. Today evangelicals in America are having to reevaluate their identity in light of their relationship with Orthodoxy on an "as needed" basis. There is not a large movement in this direction, but the problems outlined above reveal that the Orthodox church in America is indeed having a discernable impact on evangelical schools and that such schools are struggling to understand the true identity of Orthodoxy as well as their own evangelical identity in light of that discovery. Oftentimes their understanding of the Orthodox church is mediated simply through introductory books that do not adequately deal with evangelical questions, through conversations with theologically unsophisticated Orthodox leaders, or through fellow evangelical professors who themselves have only a superficial knowledge of the church's tradition. Few Orthodox or evangelical scholars are able to speak each other's language fluently or build bridges based on an authentic grasp of each other's theological history. This adversely impacts the private opinions of evangelical faculty members who are at the helm of the hiring process when reviewing job applicants of Orthodox scholars. Often evangelical faculties do not currently possess the conceptual categories in which to fit the Orthodox, as they appear as neither fish nor fowl. However, as more of the younger generation of evangelical scholars complete doctoral degrees in Greek patristics, liturgical studies, and Byzantine/modern history, the evangelical institutions that hire them may become increasingly open to acquiring the rich intellectual resources of Orthodox faculty members in the coming decades. Clearly, however, that will not happen in the near future. In fact, American evangelicalism is moving in the opposite direction! The irony is that most of these evangelical schools have aspired to greatness but lack the courage to take the associated risks. One can only humbly pray for the day when evangelical schools will welcome Orthodox theologians into their evangelical ranks with full faculty status as valued brothers in Christ.

Sadly, Orthodox schools fare no better. Orthodox institutions only number five in all of North America. It would be wrong to expect them to open their doors to evangelicals to the same degree that evangelicals should be able to do with the Orthodox due to the nature of the two being compared: Orthodoxy is a church that makes no claim to being interdenominational or theologically inclusive. Evangelicalism, on the other hand, is not a church but a spiritual movement. As such its theological distinctives are comprised of a core of spiritual and theological beliefs that embrace and transcend a wide range of denominational boundaries. These differences do not excuse the Orthodox from seriously engaging and uniting with evangelicalism in vitally important areas, but it does legitimize the limits of their cooperation so that there is a rational imbalance of what can and cannot be achieved with integrity.

Conclusion

The sum of these developments demonstrate that we are only at the start of an emerging global dialogue between the Eastern Orthodox and evangelical communities. The Orthodox tradition is fast becoming a vital issue in modern theology and world missions. An unprecedented opportunity for growth, realignment, and renewal now lies before us. The historic dialogue and ecumenical encounters that occurred at all levels during the decade of the 1990s between Orthodoxy and evangelicalism has grown strangely quiet at the turn of the twenty-first century. We now lie in the wake of a broken courtship initiated chiefly from the evangelical side. What was once a promising engagement has cooled into an estranged relationship. Evangelical seminaries that have the foresight to develop curricular emphases in Eastern Christianity will be better able to offer a fuller perspective on global theology and thus will be on the cutting edge of the future of theological education. Orthodox seminaries must do the same with evangelicalism. While the fledgling dialogue is fraught with potentially fatal hazards, it is my conviction that if our relationship is patiently nurtured with humility, courage, determination, and the laying aside of personal and ecclesial pride, it may well turn out to be one of the most fruitful and significant ecumenical encounters of all at the beginning of the third millennium. If Alister McGrath is correct in asserting that evangelicalism will increasingly become the most viable theological option on the religious landscape in the coming years,[75] I humbly believe that Eastern Orthodoxy, despite its human frailties and current weaknesses, may very well end up as the dialogue partner that can offer evangelicals the

75. Alister McGrath, *Evangelicalism and the Future of Christianity* (Downers Grove, Ill.: Inter-Varsity, 1995).

greatest abundance of fresh theological resources to nourish its ongoing maturity and creative relevance throughout the twenty-first century. However, in this dialogue evangelicals will need to develop a strategy for dealing with the poor external conditions of contemporary Orthodoxy— conditions that are partly due to a legacy of Islamic and communist domination over the Orthodox, as well as plain religious snobbery and the lack of desire to understand and communicate with the Christian West.

A renowned British Byzantinologist said that the twenty-first century will be the century of the Orthodox. This should not make the Orthodox boast, but rather it should make us feel even more strongly the immense responsibility placed on our weak shoulders to witness to the Church's faith. The theological treasures of Byzantium are just beginning to be discovered by Colin Gunton's reappropriation of classical Byzantine Christology and by Miroslav Volf's and the Torrance brothers' work on Cappadocian trinitarian theology, to name just a few of the better known evangelicals. It must also be said as it so often happens in Protestant encounters with Orthodoxy, that evangelicals may well end up feeling disappointed with the quality of their conversation with some contemporary Orthodox dialogue partners, many of whom lack a sophisticated appreciation for the theological emphases of the Reformers and their children. But it is precisely at that moment of disillusionment, when evangelicals will be tempted to turn away from the Orthodox, that evangelicals must summon the intellectual courage to move beyond the sins and weaknesses of modern Orthodoxy and go back to the primary sources themselves, which have formed the church's faith, no matter how much or how little the modern Orthodox are able to help them with the journey. The fortress mentality that now dominates evangelical institutions will need to be overcome by the truth of the gospel, a truth that the Orthodox church invites evangelicals to explore in greater depth. I am personally convinced that the reasons why evangelicals have rejected the Orthodox are due to their own unsophisticated grasp of Orthodox theology, as well as the failure of Orthodox pastors and scholars to make their faith known and understood in terms that satisfy the legitimate concerns of the Protestant Reformers and their modern children. In short, what is lacking is theological knowledge, effective "bilingual" theological communication skills, patience, dedication, love, and, above all, humility. Mutual repentance is needed on both sides for the sins and failures for which we are all responsible. The future is only as hopeful as the depth of our own repentance.

The decade of the 1990s laid the foundation for a new beginning. The stalled communication and negative conclusions we have drawn have now put us in danger of returning to the isolationist conditions of a preecumenical era. I can only urge evangelicals not to give up on their dialogues with the Orthodox but to go back to the table and explore more thoroughly the borders of their evangelical identity. Likewise the Orthodox need to return to the table with a deeper knowledge of the evangelical identity of their own faith and how it relates to that of their evangelical brethren.

15

Looking for Home

Evangelical Orthodoxy and the Search for the Original Church

Timothy P. Weber

Timothy P. Weber is professor of church history and dean of Northern Baptist Theological Seminary in Chicago. After studies at UCLA (history) and Fuller Theological Seminary (M.Div.), he earned his Ph.D. at the University of Chicago in American religious studies under Martin Marty. Before moving to Northern Baptist, Weber taught at Denver Seminary for sixteen years and at Southern Baptist Theological Seminary for five years. In the following chapter Weber explores the fascinating conversion of two thousand evangelical Protestants to Orthodoxy, a conversion that in many ways has served as a paradigm of sorts for thousands of subsequent conversions to Orthodoxy.

In 1987 about two thousand members, both lay and clergy, from seventeen parishes of the Evangelical Orthodox Church entered the Antiochian Orthodox Church amid much fanfare and public notice. Metropolitan Philip Saliba, head of the Antiochian Church's North American archdiocese, hailed their coming as an event of historic significance. The religious and secular press took notice too, declaring that it was the first time since the founding of the church in the ancient city of Antioch that an already-existing denomination had entered it. Both received and receiving called the event a "coming home."[1]

From Bradley Nassif, ed., *New Perspectives on Historical Theology: Essays in Memory of John Meyendorff* (Grand Rapids: Eerdmans, 1996), 95–121. Reprinted by permission.

1. An insider's version of this story is found in Peter Gillquist, *Becoming Orthodox: A Jour-*

Despite the obvious importance to those directly involved, within the large and complex world of American evangelicalism, which is commonly numbered at about 40 million adherents, the departure of two thousand pilgrims to Orthodoxy hardly seemed earthshaking. After all, the sanctuary of a single evangelical megachurch could easily accommodate the total number of converts with room to spare; and Southern Baptists on an average Sunday baptize over three times as many converts. Nevertheless, this modest and still-growing transference of religious allegiance is both curious and revealing. Many of the converts claimed that being evangelical had actually contributed to their becoming Orthodox. In ways that seemed surprising even to themselves, the road to Orthodoxy had been paved with evangelical beliefs and religious experience. What is even more curious is that the children of evangelicalism, who have been so thoroughly shaped by their American context, should be attracted to Orthodoxy, the least Americanized form of Christianity in the United States.

This essay will seek to do three things: (1) It will show that this turn toward Orthodoxy occurred at a time of widespread crisis over identity among evangelicals; (2) it will argue that while the reasons for "becoming Orthodox" were complex, at their root was the long-standing evangelical desire to be identified with the original New Testament church; and (3) it will demonstrate some of the ironies involved in the attempts of the evangelical converts to make Orthodoxy something that it has never been before—a church that is at home in America.

The Evangelical Search for Identity

The process that led two thousand evangelicals to enter the Antiochian Orthodox Church must be seen as part of a much larger crisis over evangelical identity. The 1970s were a monumental turning time for American religion, evangelicalism included. While the Protestant mainline churches were showing early signs of declining numbers and cultural influence, the evangelical movement experienced what some people called a "renaissance." Thanks in large part to the election of Jimmy Carter in 1976, the evangelical subculture suddenly came into view. *Time* and *Newsweek* devoted feature articles to the movement;[2] and Martin Marty declared that no one could do justice to contemporary American religion without giving evangelicalism its due.[3]

---

ney to the Ancient Christian Faith (revised and updated, Ben Lomond, Calif.: Conciliar Press, 1992).

2. Kenneth Woodward, "Born Again!" *Newsweek* (Oct. 25, 1976): 68–78; "Back to that Oldtime Religion," *Time* (Dec. 26, 1977): 52–58.

3. Martin E. Marty, *A Nation of Behavers* (Chicago: University of Chicago Press, 1976), 80.

After years of being ignored by nearly everyone else, evangelicals hurried to explain their movement to outsiders and to each other.[4] Such efforts demonstrated that it was not easy to find the institutional limits of evangelicalism or to define the movement in precise theological terms.[5] If one stepped back far enough, one could see a vibrant subculture unified around a complex network of institutions and some core convictions: that salvation comes through faith in Jesus Christ (not human works), and each person needs to experience it through an act of personal conversion; that the Bible (not church tradition) is divinely inspired and authoritative in all matters of living and believing; and that those who have personally experienced the grace of God need to share it actively with others. But if one moved closer, one could see complexities and even deep cleavages based on different histories, theological orientations, and styles. Even those who wanted to affirm that there was an evangelical "whole" had to admit that it contained many parts.[6]

It was only natural, then, that when evangelicals began to explain themselves to outsiders during the 1970s, a war over definitions broke out. Long-standing differences, deeply rooted in nineteenth-century evangelical life, resurfaced with new urgency. As in all "we're-truer-than-you" arguments, ultimately at stake were matters of identity, authenticity, and the power to control institutions.

No one was more concerned about evangelical identity than Harold Lindsell, whose *The Battle for the Bible* argued that some evangelicals were abandoning what he considered the *sine qua non* of historic evangelicalism—the doctrine of biblical inerrancy.[7] Lindsell believed that without inerrancy, evangelicals were sure to reject additional theological commitments; so he named names and warned that unless inerrantists took decisive action, evangelicalism would lose its distinctiveness and historic identity.[8] Supporters of inerrancy organized themselves into the interde-

4. Donald G. Bloesch, *The Evangelical Renaissance* (Grand Rapids: Eerdmans, 1973); Bernard Ramm, *The Evangelical Heritage* (Waco: Word, 1973); Richard Quebedeaux, *The Young Evangelicals* (New York: Harper and Row, 1974); David Wells and John Woodbridge, eds., *The Evangelicals* (Nashville: Abingdon, 1975); Donald Dayton, *Discovering an Evangelical Heritage* (New York: Harper and Row, 1976).

5. Donald W. Dayton and Robert K. Johnston, eds., *The Variety of American Evangelicals* (Downers Grove, Ill.: Inter-Varsity Press, 1991).

6. George Marsden, "The Evangelical Denomination," in Marsden, ed., *Evangelicalism in Modern America* (Grand Rapids: Eerdmans, 1984), vii–xvi.

7. Harold Lindsell, *The Battle for the Bible* (Grand Rapids: Zondervan, 1976); *The Bible in the Balance* (Grand Rapids: Zondervan, 1978).

8. Lindsell did not start the battle for the Bible. For over a decade evangelical scholars had been debating the relationship between inerrancy and biblical scholarship. See, for example, Dewey Beegle, *The Inspiration of Scripture* (Philadelphia: Westminster, 1963), and *Scripture, Tradition, and Infallibility* (Grand Rapids: Eerdmans, 1973). For an overview

nominational International Council on Biblical Inerrancy and into purposive groups in various denominations in order to protect the doctrine from its detractors and eliminate noninerrantists from leadership positions within evangelical organizations.[9]

Though it was difficult to ignore the inerrancy crusade, a few evangelical leaders understood that other things contributed to the identity crisis. Carl F. H. Henry claimed that evangelicals were at odds on a number of fronts. "While he is still on the loose, and still sounding his roar, the evangelical lion is nonetheless slowly succumbing to an identity crisis. The noteworthy cohesion that American evangelicals gained in the sixties has been fading in the seventies through multiplied internal disagreements and emerging counterforces."[10]

In addition to the conflict over biblical inerrancy, Henry cited the disagreements over the relationship between evangelicalism and political action and the place of charismatic religious experience in modern church life. He lamented the fact that "Evangelicalism has shown itself painfully weak in shaping American national conscience, despite the massive impact of the Graham crusades and the personal popularity of the evangelist."[11] He noted that many young evangelical scholars who had not personally experienced the fundamentalist war with modernism were less inclined to contend for the faith than the older leadership had been. With rare insight, he predicted that "the evangelical far right is regathering for a massive initiative all its own"[12] and counseled special care as evangelicals explored the latest "media frontiers" in television and mass communications. Though Henry himself did not see the positive side of the identity crisis, there was one: evangelicalism's "coming of age" meant that it had to reassess its core commitments, its varied histories, and its connections to other movements.

Unnoticed by either Lindsell or Henry was the growing interest in evangelicalism's relationship to historic, catholic traditions. Evangelicals had always considered themselves *orthodox*—either because they affirmed more-or-less historic Christian dogma (as interpreted through the Protestant Reformation) or because they adhered to the teachings of the Bible—but rarely had they described themselves in *catholic* terms.[13] For most of

---

of evangelical biblical scholarship, see Mark A. Noll, *Between Faith and Criticism,* 2d ed. (Grand Rapids: Baker, 1991).

9. The International Council on Biblical Inerrancy was founded in Chicago in 1978; and in 1979 inerrantists within the Southern Baptist Convention started a movement to establish their control of the denomination.

10. Carl F. H. Henry, *Evangelicals in Search of Identity* (Waco: Word, 1976), 22.

11. Ibid., 42.

12. Ibid., 22.

13. The big exception to this statement in the nineteenth century was the "evangelical catholicism" of Philip Schaff in the Mercersburg Theology. See James Hastings Nichols,

their history in America, evangelicals had defined themselves over against catholicism, by which they meant Rome.[14] From the evangelical perspective, Roman Catholicism was wholly other and therefore defective; papal infallibility, the veneration of Mary and the saints, the mysterious (and probably superstitious) sacramental system, and its strange pieties were considered nonbiblical and completely outside evangelical parameters.

At the beginning of the 1970s, most rank-and-file evangelicals probably still viewed Catholicism in such negative terms; but a growing number were ready to reconsider. The reasons for this more open attitude were many. For some, the charismatic movement had broken down old barriers between evangelicals and Catholics. For others, formal study of early church history or deep dissatisfaction with evangelical low-church and often anti-sacramental worship styles raised new questions. Still others realized that assertions of evangelicalism's orthodoxy were meaningless apart from some connection to historic Christian churches. Finding one's identity within the one, holy, catholic, and apostolic church meant examining the differences that still divided evangelicals and catholics of various kinds.

A relatively easy way for some evangelicals to "go catholic" was to become Episcopalian. After all, American evangelicalism had always been big enough to include Episcopalians;[15] and a number of British Anglicans (J. I. Packer, John R. Stott, and, of course, C. S. Lewis) were well known and admired by American evangelicals. Because Anglicanism on both sides of the Atlantic included an "evangelical party," a niche already existed for evangelicals who wanted to join. Robert Webber was one of the early and most vocal converts to Episcopalianism. His scholarly and popular studies of the history and theology of worship[16] were important in leading numerous others (including many of his students from Wheaton College) down "the Canterbury trail."[17] Those converts who explained

---

Romanticism in American Theology: Nevin and Schaff at Mercersburg (Chicago: University of Chicago Press, 1961).

14. To understand how Catholics used their outsider status to fashion their own identity in America, see R. Laurence Moore, *Outsiders and the Making of Americans* (New York: Oxford University Press, 1986), 48–71.

15. Allen Guelzo, *For the Union of Evangelical Christendom: The Irony of the Reformed Episcopalians* (University Park, Penn.: Pennsylvania State University Press, 1994).

16. Robert E. Webber, *Common Roots: A Call to Evangelical Maturity* (Grand Rapids: Zondervan, 1978); *Worship Old and New* (Grand Rapids: Zondervan, 1982); *The Biblical Foundations of Christian Worship*, The Complete Library of Christian Worship, vol. 1 (Nashville: Star Song, 1993); *Twenty Centuries of Christian Worship*, The Complete Library of Christian Worship, vol. 2 (Nashville: Star Song, 1994); *The Renewal of Sunday Worship*, The Complete Library of Christian Worship, vol. 3 (Nashville: Star Song, 1993).

17. Robert E. Webber, *Evangelicals on the Canterbury Trail: Why Evangelicals Are Attracted to the Liturgical Church* (Waco: Word, 1985).

their reasons for becoming Episcopalian all said much the same thing: they desired a sense of mystery, which was absent in "propositional" evangelicalism; they longed for meaningful worship experiences, including a more profound appreciation of the sacraments; they felt cut off from the long memories and practices of historic Christianity; and they lacked a sense of belonging to the whole church.[18] In the words of Thomas Howard, whose own walk down the Canterbury trail finally ended up in Rome, being "evangelical is not enough."[19]

But one did not have to become an Episcopalian to explore evangelicalism's catholic connections. In May, 1977, at the urging of Robert Webber, Donald Bloesch, and Thomas Howard, forty-five evangelical professors, pastors, editors, authors, and graduate students from a variety of denominations gathered in Chicago.[20] The result was "The Chicago Call: An Appeal to Evangelicals."[21] In his personal account of the events leading up to the Chicago meeting, Webber described how he and other conferees "have been growing beyond the borders of what has, until now, been regarded as the limits of evangelicalism." Just as evangelical leaders like Billy Graham, Harold John Ockenga, Harold Lindsell, and C. F. H. Henry had moved beyond the borders of fundamentalism in the forties and fifties, so other "orthodox evangelicals" have "continued to look beyond present limitations toward a more inclusive and ultimately more historic Christianity."[22]

The Chicago Call was an amazing document in many ways. In its prologue, it declared that evangelicals had "a pressing need to reflect upon the substance of the biblical and historic faith and to recover the fullness of this heritage."[23] The main body of the document consisted of eight "calls" to historic roots and continuity, biblical fidelity, creedal identity, holistic salvation, sacramental integrity, spirituality, church authority, and church unity. Each of the eight statements posed a problem and then proposed a solution.[24]

Even a casual reading of the Chicago Call reveals that its signers had a much broader definition of evangelicalism than did most people who applied the label to themselves. The Call recognized that throughout church history there has been an "evangelical impulse to proclaim the saving, unmerited grace of Christ, and to reform the church according to the

    18. Ibid., 19–161.
    19. Thomas Howard, *Evangelical Is Not Enough* (Nashville: Thomas Nelson, 1984).
    20. For media accounts of the meeting, see *Newsweek* (May 23, 1977): 76; *Christian Century* (June 1, 1977): 527; *Christianity Today* ([June 17, 1977]: 27, and [July 29, 1977]: 8).
    21. Robert E. Webber and Donald Bloesch, eds., *The Orthodox Evangelicals: Who They Are and What They Are Saying* (Nashville: Thomas Nelson, 1978).
    22. Ibid., 19.
    23. Ibid., 11.
    24. The entire Chicago Call can be found in ibid., 11–18.

Scriptures." This evangelical emphasis could be seen not only in the work of the Protestant Reformers and their heirs, but also in the theology of the ecumenical councils, the piety of the early church fathers, Augustine's theology of grace, the reforming work of monastics and mystics, and the theology of the Christian humanists. In fact, the Call went on to say that the evangelical impulse is evident whenever "the Gospel has come to expression through the operation of the Holy Spirit," including renewal movements within Eastern Orthodoxy, Roman Catholicism, and ecumenical Protestantism. "We dare not move beyond the biblical limits of the Gospel; but we cannot be fully evangelical without recognizing our need to learn from other times and movements concerning the whole meaning of the Gospel."[25]

The Call was long on critique but rather short on concrete, specific proposals for action. It rejected evangelicalism's tendency toward individualistic interpretation of the Bible in favor of an approach that was both scholarly and in touch with "the historic understanding of the church." The authors stated that historic confessions should serve as "a guide for the interpretation of the Scriptures," but they did not specify which confessions or exactly how their guidance would work.[26]

Likewise, the Call decried the "poverty of sacramental understanding" among American evangelicals, who did not recognize that "the grace of God is mediated through faith by the operation of the Holy Spirit in a notable way in the sacraments of baptism and the Lord's Supper."[27] But the authors did not define how the Spirit worked in the sacraments or how the sacraments should be observed. Furthermore, the Call criticized evangelicals' "disobedience to the Lordship of Christ as expressed through authority in his church," which resulted in a spirit of autonomy and even anarchy. All Christians should be in practical submission to each other and "to designated leaders in a church under the Lordship of Christ." But the Call took no position on the form of such leadership or how submission should take place. The Call also deplored the "scandalous isolation and separation of Christians from one another" and evangelicalism's "ahistorical, sectarian mentality," which failed "to appropriate the catholicity of historic Christianity, as well as the breadth of the biblical revelation." Accordingly, evangelicals must "recognize that God works within diverse historical streams." While the Call rejected "church union-at-any-cost," it did advocate "encounter and cooperation within Christ's church" by "earnestly seeking common areas of agreement and understanding."[28]

25. Ibid., 12.
26. Ibid., 12–13.
27. Ibid., 14.
28. Ibid., 14–16.

In retrospect, the Call bore witness to a growing catholic awareness among certain evangelicals and their inability to decide what in particular to do about it. Robert Webber and Donald Bloesch both admitted that the "orthodox evangelicals" at Chicago were deeply divided over what to do with the Reformation: were the Protestant Reformers in continuity or discontinuity with the early church? To be authentically orthodox did one have to disavow the Protestant revolt against Catholicism, or should one embrace Reformation concerns as a needed corrective to earlier Catholic corruptions?[29] A Roman Catholic participant-signer noted that the Call was a "consensus statement drafted and signed by people who were coming from very different theological places" and that those differences often grew out of the "old Reformation problem of Scripture and tradition."[30] That basic disagreement in perspective accounted for the Call's ambiguity and was the primary reason that a few conference participants refused to sign it.[31]

The Search for the Original Church

A few of the "orthodox evangelicals" at Chicago were already well down the road to "Evangelical Orthodoxy." Of the forty-five who drew up the Chicago Call, five were identified with the New Covenant Apostolic Order,[32] a group of evangelicals who were essentially "storming orthodoxy by the back door,"[33] or rather making up Orthodoxy as they went along.

The road that led this group into the Antiochian Orthodox Church in 1987 started in the 1960s at Arrowhead Springs, California, the headquarters of Campus Crusade for Christ.[34] Founded in the early 1950s by Bill Bright, Crusade had become one of the most successful parachurch organizations to grow out of the "new evangelical" movement after World War II. By the late 1960s hundreds of staff members were conducting Bible studies in dormitories and in fraternity and sorority houses and leading students to Christ by means of the "Four Spiritual Laws."[35] As a para-

29. Ibid., 25–27; Donald Bloesch, *The Future of Evangelical Christianity* (Garden City, N.Y.: Doubleday, 1983), 48–52.

30. See Webber and Bloesch, *The Orthodox Evangelicals*, 225–33, for Benedict Viviano's reflections on the conference and 16–17 for a list of the signers.

31. David Wells did not sign the Call. For his reasons, see ibid., 213–24.

32. Jon Braun, Peter Gillquist, Kenneth Jensen, Ray Nethery, and Gordon Walker. See Webber and Bloesch, *The Orthodox Evangelicals*, 16–17.

33. With apologies to Nathan Hatch, whose wonderful phrase "storming heaven by the back door" I am adapting here. See Hatch, *The Democratization of American Christianity* (New Haven: Yale University Press, 1989).

34. The outlines of the story are taken from Gillquist, *Becoming Orthodox*.

35. Richard Quebedeaux, *I Found It! The Story of Bill Bright and Campus Crusade* (San Francisco: Harper and Row, 1979).

church organization, one of those "voluntary associations" that evangelicals have used to accomplish specialized ministries outside of churchly structures, Crusade had problems turning college-age converts into churchgoing Christians. During the sixties, campus ministries often took on the countercultural ethos of the campuses. Many new converts recoiled at the stodgy "establishment" evangelical congregations to which their Crusade leaders directed them. Radically committed to Christ, many students felt alienated from the church.

Many Crusade leaders agreed with these antichurch sentiments; but they also believed that their converts needed what only churches could provide, a nurturing *community* of faith that could sustain them through all the stages of their lives. Without such community connections, most converts soon fell by the wayside. According to Peter Gillquist, one of the "stars" of Crusade's staff, "we didn't like the institutional Church and we didn't like the world system, and we were out to change them both."[36]

By the middle of the sixties, many Crusade campus leaders had concluded that a parachurch organization could not reform either world or church. During the annual training session at Arrowhead Springs in the summer of 1966, a number of Crusade's area directors decided that Campus Crusade needed to move from parachurch to church. "We sensed a lack of freedom. We wanted to pull out all the stops and do 'everything they did in the first century'—baptize our converts, serve communion, take more vocal stands against evil. In short, we wanted above all else to be the New Testament Church."[37]

That program was completely out of step with the founding vision of Bill Bright, so by 1968 a group of extremely frustrated Crusade leaders left the organization. By then most of them were thoroughly disillusioned with the institutional church. They knew what they wanted but had not found it in any of the existing denominations. "The Church was the answer, but not any Church we had ever seen. It was the New Testament Church that we sought. And we were soon to find that countless others were looking for the same things. We were beginning what we soon began to call *The Phantom Search for the Perfect Church*."[38]

For the next five years, the former Crusaders pursued other occupations but kept alive their dream of the True Church by founding "house churches" in the Midwest, South, and West Coast. These house churches took the New Testament as their only guide and tried to reproduce not only the form but also the power and commitment of the original church.

36. Gillquist, *Becoming Orthodox*, 5.
37. Ibid., 17.
38. Ibid., 19.

Eastern Orthodox Theology

This pursuit of original New Testament Christianity is common in American religion. Historians have noted the strong strains of *primitivism* and *restorationism* in American history.[39] Though the two concepts are sometimes difficult to distinguish, their adherents agree that some time shortly after the apostolic age, the church "fell" on account of its own corruptions and superstitious practices. Often the church's fall was located in the rise of Constantine, through whom the Catholic Church and the Roman state became unholy allies. Thus the story of postapostolic Christianity was mainly one of decline and defection from the pure forms and beliefs of the New Testament period.

Accordingly, the reform of the church consisted of putting it back into its prefall condition. In America such sentiments have produced powerful "back to the Bible" or "no creed but Christ" movements. Some reformers were "restorationists" who believed that since the church's fall no true church existed in the world—until it was finally restored in their own movements.[40] "Primitivists" believed that New Testament Christianity was reproducible whenever people faithfully followed the Bible, not ecclesiastical traditions.[41] Both groups were convinced that the best church was the first church, which was completely recoverable.

Twentieth-century evangelicals and fundamentalists often sounded like restorationists and primitivists. They claimed to put the Bible above all other authorities and often called themselves simple, New Testament Christians. But in most cases their primitivism was not pure. Parts of the historic Christian tradition they fully embraced. Though most probably believed that the church fell sometime after the apostles, they also believed that the original gospel was more or less restored by the Reformation. Consequently, to them "that old time religion" meant more than the New Testament church; it also referred to the legacy of the Reformation.[42]

It was this primitivistic search for the original New Testament church that drove the former Campus Crusaders in new directions. By the end of 1973, the old Crusade network reconnected to lend support for the com-

39. Richard T. Hughes and C. Leonard Allen, *Illusions of Innocence: Protestant Primitivism in America, 1630–1875* (Chicago: University of Chicago Press, 1988); Richard T. Hughes, ed., *The American Quest for the Primitive Church* (Urbana and Chicago: University of Illinois Press, 1988).

40. Committed to this perspective were Alexander Campbell's Disciples, Barton W. Stone's Christians, Joseph Smith's Church of Jesus Christ of Latter Day Saints, and the Pentecostals of the early twentieth century.

41. See Hatch, *The Democratization of American Christianity*, for a study of how such notions produced powerful populist movements in the early nineteenth century.

42. Joel A. Carpenter, "Contending for the Faith Once Delivered: Primitivist Impulses in American Fundamentalism," in Hughes, ed., *The American Quest for the Primitive Church*, 99–119.

mon experiment with house churches. Seven men over forty were designated "elders" and agreed to meet together once a quarter to study and strategize. According to Peter Gillquist, one of the newly designated elders, at one of the group's first meetings the discussion took an unexpected turn. Jack Sparks, who had the advantage (according to Gillquist) of not having had any formal theological education, raised a new issue: "As Protestants, we know our way back to A.D. 1517 and the Reformation. As evangelicals—Bible people—we know our way up to A.D. 95 or so, when the Apostle John finished writing the Revelation. It's time to fill the gap in between."[43] What happened to the New Testament church between its fall in the second century and its restoration in the Reformation?

None of the assembled elders claimed to know *where* the New Testament church had gone. Jon Braun said, "In all honesty, I was taught that the minute the Apostle John drew his last breath, the Church began to head downhill. Is that really right? And if it isn't, then where and when did the Church go wrong? How could the Reformation have been avoided, anyway?"[44] The elders then assigned topics: Sparks took worship, Braun early church history, Richard Ballew doctrine, Ken Berven the pre-Reformation period, and Ray Nethery the post-Reformation era. Gordon Walker was assigned to check all conclusions by the Bible, and Peter Gillquist acted as administrator for the project. "Our basic question was, whatever happened to that Church we read about in the pages of the New Testament? Was it still around? If so, where? We wanted to be a part of it."[45]

The group reconvened in February, 1975 and shared findings. Much to everyone's surprise, they discovered that the church of the New Testament period kept on going into the second, third, and fourth centuries and was liturgical, sacramental, hierarchical, and conciliar. Thus, they concluded, the New Testament church had been "catholic" from the beginning. Here were some rather uncritical assumptions and untested conclusions about the nature of both the church and history. That the apostolic church continued after the apostles comes as no surprise to any beginning student of church history; but the former Crusaders evidently assumed that continuation meant changeless continuity.

On the basis of this discovery, the elders decided that their house churches needed to change. They organized the New Covenant Apostolic Order (NCAO), which adopted a hierarchical structure (one bishop presiding over each congregation) and a more liturgical worship style.[46] Such

---

43. Gillquist, *Becoming Orthodox*, 24.
44. Ibid., 24–25.
45. Ibid., 28.
46. The NCAO's views of episcopal authority were roundly criticized in some evangelical circles as authoritarian and abusive. See Bill Counts, *The Evangelical Orthodox Church and the New Covenant Apostolic Order* (Berkeley: The Spiritual Counterfeits Project, 1979).

changes reflected a deeper shift in the group's evangelical identity. Instead of defining themselves primarily in terms of the Bible and the Protestant Reformation, the people in NCAO began to identify more with the historic, pre-Protestant church and its practices. They set out on the difficult task of tracing the pure, unaltered New Testament church through time.

Such an enterprise is filled with hazards. The history of Christianity is complicated, to say the least. Even for those with deep loyalties to the historic Christian tradition, unraveling the relationship between continuity and change can be daunting. Students of early Christianity must face up to certain difficult issues. For example, what difference did the Gentile mission make in the early church's identity? What impact did adopting Greek philosophical categories have in the development of Christian theology? How did living under an imperial political structure influence the church's approach to hierarchical leadership? And how did the church's expansion into "barbarian" territories affect its piety and liturgy? It is important to emphasize that leading Orthodox scholars do understand these issues and are careful to nuance their discussions about the church's continuity with the apostolic church.[47] In contrast, the leaders of the NCAO took a naïve and unsophisticated approach that failed to take the church's complex passage through time seriously.

As Grant Wacker has pointed out, from the late nineteenth century on, evangelicals have been deeply troubled by what he calls "historical consciousness," the realization that movements are unavoidably shaped by their contexts, that nothing in history is free from forces that both expand and limit.[48] Large segments of American evangelicalism have never come to terms with this perspective, preferring to stress the supernatural over the natural or to separate the two until the supernatural operates apart from the natural. Consequently, by this perspective, a church is either pure or impure, apostolic or nonapostolic, "New Testament" or some cor-

47. See, for example, George Florovsky, *Bible, Church, Tradition: An Eastern Orthodox View* (Belmont, Mass.: Nordland Publishing, 1972); idem, "The Predicament of the Christian Historian," reprinted in C. T. McIntire, ed., *God, History, and Historians* (New York: Oxford, 1977), 406–42; idem, "The Limits of the Church," *Church History Review* 117 (1933): 129ff.; Alexander Schmemann, *The Historical Road of Eastern Orthodoxy* (Crestwood, N.Y.: St. Vladimir's Seminary Press, 1992); John Meyendorff, *Living Tradition: Orthodox Witness in the Contemporary World* (Crestwood, N.Y.: St. Vladimir's Seminary Press, 1978); idem, *Catholicity and the Church* (Crestwood, N.Y.: St. Vladimir's Seminary Press, 1983); S. Breck, J. Meyendorff, and E. Silk, *The Legacy of St. Vladimir* (Crestwood, N.Y.: St. Vladimir's Seminary Press, 1990), 14–20; Bradley Nassif, "New Dimensions in Eastern Orthodox Theology," in David Dockery, ed., *New Dimensions in Evangelical Thought* (Downers Grove, Ill.: Inter-Varsity, 1998).

48. Grant Wacker, *Augustus H. Strong and the Dilemma of Historical Consciousness* (Macon, Ga.: Mercer University Press, 1985).

rupt defection. At its base, then, such a view attempts to keep the church free from historical contingencies and corrupting influences. The real church is *in* history, but it is not *of* history.

In their search for the original church, the NCAO adopted such an approach. For them, the history of the New Testament church through time looked remarkably straightforward and uncomplicated. For a millennium, the church carried on virtually unscathed, able to ward off anything that might compromise its essential purity and its continuity with the original church. But then, in 1054, the unity of the New Testament church was broken by the Great Schism, in which papal pretensions and the Western church's addition of *filioque* to the Creed drove a wedge between the Eastern and Western churches. Not even the Protestant Reformation could overcome the schism and reestablish unified New Testament Christianity. In their zeal to correct the abuses of Roman Catholicism, many Protestants rejected crucial elements of the original church, such as hierarchy, liturgy, the sacraments, and the like.

> Thus, while retaining in varying degrees portions of foundational Christianity, neither Protestantism nor Catholicism can lay historic claim to being the true New Testament Church. In dividing from the Orthodox Church, Rome forfeited its place in the Church of the New Testament. In the divisions of the Reformation, the Protestants—as well meaning as they might have been—failed to return to the New Testament Church.[49]

This view of church history can be clearly seen in "A Time Line of Church History."[50] It shows the "one holy catholic and apostolic church" stretching out in a straight line from Pentecost to the Great Schism in 1054, where a branch labeled the Roman Catholic Church splits off. From that branch other splits emerge, including those of the Reformation. While the Roman Catholic Church and Protestant churches head off in other directions, the one holy catholic and apostolic church continues in its straight line, which after 1054 is labeled "the Orthodox Church."

Historians of American religious history will recognize this plot line as a kind of "successionism." Unlike restorationists who teach that the church fell early on and had to be restored in more recent times, successionists hold that the true church never ceased to exist. While the rest of "Christendom" degenerated, a remnant of the New Testament church continued on, alive, pure, and uncompromising. Landmarkist Baptists, for

49. Jon Braun, *Finding the New Testament Church* (Ben Lomond, Calif.: Conciliar Press, 1992), 16–17.

50. The time line can be found in Gillquist, *Becoming Orthodox*, 48–49, or in a pamphlet entitled *A Time Line of Church History*, available separately from Conciliar Press.

example, trace a pure "trail of blood" through the history of corrupt Christianity into the present day, thereby providing that only Baptists have New Testament legitimacy.[51] Of course, to arrive at such conclusions, successionists must be highly selective and ignore all evidence to the contrary. They must also maintain an idealized and naïve view of the past. In the end, successionism is based on one's theology or ideology, not on any critical historical analysis.[52]

This orientation to the past is common among the evangelical Orthodox. A number of evangelical clergy who converted to Orthodoxy told their stories in Coming Home.[53] According to the book's editor, "Almost every author shares his fervent desire for the New Testament Church, the Faith of the Apostles, the Pearl of Great Price, authentic worship in spirit and in truth—in short, original Christianity."[54] A former Presbyterian and graduate of Westminster Theological Seminary claimed, "I am now serving Him in the very Church of Antioch which Saint Luke describes so vividly in Acts, and which has continued on unabated for almost two thousand years."[55] A former Baptist minister exclaimed, "I had found the Church which our Lord said would stand the test of time and assault the very gates of hell."[56] According to a former Lutheran, "The Church of the New Testament, the Church of Peter and Paul and the Apostles, the Orthodox Church—despite persecution, political oppression, and desertion on certain of its flanks—miraculously carries on today the same faith and life of the Church of the New Testament."[57]

Fashioning an Orthodox Church for America

By the mid-1970s, then, the NCAO's search was clearly leading in the direction of Orthodoxy. But none of the church's leaders knew anything about Orthodoxy in the modern world. "Where was this Orthodox

51. Because successionist groups consider themselves to be in the unbroken line of New Testament churches, they do not consider themselves Protestants: if one's church has never been corrupted, there is no need to reform it. On Baptist successionism, see James Edward McGoldrick, Baptist Successionism: A Crucial Question in Baptist History, ATLA Monograph Series 32 (Metuchen, N.J.: American Theological Library Association/Scarecrow Press, 1994).

52. Of course, the Evangelical Orthodox successionist claims have much more warrant than those of Landmarkist Baptists; but both groups view the past in remarkably similar terms and build their cases in selective and uncritical ways.

53. Peter E. Gillquist, ed., Coming Home: Why Protestant Clergy Are Becoming Orthodox (Ben Lomond, Calif.: Conciliar Press, 1992).

54. Ibid., 14.

55. Ibid., 42.

56. Ibid., 99–100.

57. Gillquist, Becoming Orthodox, 57.

Church today? Was it still around? Or had it quietly died away sometime in the late Middle Ages? The truth is, *none* of us had ever to our knowledge been inside an Orthodox Church. Most of us did not know it existed. For that reason, I am chagrined to report that we decided to try to start it over again!"[58]

The year 1977 was a turning point for the NCAO. First, it founded a school of its own, the Academy of Orthodox Theology (later renamed after St. Athanasius) in Santa Barbara, under the leadership of Jack Sparks.[59] Second, it started its own publishing house, Conciliar Press, which issued *Again* magazine.[60] Third, it made its first contacts with contemporary Orthodoxy. Alexander Schmemann of St. Vladimir's Seminary in New York heard about the group in Santa Barbara, then informed Bishop Dmitri of the Orthodox Church of America, who asked Ted Wojcik, pastor of the Saint Innocent Orthodox Church in a Los Angeles suburb, to call on the Academy.

That single visit opened many other doors. During the next year (1978), the contacts with Orthodoxy dramatically increased. A group of NCAO leaders visited Fr. Wojcik's parish in Los Angeles and saw for the first time an Orthodox liturgy. Then a delegation visited St. Vladimir's Seminary to consult with professors there, including Alexander Schmemann, Thomas Hopko, and John Meyendorff. Schmemann took a special interest in the group and traveled to Santa Barbara to advise NCAO leaders. Bishop Dmitri, who had grown up a Texas Southern Baptist, also visited the Academy during 1978 and lent his support.

By 1979, their minds were made up: Orthodoxy was the New Testament church; and they must be a part of it. Accordingly, the NCAO, which had been a rather informal network of congregations, became the Evangelical Orthodox Church (EOC), "a Denomination within the One Holy Catholic and Apostolic Church."[61] Doctrinally, the EOC affirmed the Apostles', Nicene, and Chalcedonian Creeds. It declared itself against abortion, divorce, homosexuality, and women serving as spiritual leaders. It also rejected "as a mark of apostacy [sic] the spread of parachurch movements as a substitute means of accomplishing the great commission of the Church."[62] The EOC's highest governing authority was the Council of

---

58. Ibid., 54.

59. After the Evangelical Orthodox joined the Antiochian Church, the Academy became a correspondence school.

60. The magazine is still published quarterly, with about five thousand copies of each issue printed.

61. George Vecsey, "New Group Combines Evangelism and Orthodoxy," *New York Times*, 11 May 1979, 25. The quotation is from a promotional brochure distributed by the EOC. The brochure is hereafter referred to as *The Evangelical Orthodox Church*.

62. *The Evangelical Orthodox Church*.

Bishops, on which nineteen bishops served, including Peter Gillquist, who was appointed presiding bishop.[63]

If these evangelicals wanted to become Orthodox, why did they not simply join existing Orthodox parishes?[64] The answer is not difficult. First, by the time the leaders decided to become Eastern Orthodox, they were presiding over congregations with histories of their own and a strong sense of their own identity. To join existing Orthodox parishes would mean breaking up closely knit religious communities with established authority structures.

Second, they discovered that the road to Orthodoxy was strewn with perils of various kinds. To be in love with Orthodoxy as a historical abstraction was one thing, but to come in contact with it as a contemporary reality was something else again. When the Evangelical Orthodox finally started to visit Orthodox parishes, their first impressions were often negative and disillusioning. The liturgies were not in English; the congregations were ethnic and apparently uncommitted; and the worship practices were exotic.[65] The search for the original church had led these unsuspecting American evangelicals into a world of strange sights, sounds, and smells: clouds of incense, elaborate vestments, prayers to the saints and for the dead, and veneration of the Mother of God and the holy icons, some of which even wept occasionally. Historically, evangelicals had considered such practices as clear evidence of Orthodoxy's *fallenness*. Where were such things found in the New Testament? But if the evangelicals were going to complete their pilgrimage, they had to find a way of embracing them. "Becoming Orthodox" in the full sense meant accepting the tradition whole; the faithful were not allowed to pick and choose what they liked.

63. The brochure listed the books published by its bishops: J. Richard Ballew, *The Place Where God Lives* (Seattle: Conciliar Press, 1976); idem, *Coming in Out of the Cold* (Seattle: Conciliar Press, 1976); Kenneth A. Berven, *Blest Be the Tie that Frees* (Minneapolis: Augsburg, 1973); idem, *I Love Being Married to a Grandma* (Nashville: Thomas Nelson, 1978); Jon E. Braun, *It Ain't Gonna Reign No More* (Nashville: Thomas Nelson, 1978); idem, *Whatever Happened to Hell?* (Nashville: Thomas Nelson, 1979); Peter E. Gillquist, *Love Is Now*, rev. ed. (Grand Rapids: Zondervan, 1978); idem, *The Physical Side of Being Spiritual* (Grand Rapids: Zondervan, 1979); Jack N. Sparks, *The Mindbenders* (Nashville: Thomas Nelson, 1977); idem, *The Apostolic Fathers* (Nashville: Thomas Nelson, 1978); idem, *Going Back Home* (Seattle: Conciliar Press, 1979); idem, *The Resurrection Letters* (Nashville: Thomas Nelson, 1980); Gordon T. Walker, *Twentieth Century Apostleship* (Seattle: Conciliar Press, 1976).

64. It must be remembered that numerous evangelical Protestants had converted to Orthodoxy before the dramatic entry of the Evangelical Orthodox in 1987. For them, there had been no other alternative but to join existing congregations.

65. Gillquist, *Coming Home*, 87, 117, 123–24, 156; Frank Schaeffer, *Dancing Alone: The Quest for Orthodox Faith in the Age of False Religions* (Brookline, Mass.: Holy Cross Orthodox Press, 1994), 297–315.

That took some time. In 1981, for example, Gillquist reflected on where the EOC stood on a number of issues. "From what I can tell of the relationship in Orthodoxy between Holy Scripture and tradition, we have no problems. We have read Timothy Ware's *The Orthodox Church* and concur with its stance." Concerning the saints, Gillquist affirmed that "the righteous dead are far from dormant. If they can intercede for us as earthly saints, they can certainly pray for us as saints in their heavenly state as well." He struggled a bit more with Orthodoxy's teachings about Mary. While he could affirm Mary as *theotokos* against the Nestorian heresy, the matter of her "ever-virginity" was more of a problem: "We would give our eye-teeth, however, for a verse or two in Scripture to back this up—that would certainly make it much easier for us to communicate orthodoxy with our Protestant assailants." On icons Gillquist said, "We feel that in the West, it would be helpful if the iconography were *a bit more* in keeping with our culture, rather than with 9th Century Byzantium. But we are certainly flexible on that particular issue."[66]

The EOC bishops forged ahead in their attempt to reconnect with historic Orthodoxy. They consulted with Orthodox leaders from the three jurisdictions in North America, they asked questions, and they set up altars and icons in their parishes. They worked hard to develop an Orthodox *phronema* (mind-set). By 1985 the EOC decided to seek formal entry into the Orthodox church; but they quickly discovered that the leaders of the Greek and Russian jurisdictions were reluctant to receive them. Discouraged by the poor reception in America, the EOC decided to seek the approval of the ecumenical patriarch and his advice about the best way to enter the church. After considerable planning, in June 1985 a contingent of EOC bishops traveled to Constantinople (Istanbul); but before they arrived, a number of Greek Orthodox clergy had persuaded the patriarch not to meet with the EOC group because they feared that evangelicals would subvert the Hellenic culture of parishes in America. Disillusioned and angry, the EOC bishops returned home empty-handed.[67]

A few days after their return, Peter Gillquist, Jon Braun, and Richard Ballew met in Los Angeles with Metropolitan Philip Saliba and Patriarch Ignatius, who were enthusiastic about the possibility of receiving the EOC into the Antiochian Archdiocese of North America. Over the next year and a half, the details unfolded. Both sides agreed on a proposal for how the EOC should be received, the EOC's liturgical practices were reviewed

66. Peter Gillquist, "The Evangelical Orthodox Church," *Theosis* (February 1981): 3–6. Later on, Gillquist was less tentative. He vigorously defended the perpetual virginity of Mary, along with her assumption and her heavenly intercession for sinners. See Peter Gillquist, *Facing Up to Mary* (Ben Lomond, Calif.: Conciliar Press, n.d.), 9–10, 13–14.

67. I am following the account in Gillquist, *Becoming Orthodox.*

and adjusted, and final arrangements were made for early 1987. From February through March, Antiochian bishops received clergy and laypeople from the EOC into the church. Because Orthodox tradition does not allow married bishops, the EOC bishops could not maintain their episcopal rank. They were ordained first as deacons, then as priests of the Antiochian Church. Seventeen of the EOC parishes were received and allowed to remain intact. The movement that had begun with Campus Crusade for Christ had now become the Antiochian Evangelical Orthodox Mission (AEOM), a full-fledged part of Orthodoxy.[68]

When Metropolitan Philip Saliba welcomed the evangelicals, he expressed hope that they would spearhead an Orthodox evangelistic outreach into American culture.

> In America, our various Orthodox jurisdictions have been ministering to ethnic communities. We have lost some of the Church's missionary spirit, and so far have not made any breakthrough in American society.
>
> I think the main task of the EOM is to preach the gospel to America. I don't want them to lose their identity as an evangelical missionary group. I feel strongly that our best gift to America will be a stable Christianity that is rooted in the Bible, holy tradition, and the fathers of the Church.[69]

The AEOM took this mandate seriously. The year after entering the church, they sponsored a conference on missions and evangelism; but no one outside the Antiochian Archdiocese came. In 1990 representatives of the Orthodox Church of America (the Russian Orthodox jurisdiction) attended and offered to join forces with the AEOM. In 1991, an observer from the Greek Orthodox Church came and almost immediately got permission from Archbishop Iakavos to align the Greek Church with the annual conferences. By 1992, the gathering was renamed the "Pan-Orthodox Conference on Missions and Evangelism" and marked a new level of cooperation among the three Orthodox jurisdictions. This kind of networking around mission concerns is historically what American evangelicals do best and indicates something of the zeal and contagious enthusiasm of the evangelical converts.[70]

---

68. Not everyone in the EOC went along. Five of the nineteen bishops and about 1,200 laypeople declined the invitation to join. The main problem seemed to be ecclesiological: some did not want to put themselves under the control of "foreign" jurisdictions, and others resisted having to submit to an outdated canon law that forbade married bishops when the Bible allowed the practice (1 Tim. 3:2). See James Mark Kushiner, "The Evangelical Orthodox," *Touchstone* (Fall 1987): 20–21, 24. Kenneth Samuel Jensen, "The Case for a Living Orthodoxy," *Touchstone* (Winter 1989): 14–18.

69. Quoted in Bradley Nassif, "Evangelical Denomination Gains Official Acceptance into the Orthodox Church," *Christianity Today* (Feb. 6, 1987): 40.

70. Telephone interview with Peter Gillquist, August 16, 1994.

Another significant accomplishment of the AEOM is the *Orthodox Study Bible: New Testament and Psalms*, which was published in 1993.[71] The *Study Bible's* purpose is obvious: to encourage Bible study among the Orthodox and to demonstrate that Orthodoxy is rooted in biblical teaching. Thus the notes at the bottom of each page often quote from Orthodox sources or explain how the text relates to Orthodox teaching or practice. Following the basic format of other evangelical study Bibles (e.g., the *Scofield Reference Bible* and the *Ryrie Study Bible*), the *Orthodox Study Bible* also includes brief introductions and outlines for each biblical book, cross references, a concordance, a glossary, a harmony of the Gospels, articles on various themes, a lectionary, a collection of morning and evening prayers, maps, and numerous icons to illustrate the text. Peter Gillquist served as project director, and first drafts of the textual notes were prepared by people at the AEOM's St. Athanasius Academy. Their work was then reviewed by other Orthodox biblical scholars and hierarchs. In its first year, the *Orthodox Study Bible* sold 75,000 copies and is the first Bible of its kind produced by and for the Orthodox in America.

No activities are more typically evangelical than strategizing for evangelism and putting the Bible into the hands of laypeople—and no activities have more potential for disturbing established ecclesiastical hierarchies. In the history of American religion, evangelism—especially the kind that works—has tended to challenge traditional structures and the theologies behind them. Likewise, putting the Bible into the hands of common people—especially those who like to read it on their own—has sometimes had revolutionary and unintended consequences. Bible reading by laypeople, some creedal churches have learned to their cost, can cause more trouble than it is worth. Furthermore, ethnic churches that try to evangelize the broader American culture often end up being Americanized themselves.

As sincere as evangelical Orthodox mission to America is, many questions remain. What if the AEOM succeeds? What if Americans begin to respond to the evangelistic program in significant numbers? Will they be welcomed in non-AEOM, ethnic Orthodox parishes? What kinds of cultural and religious identity crises will result from a successful mission to America? What if American Orthodox laity read their Bibles and come to conclusions different from those of their bishops? How long will it be before those in charge stop dreaming of turning America Orthodox and start worrying about Orthodoxy becoming too American? Before 1987, evangelical Protestant converts to Orthodoxy joined existing congrega-

71. *The Orthodox Study Bible: New Testament and Psalms* (Nashville: Thomas Nelson, 1993). The translation is the New King James Version.

tions and had to cope with ethnic realities, but what will happen now that the evangelicals have their own parishes, where a distinctly American style can develop?

Of course, it is much too early to answer such questions. As things now stand, the AEOM seems to be no threat to the Orthodox establishment. Their parishes are growing but not explosively. As recent converts, the evangelicals are enthusiastic, loyal, and obedient. Though their style is sometimes not what most Orthodox are accustomed to—an Orthodox *phronema* is not achieved overnight—their theology is unabashedly Orthodox.[72] In fact, on some crucial doctrines, they no longer sound like Protestant evangelicals at all.

For example, no issue is more important to evangelicals than the doctrine of salvation. At the heart of evangelicalism is the conviction that salvation is a gift of God's grace that comes to sinners through their faith in Christ. Salvation cannot be earned or merited; it must be received by faith, apart from human works. Evangelicals believe that being baptized or holding church membership or even believing the right things is not enough. Each person needs to repent and trust in Christ. This is what evangelicals mean by being "saved" or "born again" and why they invite others to receive Christ and experience conversion by the power of the Holy Spirit.[73]

The leaders of the AEOM no longer teach this doctrine. In fact, they are quite critical of it. Frank Schaeffer, a former evangelical whose pilgrimage did not follow the Campus Crusade-NCAO-EOC-AEOM route, calls the standard evangelical doctrine a "false bill of goods." "The simplistic 'born-again' formula for instant painless 'salvation' is not only a misunderstanding, I believe it is a heresy. It contradicts the teaching of Christ in regard to the narrow, hard, ascetic, difficult way of salvation." Real salvation "is not found in simplistic formulas but in choosing to grow into the people God created us to be and by a life-long ascetic, sacramental struggle for holiness."[74]

In his booklet on "Entering God's Kingdom," Pete Gillquist sounds like the old Campus Crusade evangelist when affirming that salvation is God's

---

72. Conciliar Press, the AEOM's publishing arm, publishes a series of booklets that explain Orthodox doctrine to outsiders, especially Protestant evangelicals. Titles include: *Finding the New Testament Church; No Graven Image; Which Came First: The Church or the New Testament? Entering God's Kingdom; Facing Up to Mary;* and *Scripture and Tradition.*

73. For two typical Protestant evangelical theologies of conversion, see Donald Bloesch, *Essentials of Evangelical Theology: God, Authority, and Salvation,* vol. 1 (New York: Harper and Row, 1978), 181–252; Stanley J. Grenz, *Theology for the Community of God* (Nashville: Broadman and Holman, 1994), 528–99.

74. Schaeffer, *Dancing Alone,* 256–57. Frank Schaeffer and his father Francis Schaeffer were well-known evangelical apologists and social critics during the seventies and eighties.

gift, impossible to earn by our own merit; but then he adds a distinctly Orthodox perspective: "Through Christ, we are born from above through Holy Baptism into newness of life." For salvation to be authentic, it must be lived out within the Orthodox church: "For one must live within the body of Christ, be fed by her sacraments, be instructed in her true faith, and worship at her altar to attain the godliness and righteousness that lead to the Kingdom's open doors."

> Let me ask you a sincere question. Are you willing to flee to Jesus Christ for protection in His Holy Church, to learn to know Him, to be cleansed and changed? If so, a new life in Christ lies ahead for you. Your next step is to get to know an Orthodox priest in your area who can guide you through a time of preparation and instruction in the Christian faith, and then union with Christ in holy baptism.[75]

In the *Orthodox Study Bible*, the Protestant evangelical doctrine of salvation is often used as a foil for Orthodox teaching. Even common evangelical phraseology is criticized: "Becoming a Christian is not so much inviting Christ into one's life as getting oneself into Christ's life."[76] Justification is *not* by faith *alone*, since from apostolic times Orthodox have believed that "salvation was granted by the mercy of God to righteous men and women."

> This is why the modern evangelical Protestant question, "Are you saved?" gives pause to an Orthodox believer. As the subject of salvation is addressed in Scripture, the Orthodox Christian would see it in at least three aspects: (a) I have been saved, being joined to Christ in baptism; (b) I am being saved, growing in Christ through the sacramental life of the Church; and (c) I will be saved, by the mercy of God at the Last Judgment.[77]

Such statements make it obvious that the evangelical Orthodox have left their former views of evangelism far behind. Whereas some evangelicals in sacramental traditions (e.g., the Lutherans and Episcopalians) might view the relationship between conversion and sacraments in similar ways, most evangelicals would not. In an effort to correct what they believe was their earlier error—of leading people to Christ without adequately stressing the importance of the church or the need for obedience to Christ's commands—the evangelical Orthodox now affirm a doctrine of salvation that most evangelicals cannot accept. From an evangelical

---

75. Peter Gillquist, *Entering God's Kingdom* (Ben Lomond, Calif.: Conciliar Press, 1987), 7, 13–14.

76. *Orthodox Study Bible*, 439.

77. From an article on "Justification by Faith" in *The Orthodox Study Bible*, 348.

perspective, their teaching does not make distinct *enough* the absolute importance of personally receiving by faith the gracious gift of God in Christ, apart from all human works—even good religious ones. Such a "Catholic" view of faith and works dangerously confuses the closely connected but still distinct doctrines of justification and sanctification: once justified, the redeemed are able to do works of righteousness (Eph. 2:8–10); but good works play no role in the sinner's justification before God. Sanctification (becoming holy) follows justification; it is not the basis for justification. One thing seems clear: in their mission to America, the evangelical Orthodox will not preach the same message that they used to preach.

What about the AEOM's relationship to the Orthodox "system"? Many of the evangelicals are bewildered by the three Orthodox jurisdictions in America and a bit put off by the church's ethnic identity. But their successful bridge building between the jurisdictions through the Pan-Orthodox Conferences on Missions and Evangelism and their ability to fashion their own nonethnic congregations have mitigated those concerns to some extent. Likewise, the evangelical Orthodox seem to be on the best of terms with the bishops. In fact, some reform-minded "cradle Orthodox" have accused the AEOM of being too compliant. Archimandrite Fr. Eusebius Stephanou, whose Orthodox Brotherhood of St. Symeon the New Theologian promotes charismatic renewal within the church, has criticized the AEOM for preaching Orthodoxy rather than Christ and viewing "everything in the Orthodox Church through rose-colored glasses." So concerned to appear loyal to the bishops and the tradition, the evangelicals are, he says, unrealistic about the real state of the church, blind to its desperate need for renewal, and too uncritically obedient to the hierarchy.[78]

Nevertheless, there are already signs that the evangelicals are willing to address some problems. In addition to saving souls, evangelicals have historically also been interested in the renewal of churches, which requires a willingness to engage in prophetic critique. As delighted as they were to finally be part of the New Testament church, the evangelicals were shocked to discover that many Orthodox did not appreciate the "pearl of great price" that they already possessed. The Orthodox church was true, but it was not perfect.

No one has been more outspoken on such matters than Frank Schaeffer, who was an often abrasive critic within and against evangelicalism before his conversion to Greek Orthodoxy in 1990. Now a frequent speaker in Orthodox circles, Schaeffer has turned his critical eye on his

---

78. Eusebius Stephanou, "Converts to Orthodoxy: A Grave Concern," *The Logos* 25 (November/December 1992), 1–2, 4.

new spiritual home.[79] Like the other evangelical converts, Schaeffer is convinced that he has finally found the New Testament church: "Our altars are clean, our liturgies are pure, the Spirit dwells within our sanctuaries. We have not changed."[80] Yet Schaeffer sees two Orthodox churches in the United States. One is the historic church, unchanging and undefiled; the other is "a sort of social-ethnic club" infected with nominalism, materialism, ethnic pride and exclusivism, indifference to the sacraments, and "the Protestant disease of individualism and democracy." Many recent converts, eager to experience New Testament Christianity in the modern world, have felt unwelcome in Russian, Greek, or Middle Eastern congregations. Schaeffer calls this division of Orthodoxy into ethnic jurisdictions the "Protestantizing" of Orthodoxy in America.

"Becoming Protestant" is a great temptation for Orthodoxy in America, according to Schaeffer. This tendency can be clearly seen in the way parish councils quarrel with their dioceses over financial matters and show disrespect to local priests who stand "in the place of the bishop, and ultimately of Christ."[81] It can also be seen in Orthodoxy's participation in the ecumenical movement, desiring to fit into the broader Christian community in America. This is a serious mistake, says Schaeffer, who calls Orthodox ecumenist Fr. George Florovsky "misguided" and "blinded by his own innocent good will."[82]

Though Schaeffer does not speak for all of the evangelical converts to Orthodoxy, his analysis of the church and his hopes and fears for Orthodoxy's future in the United States are probably widespread. While he urges Orthodoxy to mount a crusade to win America to Christ, he also wants the church to remain free of corrupting American and Protestant values, unchanged in its ancient theology, and firmly under the authority of its bishops and to become less ethnic at the local level and more aggressive in making its case against other Christian groups.[83]

As the history of the Orthodox church demonstrates, it is not easy to contextualize the faith in a given culture without accommodating to its values. From Constantine on, in the many places where Orthodoxy aligned with state powers, the church became identified with the surrounding culture. During subsequent centuries of persecution and marginalization, the church's isolation only deepened its ethnic identities. Thus

79. Schaeffer, *Dancing Alone*, 297–315.
80. Ibid., 311.
81. Ibid., 298–99. The use of parish councils in local Orthodox parishes grew out of the legal requirements of incorporation. As other episcopal churches (e.g., Roman Catholic and Episcopalian) in America have discovered, local lay control is difficult to avoid.
82. Ibid., 307–9.
83. Ibid., 310–15.

the differences within the Orthodox family of churches are cultural, linguistic, and social, not essentially theological. Such "ethnic" differences
have undercut attempts to evangelize the American people in any effective way. Will the coming of the evangelical Orthodox provide this entree
into American life? And is the church ready for the changes that contex-
tualizing its message in America will bring?

No one can say, but therein lies the irony. The hierarchy welcomed the
evangelicals in hopes that they might help Orthodoxy become something
it has never been: a church that is at home in America. But the evangelicals converted in large part because Orthodoxy was *not* identified with
American culture: it was the New Testament church, unstained by history
and modernity, not just another watered-down and Americanized version
of the original church. Maybe the most important question is whether the
evangelical Orthodox still have what it takes to mount a popular mission
to post-Christian America. For the AEOM to succeed, it will have to
preach Christ more than Orthodoxy—at least as it presently exists.

One other irony needs to be mentioned. In the 1990s, the growing edge
within otherwise declining mainline churches is found in vibrant ethnic
congregations, in which African-American, Latino, Korean, and Chinese
people create their own distinctive kinds of Christianity. In Orthodoxy,
the best chance for future growth lies in creating new "American ethnic"
congregations that have their own distinctive style. Whether or not this
mission to America can be embraced and affirmed by the other ethnic
Orthodox is uncertain.

Still, the hierarchy's hopes for the AEOM might be realized. After all,
according to some experts the current big winners in the American free-
market religious economy are those groups that build high walls, make
high demands, and never waiver from their convictions.[84] Because of their
successful search for the New Testament church, the evangelical Orthodox believe they can make the most exclusive claims of them all.

---

84. Roger Finke and Rodney Stark, *The Churching of America, 1776–1990: Winners and
Losers in Our Religious Economy* (New Brunswick, N.J.: Rutgers University Press, 1992).

Bibliography

Alexeev, Wassilij, and Theofanis G. Stavrou. *The Great Revival: The Russian Church under German Occupation*. Minneapolis: Burgess, 1976.

Anglican-Orthodox Dialogue: The Dublin Agreed Statement of 1984. Crestwood, N.Y.: St. Vladimir's Seminary Press, 1985.

Anglican-Orthodox Dialogue: The Moscow Agreed Statement of 1976. London: S.P.C.K., 1977.

Arseniev, Nicholas. *Mysticism and the Eastern Church*. Crestwood, N.Y.: St. Vladimir's Seminary Press, 1979.

Atiya, Aziz S. *A History of Eastern Christianity*. Notre Dame: University of Notre Dame Press, 1968.

Bajis, Jordan. *Common Ground: An Introduction to Eastern Christianity for the American Christian*. Minneapolis: Light and Life, 1991.

Baker, Derek. *The Orthodox Churches and the West*. Oxford: Basil Blackwell, 1976.

Beeson, Trevor. *Discretion and Valour: Religious Conditions in Russia and Eastern Europe*. Rev. ed. Philadelphia: Fortress, 1982.

Benz, Ernst. *The Eastern Orthodox Church: Its Thought and Life*. Translated by Richard and Clara Winston. Garden City, N.Y.: Anchor Books, 1963.

Billington, James H. *The Icon and the Axe: An Interpretive History of Russian Culture*. New York: Random House, 1966.

———. *Russia Transformed: Breakthrough to Hope*. New York: Free, 1992.

Blackmore, R. W., et al. *The Doctrine of the Russian Church*. Willits, Calif.: Eastern Orthodox Books, 1973.

Bociurkiw, Bohdan R., and John W. Strong, eds. *Religion and Atheism in the U.S.S.R. and Eastern Europe*. Toronto: University of Toronto Press, 1975.

Bourdeaux, Michael. *Gorbachev, Glasnost and the Gospel*. London: Hodder and Stoughton, 1990.

———. *Patriarch and Prophets: Persecution of the Russian Orthodox Church Today*. New York: Praeger, 1970.

———. *Religious Ferment in Russia: Protestant Opposition to Soviet Religious Policy*. New York: St. Martin's, 1968.

———. *Risen Indeed: Lessons in Faith from the USSR*. Crestwood, N.Y.: St. Vladimir's Seminary Press, 1983.

———, and Lorna Bourdeaux. *Ten Growing Soviet Churches*. Bromley, Kent: MARC Europe, 1987.

Bratsiotis, Panagiotes. "Fundamental Principles and Main Characteristics of the Orthodox Church." In *The Orthodox Ethos*, edited by A. J. Philippou, 23–31. Oxford: Holywell, 1964.

———. *The Greek Orthodox Church*. Notre Dame: University of Notre Dame Press, 1968.

Bulgakov, Sergius. *The Orthodox Church*. Rev. ed. Crestwood, N.Y.: St. Vladimir's Seminary Press, 1988.

———. *The Wisdom of God: A Brief Summary of Sophiology*. New York: Paisley, 1937.

Buss, Gerald. *The Bear's Hug; Christian Belief and the Soviet State, 1917–86*. Grand Rapids: Eerdmans, 1987.

Calian, Carnegie S. *Icon and Pulpit: The Protestant-Orthodox Encounter*. Philadelphia: Westminster, 1968.

273

————. *Theology without Boundaries: Encounters of Eastern Orthodoxy and Western Tradition.* Louisville: Westminster/John Knox, 1992.

Carroll, Colleen. *The New Faithful: Why Young Adults Are Embracing Christian Orthodoxy.* Chicago: Loyola Press, 2002.

Cavarnos, Constantine. *The Icon: Its Spiritual Basis and Purpose.* Belmont, Mass.: Institute for Byzantine and Modern Greek Studies, 1973.

Chmykhalov, Timothy, and Danny Smith. *The Last Christian: The Release of the Siberian Seven.* Grand Rapids: Zondervan, 1986.

Chrestou, Panagiotes. *Partakers of God.* Brookline, Mass.: Holy Cross Orthodox, 1984.

Chrysostomos, Archimandrite. *Contemporary Eastern Orthodox Thought: The Traditionalist Voice.* Belmont, Mass.: Nordland, 1982.

Clendenin, Daniel. "Why I'm Not Orthodox." *Christianity Today* 41.1 (Jan. 6, 1997).

Coniaris, Anthony M. *Introducing the Orthodox Church: Its Faith and Life.* Minneapolis: Light and Life, 1982.

Conquest, Robert. *The Great Terror: Stalin's Purge of the 1930s.* New York: Oxford University Press, 1990.

————. *The Harvest of Sorrows: Soviet Collectivization and the Terror-Famine.* New York: Oxford University Press, 1986.

————. *Religion in the U.S.S.R.* New York: Praeger, 1968.

————, ed. *The Last Empire: Nationality and the Soviet Future.* Stanford, Calif.: Hoover Institution Press, 1986.

Constantelos, Demetrios J. *The Greek Orthodox Church: Faith, History, and Practice.* New York: Seabury, 1967.

Copleston, Frederick C. *Philosophy in Russia.* Notre Dame: University of Notre Dame Press, 1986.

————. *Russian Religious Philosophy.* Notre Dame: University of Notre Dame Press, 1988.

Curtiss, John S. *Church and State in Russia: The Last Years of the Empire, 1900–1917.* New York: Octagon, 1940.

————. *The Russian Church and the Soviet State, 1917–1950.* Boston: Little, Brown, 1953.

Cutsinger, James, ed. *Reclaiming the Great Tradition: Evangelicals, Catholics and Orthodox in Dialogue.* Downers Grove, Ill.: Inter-Varsity, 1997.

Demetrakopoulos, George H. *Dictionary of Orthodox Theology: A Summary of the Beliefs, Practices, and History of the Eastern Orthodox Church.* New York: Philosophical Library, 1964.

Doulis, Thomas, ed. *Journeys to Orthodoxy: A Collection of Essays by Converts to Orthodox Christianity.* Minneapolis: Light and Life, 1986.

Dudko, Dmitrii. *Our Hope.* Crestwood, N.Y.: Saint Vladimir's Seminary Press, 1977.

Durasoff, Steve. *Pentecost behind the Iron Curtain.* Plainfield, N.J.: Logos International, 1972.

————. *The Russian Protestants: Evangelicals in the Soviet Union, 1944–1964.* Rutherford, N.J.: Fairleigh Dickinson University Press, 1969.

Dvornik, Francis. *Byzantium and the Roman Primacy.* New York: Fordham University Press, 1966.

Ellis, Jane. *The Russian Orthodox Church: A Contemporary History.* Bloomington: Indiana University Press, 1986.

Evdokimov, Paul. *The Art of the Icon: A Theology of Beauty.* Torrance, Calif.: Oakwood, 1990.

————. *L'Orthodoxie.* Paris: Delachaux and Niestlé, 1959.

Fairbairn, Donald. *Eastern Orthodoxy through Western Eyes.* Louisville: Westminster John Knox, 2002.

Fedotov, George P. *The Russian Religious Mind.* New York: Harper and Row, 1965. (2 vols. Cambridge, Mass.: Harvard University Press, 1946, 1966. Vol. 1, *Kievan Christianity: The Tenth to the Thirteenth Centuries*; Vol. 2, *The Middle Ages: The Thirteenth to the Fifteenth Centuries.*)

————. *A Treasury of Russian Spirituality.* 2 vols. Belmont, Mass.: Nordland, 1975.

Feuter, Paul. "Confessing Christ through the Liturgy: An Orthodox Challenge to Protestants." *International Review of Missions* 65 (1976): 123–28.

Fletcher, William C. *Religion and Soviet Foreign Policy, 1945–1970.* New York: Oxford University Press, 1973.

———. *The Russian Orthodox Church Underground, 1917–1970*. New York: Oxford University Press, 1971.

———. *Soviet Believers: The Religious Sector of the Population*. Lawrence, Kans.: Regents Press of Kansas, 1981.

———. *Soviet Charismatics*. New York: Peter Lang, 1985.

———. *A Study in Survival: The Church in Russia, 1927–1943*. New York: Macmillan, 1965.

Florensky, Pavel. *The Pillar and Ground of the Truth* (in Russian). Godstone, Eng.: Gregg, 1971.

Florovsky, George. *Collected Works*. 14 vols. Belmont, Mass.: Nordland, 1972–79 (vols. 1–5); Vaduz, Liech.: Büchervertriebsanstalt, 1987–89 (vols. 6–14). Vol. 1, *Bible, Church, Tradition* (1972); Vol. 2, *Christianity and Culture* (1974); Vol. 3, *Creation and Redemption* (1976); Vol. 4, *Aspects of Church History* (1975); Vols. 5–6, *The Ways of Russian Theology* (1979, 1987); Vol. 7, *Eastern Fathers of the Fourth Century* (1987); Vol. 8, *Byzantine Fathers of the Fifth Century* (1987); Vol. 9, *Byzantine Fathers of the Sixth to Eighth Centuries* (1987); Vol. 10, *Byzantine Ascetic and Spiritual Fathers* (1987); Vol. 11, *Theology and Literature* (1989); Vol. 12, *Philosophy* (1989); Vols. 13–14, *Ecumenism* (1989).

Fouyas, Methodios. *Orthodoxy, Roman Catholicism, and Anglicanism*. New York: Oxford University Press, 1972.

French, Reginald M. *The Eastern Orthodox Church*. New York: Hutchinson's University Library, 1951.

Gill, Joseph, and Edmund Flood. *The Orthodox: Their Relations with Rome*. London: Darton, Longman, and Todd, 1964.

Gillquist, Peter E. *Becoming Orthodox: A Journey to the Ancient Christian Faith*. Brentwood, Tenn.: Wolgemuth and Hyatt, 1989.

———. *Making America Orthodox: Ten Questions Most Asked of Orthodox Christians*. Brookline, Mass.: Holy Cross Orthodox, 1984.

———, ed. *Coming Home: Why Protestant Clergy Are Becoming Orthodox*. Ben Lomond, Calif.: Conciliar Press, 1992.

Goricheva, Tatiana. *Talking about God Is Dangerous: The Diary of a Russian Dissident*. New York: Crossroad, 1987.

Greek Orthodox Theological Review 22.1 (1977): 357–463; 27.1 (1982): 2–82 (Orthodox–Southern Baptist dialogues).

Hadjiantoniou, George A. *Protestant Patriarch: The Life of Cyril Lucaris*. Richmond: John Knox, 1961.

Harper, Michael and Peter Gillquist, eds. *A Faith Fulfilled: Why Are Christians across Great Britain Embracing Orthodoxy?* Ben Lomond, Calif.: Conciliar Press, 1999.

Hebly, J. A. (Hans). *Protestants in Russia*. Grand Rapids: Eerdmans, 1976.

Hill, Kent R. *The Soviet Union on the Brink: An Inside Look at Christianity and Glasnost*. Portland: Multnomah, 1991.

———. *Turbulent Times for the Soviet Church*. Portland: Multnomah, 1991.

Hopko, Thomas. *All the Fulness of God: Essays on Orthodoxy, Ecumenism and Modern Society*. Crestwood, N.Y.: St. Vladimir's Seminary Press, 1982.

———. "Criteria of Truth in Orthodox Theology." *St. Vladimir's Theological Quarterly* 15.3 (1971): 121–29.

———. *Lenten Spring: Readings for Great Lent*. Crestwood, N.Y.: St. Vladimir's Seminary Press, 1983.

———. *The Orthodox Faith*. 4 vols. Crestwood, N.Y.: St. Vladimir's Seminary Press, 1984.

———. *Winter Pascha: Readings for the Christmas-Epiphany Season*. Crestwood, N.Y.: St. Vladimir's Seminary Press, 1984.

———. *Women and the Priesthood*. Crestwood, N.Y.: St. Vladimir's Seminary Press, 1983.

House, Francis. *Millennium of Faith: Christianity in Russia, 988–1988*. Crestwood, N.Y.: St. Vladimir's Seminary Press, 1988.

Hussey, Joan M. *The Orthodox Church in the Byzantine Empire*. New York: Oxford University Press, 1986.

Karmiris, John. *A Synopsis of the Dogmatic Theology of the Orthodox Catholic Church*. Scranton, Pa.: Christian Orthodox Edition, 1973.

Kline, George L. *Religious and Anti-Religious Thought in Russia*. Chicago: University of Chicago Press, 1968.

Landmarks: A Collection of Essays on the Russian Intelligentsia, trans. Marian Schwartz (New York: Karz Howard, 1977).

Lane, Christel. *Christian Religion in the Soviet Union: A Sociological Study*. Winchester, Mass.: Allen and Unwin, 1978.

Lapeyrouse, Stephen L. *Towards the Spiritual Convergence of America and Russia*. Santa Cruz, Calif.: Stephen L. Lapeyrouse, 1990.

Lossky, Vladimir. *In the Image and Likeness of God*. Crestwood, N.Y.: St. Vladimir's Seminary Press, 1974.

———. *The Mystical Theology of the Eastern Church*. Crestwood, N.Y.: St. Vladimir's Seminary Press, 1976.

———. *Orthodox Theology: An Introduction*. Crestwood, N.Y.: St. Vladimir's Seminary Press, 1978.

———. *The Vision of God*. Crestwood, N.Y.: St. Vladimir's Seminary Press, 1963.

Makrakis, Apostolos. *An Orthodox-Protestant Dialogue*. Chicago: Orthodox Christian Educational Society, 1966.

Maloney, George A. *A History of Orthodox Theology since 1453*. Belmont, Mass.: Nordland, 1976.

Mantzaridis, Georgios I. *The Deification of Man*. Crestwood, N.Y.: St. Vladimir's Seminary Press, 1984.

Marshall, Richard H., Jr., ed. *Aspects of Religion in the Soviet Union, 1917–1967*. Chicago: University of Chicago Press, 1971.

Mathewes-Green, Frederica. *At the Corner of East and Now: A Modern Life in Ancient Christian Orthodoxy*. New York: Putnam, 2000.

———. *Facing East: A Pilgrim's Journey into the Mysteries of Orthodoxy*. San Francisco: Harper, 1997.

Medvedev, Roy A. *Let History Judge: The Origins and Consequences of Stalinism*. Rev. ed. New York: Columbia University Press, 1989.

———. *On Stalin and Stalinism*. New York: Oxford University Press, 1979.

Meyendorff, John. *The Byzantine Legacy in the Orthodox Church*. Crestwood, N.Y.: St. Vladimir's Seminary Press, 1982.

———. *Byzantine Theology: Historical Trends and Doctrinal Themes*. New York: Fordham University Press, 1974.

———. *Byzantium and the Rise of Russia*. Crestwood, N.Y.: St. Vladimir's Seminary Press, 1989.

———. *Catholicity and the Church*. Crestwood, N.Y.: St. Vladimir's Seminary Press, 1983.

———. *Christ in Eastern Christian Thought*. Crestwood, N.Y.: St. Vladimir's Seminary Press, 1975.

———. *Imperial Unity and Christian Divisions*. Crestwood, N.Y.: St. Vladimir's Seminary Press, 1989.

———. *Living Tradition*. Crestwood, N.Y.: St. Vladimir's Seminary Press, 1978.

———. *The Orthodox Church*. Crestwood, N.Y.: St. Vladimir's Seminary Press, 1981.

———. *Orthodoxy and Catholicity*. New York: Sheed and Ward, 1966.

———. *St. Gregory Palamas and Orthodox Spirituality*. Crestwood, N.Y.: St. Vladimir's Seminary Press, 1974.

———. *The Vision of Unity*. Crestwood, N.Y.: St. Vladimir's Seminary Press, 1987.

———, ed. *The Primacy of Peter in the Orthodox Church*. Crestwood, N.Y.: St. Vladimir's Seminary Press, 1992.

———, and Joseph McLelland, eds. *The New Man: An Orthodox and Reformed Dialogue*. New Brunswick, N.J.: Agora Books, 1973.

———, and Robert Tobias. *Salvation in Christ: A Lutheran-Orthodox Dialogue*. Minneapolis: Augsburg, 1992.

Nassif, Bradley. "Eastern Orthodoxy and Evangelicalism: The Status of an Emerging Dialogue." *Scottish Bulletin of Evangelical Theology* 18.1 (Spring 2000): 21–55.

————, ed. *New Perspectives on Historical Theology: Essays in Memory of John Meyendorff*. Grand Rapids: Eerdmans, 1996.

Nesdoly, Samuel J. *Among the Soviet Evangelicals*. Carlisle, Pa.: Banner of Truth, 1986.

New Valamo Consultation: The Ecumenical Nature of Orthodox Witness. Geneva: World Council of Churches, 1978.

Nichols, Robert L., and Theofanis G. Stavrou. *Russian Orthodoxy under the Old Regime*. Minneapolis: University of Minnesota Press, 1978.

Niesel, Wilhelm. *Reformed Symbolics: A Comparison of Catholicism, Orthodoxy, and Protestantism*. London: Oliver and Boyd, 1962.

Nissiotis, Nikos. "The Unity of Scripture and Tradition." *Greek Orthodox Theological Review* 11.2 (Winter 1965–66): 183–208.

O'Callaghan, Paul. *An Eastern Orthodox Response to Evangelical Claims*. Minneapolis: Light and Life, 1984.

Oden, Thomas. *The Rebirth of Orthodoxy*. San Francisco: Harper, 2002.

————. *Two Worlds: Notes on the Death of Modernity in America and Russia*. Downers Grove, Ill.: Inter-Varsity, 1992.

The Orthodox Church and the Churches of the Reformation: A Survey of Orthodox-Protestant Dialogue. Faith and Order paper 76. Geneva: World Council of Churches, 1975.

The Orthodox Church in the Ecumenical Movement: Documents and Statements, 1902–1975. Edited by Constantin G. Patelos. Geneva: World Council of Churches, 1978.

Orthodox Study Bible. Nashville: Thomas Nelson, n.d.

Ouspensky, Leonid. *Theology of the Icon*. Crestwood, N.Y.: Saint Vladimir's Seminary Press, 1978. (2 vols. Crestwood, N.Y.: St. Vladimir's Seminary Press, 1991.)

————, and Vladimir Lossky. *The Meaning of Icons*. Rev. ed. Crestwood, N.Y.: St. Vladimir's Seminary Press, 1982.

Pain, James, and Nicolas Zernov, eds. *A Bulgakov Anthology*. Philadelphia: Westminster, 1976.

Paraskevas, John E., and Frederick Reinstein. *The Eastern Orthodox Church: A Brief History*. Washington, D.C.: El Greco, 1969.

Parsons, Howard L. *Christianity Today in the U.S.S.R.* New York: International Publishers, 1987.

Paul of Finland, Archbishop. *The Faith We Hold*. Crestwood, N.Y.: St. Vladimir's Seminary Press, 1980.

Pelikan, Jaroslav. "Fundamentalism and/or Orthodoxy." In *The Fundamentalist Phenomenon*, edited by Norman J. Cohen, 3–21. Grand Rapids: Eerdmans, 1990.

————. *Imago Dei: The Byzantine Apologia for Icons*. Princeton: Princeton University Press, 1990.

————. *The Spirit of Eastern Christendom (600–1700)*. Chicago: University of Chicago Press, 1974.

Petro, Nicolai N., ed. *Christianity and Russian Culture in Soviet Society*. Boulder, Colo.: Westview, 1990.

Philokalia. Translated and edited by G. E. H. Palmer, Philip Sherrard, and Kallistos Ware. 3 vols. London: Faber and Faber, 1979–90.

Pollock, John C. *The Faith of Russian Evangelicals*. New York: McGraw-Hill, 1964.

————. *The Siberian Seven*. Waco: Word, 1979.

Pomazansky, Michael. *Orthodox Dogmatic Theology: A Concise Exposition*. Platina, Calif.: St. Herman of Alaska Brotherhood, 1983.

Pospielovsky, Dimitry V. *A History of Marxist-Leninist Atheism and Soviet Antireligious Policies*. 3 vols. New York: St. Martin's, 1987–88.

————. *The Russian Church under the Soviet Regime, 1917–1982*. 2 vols. Crestwood, N.Y.: St. Vladimir's Seminary Press, 1984.

Powell, David E. *Antireligious Propaganda in the Soviet Union*. Cambridge, Mass.: MIT Press, 1975.

Pushkarev, Sergei, and Gleb Yakunin. *Christianity and Government in Russia and the Soviet Union: Reflections on the Millennium*. Boulder, Colo.: Westview, 1989.

Quenot, Michel. *The Icon: Window on the Kingdom.* Crestwood, N.Y.: St. Vladimir's Seminary Press, 1991.

Ramet, Pedro. *Cross and Commissar: The Politics of Religion in Eastern Europe and the U.S.S.R.* Bloomington: Indiana University Press, 1987.

Sahas, Daniel J. *Icon and Logos: Sources in Eighth-Century Iconoclasm.* Toronto: University of Toronto Press, 1986.

Sawatsky, Walter. *Soviet Evangelicals since World War II.* Scottdale, Pa.: Herald, 1981.

Schaeffer, Frank. *Dancing Alone: The Quest for Orthodox Faith in the Age of False Religions.* Brookline, Mass.: Holy Cross Orthodox Press, 1994.

Scheffbuch, Winrich. *Christians under the Hammer and Sickle.* Grand Rapids: Zondervan, 1974.

Schmemann, Alexander. *Church, World, Mission: Reflections on Orthodoxy in the West.* Crestwood, N.Y.: St. Vladimir's Seminary Press, 1979.

————. *The Eucharist: The Sacrament of the Kingdom.* Crestwood, N.Y.: St. Vladimir's Seminary Press, 1988.

————. *For the Life of the World: Sacraments and Orthodoxy.* Crestwood, N.Y.: St. Vladimir's Seminary Press, 1973.

————. *The Historical Road of Eastern Orthodoxy.* Crestwood, N.Y.: St. Vladimir's Seminary Press, 1977.

————. *Introduction to Liturgical Theology.* Crestwood, N.Y.: St. Vladimir's Seminary Press, 1986.

————. *Of Water and the Spirit: A Liturgical Study of Baptism.* Crestwood, N.Y.: St. Vladimir's Seminary Press, 1974.

————. "Russian Theology: 1922–1972." *St. Vladimir's Theological Quarterly* 16.4 (1972): 172–94.

————. "Towards a Theology of Councils." *St. Vladimir's Theological Quarterly* 6.4 (1962): 170–84.

————, ed. *Ultimate Questions: An Anthology of Modern Russian Religious Thought.* Crestwood, N.Y.: St. Vladimir's Seminary Press, 1977.

Schneirla, William. "Orthodoxy and Ecumenism." *St. Vladimir's Theological Quarterly* 12.2 (1968): 86–88.

Sherrard, Philip. *The Greek East and the Latin West.* New York: Oxford University Press, 1959.

Solovyev, Vladimir. *Lectures on Godmanhood.* New York: Hillary, 1948.

————. *Russia and the Universal Church.* London: N.p., 1948.

————. *A Solovyev Anthology.* Edited by S. L. Frank. Westport, Conn.: Greenwood, 1974.

Solzhenitsyn, Alexander, ed. *From under the Rubble.* Chicago: Regnery Gateway, 1981.

Spinka, Matthew. *The Church and the Russian Revolution.* New York: Macmillan, 1927.

————. *The Church in Soviet Russia.* Westport, Conn.: Greenwood, 1980.

Stamoolis, James J. *Eastern Orthodox Mission Theology Today.* Maryknoll, N.Y.: Orbis, 1986.

————, ed. *Three Views on Eastern Orthodoxy and Evangelicalism.* Grand Rapids: Zondervan, forthcoming.

Staniloae, Dumitru. *Theology and the Church.* Crestwood, N.Y.: St. Vladimir's Seminary Press, 1980.

Stavropoulos, Christoforos. *Partakers of Divine Nature.* Minneapolis: Light and Life, 1976.

Stroyen, William B. *Communist Russia and the Russian Orthodox Church, 1943–1962.* Washington, D.C.: Catholic University of America Press, 1967.

Struve, Nikita. *Christians in Contemporary Russia.* New York: Scribner, 1967.

Szczesniak, Boleslaw, ed. *The Russian Revolution and Religion: A Collection of Documents concerning the Suppression of Religion by the Communists, 1917–1925.* Notre Dame: University of Notre Dame Press, 1959.

Tarasar, Constance, ed. *Orthodox America, 1794–1976: Development of the Orthodox Church in America.* Syosset, N.Y.: Orthodox Church in America, 1975.

Theological Dialogue between Orthodox and Reformed Churches. Edited by Thomas F. Torrance. Edinburgh: Scottish Academic Press, 1985.

Thrower, James. *Marxist-Leninist "Scientific Atheism" and the Study of Religion and Atheism in the U.S.S.R.* Hawthorne, N.Y.: Mouton, 1983.

Ugolnik, Anthony. *The Illuminating Icon*. Grand Rapids: Eerdmans, 1989.

————. "The Orthodox Church and Contemporary Politics in the USSR." Unpublished paper, 1991.

Ware, Timothy. *The Orthodox Church*. Baltimore: Penguin, 1964.

————. *The Orthodox Way*. Crestwood, N.Y.: St. Vladimir's Seminary Press, 1990.

Yancey, Phil. *Praying with the KGB: A Startling Report from a Shattered Empire*. Portland: Multnomah, 1992.

Zernov, Nicolas. *Eastern Christendom: A Study of the Origin and Development of the Eastern Orthodox Church*. New York: Putnam, 1961.

————. *Moscow, the Third Rome*. New York: Macmillan, 1937.

————. *The Russian Religious Renaissance of the Twentieth Century*. New York: Harper, 1963.

————. *The Russians and Their Church*. Crestwood, N.Y.: St. Vladimir's Seminary Press, 1978.

Scripture Index

Subject Index

Abyss of the Father, 154, 155, 156, 157
ACUTE, 219
Adam, 186–87; Christ as the new, 37, 39, 45, 187
Adoption, divine, 185
Afanasieff, Nicolai, 93
A Filio, 164
Again magazine, 214, 263
Alaxanian, Joseph, 242
Albinus, 154, 155
Allen, Joseph, 240
Allison, Dale, 216
All Saints, Feast of, 69
Altar, 18
America, theology in, 94–96
American Academy of Religion, 212, 220
Americanization, of Orthodoxy, 234–35, 267–72
American Mission to the Greeks, 222n
Anabasis, 151
Analogy (third way), 154
Analysis (first movement of apophasis), 154
Anastasius of Sinai, 184
Ancient Christian Commentary on Scripture, 223, 225–26
Angels, 73–75
Anglicanism, 214, 215, 253–54
Animals in icons, 60
Annunciation, 66–67
Anointing, 25–26
Anthony the Great, 54, 56
Antiochian Evangelical Orthodox Mission, 266–70, 272
Antiochian Orthodox Church, 214, 215n, 217, 240, 244, 249, 256
Antiquitas, 98
Antiquity, argument from, 120–21
Anthropology, Orthodox, 230
A Patre Filioque, 164, 167
Apocrypha, 82, 138
Apologetic, theology as, 91
Apophasis, 149–62, 169–70, 171
Apostles and Fathers, 122
Apostolic succession, 30, 85, 103
Aquinas, Thomas, 157, 159, 166, 167
Architecture: church, 16–18; in icons, 60–61
Arianism, 88, 104–7, 108, 111
Ascension in Eucharist, movement of, 200
Ascetic experience and icons, 54–55, 56–57, 59
Assumption of Mary, 90
Athanasius, 8, 29, 40n, 88, 104–7, 108, 112, 185, 187

Athos, Mount, 20
Augustine, 40n, 110, 112, 114, 120, 182, 255
Authority: Augustine and catholic, 114; conciliar, 118; of Fathers, 123; vested in the church, ultimate, 118, 124; in Western Christianity, critique of external, 87
Autocephalous churches, 81n

Ballew, Richard, 259, 265
Baptism, 15, 22, 24–25, 38, 75, 110, 192; of necessity, 25
Baptismal profession of faith, 100, 102, 109; in the Trinity, 111, 130
Baptists, 214
Basil the Great, 24, 40, 82, 84, 108–12, 114, 128–31, 133, 142n, 151, 157, 179, 181, 184, 189
Barth, Karl, 220
Beauty: emphasis on, 12; in icons, 58; Orthodox understanding of, 42
Bell ringing, 16
Berven, Ken, 259
Biblical inerrancy, 251–52
Billy Graham Center, 216, 244
Billy Graham Crusades, 213
Biola University, 242–43
Bishops: collegiality of, 116; as guardians of tradition, 85–86, 103, 116; succession of, 86n, 102, 122. *See also* Apostolic succession
Blaising, Craig, 216
Bloesch, Donald, 216, 228, 233, 254, 256
Body: problem of representing the human, 58n–59n; representation of, in icons, 61; and soul as image of God, 186
Bolotov, V. V., 118, 164–65
Borisov, Alexander, 230n
Borromeo, Charles, 59n
Bradley, James, 239
Braun, Jon, 259, 265
Bray, Gerald, 216, 223–24
Bread and wine, 28
Bria, Ion, 221
Bright, Bill, 217, 244–45, 256
Brigs, John, 219n
Brown, Harold O. J., 216, 228
Bulgakov, Sergius, 65, 93, 178, 180
Byzantine Orthodox Church, 224

Campus Crusade for Christ, 213, 214, 256–57, 258, 266, 268
Canon: detachment of Orthodoxy regarding the problem of the scriptural,

82; of Scripture as dynamic, preservation of the, 137; of truth, 101–3
Canonization, 71
Canterbury Trail, 253–54
Cappadocian fathers, 95, 108, 157, 160, 161, 247
Carthage, Council of, 120
Cassian, John, 131
Catherine II, 92
Catholic authority, Augustine and, 114
Catholicity, evangelicals on, 252–53
Cause of the other hypostases, the Father as, 170–73, 176, 178
Celestine I, Pope, 7
Celsus, 154
Chalcedon (451), Council of, 35, 88, 89, 119, 123, 143
Chapters, Three, 121
Charismatic movement, 253
Charisma veritatis, 102
Chesterton, G. K., 224
"Chicago Call: An Appeal to Evangelicals, The," 254–56
Chrism, 25–26
Chrismation, 22, 25–26
Christ: as criterion of truth, 119–21; in the Eucharist, real presence of, 27–28; Eucharist as union with, 26–28; majesty of (second movement of apophasis), 154–55; as the New Adam, 37, 39, 45, 187; union with, 69
Christendom, 261
Christian and Missionary Alliance, 214
Christian humanists, 255
Chrysostom, 24
Church: authority of, 114; as context of tradition, 85; as council, 118; critical spirit of the, 137; as fullness, 198, 199; infallibility of the, 124, 136; as only interpreter of Scripture, 99–101, 107, 112–14, 119; Orthodox doctrine of the, 196–99, 200; as response, 198–99; to sacraments, indispensability of, 23, 30; Slavonic, 15; ultimate authority vested in the, 118, 124; unity of the, as focus of early councils, 116; universality of the, 117
Church Mission Society (Church of England), 219
Clapsis, Emmanuel, 216, 232, 242
Clement VIII, Pope, 58n
Clement of Alexandria, 152, 153–57, 161
Clendenin, Daniel, 228
Clericalism, lack of professional, 92
Clothing in icon, representation of, 59, 61

283